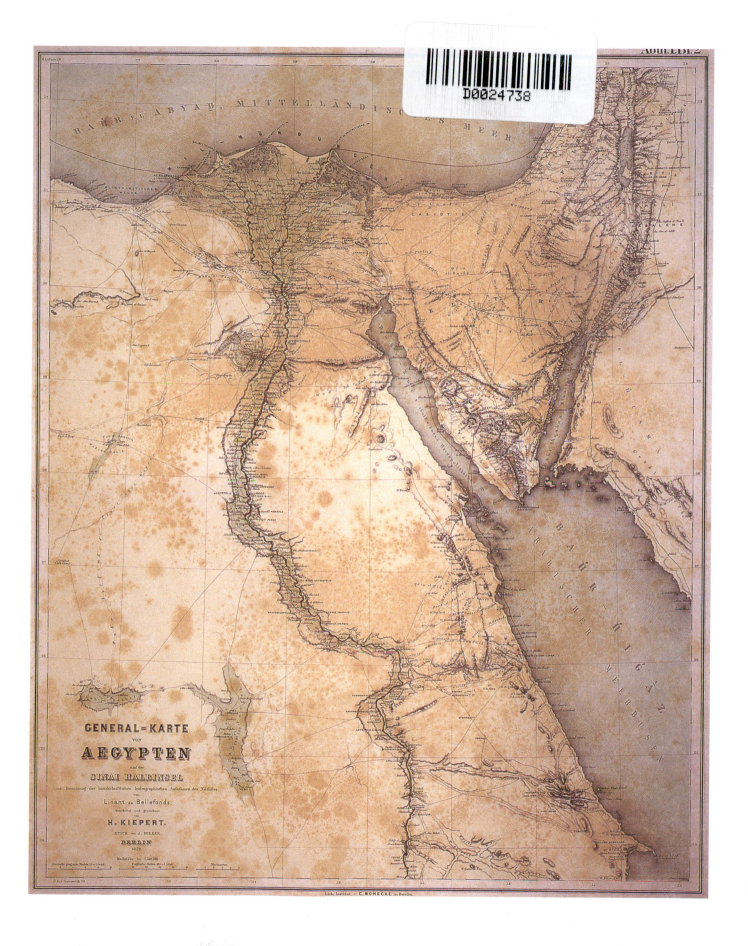

GENERAL=KARTE

von

AEGYPTEN

und der

SINAI HALBINSEL

mit Benutzung der handschriftlichen hydrographischen Aufnahmen des Nilthales

von

Linant de Bellefonds,

bearbeitet und gezeichnet

von

H. KIEPERT.

STICH von J. SULZER.

BERLIN

1828.

Lith. Institut. v. C. NONECKE in Berlin.

TEMPLES OF THE LAST PHARAOHS

TEMPLES OF THE LAST PHARAOHS

DIETER ARNOLD

New York   Oxford

Oxford University Press

1999

Oxford University Press

Oxford   New York

Athens   Auckland   Bangkok   Bogotá   Buenos Aires   Calcutta
Cape Town   Chennai   Dar es Salaam   Delhi   Florence   Hong Kong   Istanbul
Karachi   Kuala Lumpur   Madrid   Melbourne   Mexico City   Mumbai
Nairobi   Paris   São Paulo   Singapore   Taipei   Tokyo   Toronto   Warsaw

and associated companies in
Berlin   Ibadan

Library of Congress Cataloging-in-Publication Data
Arnold, Dieter, 1936–
Temples of the last pharaohs / Dieter Arnold.
p.   cm.
Includes index.
ISBN 0-19-512633-5
1. Architecture, Ancient—Egypt.
2. Temples—Egypt.   I. Title.
NA215.A75   1999
726'.1931—dc21   99-24117

Endpaper maps: Egypt 1842/45 (Richard Hepsius, Denkmaeler

aus Aegupten und Aethipien, vol. 1, pl. 2, Berlin 1849).

9 8 7 6 5 4 3 2 1
Printed in Hong Kong
on acid-free paper

ACKNOWLEDGMENTS

I wish to express my gratitude to the Oxford University Press, New York, for the publication of this book and to Joyce Berry, senior editor, for her valuable help. I further want to thank Adela Oppenheim, who took a considerable number of photographs in Upper Egypt—often under difficult conditions— and contributed to the text through essential observations. Her photos are marked (A.O.). I also wish to mention gratefully my late friend Artur Brack, who put his ample photographic collection at my disposal. His photos are marked (A.B.). And I thank Marilyn Bridges, in New York, for lending me copies of her breathtaking collection of aerial photos of Egyptian temple sites. I also wish to thank The Metropolitan Museum of Art, New York, for granting me a travel stipend in 1996 to visit Late Period temples in Upper Egypt.

New York, New York   D. A.
March 1999

CONTENTS

PART II: CHARACTERISTICS OF THE ARCHITECTURE
            OF THE LATE PERIOD

TEMPLES OF THE LAST PHARAOHS

INTRODUCTION

This book deals with the last 1,300 years of the nearly 3,000-year-long history of temple building in ancient Egypt, undertaken by about fifty kings, from the collapse of the New Kingdom to the end of Roman rule. The flow of historical data from this period—at least from the eighth century B.C. on—is so much stronger than in all preceding periods, and the sheer number of buildings seems formidable; however, the distribution and preservation of monuments of the Late Period is erratic. The Nile valley of Upper Egypt and Nubia is relatively rich in these monuments; so are the Faiyum and the western oases. By contrast, Middle and Lower Egypt, and especially the Nile Delta, are depleted of temples. The rise of modern cities like Cairo, Alexandria, Zagazig, Beni Suef, Miniyia, and others, with their demand for building material, led to the total destruction of nearby monuments. This disappearance is especially unfortunate for tracing the building history of the 26th and 30th Dynasties, which built most of their temples in Lower Egypt.

This rarity of late Egyptian temples should actually have prompted an eager study of the few surviving remains. This has, however, rarely happened. Egyptologists who thoroughly study the sculpture of the Egyptian Late Period mostly omit contemporary temple architecture from their attention.[1] The main reason is that temples of the Late Period are—because of their lavish decoration and inscriptions—considered less as architectural monuments and more as carriers of reliefs and inscriptions. This neglect of architecture is no wonder where all that sometimes remains of a temple is a pile of inscribed building blocks.

The remaining buildings, however, not only bear witness to the high standard of Late Egyptian temple building in general but also demonstrate that architecture took significant steps in development, creating a new world of pharaonic temples that compares well with the achievements of preceding periods. In addition to their outstanding artistic value, some of these temples still convey the unforgettable notion of proximity to ancient times, when ceremonial life still filled their interiors. This sensation is supported by eyewitness reports of visiting Greek and Roman travelers.[2] The Greek historian Herodotus of Halicarnassus visited Egypt ca. 450–444 B.C., when the country was under the rule of the Persian king Artaxerxes I, and in his second book recorded his experiences at Egypt's temples. His descriptions of Buto, Sais, Bubastis, and Memphis portray the temples as functioning sanctuaries, still alive with ritual activity. Another Greek writer, Strabo of Amasia, traveled in Egypt ca. 27/26 B.C., shortly after the Roman conquest. In the seventeenth volume of his *Geography*, Strabo discloses important information about sites like Heliopolis, Memphis, and Alexandria. The opulence of temples and chapels governing the landscape of Egypt in classical antiquity is further demonstrated by picturesque representations of Egypt and the Nile in Roman mosaics and wall paintings. Even after centuries of destruction of Egyptian temples, Arab writers were still able to visit and describe in good detail the temples of Sebennytos and Akhmim.

Even more than temples of earlier periods, those of the Egyptian Late Period were characterized by the two typical conflicting intentions of maintaining the traditional and developing contemporary forms. This aspect will be addressed repeatedly in the following chapters.

During the Late Period, Egyptian cults and their specific building forms were spreading over the whole range of the Mediterranean; simultaneously, Egypt was being exposed to foreign influences as never before. These foreign connections cannot be entirely ignored and require repeated glimpses at the contemporary architecture of Egypt's neighbors.[3] Indeed, two prominent side branches of Egyptian Late Period architecture developed into such extensive and specific architectural entities that they cannot properly be treated in the framework of a book about Late Egypt: the building of the Kushites in the Sudan and the Hellenistic architecture of Alexandria. The presentation of traditional architecture in Egypt leaves no room for these two fascinating architectural worlds.

The reader should comprehend that in Egyptological convention Arabic or Greek and Roman topographical names often change surprisingly and not always logically. Greek and Roman names are preferred when no important modern city is in the neighborhood, whereas the Arabic name comes into use when a major modern city is placed on the ancient site. In the following text, both names are given in most of the cases, but Greek and Roman names are preferred because the book deals with a period in which ancient Egyptian names were transformed into Greek and Latin. Site or temple names are capitalized in the text to indicate a more profound discussion of the building activity at a specific site. Uncommon technical, architectural, and Egyptological terms that are explained in the glossary are italicized where they first occur in the text. Question marks (?) indicate doubts about the proposed date or allocation. "Augustus(?)" therefore means that we are not sure that Augustus was the builder. Exclamation marks (!) should attract attention to a remarkable fact or dimension.

PLANS & MAPS

The fifteen plans that follow depict the main Egyptian sanctuaries of the Late Period and are referenced throughout the text as plans I–XV. These are not plans of the existing ruins but reconstructions that should assist the reader in imagining the ancient layout of the buildings and the paths of movement within the sanctuaries.

Following the plans, three maps show the distribution of Late Period temples in Lower Egypt, the Faiyum, and Upper Egypt and lower Nubia.

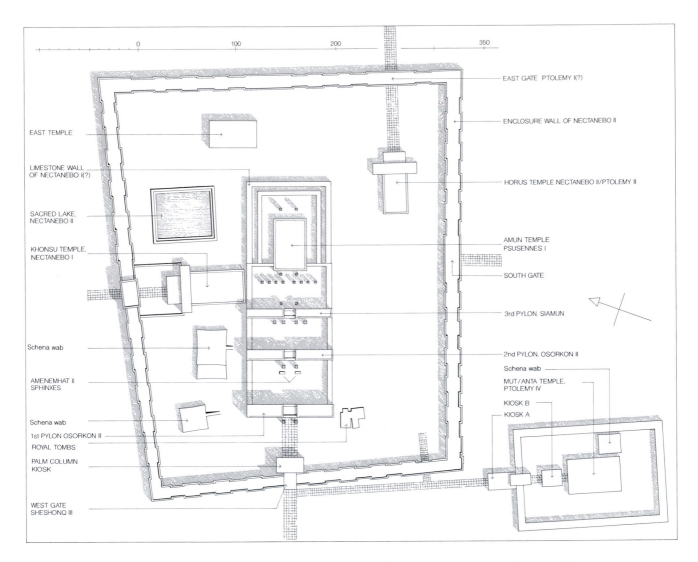

EAST GATE PTOLEMY I(?)

ENCLOSURE WALL OF NECTANEBO II

EAST TEMPLE

LIMESTONE WALL
OF NECTANEBO I(?)

HORUS TEMPLE NECTANEBO II/PTOLEMY II

SACRED LAKE,
NECTANEBO II

KHONSU TEMPLE,
NECTANEBO I

AMUN TEMPLE
PSUSENNES I

SOUTH GATE

3rd PYLON, SIAMUN

Schena wab

2nd PYLON, OSORKON II

AMENEMHAT II
SPHINXES

Schena wab

MUT/ANTA TEMPLE,
PTOLEMY IV

KIOSK B

Schena wab

KIOSK A

1st PYLON OSORKON II
ROYAL TOMBS

PALM COLUMN
KIOSK

WEST GATE
SHESHONQ III

I. Reconstructed plan of the temple precincts of Amun and Anta at Tanis.

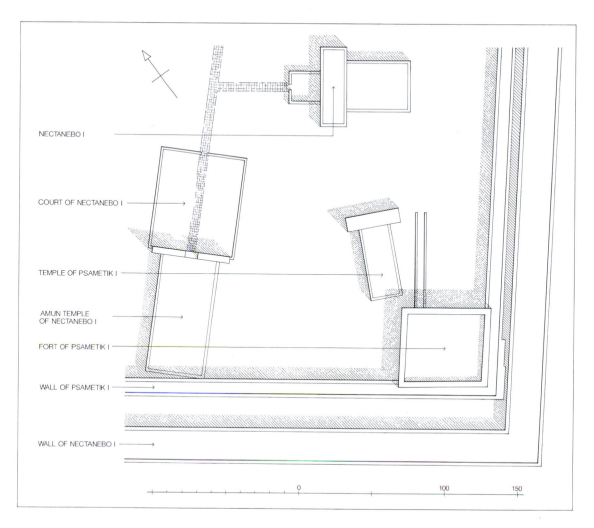

NECTANEBO I

COURT OF NECTANEBO I

TEMPLE OF PSAMETIK I

AMUN TEMPLE
OF NECTANEBO I

FORT OF PSAMETIK I

WALL OF PSAMETIK I

WALL OF NECTANEBO I

0   100   150

II. Reconstructed plan of the temple precinct of Amun at Balamun.

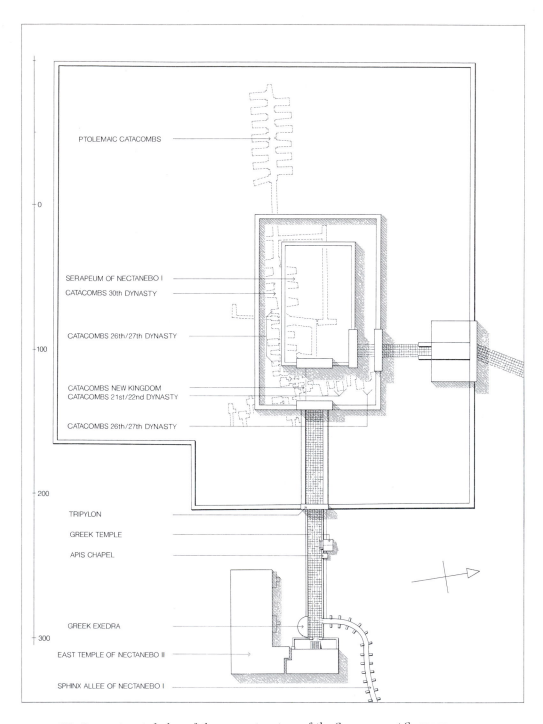

PTOLEMAIC CATACOMBS

SERAPEUM OF NECTANEBO I

CATACOMBS 30th DYNASTY

CATACOMBS 26th/27th DYNASTY

CATACOMBS NEW KINGDOM
CATACOMBS 21st/22nd DYNASTY

CATACOMBS 26th/27th DYNASTY

TRIPYLON

GREEK TEMPLE

APIS CHAPEL

GREEK EXEDRA

EAST TEMPLE OF NECTANEBO II

SPHINX ALLEE OF NECTANEBO I

III. Reconstructed plan of the superstructure of the Serapeum at Saqqara.

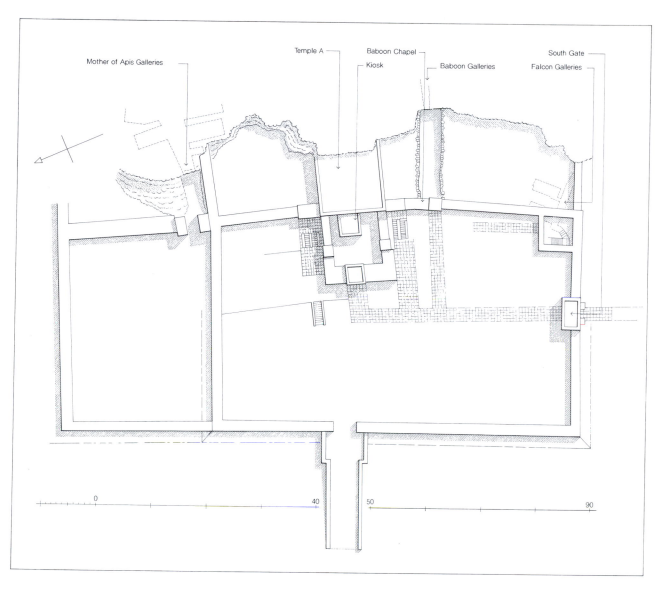

Mother of Apis Galleries

Temple A

Baboon Chapel

South Gate

Kiosk

Baboon Galleries

Falcon Galleries

0   40   50   90

IV. Reconstructed plan of the enclosure and temple for the sacred animals of
Nectanebo II at North Saqqara.

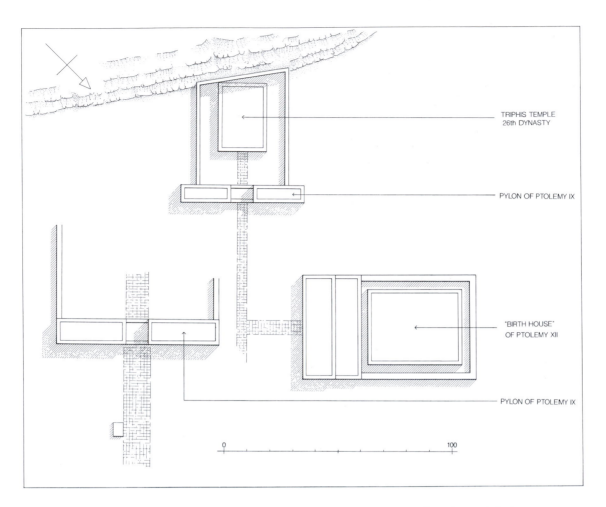

TRIPHIS TEMPLE
26th DYNASTY

PYLON OF PTOLEMY IX

"BIRTH HOUSE"
OF PTOLEMY XII

PYLON OF PTOLEMY IX

0   100

V. Reconstructed plan of the temple precinct of Triphis at Athribis (Wannina).

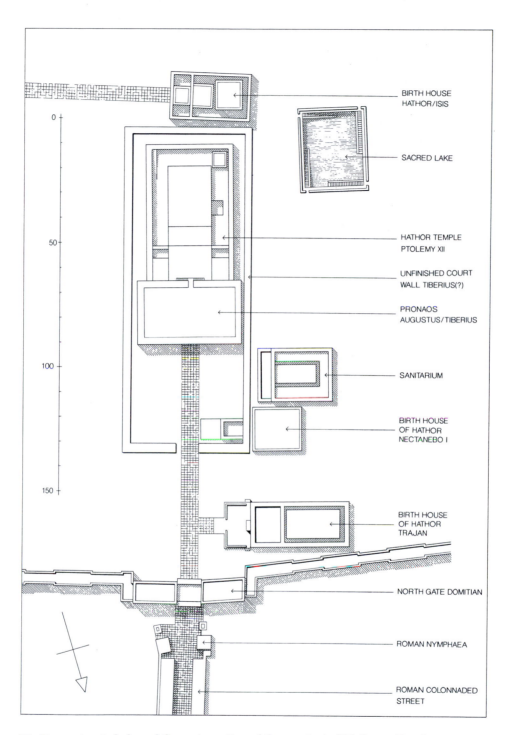

BIRTH HOUSE
HATHOR/ISIS

SACRED LAKE

HATHOR TEMPLE
PTOLEMY XII

UNFINISHED COURT
WALL TIBERIUS(?)

PRONAOS
AUGUSTUS/TIBERIUS

SANITARIUM

BIRTH HOUSE
OF HATHOR
NECTANEBO I

BIRTH HOUSE
OF HATHOR
TRAJAN

NORTH GATE DOMITIAN

ROMAN NYMPHAEA

ROMAN COLONNADED
STREET

VI. Reconstructed plan of the main section of the precinct of Hathor at Dendera.

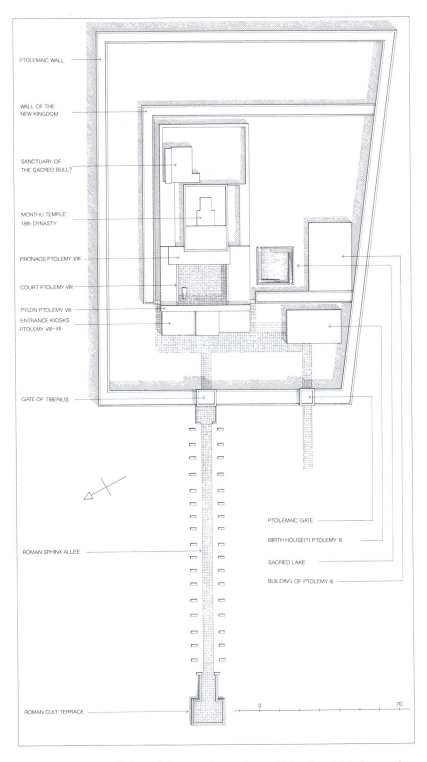

PTOLEMAIC WALL

WALL OF THE
NEW KINGDOM

SANCTUARY OF
THE SACRED BULL?

MONTHU TEMPLE
18th DYNASTY

PRONAOS PTOLEMY VIII

COURT PTOLEMY VIII

PYLON PTOLEMY VIII
ENTRANCE KIOSKS
PTOLEMY VIII–XII

GATE OF TIBERIUS

ROMAN SPHINX ALLEE

ROMAN CULT TERRACE

PTOLEMAIC GATE

BIRTH HOUSE(?) PTOLEMY III

SACRED LAKE

BUILDING OF PTOLEMY III

0   70

VII. Reconstructed plan of the temple precinct of Monthu at Medamoud
(see also fig. 145).

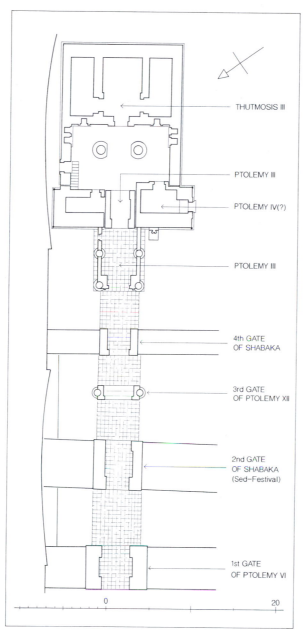

THUTMOSIS III

PTOLEMY III

PTOLEMY IV(?)

PTOLEMY III

4th GATE
OF SHABAKA

3rd GATE
OF PTOLEMY XII

2nd GATE
OF SHABAKA
(Sed-Festival)

1st GATE
OF PTOLEMY VI

0   20

VIII. Plan of the processional approach to the temple of Ptah at Karnak.

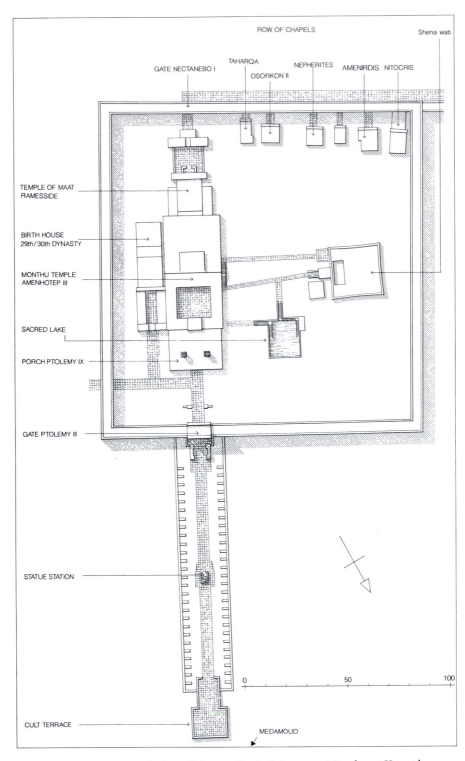

ROW OF CHAPELS

Shena wab

GATE NECTANEBO I
TAHARQA
OSORKON II
NEPHERITES
AMENIRDIS NITOCRIS

TEMPLE OF MAAT
RAMESSIDE

BIRTH HOUSE
29th / 30th DYNASTY

MONTHU TEMPLE
AMENHOTEP III

SACRED LAKE

PORCH PTOLEMY IX

GATE PTOLEMY III

STATUE STATION

0   50   100

CULT TERRACE

MEDAMOUD

IX. Reconstructed plan of the precinct of Amunra-Monthu at Karnak.

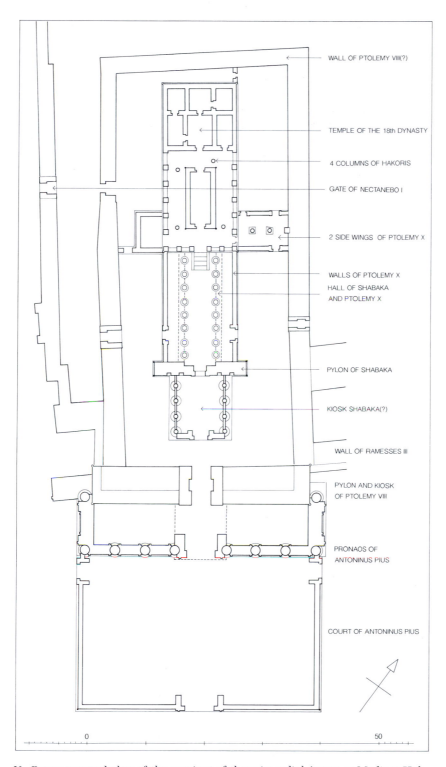

WALL OF PTOLEMY VIII(?)

TEMPLE OF THE 18th DYNASTY

4 COLUMNS OF HAKORIS

GATE OF NECTANEBO I

2 SIDE WINGS OF PTOLEMY X

WALLS OF PTOLEMY X

HALL OF SHABAKA
AND PTOLEMY X

PYLON OF SHABAKA

KIOSK SHABAKA(?)

WALL OF RAMESSES III

PYLON AND KIOSK
OF PTOLEMY VIII

PRONAOS OF
ANTONINUS PIUS

COURT OF ANTONINUS PIUS

0   50

X. Reconstructed plan of the precinct of the primordial Amun at Medinet Habu.

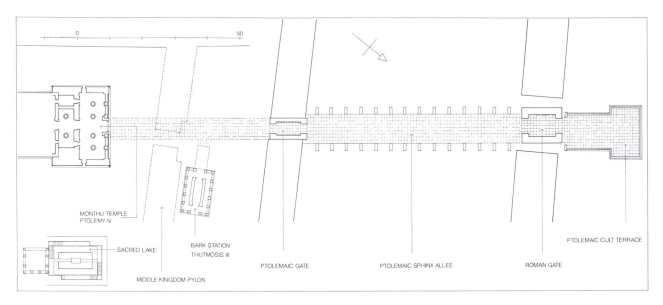

XI. Reconstructed plan of the processional approach of the temple of Monthu at El-Tôd.

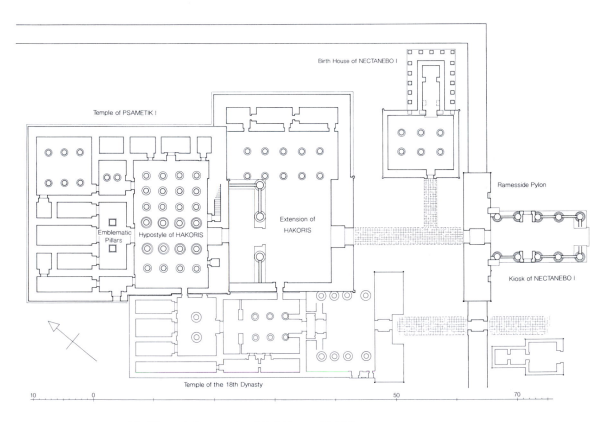

XII. Plan of the temple of Nekhbet at El-Kâb.

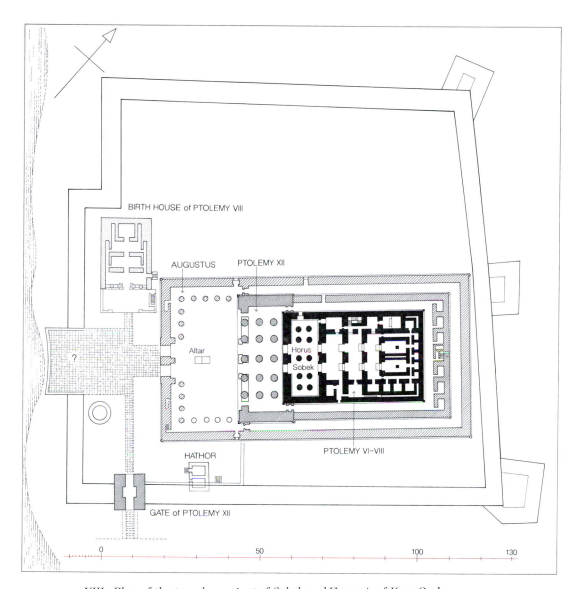

BIRTH HOUSE of PTOLEMY VIII

AUGUSTUS   PTOLEMY XII

Altar

Horus

Sobek

PTOLEMY VI–VIII

HATHOR

GATE of PTOLEMY XII

0   50   100   130

XIII. Plan of the temple precinct of Sobek and Haroeris of Kom Ombo.

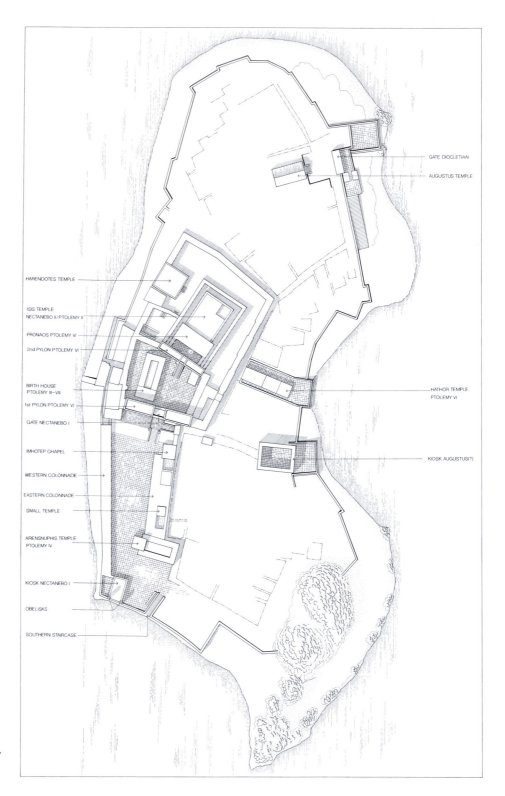

GATE DIOCLETIAN

AUGUSTUS TEMPLE

HARENDOTES TEMPLE

ISIS TEMPLE
NECTANEBO II/PTOLEMY II

PRONAOS PTOLEMY VI

2nd PYLON PTOLEMY VI

HATHOR TEMPLE
PTOLEMY VI

BIRTH HOUSE
PTOLEMY III–VIII

1st PYLON PTOLEMY VI

GATE NECTANEBO I

IMHOTEP CHAPEL

KIOSK AUGUSTUS(?)

WESTERN COLONNADE

EASTERN COLONNADE

SMALL TEMPLE

ARENSNUPHIS TEMPLE
PTOLEMY IV

KIOSK NECTANEBO I

OBELISKS

SOUTHERN STAIRCASE

XIV. Plan of the island of
Philae in Roman times.

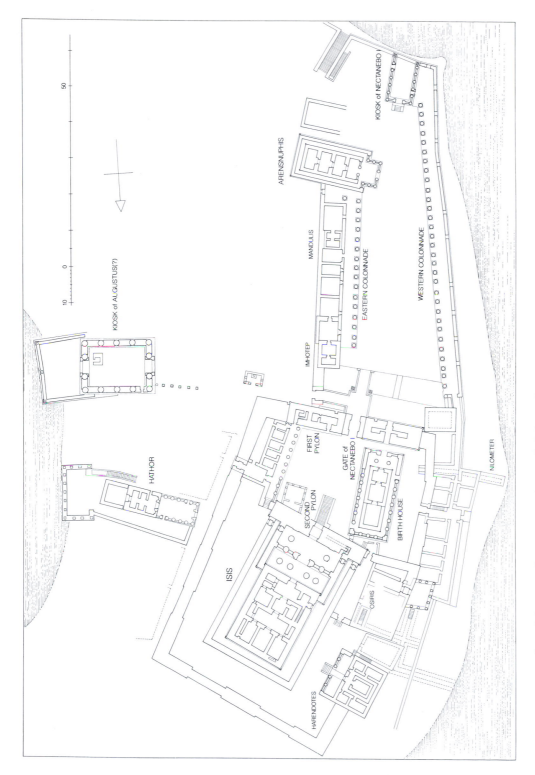

KIOSK of NECTANEBO

ARENSNUPHIS

MANDULIS

IMHOTEP

EASTERN COLONNADE

WESTERN COLONNADE

NILOMETER

KIOSK of AUGUSTUS(?)

50

0

10

HATHOR

FIRST PYLON

GATE of NECTANEBO

SECOND PYLON

BIRTH HOUSE

ISIS

OSIRIS

HARENDOTES

XV. Plan of the central monumental area of Philae in Roman times.

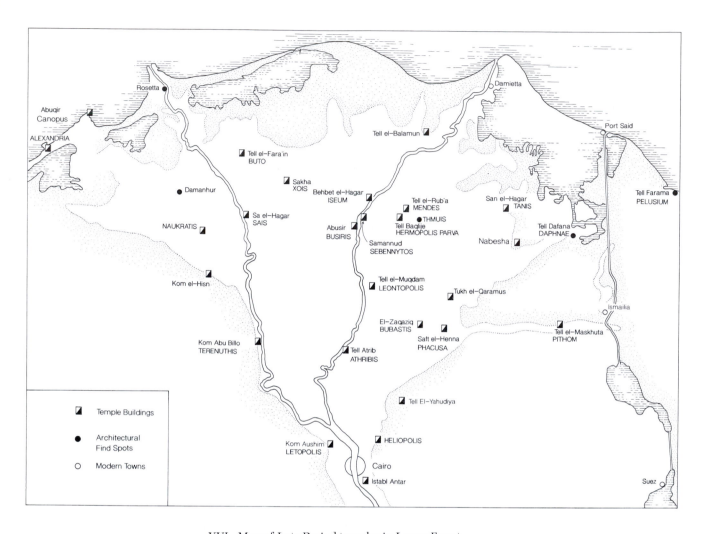

Abuqir
Canopus

ALEXANDRIA

Rosetta

Damietta

Port Said

Tell el-Balamun

Tell Farama
PELUSIUM

Tell el-Fara'in
BUTO

Damanhur

Sakha
XOIS

Behbet el-Hagar
ISEUM

Tell el-Rub'a
MENDES

San el-Hagar
TANIS

Sa el-Hagar
SAIS

NAUKRATIS

Abusir
BUSIRIS

THMUIS

Tell Baqlije
HERMOPOLIS PARVA

Tell Dafana
DAPHNAE

Samannud
SEBENNYTOS

Nabesha

Kom el-Hisn

Tell el-Muqdam
LEONTOPOLIS

Tukh el-Qaramus

Ismailia

Kom Abu Billo
TERENUTHIS

El-Zaqaziq
BUBASTIS

Saft el-Henna
PHACUSA

Tell el-Maskhuta
PITHOM

Tell Atrib
ATHRIBIS

Tell El-Yahudiya

Kom Aushim
LETOPOLIS

HELIOPOLIS

Cairo

Istabl Antar

Suez

Temple Buildings

Architectural
Find Spots

Modern Towns

XVI. Map of Late Period temples in Lower Egypt.

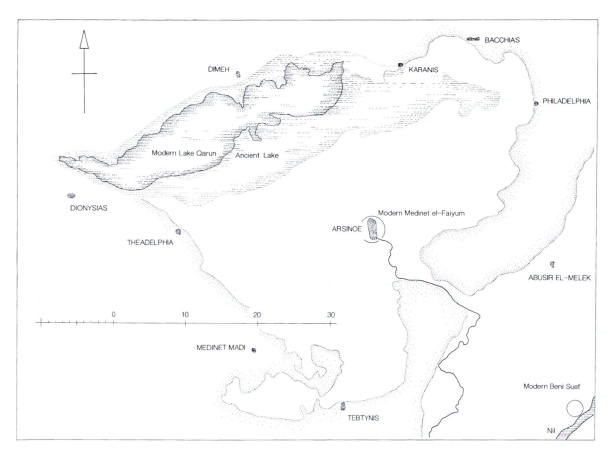

XVII. Map of Late Period temples in the Faiyum.

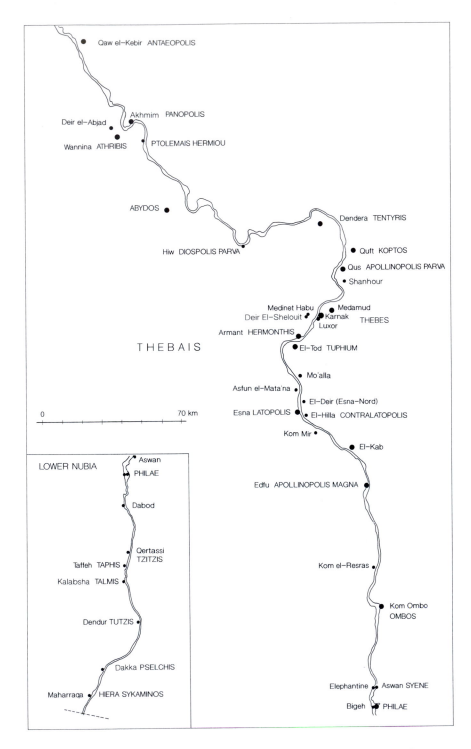

Qaw el–Kebir ANTAEOPOLIS

Akhmim PANOPOLIS
Deir el–Abjad
Wannina ATHRIBIS
PTOLEMAIS HERMIOU

ABYDOS

Dendera TENTYRIS

Hiw DIOSPOLIS PARVA

Quft KOPTOS

Qus APOLLINOPOLIS PARVA
Shanhour

Medinet Habu   Medamud
Deir El–Shelouit   Karnak   THEBES
Armant HERMONTHIS   Luxor

THEBAIS

El–Tod TUPHIUM

Mo'alla

Asfun el–Mata'na

El–Deir (Esna–Nord)

Esna LATOPOLIS   El–Hilla CONTRALATOPOLIS

Kom Mir

El–Kab

0   70 km

Edfu APOLLINOPOLIS MAGNA

LOWER NUBIA   Aswan
                   PHILAE

Dabod

Qertassi
TZITZIS
Taffeh TAPHIS   Kom el–Resras
Kalabsha TALMIS

Kom Ombo
OMBOS
Dendur TUTZIS

Dakka PSELCHIS

Maharraqa HIERA SYKAMINOS   Elephantine Aswan SYENE

                                 Bigeh PHILAE

XVIII. Map of Late Period temples in Upper Egypt and lower Nubia.

PART I

THE DEVELOPMENT OF THE
ARCHITECTURE OF THE LATE PERIOD

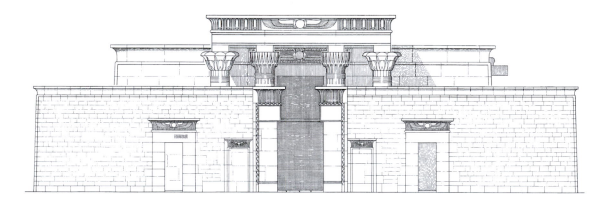

Reconstructed frontal view of the temple of Hibis in Ptolemaic times
(after L. F. Hall, courtesy of MMA).

I

THE LAST TEMPLES OF THE NEW KINGDOM
(1550–1070 B.C.)

The New Kingdom, with such fascinating temples as Deir el-Bahari, Karnak, and Luxor, was certainly the golden age of Egyptian temple building. The last great temples of this period were erected under Ramesses III and were meticulously listed in the Papyrus Harris[1] in impressive numbers: the king's mortuary temple of Medinet Habu; two smaller temples and the Khonsu temple at Karnak; royal temples in remote Nubia and Canaan; a sanctuary, colossal sphinxes, and other buildings in the temple of Heliopolis; the temples for Ptah in Memphis, Onuris at Thinis, Thoth at Hermopolis magna, Osiris at Abydos, Upuaut at Asyut, Seth at Ombos; and an enclosure of the temple of Khenti-khety at Athribis—altogether over a dozen presumably larger building projects. The well-preserved royal mortuary temple of Medinet Habu and the remains of two smaller temples at Karnak confirm that the volume of building listed in the papyrus was not exaggerated.

Fortunately, the "royal mortuary temple" of Ramesses III of Medinet Habu and the temple of Khonsu at Karnak are well preserved (figs. 1–3).[2] The temple of Medinet Habu was begun and completed within the reign of Ramesses III and was dedicated to the joint cult of Amun, the king, and several other deities traditionally assembled around the king. The temple of the moon god Khonsu has an extended building history. Ramesses III presumably replaced an older Khonsu temple, and Ramesses IV completed the building. The decoration was only completed under Ramesses IX and Herihor.

Both temples summarize the basic ideas of Egyptian temple building of the New Kingdom. The central processional axis is the structural backbone of the complex. At the same time, the axis of the Medinet Habu temple follows the path of the sun and links the temple with the order of the Egyptian cosmos. A sequence of monumental gates along this axis organizes the building as a linear series of spaces, reinforcing direction and movement. Whereas the

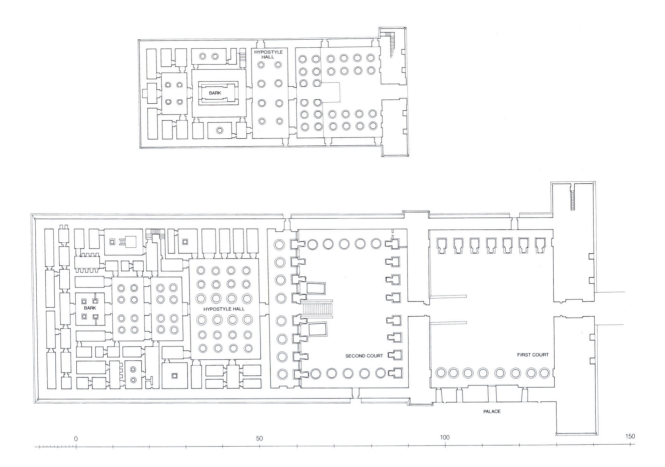

Figure 1.
Plans of the temple of Khonsu
at Karnak (*top*) and of
Ramesses III at Medinet Habu.

modern viewer tends to experience the direction of the path of movement
from the outside to the inside, the Egyptians saw it differently. The center of
movement was located in the sanctuary, from where the image of the deity
moved outward. In both temples, a large group of secondary sanctuaries
is gathered around the bark shrine of Amun. The clustered organization of
these diminutive and convoluted rooms surrenders geometrical regularity
to intricate cultic requirements. The spatial grandeur that dominated the
temples of the late 18th Dynasty is transformed into a tomblike narrowness.
The next spatial component following to the front is a *hypostyle hall* with a
towering central nave. Voluminous, unstructured, and, to our eyes, ungrace-
ful columns intimidate the viewer, who feels crushed between their narrow
intercolumniations. They display the oppressive narrowness of the Ramesside
building style, which can be felt even in the courts in front. They were in the
tradition of the royal mortuary temples of the New Kingdom, dominated by
rows of pillars with a colossal statue of the king. Ramesside architectural
ideas were marked by the striving for inflated monumentality, bolstered by the
unrestrained usurpation of older obelisks and colossal statues. These tendencies introduce dramatic, startling—perhaps even "baroque-like"—elements
into temple architecture that hitherto had been determined by the more

Figure 2.
Heavy-handed, narrowly
spaced columns in the interior
of the temple of Khonsu at
Karnak (photo A.O.).

Figure 3.
Built history dis-
played at the late
New Kingdom
temple of Khonsu
at Karnak with the
entrance porch of
Taharqa and the
gate of Ptolemy II
(*lower right*) and
temple of Opet
(*left*) (courtesy of
Marilyn Bridges,
New York).

restrained and motionless qualities of the building style of the 18th Dynasty. The court of the Khonsu temple is compressed on three sides by plain papyrus columns. The temple of Medinet Habu has two courts with a combination of papyrus columns and statue pillars. In both temples, the rear hall of the court rises on a flat platform articulated by a *cavetto*. Broad, high pylons precede in front and, with their huge wall planes, clearly seal the sacred interior from the outside world.

The megalithic masses of whitewashed stone surfaces stress the everlasting indestructibility of the Egyptian world order. The huge, whitewashed surfaces of the walls were articulated by the yellow, brown, and blue reliefs and inscriptions. Their most outstanding property was the extremely deep carving, which rendered these reliefs and hieroglyphs into nearly three-dimensional shapes suspended in front of the scarcely noticeable wall surface. This seemingly stylistic quality is actually an attempt to vitalize the magic power of the animated world of images. The temple walls' elaborate decoration program activates the principle of exchange whereby the observance of the gods' demands by the Egyptian chief priest, the king, translates into the maintenance of the world order and the prosperity of Egypt by the gods.

The careful study of Medinet Habu by the Oriental Institute of the University of Chicago demonstrated that the above-described temple was the center of a sacred city enclosed by strong defensive walls.[3] The city contained living quarters for priests and guards, offices, stables, workshops, magazine buildings, and gardens. A ritual palace was attached to the south side of the temple. One can assume that Egyptian temples of all periods were surrounded by similar facilities.

The oversized "royal mortuary temple" of King Ramesses IV, at the entrance into the Asasif valley of the Theban west bank, remained unfinished at the king's early death. The temple would have been the last monumental representative of a specific type of royal cult installation, which had its roots in the Middle Kingdom and was never revived again in later times. Soon after, public building in the country ceased altogether. Instead, demolition and stone robbery spread, and the pillaging of temples and royal tombs—as described in the tomb robbery papyri—raged out of control.

2

THE THIRD INTERMEDIATE PERIOD
(CA. 1070–730 B.C.)

At the end of the 20th Dynasty (ca. 1070 B.C.) the political unity of the centralized pharaonic state dissolved into several fragmentary provinces. Dynasties of foreign, partially Libyan, origin constituted themselves for a longer period in Thebes, Middle Egypt, Heracleopolis, Bubastis, and Tanis. As a result of this disarray, many problems of the sequence of rulers and the evaluation of their territorial distribution have not yet been resolved. Such questions have less impact on our studies because only nine out of the thirty-seven rulers of this period were builders. Since the entire building volume of this Third Intermediate Period could have been accomplished in a few generations, one would hesitate to assign it the traditionally accepted 350 years.

Thebes was controlled by the high priest of Amun,[1] who soon usurped royal ranks. Their resources permitted only the restoration of decaying buildings, the donation of statues and small chapels, or the addition of their names onto older monuments. Simultaneously and in peaceful agreement with these priest-kings of Thebes, a Libyan dynasty ruled in the north. Their first king Nesubenebded (1070–1044) developed as his residence Tanis, which is located in the marshes of the northeast corner of the Delta. The so-called Third Intermediate Period was not—in spite of its alleged length and the peaceful conditions in the country—a period of large public building. On the other hand, smaller workshops for sculpture, bronze casting,[2] gold-works, and coffin painting flourished, and the production of painted wooden stelae and the inscription and decoration of papyri suggest a continuation of the New Kingdom tradition.

The evaluation of the artistic achievement of architecture of the period is impaired not only by the meager building activity in general but also by the lack of preserved buildings. The few remains that did survive suggest that little had changed since the Ramessides. Quite in contrast to the following

Kushite, Saite, Mendesian, and Ptolemaic building programs, the buildings of the Third Intermediate Period do not reflect a royal proclamation of a new governmental program and therefore lack distinctiveness. The temple builders of the Third Intermediate Period obviously wished to continue the New Kingdom tradition as closely as possible, ignoring any political, and potential religious and cultic, changes. One might suspect that this standstill even reflects an intention to block out political and cultural changes that threatened to shatter the Egyptian view of life by artificially preserving the forms of the Ramesside past. This attitude is surprising because Egypt was ruled by kings of foreign, Libyan origin. However, one architectural element points at least to a future development. The freestanding sanctuary that will play a major role in the architecture of the Ptolemaic and Roman Periods appears in the temple of Sheshonq I at El-Hibe (fig. 5).

Beginning in the twelfth century—and notwithstanding the unfavorable conditions inside Egypt—the country's contacts with the outside world favored the export of Egyptian technologies and artistic motives and influenced the minor arts of Canaan and the Levant (such as ivory carving and metalworking) that flourished onwards from the ninth century in Phoenicia. The Egyptian influence in the field of architecture remained not insignificant but more marginal.[3] Egyptian building elements such as the cavetto were, of course, widely adapted abroad from the tenth century on.[4] An open papyriform capital of early Israelite time was found at Beth Shan.[5] In the first millennium B.C. a new capital type—the so-called Proto-Aeolic, Proto-Ionic, or Timorah-capital—made its appearance in countries around the eastern Mediterranean. Its main features, a central triangle flanked by two spiraling *volutes*, also characterize the Egyptian lily capital known since the late 18th Dynasty. Nevertheless, scholars question a significant Egyptian contribution.[6]

A similar, more international phenomenon was the spreading of *ashlar* masonry in the tenth and ninth centuries in Phoenicia, Cyprus, and Palestine.[7] Again, the development of this technique—with rectangular blocks arranged in horizontal courses—is somewhat controversial, but its origin in Egypt, a country with a long tradition in stone construction, cannot be overlooked.[8]

Pinodjem I of Thebes (1071–1033)

Herihor and his successor, Pinodjem I, completed the old Theban Khonsu temple of Ramesses III, which was under construction for several generations. When the temple was approaching completion, it was supplied with a sphinx allée, for which Pinodjem I had sphinxes of Amenhotep III transferred from his mortuary temple at Kom el-Heitan on the west bank. The new allée was part of a Theban network of processional roads and led to a bark basin 250 m southwest at the processional road to the Luxor temple. Pinodjem I also presented statues of the lion goddess Sakhmet to the precinct of Mut, apparently continuing similar donations by the great Theban builder-kings Amenhotep III and Ramesses II.

At EL-HIBE in Middle Egypt, which so far had not played a significant role at all, a stronghold for a kind of secondary residence for the Theban rulers was built under Pinodjem I and later extended by the high priest of Amun, Menkheperra.

Psusennes I, King of Tanis (1040–992)

In the forty-eight-year reign of Psusennes I, construction activity naturally concentrated on the development of the new residence city of TANIS.[9] Compelling for military reasons was the erection of a huge, 20 m thick brick enclosure. However, a temple for the traditional Amun also was built, consisting of a large 38 x 50 m temple house (plan I). The front part of the building, which seems to have made use of much granite, was a colonnaded porch with *monolithic*, closed papyrus bundle columns of granite—spoils from Middle Kingdom buildings of older Delta cities.

Psusennes I also founded the royal cemetery of Tanis. Perhaps for better protection, the kings of the Late Period were buried within temple enclosures that differed considerably from the complex royal tombs of the Ramessides at Thebes. The Tanis tombs consisted of three larger and two smaller buildings for a dozen royal burials. The aboveground structures are now lost, but one may assume that they consisted of chapels with funerary offering rooms and entrances into the shafts. Directly below ground, simple sarcophagus chambers were built from huge blocks (mostly spoliated) and supplemented by a small antechamber or side chamber. The crypts were filled with large stone sarcophagi. These underground apartments, being reduced to the minimal function of housing a sarcophagus and its funerary equipment, are architecturally speaking insignificant.

Siamun, King of Tanis (979–960)

Only at the end of the Twenty-first Dynasty, under Siamun, the Amun temple at TANIS, founded under Psusennes I, was enlarged. In front of the older temple house Siamun built an approximately 40 x 75 m wide colonnaded court, again amply usurping older building elements from neighboring sites (plan I). This court probably contained a Ramesside obelisk pair, a row of royal statues of the Middle Kingdom, and an imposing phalanx of eight or ten more obelisks in front of the temple house of Psusennes I. A pylon, possibly cased with granite and with four obelisks in front, shielded the front of the court.

Siamun probably also built at Tanis the oldest temple for the foreign goddess Anta, identified with the Theban goddess Mut. The temple was later replaced by Apries and again by Ptolemy IV. A 80 x 120 m wide brick enclosure of the sanctuary might have belonged to the early project because the monumental gate in the northern wall is dated by a foundation deposit of Siamun.

No building activity outside the residence is known except for a door frame of a chapel dedicated by a private person, Ptah-kha, to the king in the Ptah temple at MEMPHIS.[10]

Sheshonq I, Hedjkheperre setepenre (945–924)

Sheshonq I established his rule as the first king of the 22nd Dynasty at Bubastis but soon achieved recognition beyond his hometown, first at Tanis and later at Memphis and Thebes. He finally became the most powerful ruler and prolific builder of the period between the end of the New Kingdom and the 25th Dynasty. The "Bubastide" king did not choose Bubastis for his residence; he chose Tanis, the city in which he was also finally buried.

Sheshonq I, King Shishak of the Old Testament, acquired international attention through his devastating campaign against Judah and Israel, undertaken in the fifth year of Rehoboam king of Judah (ca. 925 B.C.). He marched with 1,200 chariots and 3,000 horsemen to Megiddo and the Mediterranean coast near modern Haifa, plundered extensively, and finally seized the treasures of the temple and royal palace of Jerusalem (1 Kings, 14:25–29). The outcome of this predatory attack was guarded by a chain of fortresses along the coastal road, which was meant to secure fast access to the Negev and Canaan. Remains of these forts have been found between Gaza and El-Arish (at Bethpelet and Gerar).

In Egypt's residence TANIS the completion of the Amun temple was still carried on (fig. 4). A pair of giant sphinxes of King Amenemhat II was hauled in front of the court of Siamun.[11] An inscribed block from TELL BAL-ALA (Tell Tebilla) suggests an unexplored Osiris temple of Sheshonq I northwest of Tanis.[12]

Figure 4.
The ruins of the Amun temple of Tanis (photo A.O.).

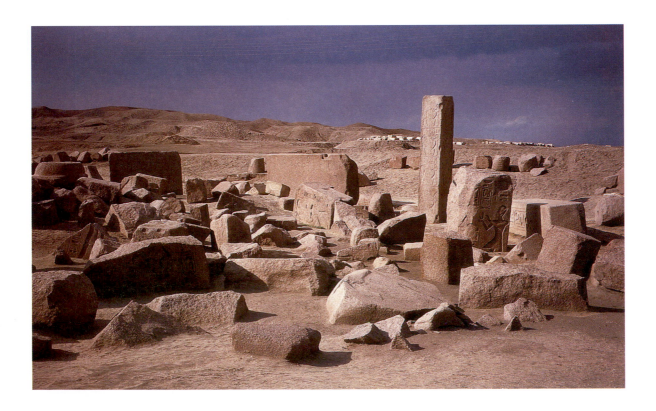

Sheshonq I apparently also enlarged the famed New Kingdom temple of the ancient creator god Ptah at MEMPHIS by a monumental element, probably a huge gate, as indicated by the fragment of a large cavetto with a row of cartouches.[13]

Sheshonq I also dedicated a small temple to Amun at EL-HIBE (ancient Ibeon), the Middle Egyptian outpost of the priest-kings of Thebes.[14] Inside a brick enclosure with projecting bastions stood the 17.65 x 30 m temple house with a hypostyle hall of two-by-four pillars, an offering chamber, and a bark sanctuary with four side rooms for the cult images (fig. 5). Some very fine reliefs of Sheshonq I were preserved in the ruin of the temple.[15]

The building was small and would not be of great importance except for its *pronaos* with papyrus bundle columns. If this pronaos dates to the reign of Sheshonq I, it would represent the earliest example of a building type popular not before the 30th Dynasty. However, the sloping rear wall of the pronaos, with the representations of the king smiting enemies—a typical scene for a temple facade—suggests that this wall originally formed the facade of the temple and that the pronaos was added later. Since papyrus bundle columns appear in the pronaos of the 30th Dynasty at Hermopolis magna, one would prefer to date the pronaos of El-Hibe to the same period. Since the decoration of the pronaos was left unfinished, one further thinks of the time of Nectanebos II, whose building projects were interrupted by the second Persian invasion of 343. The sanctuary of the temple stood free in a tiny ambulatory and

Figure 5.
Longitudinal section and plan of the temple of Sheshonq I at El-Hibe with later additions (*left*) and capital of pronaos (after Hermann Ranke, *Koptische Friedhöfe bei Karâra und der Amontempel Scheschonks I bei El Hibe* [Berlin, 1926], pls. 9–11).

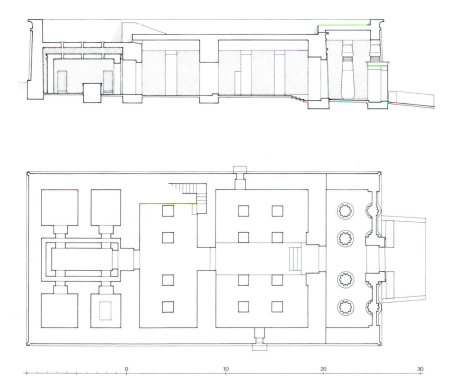

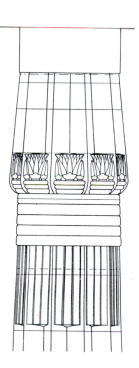

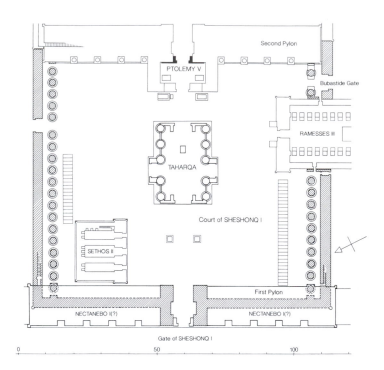

Figure 6.
The Ramesside monuments in front of
the Amun temple at Karnak structured
by the colonnades and gate of Sheshonq I,
the kiosk of Taharqa, and the pylon of
Nectanebo I(?).

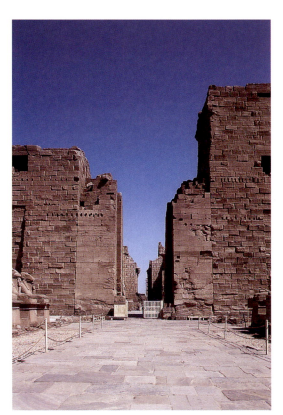

Figure 7.
The unfinished gate of Sheshonq I(?) at
Karnak flanked by the unfinished pylon
towers of Nectanebo I(?) (photo A.O.).

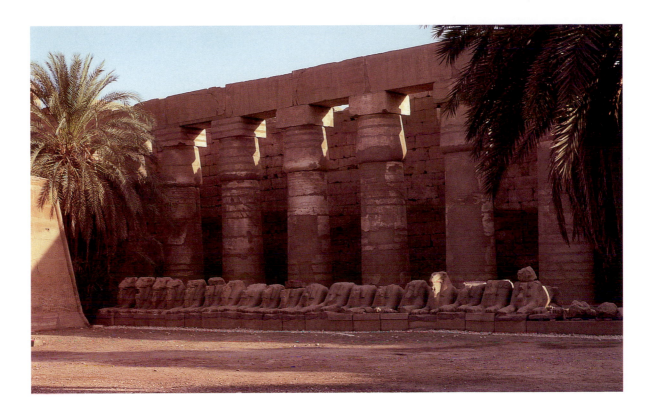

reminds one of the sanctuaries popular from the Macedonian period on, for example, at Karnak. Was even the sanctuary added at a later date?

A detail of the papyrus bundle columns also points to a 30th Dynasty date of the El-Hibe pronaos (fig. 5). The capitals replace the traditional simple papyrus buds inserted between the main stems with the more advanced version with small bundles of one open and two closed papyrus blossoms.

Sheshonq I imitated the kings of the New Kingdom not only with his Israel campaign but also with his devotion to Amun of Karnak. After his campaign against Israel in 925 B.C., Sheshonq I enlarged the Amun temple at KARNAK by adding a huge festival court in front of the Ramesside (now second) pylon (figs. 6–8). The new court measures 81.01 x 101.11 m, which corresponds to 152 x 190 cubits and a proportion of 4:5 modules of 38 cubits each.[16] Virtually following Ramesside architectural tradition, the court was flanked on both sides by colonnades and enclosed the Ramesside festival arena with the bark stations of Sethos II and Ramesses III. Between the temple of Ramesses III and the second pylon, room was available for a side entrance flanked by two columns, the so-called Bubastide Gate. The court was probably closed at the front by a plain wall with a monumental, central gate (now in the first pylon). Due to the lack of inscriptions the unfinished gate cannot be dated (fig. 7).[17] It is certainly older than the two flanking towers of the first pylon (see fig. 72), however, which are part of the enclosure of Nectanebo I. The 7.40 m wide doorway would have required roofing beams of 9 m length, overstraining the

Figure 8.
The colonnades of the Bubastide court at Karnak follow the style and proportions of the late New Kingdom (photo A.O.).

strength of sandstone and necessitating granite or wooden beams. The height of the opening was 17.70 m, suggesting a total height of the gate of 27.50(!) m. The untimely death of Sheshonq I terminated this ambitious project. Only the wall decoration of the side gate could be executed; the decoration of the enormous wall surfaces of the court would have overtaxed the available resources.

The court of Sheshonq I reveals that nothing had changed in constructing huge temple courts since the last building projects of the Ramesside kings. After the works of Sheshonq I, for 200 years no other significant building project was undertaken at Thebes until the Kushite period.

Osorkon I, Sekhemkheperre setepenre (924–889)

Sheshonq I's son Osorkon I began his reign with generous donations to the main sanctuaries of the country, probably to secure the favor of the gods and their priesthood, and presumably using up his father's Jerusalem booty. His main architectural contribution ameliorated the Bastet temple of the family's hometown of BUBASTIS. Since the Old Kingdom, great rulers like Kheops, Khephren, Senwosret III, Amenhotep III, Sethos I, and Ramesses II had erected monuments for the lioness deity Bastet of Bubastis. After the Ramesside period, her aged temple probably fell into disrepair. No wonder that the Bubastide Osorkon I made the renewal of her sanctuary a priority of his building program. His works, and later additions by Osorkon II and Nectanebo II, upgraded this temple to a leading position (fig. 9). Unfortunately, the temple is so greatly destroyed that its exact form remains unknown (fig. 10).[18] The range of the debris mounds covering the temple area suggests that Osorkon I began a new temple consisting of a temple house and a court. Gates and columns consisted of granite; the walls were probably of limestone.[19] The front part of the temple contained a hypostyle hall with a central row of 8.55 m high papyrus-bundle columns of granite.[20] They probably were flanked by smaller (6.71 m high) palm columns. The hypostyle hall, therefore, seems to have had a high central nave. Nothing is known about the plan of the temple house behind.[21]

A temple of Atum, who was considered the spouse of Bastet, stood about 600 m away from the Bastet temple. On the connecting processional road, according to Herodotus (II.138), were "here and there . . . trees which seem to touch the sky." The Atum temple was initially built by Ramesses II and enlarged or renewed by Osorkon I. E. Naville started to excavate decorated granite blocks but was prevented from further work by the owner of the land.[22]

MEMPHIS received only a small chapel, of which an *architrave* is still preserved with the names of Bastet and Horus.[23]

At ATFIH, on the east bank of the Nile, opposite El-Wasta, Osorkon I probably enlarged the sanctuary of an ancient cow cult identified with Hathor-Isis, as can be inferred from a relief block showing the goddess.[24]

Farther to the south, a fortress was built on the west bank of the Nile, presumably near Heracleopolis magna, to control the road junction between Upper and Lower Egypt and the Faiyum.

Figure 9.
The giant ruins of the temple of Bastet at Bubastis looking west (photo A.O.).

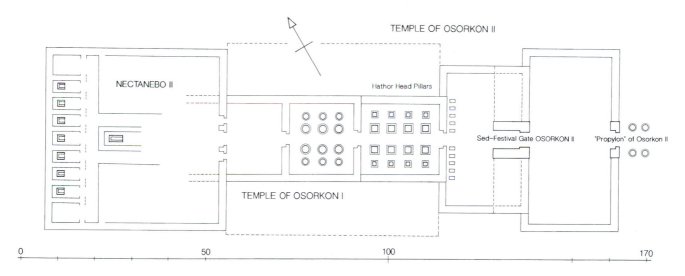

Figure 10. Hypothetical reconstruction of the Bastet temple of Bubastis in the Third Intermediate Period and 30th Dynasty.

Osorkon II, Usimare setepenamun (874–850)

During the twenty-four-year reign of Osorkon II, a group of interesting buildings were erected in Egypt. At TANIS, Osorkon II enlarged the 150-year-old Amun temple, founded by Psusennes I, by adding two pylons and the associated courts. The temple now reached an imposing double length of 234 m (plan I). The emplacement of all pylons at Tanis is only suggested by the location of a number of fallen obelisks that were usurped from buildings of Ramesses II at Qantir. In front of the first pylon of Osorkon II stood the obelisks nos. 1 and 2. In the court behind followed the obelisk pair nos. 3–4. This court also enclosed two colossal sphinxes of Amenemhat II, which had been brought there by Sheshonq I (now in the Louvre [A 23]).

Behind the temple house of Psusennes I and its enclosure wall, Osorkon II built another monument, including the obelisk pair nos. 9 and 10. Of this eastern temple mainly ten 7 m high granite palm columns are preserved. They came originally from an Old Kingdom temple, usurped by Ramesses II before they were reinscribed by Osorkon II.[25] No traces of the walls of this temple were found.

Osorkon II built his granite tomb chamber containing his huge, 3.5 m long granite sarcophagus close to the southwest corner of the first pylon of the Amun temple. No superstructure is preserved.

At BUBASTIS Osorkon II continued the temple of Osorkon I. From remains of four different column and pillar capitals found in front of the area of the temple of Osorkon I, one can conclude that the temple received a new hypostyle hall. The granite pillars had old-fashioned double-faced Hathor heads appropriate for a female deity (fig. 11). The higher central row of pillars was probably flanked by somewhat smaller ones.[26] The hypostyle hall apparently was built in connection with the erection of a more famous structure, the Sed-festival gate (see below). The gate apparently commemorates the king's Sed festival in the year 853. The gate probably stood at the front of a court which led to the hypostyle hall. In 1887–1889 E. Naville found several dozen disconnected blocks of the gate and used them to reconstruct (regrettably only on paper, fig. 12) one of the most outstanding Sed-festival monuments known to us from ancient Egypt. The gate was decorated on the front, the interior, and inside the doorway with several registers depicting a Sed-festival cycle.[27] The width of the passage was probably 5 m and the total height of the gate, including architrave and cavetto, 15 m.

The complete Sed-festival cycle on Osorkon's gate is unique, since functionally related predecessors of the 12th and 18th Dynasties and comparable successors of the 22nd and 25th Dynasties have a simpler decorative program.[28] The last known example was that of Ptolemy II at Medamoud.[29] These Sed-festival gates led to temples in which, at the feast, the gods of the two countries were supposed to assemble around the king.[30] At the same time, the king may have been rejuvenated by passing the depictions of the rites.

In addition, Osorkon II dedicated at Bubastis a *naos* of red granite.[31] Herodotus (I.138) later saw a *propylon* that was "ten fathoms high," or an amazing 17.76 m, and adorned with 6 cubit high (2.66 m) figures (II.138). Traces of such an entrance kiosk, which Osorkon II probably added to the front of the first temple court, have been noticed.

Figure 11. Granite Hathor capital of the temple of Osorkon II at Bubastis in the garden of the Egyptian Museum, Cairo.

Figure 12.
Naville's reconstruction model of the
granite Sed-festival gate of Osorkon II
at Bubastis showing the south side.

Osorkon II also built a small Mihos (Miysis) temple, 60 m north and behind
the Bastet temple. Since Mihos was considered the child of Bastet and Atum,
his temple may have been an early version of the later birth houses. Excavation by L. Habachi in 1943 recovered red granite palm and papyrus bundle
columns, but not the shape and dimensions of the temple.[32]

A larger building project may be postulated for LEONTOPOLIS (Tell el-
Muqdam), where Osorkon II renewed the Mihos (Miysis) temple with numerous spoils of the Old and Middle Kingdoms. The temple already was so badly
demolished by 1892 that its size and shape remain unknown.[33]

At PITHOM Osorkon II apparently dedicated sanctuaries for the primordial
gods Atum, Shu, Tefnut, Reharakhte, and the Theban Triade. Unfinished cornices with his name only painted in red were found by Naville.[34] In MEMPHIS
some insignificant works were carried out.

At KARNAK a small but architecturally interesting gate was dedicated by
Nimrod, the high priest of Amun, son of Osorkon II. The gate stood at the processional approach of the Amunra-Monthu temple.[35] From a few blocks
reused in a Kushite porch (see figs. 30, 243; plan IX), the shape of the gate can
be recognized as consisting of two columns bridged by an architrave (fig. 13).
The gate anticipated the shape of a gate of the same type built under Ptolemy
XII at the Ptah temple at Karnak (figs. 168–169).

0   5

Figure 13.
Plan of the two-column gate
of Nimrod, the high priest of
Amun, at Karnak.

Sheshonq III, Usimare setepenre/Amun (825–773)

The main monuments of the long-ruling king were built in the Delta, the heartland of the dynasty. The most eminent structure was the main gate of the enclosure of Amun at TANIS leading through the earlier 15.5 m thick brick enclosure of Psusennes I (plan I). The huge granite gate contained several blocks of Kheops and Ramesses II, some of which have been reassembled now. The width of the passage was 5 m, its height 12.85 m. The relatively thin and not very strong construction shows that the gate was not freestanding but was engaged in the brick wall. Behind the gate and slightly apart from the earlier royal tombs, Sheshonq III built his own crypt.

Not far from Tanis, Sheshonq III also started considerable building activity at Diospolis inferior, the city of AMUN (modern Tell el-Balamun, west of the Damietta branch of the Nile).[36] Reports on the recent excavations of the British Museum under J. Spencer grant important new insights into the building history of the main temple A. This presumably Ramesside Amun temple was enlarged by adding two pairs of pylons with two courts (plan II). With its breadth of 75 m, the front pylon surpassed even the 68 m pylon of Ramesses III at Medinet Habu. Both pairs of pylons were apparently linked by a double row of columns leading through the first court. Such colonnaded passages had prototypes in the New Kingdom, most prominently the gigantic late–18th Dynasty colonnade of the Luxor temple.[37]

Blocks bearing the name of Sheshonq III suggest that he also initiated the building of the temple of TÛKH EL-QARÂMÛS (between Bubastis and Tanis).[38] As indicated by a foundation deposit, the 136 m long limestone temple was later renewed under Philippus Arrhidaeus. The 454 x 514 m enclosure may belong to the 30th Dynasty, the period of great enclosure-wall building.

In the sanctuary of Thoth of MESDET, Sheshonq III replaced a Ramesside temple with a new building. We know about this project from over thirty inscribed limestone blocks of Sheshonq III found in the ruins of the nearby TELL UMM HARB (Tell Mustâi, between Zifta and Benha).[39] Blocks that carry his cartouches were also found at MENDES.[40] Sheshonq III also seems to have contributed to the Sakhmet-Hathor temple at KOM EL-HISN (ancient Imu, capital of the third nome), where blocks of a gateway with his name were found.[41] Another block with the name of the king was noticed in a huge, unexplored temple enclosure near EL-BINDARÎA (between Zifta and Kom el-Hisn).[42]

Osorkon III, Usermaatre setepen-Amun (777–749)

Under Osorkon III and Takelothis III, in a period that is understood neither chronologically nor historically, a small two-room chapel was built for Osiris-Heka-djet, the "ruler of eternity," 100 m northeast of the Amun temple at KARNAK. An interesting feature is a huge false door, inserted into the facade of the chapel. Its cavetto moldings depict seven superimposed chapel facades (fig. 14).[43] The building started a certain pattern of chapels for Osiris, built at Karnak, mainly during the 25th Dynasty (see chapter 3, under Shabaka, and chapter 4, under Psametik I).

Sheshonq V (former IV), Akheperre (767–730)

Using numerous spoils, Sheshonq V of Leontopolis built at TANIS another temple for the Theban Triad north of the precinct of Amun. Apparently, the temple was distinguished by a Sed-festival structure for the celebration of his jubilee, perhaps a gate, of which seventeen blocks were discovered reused at the sacred lake of Tanis.[44]

The kings and kinglets of the 23rd and 24th Dynasties, whose rule overlapped with the later part of the 22nd Dynasty were too impoverished to build any temple worth mentioning.

Figure 14.
The false door of the chapel of Osorkon III at Karnak representing a sequence of seven superimposed chapel facades (photo A.O.).

3

THE KUSHITE PERIOD
(CA. 716–664 B.C.)

During the period of declining Egyptian domination over Nubia in the tenth century, the Kushite kingdom of Napata established itself along the upper Nile.[1] The local rulers stood in the tradition of the bygone Egyptian authority and under the influence of the cult of Amun at Napata, and they saw themselves as legitimate successors of the pharaohs. They finally succeeded in 736 or before by hitherto unknown means to gain control over Upper Egypt. In 728/727 their king, Piankhi, defeated a Lower Egyptian coalition under Tefnakht, the king of Sais, and finally conquered Memphis.[2] From this event on, Egypt was for sixty-three years united under Kushite rule. The reigns of the kings Shabitku, Shabaka, and Taharqa generated a political and cultural flowering, enhanced by the strong Kushites' inclination toward Egyptian religion and culture. Although the Kushite rulers did not reside continuously in Egypt, they considered themselves instigators of a historical renewal and followed the Egyptian tradition, choosing their titulary from Old Kingdom royal examples.

After an ebb in public building in Upper Egypt of about 250 years, the conquest of Egypt by the Kushites released a new wave of monumental building in Thebes.[3] A promising initiative was first signaled by the still modest building activity under Shabaka and Shabataka. Under Taharqa, however, temple building at Thebes reached the level of his royal predecessors of the New Kingdom. Disregarding buildings in the Kushite heartland (i.e., the Sudan, which cannot be discussed here; see introduction), royal commissions were limited to Upper Egypt, however,[4] and there especially to Thebes. For unknown reasons, outside Thebes only modest buildings were erected in places like Tanis, Memphis, Baharia Oasis, and Philae.

Building Form and Style in the Kushite Period

Altogether, the Kushite royal commissions were exclusively enlargements and modifications of existing buildings that expressed admiration and respect for pharaonic sacred building.[5] Had the Kushites built new temples in Egypt, they probably—as indicated by the temples of Taharqa at Tabo, Kawa, and Sanam in the Sudan—would have copied prototypes of the New Kingdom, perhaps enhanced by Old Kingdom decorative elements.[6] The Kushite rule in Egypt, lasting only three generations, nevertheless was a productive phase of temple building. For example, additions to most of the Theban temples of the New Kingdom brought about significant optical and functional alterations. Three types of additions catch the eye (see fig. 242). One is the kiosk standing free in the forecourt or some distance from the main temple. The second type is a kiosk adjoining the temple facade with its back wall. The third building type is a porch of several parallel rows of columns, also leaning against the temple but with a fully open front. With kiosks and porches an element was introduced into temple building that finally redefined the appearance of Late Egyptian temples. The creation of these forms must reflect transformations in ritual practices. Temple gates must have become gathering places of huge crowds of laymen who were not admitted into the actual sanctuary but summoned to the gates. Kiosks and porches therefore served as monumental, shady rooms for the gathering of these visitors and the organization of participants in ceremonial processions.

In continuation of a practice of the 22nd Dynasty (see chapter 2, under Osorkon II), several small chapels for Osiris were built under the Kushites, mainly at Karnak. The decoration program of the chapels suggests that the resurrection of the king or the divine consorts was a primary incentive for erecting these chapels.[7]

Bernard V. Bothmer states that the Kushite

rise to power ushers in the last great era of Egyptian history and art, which is commonly called the Late Period. Far from exercising a debasing influence on Egypt, [the Kushites] effected a revival of artistic expression, and many of the works created during their rule rival in quality the best created in earlier periods.[8]

The 25th and 26th Dynasties therefore became a period of renewal of the forms and style of the glorious past, especially of the Old Kingdom. Prototypes for the reliefs of the temple of Kawa can be located in the pyramid temples of the 5th Dynasty. As M. Bietak has shown,[9] these models were not always slavishly imitated or adjusted to current perceptions but also merged into new programs. Even the proportions of human figures no longer follow the canon of the New Kingdom but were considerably elongated and reverted to those of the Old Kingdom. These changes, however, had nothing to do with a reformation of the Egyptian unit of length and the alteration of the proportion grid for the drawing of human figures.[10] That Kushite builders showed a preference for the Old Kingdom column type of the palm column may be no coincidence.

J. Leclant pointed out the more slender and elegant proportions of Kushite papyrus columns. Their diameter relates to their height at a proportion of 1:7, in contrast to Ramesside proportions of 1:5 or even 1:4.[11]

The funerary palaces of Theban officials of the period display an affluence in building rarely found in the New Kingdom.[12] The tombs confirm that their builders had an outstanding knowledge of older Theban and Memphite architecture, and the decoration and inscriptions display a deep insight into the Egyptian understanding of the otherworld. Finally, the tombs show a remarkable religious and artistic creativity[13] that elevates the Kushite Period far above the preceding Third Intermediate Period.

The Building Methods of the Kushite Period

The traditional methods of stone cutting and dressing of the New Kingdom continued unchanged during the 25th Dynasty. In the Kushite Period a few innovations can be detected, which certainly resulted from an increase in the use of iron tools. Meteoric iron appears in Egypt as a curiosity from prehistoric times. Only from the late 18th Dynasty on, the number of iron tools continuously grows, and the period from 700 on could be considered the Iron Age. Thus far, proof for iron smelting has been detected only in the Greek settlements of Naucratis and Daphnae (sixth century).[14] In the 26th Dynasty, following the Kushites, iron tools are as common in Egypt as bronze tools, although, due to the unfamiliar material, the quality of early iron products rarely reached that of the traditional bronze tools. Only during the 26th Dynasty did metal production methods improve. In consequence, preserved monuments from that period exhibit advanced stone-dressing methods. In cutting rock tombs, the traditional stone hammer, with a head of diorite or quartzite, was used far into the Late Period for the rough preparatory work. For the subsequent cleaning of the rough surface, the pointed and wide chisel was applied (fig. 15).

From about 675 B.C. on, a series of new builders' tools came into use.[15] In the Theban tombs of Nespekashuti (ca. 675 B.C.) and Pedineith (ca. 545 B.C.), traces of a 7 cm wide claw chisel with seven teeth were detected. The use of a stone plane with a toothed blade also was observed. This more refined surface treatment spared the use of the traditional surface polishing with grinding stones. As a result, however, haste replaced quality. The masonry of the Kushite Period also catches the eye; its ashlar blocks are considerably smaller than the huge building blocks used in the New Kingdom and the Third Intermediate Period. Even the huge columns of Taharqa at Karnak were pieced together from small blocks.

The appearance of true stone vaults between 750 and 720 is of great interest for architectural historians.[16] The first vaults of the 25th Dynasty are a mixture of corbel and true wedge-shaped *voussoir* vaults.[17] The lower parts of the vaults still consist of two to four corbeled courses followed on top by wedge-shaped voussoirs. A true stone vault also covers the entrance passage to the pyramid of Shabitku at Kurru (ca. 695 B.C.).[18] In the same period the chambers of monumental tomb shafts at Giza and Saqqara also were provided with true stone vaults.

Figure 15.
Unfinished masonry of the
25th Dynasty at the temple
of Taharqa at Karnak.

During the Late Period, the increasing number of buildings with wide inter-columniations could have capitalized from vault constructions. However, the repertoire of forms in Egyptian stone building had long ago been established and was so strongly fixated on flat ceilings that later builders had no use for stone vaults. True stone vaults with voussoirs set radially developed in Greece only during the Hellenistic Period, and one may suspect that they were inspired by Egyptian or western Asian examples.[19] The widest stone vaults known from Greece reach a span of 6.48 m (compared with Egyptian examples of a modest 2.8[!] m), and the largest known Roman example (the Fabricius Bridge in Rome) spans 24.5 m. It might not be coincidental, however, that during the same Kushite Period, the previously mentioned Theban tombs made extensive use of brick arches, which span the gates of their entrance pylons.

The close contact of the Kushites with Egypt proved productive not just for Kushite art in general but especially for architecture in the Sudan. Since the culture of the A and C Groups (3500–1500), local traditions produced *tumulus* tombs. From ca. 790, pyramid-shaped superstructures developed. These prevailing nomadic cultures did not, however, require temple building; this situation altered only in the reign of Taharqa, who initiated extensive temple-building activities in the Sudan as well as in Egypt. This activity culminated in the second and first centuries B.C. in Meroitic architecture, characterized by an independent, distinct style. The development of this side branch of Late Egyptian architecture, whose importance is becoming more and more apparent, cannot be followed here.[20]

The Buildings of the Kushites

Shabaka, Neferkare (716–702)

In 715 Piankhi's brother Shabaka marched again against Egypt in order to renew Kushite domination, and to subdue Bekenrenef of Sais, a vassal who had become too independent. After the restitution of law and order, a local overseer of public works was ordered to fortify the sanctuaries of the country with new enclosure walls. The old enclosures must have fallen into disrepair, perhaps through military actions during the Kushite invasions. The first works, focusing on repairs in Thebes, were modest, but they inaugurated a new phase of building activity.

Under Shabaka, many relatively small projects were carried out at KARNAK, starting with repairs undertaken at the fourth pylon. The Ptah temple outside the northern enclosure wall was honored with a Sed-festival gate (no. 2, plan VIII).[21] In the northern court of the enclosure of Amun a colonnaded hall was built, and north of the ancient Akhmenu a new "Gold House" (both destroyed now).[22] An entrance porch of perhaps four-by-five columns was erected to shelter the northern access to the court between the third and fourth pylons. The columns are now destroyed.[23]

In the area north of the great hypostyle hall, a small temple for Osiris "in the Persea-tree" was built, consisting mainly of bricks with key elements in stone.[24] The construction of this temple emphasizes the invasion of the god of the netherworld during the Late Period into the contrasting realm of Amun of Karnak. The cult of Osiris gradually spread over and dominated the northeastern quadrant of the later enclosure wall of the precinct of Amun. From the 22nd Dynasty on, six chapels for Osiris were built by the divine consorts of Amun along the northern boundary of the area of Osiris. The chapels are modest, three-room stone buildings with a pylon-like front wall. The second chapel from the west was built by Amenirdis I under Shabaka and dedicated to Osiris Nebankh.[25] The connection of the chapels with the center of the Osiride cult center was interrupted when the huge enclosure walls of the precinct of Amun and Amunra-Monthu were built in the 30th Dynasty, which included the chapels in the precinct of Amunra-Monthu.

South of the precinct of Amun and in front of the Mut temple stood the Kamutef temple of Hatshepsut. The approach to this temple was sheltered by the addition of two double rows of columns, one in front of the gate and the other inside the court. The date of the enlargement, which now is completely destroyed, is unknown, but the building type may suggest a Kushite date.[26]

At the LUXOR temple, the pylon of Ramesses II received an entrance porch consisting of four-by-five columns (now destroyed).[27] The two outer aisles were covered with a roof, but the middle one, containing the two obelisks and colossal statues of Ramesses II, had to be left open.

Ramesses III had bound the small temple of the 18th Dynasty at MEDINET HABU into his enclosure wall. Shabaka added a rectangular forecourt to this temple for the primordial Amun. The court was entered through a small pylon (figs. 16–18; plan X).[28] At the same time, the pylon facilitated a passage through a new enclosure wall. The axis of the forecourt was embellished with a double row of columns, which corresponded to similar, contemporary Kushite colonnades in Theban temples. The columns were connected in the direction of the axis by screen walls. In front of the pylon stands a kiosk of uncertain date (figs. 16, 244). Since inscriptions of Nectanebo I cover older, illegible cartouches, the kiosk must have a pre–30th Dynasty date. Because no significant buildings were erected at Thebes between the 26th and 29th Dynasties, one might suggest that the kiosk dates to the 25th Dynasty.[29]

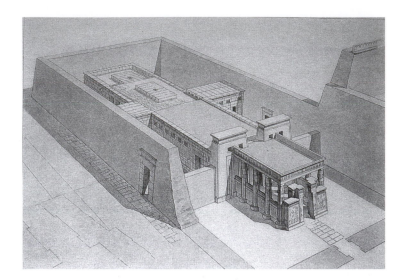

Figure 16.
Reconstruction of the Kushite(?) entrance kiosk of the temple of the primordial Amun at Medinet Habu (Uvo Hölscher, *The Temples of the Eighteenth Dynasty* [Chicago, 1939]).

Figure 17.
Actual state of the Kushite(?) entrance kiosk of the temple of the primordial Amun at Medinet Habu looking west (photo A.O.).

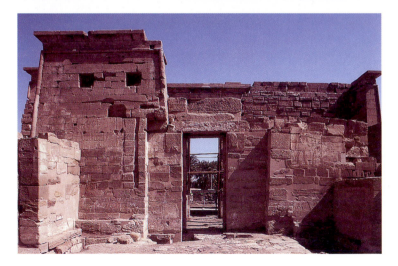

Figure 18.
Rear of the Kushite pylon of the temple of the primordial Amun at Medinet Habu (photo A.O.).

In that case, the kiosk would be one of the oldest examples of this type in Late Period architecture. It consists of two-by-four columns, which were spaced 5 cubits apart, resulting in a proportion of the ground plan of 16:15 (measured between the centers of the corner columns). The entrance gate of the kiosk stands slightly in front of the kiosk and is therefore not flanked by two columns. The frontal, 8.6 m long architrave, therefore, sat on the corner columns; it had to be made of wood, together with the rest of the roof construction, which must have carried a shallow vault.

Amenirdis I, sister of Piankhi, was established as the *divine consort* of Amun and ruler over Thebes (ca. 740–700). Her tomb chapel is still preserved at MEDINET HABU between those of the divine consorts Shepenwepet I–II and Nitocris (of the 25th and 26th Dynasties). The Amenirdis building has a pylon-like front topped by a heavy cavetto (figs. 19–20) with an interior colonnaded court followed by a sanctuary for the mortuary offerings on a slightly higher level. The offering room is freestanding and roofed by a stone barrel vault, which consists of two corbeled courses in its lower part and wedge-shaped voussoirs in the upper part. Although the vault spans only 2.18 m, it is one of the earliest examples of a true vault in the Late Period. The tomb is under the floor of the sanctuary. On one hand, these tomb chapels follow Theban and Memphite New Kingdom prototypes, modified by a freestanding offering hall covered by a vault. On the other hand, they are the fore-runners of the private tomb chapels of the Ptolemaic Period (e.g., at Tuna el-Gebel; see fig. 104).

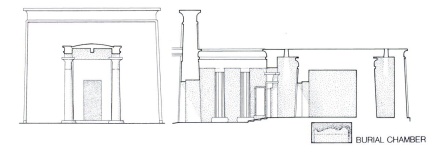

BURIAL CHAMBER

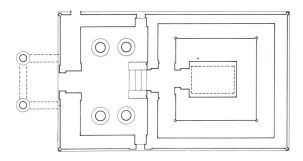

Figure 19.
Section and plan of the mortuary chapel of Amenirdis I at Medinet Habu.

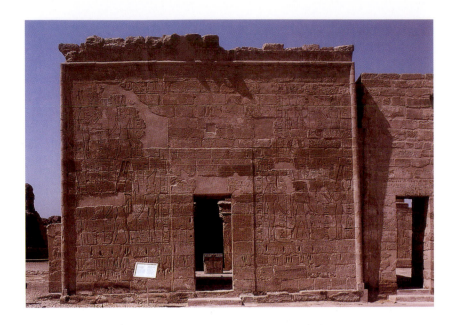

Figure 20.
Frontal view of the mortuary
chapel of Amenirdis I at
Medinet Habu (photo A.O.).

Some building projects were also started in the Upper Egyptian provinces. Blocks of a Sed-festival gate of an unknown Kushite ruler (Shabaka?) were found reused under the pavement of the Ptolemaic court of EDFU. Other remains of monuments are known from ABYDOS and ESNA.[30] Even in distant MEMPHIS the older pylons were provided with modern porches, and a chapel was built.

Following Piankhi's example, the king was buried in a pyramid tomb at El-Kurru, the earliest royal cemetery of the Kushites, some kilometers north of the Gebel Barkal.

Shabitku (Shabataka) Djedkaure (702–690)

Twenty-four years after the conquest of Egypt by the Kushites, the short ensuing peace was over and the struggle against the Assyrians started, for the time being still in Palestine. Shabitku supported an initially successful Phoenician-Palestinian uprising against the Assyrian king Sennacherib and sent the Kushite prince (and later king) Taharqa to strengthen the rebellion. Apparently, the Kushites were defeated by the more experienced Assyrians and could not prevent the siege and fall of Lakhish in 701. The probably heavy war taxation collected by the Kushites from the Egyptian population and the relatively short reign of Shabitku may explain why practically no temples were erected.

At KARNAK the small temple of Osorkon III for Osiris-Heka-djet, 100 m northeast of the Amun temple, was enlarged by a frontal broad room.[31] A small chapel built southeast of the sacred lake is now in Berlin. [32]

From MEMPHIS, a relief block and a headless statue of Shabitku are known.[33]

Taharqa, Nefertem-khu-Re (690–664)

The rule of Taharqa was marked by the fights with the Assyrians Senna-cherib, Esarhaddon, and Ashurbanipal over the Levant. In the few peaceful years between the wars, Taharqa launched building activity at a scale not seen since the New Kingdom.[34] However, the Kushite domination and their building activity in Egypt came soon to an end. After a first failed attempt in 674, Esarhaddon defeated Taharqa's army in 671, conquered Memphis, and put Taharqa to flight. At first the Assyrian victory seemed temporary, and Taharqa succeeded in reconquering Memphis. In 669 Esarhaddon again marched against Egypt, but he died on his way. In 667–666 his son Ashurbanipal appeared and defeated the Kushite-Egyptian army at Kar-baniti, conquered fortresses and towns,[35] and pursued Taharqa in an unprecedented campaign up to Thebes, whose temples were plundered for the first time in history. An ensuing rebellion by Delta rulers was crushed, and their leader, Necho, who would later cause more stir, was deported to Nineveh. After a surprise amnesty, Necho was reinstalled as an Assyrian vassal at Sais, while his son became governor of Athribis. Taharqa himself apparently fled to Napata, where he died after a few years. The pyramid of Taharqa was built at Nuri, with an underground apartment that seems to have followed the tradition of an Egyptian Osireion.

Three years after the Assyrian conquest, in 664 or 663, Taharqa's successor, Tanutamun (664–656), at once attempted to reconquer Egypt. With his troops he defeated the Assyrian vassal Necho of Sais and the other Delta vassals and for a short period reestablished Kushite rule. In 661 the Assyrian army of Ashurbanipal returned and expelled the Kushites permanently from Egypt.[36] Thebes again fell into the hands of the revengeful foreigners, and this time the destruction seems to have been so thorough that Thebes, with its cult of Amun, never recovered its former status. No wonder that no monuments are known from the few years of Tanutamun's reign.

THEBES glistened—for the last time in its glorious history—and was honored by Taharqa with monuments, a project conducted mainly by the competent major of Thebes, Montuemhat. The principal monument of the time was doubtlessly the kiosk in the Bubastide court of the Amun temple at Karnak, a daring feat of engineering that surpassed all earlier kiosks in size (figs. 21–24).[37] It consisted of two rows of gigantic columns with open papyrus capitals. Their shafts were constructed of twenty-five courses of limestone blocks and soared to a height of 18.87 m, nearly as high as the New Kingdom columns of the hypostyle hall of Karnak and the colonnade of the Luxor temple.[38] The uppermost course of the 4.93 m wide, overhanging capitals was balanced by a heavy *abacus*. The reconstruction of the entablature is conflicting. In the direction of the axis, architraves would have been possible. The transversal distance of 16.25 m would have been difficult to bridge even with timber. One scholar has also suggested that the columns were freestanding and used as pedestals for statues.[39] The columns were connected with screen walls only under Ptolemy IV Philopator.

Also at Karnak, a peculiar cult building was erected at the north side of the sacred lake (figs. 15, 25). According to the remains of the wall decoration the

Figure 21.
Reconstruction of the first court of the Amun temple of Karnak with the Taharqa kiosk (*Description* III, pl. 41).

Figure 22.
The reconstructed column of the kiosk of Taharqa kiosk in the first court of Amun at Karnak (photo A.B.).

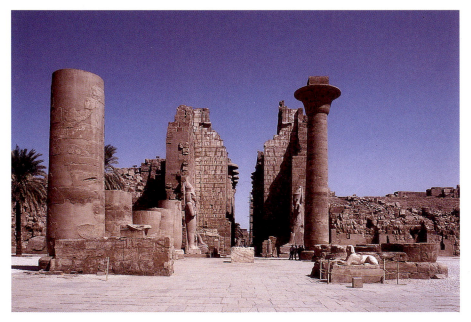

Figure 23. Frontal view of the kiosk of Taharqa in the first court of Amun at Karnak (photo A.O.).

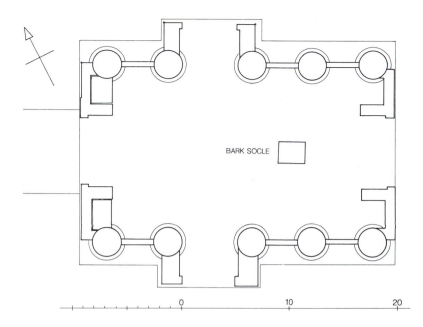

BARK SOCLE

0   10   20

Figure 24.
Plan of the Taharqa kiosk in the
first court of Amun at Karnak.

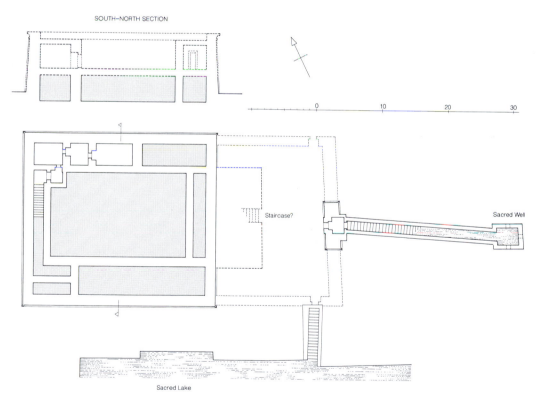

SOUTH–NORTH SECTION

0   10   20   30

Staircase?

Sacred Well

Sacred Lake

Figure 25. Section and plan of the temple of Taharqa at Karnak.

temple was dedicated to the cult of the sun and the King. The king was elevated to the role of the lord of the universe by a cultic performance, enacting the daily course of the sun.[40] The deification of the ruler, therefore, was an important aspect of the temple. The building of 25 x 29 m, the upper part of which is now destroyed, offered for these rituals an open court for the solar cult and underground crypts for the performance of the nocturnal course of the sun. The question of the location of the entrance and the reconstruction of the upper floor remain unsolved. Possibly Shabaka had already erected a similar building, blocks of which were found reused in the Taharqa temple.[41] A later formal and functional successor may have been the Opet temple built by Ptolemy VIII (see figs. 110–111).

Under Taharqa also the gates of the second and tenth pylons, which had been burned perhaps during an unheard-of military action, were restored. Their relief decoration was later reinscribed by Psametik II. Furthermore, two gates were erected on the processional approach to the Ptah temple, which stands 130 m north of the Amun temple (plan VIII).

A small, two-room chapel for Osiris Nebankh was built by the divine consorts under Taharqa north of the third pylon of Karnak and another chapel for Osiris-Ptah-Nebankh south of the tenth pylon.[42]

New structures can also be confirmed in the complex of AMUNRA-MONTHU (Karnak-North, plan IX). One of the buildings was a small temple of the divine consorts of Amun Shepenupet II and Amenirdis II (the sister and the daughter of Taharqa), built in the last years of Taharqa's reign (fig. 26). The facade of the temple can be reconstructed to some degree with the help of blocks found reused in the foundations of a nearby Ptolemaic porch.[43] The function of the temple is unclear. The emphasis in the decoration program on the cult of Osiris and its connection to the Sed festival suggest a dynastic cult center. The unusual pattern of the facade accentuates female aspects. Four engaged half-columns with Hathor capitals divide the 10 m wide facade into three sections, with the entrance in the center. This arrangement shows that the building depicts a colonnaded kiosk. It would have been easy to build such a kiosk in the round, but the builders preferred a depiction.[44] This feature also appears at a chapel in front of the LUXOR temple. Opposite the pylon of Ramesses II and east of the sphinx allée approaching from Karnak, a chapel was built at the Sed festival of Taharqa. Its northern facade was again articulated by three engaged Hathor columns, which protruded inside and out from the wall.[45] These columns seem to suggest a functional connection with the later birth houses (see the discussion in chapter 9).

A small shrine was built at the northeast corner of the Amunra-Monthu temple of Amenhotep III at Karnak-North (fig. 30). The shrine stood on a platform that was reached by a ramp.[46] Entrance was through a 2.5 m high pylon, the gate of which had a broken lintel. Numerous decorated blocks of the pylon were found built into the foundations of a Ptolemaic porch. Behind the gate was an elongated room surrounded on three sides by columns connected by screen walls. The columns, made of wood, were set at amazingly short intervals. It is difficult to determine whether the shrine was open or roofed. Although the function remains unknown, the impermanent construction suggests a throne kiosk, perhaps for administering justice.

The smaller temple of Harpare and Raittaui in the Amunra-Monthu enclosure of Karnak-North also was furnished with a new facade.

Under Taharqa, the important New Kingdom temple of MUT at Karnak was restructured (fig. 27). The old temple consisted of a huge pylon-like brick structure enclosing a court enhanced by hundreds of statues of the lion goddess Sakhmet. Behind followed a second pylon with another court with Sakhmet statues, surrounded on three sides by Hathor-headed pillars. The actual temple house at the rear side of the second court measured only approximately 24 x 38 m.

Taharqa added a 34 m wide section, containing a hypostyle hall with eight columns and some side rooms, to the front of the temple house. The new facade of the temple house was articulated by six engaged Hathor columns, reminding one of the gender of the deity and reflecting the New Kingdom Hathor pillars that surround the other three sides of the court.[47] The freestanding bark shrine, the ambulatory, and side chapels also suggest a Late Period date. How far these parts of the temple house were rebuilt is still unclear.[48]

Taharqa also seems to have added an entrance porch to the front of the first pylon. The porch was replaced in Ptolemaic times. A colonnade of four pairs of columns inside the first court may also be Kushite. A porch of four columns was built in the second court and connected with the facade of the new, Kushite temple house by screen walls decorated with the "Piankhi reliefs."[49]

Substantial alterations were carried out at the Khonspakhered temple northeast of the Mut temple (fig. 28).[50] An earlier Ramesside temple was replaced by a new building—measuring 19.52 x 40.28 m (37 x 77 cubits)—into which numerous elements of the older building were integrated. The temple house contained a sanctuary, a square offering hall, and a transversal hall, each with four papyrus bundle columns. The front third of the temple house was formed by a hypostyle hall with sixteen columns. The side aisles of the hypostyle hall consisted of palm columns, much esteemed in the Kushite Period. Later, under Taharqa, a court with a 29.40 m broad pylon was added, again with palm columns in the three colonnades.

Figure 26.
Reconstruction of the facade of a temple of the divine consorts at Karnak (25th Dynasty).

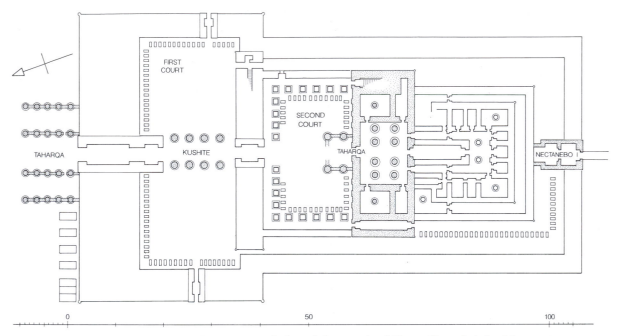

Figure 27. Reconstructed plan of the temple of Mut at Karnak (after Margaret Benson and Janet Gourlay, *The Temple of Mut in Asher* [London, 1899]).

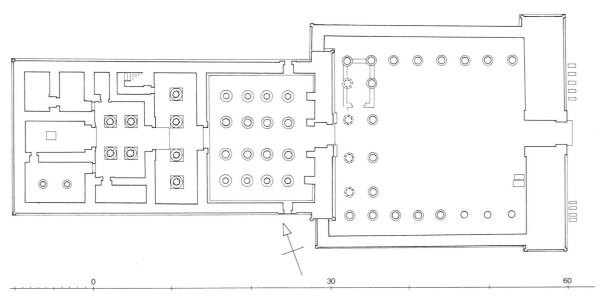

Figure 28. Plan of the Ramesside/Kushite temple of Khonspakhered in the precinct of Mut at Karnak.

The overall plan and the location of a small chamber with two columns in the northeast corner of the temple correspond to the contemporary temples at Tabo, Kawa, and Sanam in the Sudan and indicate that the building was not a birth house[51] but a fully developed temple. The Khonspakhered temple is the only one completely built by the Kushites on Egyptian soil. Its oblique angles and poor-quality masonry attest to the decline in Theban construction, which can be observed from the late New Kingdom on. Slender columns with wider spans probably produced a feeling for space which was different from that of the architecture of the Ramessides, thus heralding a new building style.

Under Taharqa the entrance pylons to the five most important Theban temples were furnished with an entrance porch. Monumental aspects were emphasized by the use of special material for the pavement: red or black granite in the center nave and alabaster or limestone in the side aisles. The following examples were built:

1. To the pylon of the Khonsu temple at Karnak an entrance porch was added, the roof of which was carried by four rows of five rather high columns (figs. 3, 243). The roof was made of timber because of the 7.20 to 8.20 m wide spans between the columns.[52]
2. Against the east end of the Amun temple of Karnak stood—facing east—a Ramesside *contra-temple* for Reharakhte. Taharqa built a porch in front of the pylon of this temple (figs. 29, 243). Four rows of five slender, 9.5 m high columns with open papyrus capitals carried the roof; decorated screen walls were placed between the columns.[53]

Figure 29.
Remains of the entrance porch of Taharqa of the temple of Reharakhte east of the Amun temple at Karnak (photo A.B.).

3. The Amunra-Monthu temple at Karnak-North faces north, in the direction of the distant Monthu temple at Medamoud.[54] The facade was furnished with a porch of four rows of five columns (figs. 30, 243; plan IX), connected by decorated screen walls. Since the front of the porch had only one entrance into the central aisle, transversal doors between the first intercolumniations led into the side aisles. The two obelisks of Amenhotep III, originally outside the temple, were integrated into the portico, but their great height created problems for the roofing of the porch.

   In connection with a raised level, the Kushite porch was removed under Ptolemy IX Soter II and replaced at a higher level by a similar portico with sturdier columns. The foundations of the Kushite porch and of numerous building elements were integrated into the Ptolemaic foundations.

4. A porch was built in front of the first pylon of the Mut temple (fig. 27). The wide column spacing required a timber roof. A few column drums of the Kushite porch survived after it was replaced by a new porch in Ptolemaic times. The Ptolemaic porch had four rows of perhaps five(?) columns, which were decorated with figures of the god Bes.

5. The porch in front of the sanctuary of the Hatshepsut temple at Deir el-Bahari may also date to the 25th Dynasty. Not only was this building type typical for the Kushite Period, but the use of columns with open papyrus capitals also was common during this era. (In Ptolemaic-Roman kiosks, columns with composite capitals were the rule). The dissonance between the screen walls and the frontal gate, which reaches up to the neck of the columns, also supports a date of the 25th Dynasty, when entrance porches were still under development.

Figure 30.
Plan of the Kushite entrance porch of the temple of Amunra-Monthu at Karnak in Kushite and Ptolemaic times.

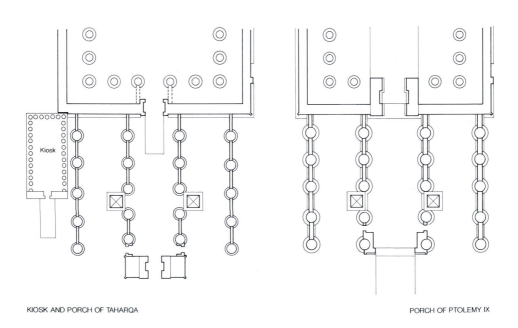

KIOSK AND PORCH OF TAHARQA

PORCH OF PTOLEMY IX

At EDFU the New Kingdom Horus temple was distinguished by a Sed-festival gate that probably stood on the access road to the temple. Four blocks of Taharqa, reused by Psametik II, were excavated in 1984–85 in the Ptolemaic court, apparently the site of these older monuments.

In the fortress of QASR IBRIM in Lower Nubia a small brick temple was built under Taharqa.[55] The 10 x 16.5 m building consisted of an anteroom, with four columns carrying the ceiling and a sanctuary. The sanctuary was separated from the exterior walls by a staircase to the roof and a secret corridor, creating an early form of the freestanding sanctuary that is characteristic of Ptolemaic temples. In late Napatan or early Meroitic times, the building became the nucleus of a larger temple complex.

At BUHEN the south temple was enlarged, and at SEMNA-WEST a small brick temple was built.

In Lower Egypt, far distant from the Kushite homeland, the presence of the Kushites is confirmed by Taharqa's restoration of a small Amun temple in MEMPHIS[56] and a granite stela from TANIS. During the wars against the Assyrians in the northeast, Taharqa must have frequented Memphis and Tanis.

At this point the building program of Taharqa in his home country, which the king inaugurated in his sixth year (684), must be mentioned. In the Sudan, Taharqa became the greatest temple builder of all times, with large temples in at least four places. These temples follow precisely pharaonic style and the temple-building tradition of the Ramesside Period. The three temples of Taharqa at TABO (on the island Argo), at KAWA (opposite Dongola), and at SANAM (Napata) were built following a common plan (fig. 31).[57] The temples of Kawa and Sanam were closer together, with Sanam apparently representing the later, slightly modified version. Both measured 38.7 x 68.5 m. Sculptors of a Memphite school seem to have decorated the Kawa temple, copying reliefs from the pyramid temples of Sahure, Niuserre, and Pepy II at Abusir and Saqqara.[58] The Old Kingdom prototypes were adapted to their—actually inapplicable—environment by a change of the depicted gods and the Nubian costumes of the king and the priests.

The plans of the three temples were divided into four sections by a larger and a smaller pylon and two following gates. The pylon of Tabo, like the rest of the temple, is largely destroyed. The pylons of Kawa and Sanam had four flagpoles. The court between the two pylons—like that of the Khonsu temple at Karnak, for example—was surrounded by colonnades, in the temple of Kawa with palm columns. A kiosk stood in the center of the court of Tabo as the kiosk of Taharqa stood in the center of the first court of the Karnak temple. All courts have two lateral gates. A hypostyle hall followed behind the second pylon. The halls of Kawa and Sanam had four-by-four, that of Tabo, four-by-five, columns. They had no raised central nave as in the New Kingdom. Kawa again had palm columns, certainly a pointer to the architecture of the Old Kingdom. The intercolumniations of the central nave, which were 7.80 m, could have scarcely been covered with stone. At Kawa and Sanam, a shrine of Taharqa was placed in the corresponding intercolumnar space.[59] All hypostyles have side exits, creating a lateral axis at Kawa and Sanam. The following room for the emplacement of statues of visiting gods[60] and the following offering hall had four columns each and no longer occupied the full width of

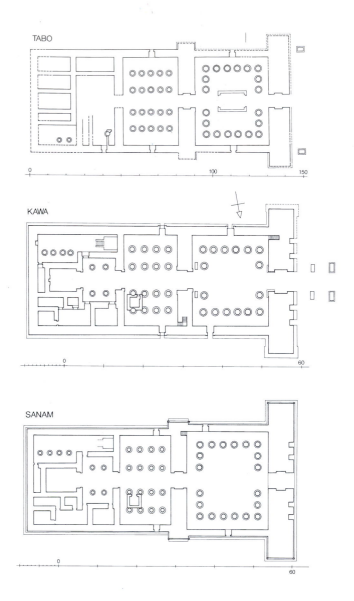

TABO

KAWA

SANAM

Figure 31.
Plans of the temples of Taharqa at Tabo, Kawa, and Sanam.

the temple house because each side was occupied by a lateral room. The right side chamber (looking inward) contained a high platform, which probably carried a shrine. A certain relationship to the *wabet*, the New Year's festival court (see discussion in chapter 9) may be suggested. The last plan section contains the large central sanctuary, which at its right side had a longitudinal hall with four palm columns[61] and opposite, at its left, a conspicuous group of four rooms. Some of these features seem to answer specific Kushite cult requirements of local origin which have no parallels in temples in Egypt. The planning and proportioning of the three temples attest to solid craftsmanship. The organization of these temples discloses that only minor details had changed in temple building since the New Kingdom and that older plans and decoration programs were purposefully followed.

These three Kushite temples in the Sudan represent a certain temple type that is represented in Egypt by the above-mentioned Khonspakhered temple in the complex of Mut at Karnak. One may assume that other temples the Kushites may have built in Egypt might have looked the same.

At the GEBEL BARKAL, rock formations of the sacred mountain show features in which modern visitors claim to recognize four gigantic statues of a king. At the foot of the rock, three temples were either newly built or reconstructed on older remains: the great Amun temple, the Hemispeos, and the "Typhonium," with Hathor columns and unusual Bes pillars (see the discussion of columns in chapter 9).[62]

4

THE SAITE PERIOD
(664–525 B.C.)

The Historical Background

Although Egypt was under the domination of the Assyrians, probably only small foreign garrisons were left to guard the country, allowing Egyptian vassals a certain autonomy, particularly Necho of Sais. Necho probably died for the Assyrian cause, when the last Kushite ruler, Tanutamun, tried to reconquer Egypt and entered the Nile Delta. In 661, Necho's son Psametik I assumed his father's position as vassal in Sais. At first, Psametik I ruled only Sais and Memphis. By 656/655 he had usurped the whole country and—benefiting from the decline of the Assyrian power—freedom from the Assyrians. The annexation of the Theban theocracy was achieved peacefully by the adoption of Psametik's daughter Nitocris through the ruling Theban divine consort, the last Kushite princesses Shepenwepet II and Amenirdis II, who somehow must have survived the Assyrian invasions. The Theban officials of the Kushite and Assyrian Period, like Montuemhet and Ibi, also kept their offices.

Psametik I apparently unified the country still as a nominal vassal of the Assyrians. For unknown political reasons, Ashurbanipal even seems to have tolerated Egypt's passage to autonomy. He gained at least Psametik I and his son Necho as supporters of the Assyrian cause.

The reign of Psametik I inaugurated a 140-year-long period of recovery from foreign intervention. The Delta town of Sais remained the capital of Psametik I and his five successors of the 26th Dynasty. The first regnal years of Psametik I were filled with more military engagements in the north: the menacing Scythian invasion of 630–625, the alleged twenty-nine-year siege and final conquest of Ashdod (16 km north of Ashkalon), and the military support for the Assyrians against the Neo-Babylonians in 615–612.[1] Psametik I is also credited for employing Ionic and Carian mercenaries, who were settled in two camps in the northeastern Delta.[2]

The rulers of the 26th Dynasty founded by Psametik I constructed at least a dozen prominent temples, a corresponding number of new smaller sanctuaries (fig. 32), and numerous additions to already standing buildings. War damage by the Assyrian invasions does not seem to have been so serious that repairs played an important part. The most conspicuous buildings were certainly the temples of the ancient creator deities Neith and Atum at Sais, the temple of the ram-god Banebdjedet at Mendes, the temple of the obscure goddess Buto, mistress of Nebesha, and the temples of Ptah and Apis at Memphis. All these buildings are destroyed now, and some cannot be located anymore because no foundations are left or no excavations have been carried out. Repeatedly, some inscribed blocks were seen at obscure places and have disappeared since. In such cases it is difficult to determine whether these blocks attest to the existence of a temple in the neighborhood or whether they were moved from a distant ruin for later reuse.[3] Occasional inscriptions mentioning deities or their cult place offer a suggestion.

Contrasting with the Kushite Period, an absolute pole-changing of the political, economic, and religious orientation from south-north to west-east materialized within Egypt and in its relation with its neighbors. No wonder that during such concentration on Lower Egypt, and its neighbors to the west (Cyrenaika), north (Ionia), and east (Israel, Persia), temple building in the south was neglected. As a consequence, no king of the 26th Dynasty built a noteworthy monument in the Theban area.[4] The dominance of Amun, whose temples were still growing under the Bubastide and Kushite rulers, was over. In contrast to the building policy of the later 30th Dynasty, which favored the eastern Delta (fig. 48), the building commissions of the Saite rulers spread

Figure 32.
Delta map with the distribution of Saite temples.

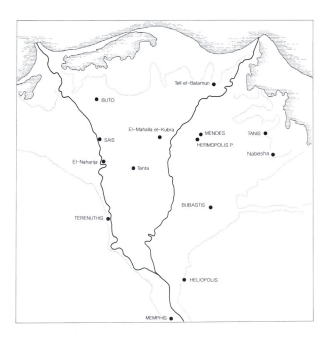

over the whole Delta. Equivalent temple building reflected the growing significance of the western oases, which were made accessible by new trade routes from the north to the Bahariya Oasis.

Building Form and Style in the Saite Period

Rulers with strong personalities often strive for manifestation in monumental architecture. The new Saite dynasty of self-willed monarchs was no exception. The political and economic recovery of Egypt under their 140-year rule favored such a dynamic building program. Without seeing larger temples of the Saite Period preserved, however, the assessment of their characteristic building style is difficult.

Works of sculpture of the 26th Dynasty exhibit a clear renewal of the arts of the Old, Middle, and New Kingdoms,[5] but they outshine similar tendencies that began in the 25th Dynasty.[6] The increasing admiration of the past intensified canonization in the arts and religion to a degree that was previously unheard of. One would assume, however, that this attitude was—under the rather favorable condition of the country during the 25th Dynasty—not an attempt to flee the present but an expression of national pride.

This tendency distinguished the sculpture of the Saite Period with beautiful perfection but also with a certain artificiality and coolness. One might assume that similar properties dominated the general impression of Saite architecture. Due to the lack of monuments, no archaizing building elements such as specific Old Kingdom forms are known. An important indicator is the increased use of hard stones like granite and quartzite as material not only for statues but also for building. The appearance of hard stone, with its sharp edges, polished surfaces, and generally dark colors, in itself invokes monumentality. This effect was certainly generated by the architecture of the Pyramid Age. The choice of the same material confirms the efforts of the Saite architects to achieve a similar monumental impression.

However, this clinging to the past cannot obscure the fact that Egyptian cults during the Late Period underwent enormous changes, which certainly influenced rituals and their architectural environment. The main aspect of this development is probably the transformation of a state dogma exclusively restricted to the encounter between gods and kings into popular belief. Evidence for this development is abundant. Temples were used as sanitariums and seats of oracles. Cult associations appeared. The cult of sacred animals became a popular attraction, and mummification and burial of crocodiles, ibises, bulls, and goats was a public affair. Magic and superstition were growing, as was the use of amulets and the donation of votives. Pictures and names of deities entered the private domain.

All these innovations must have increasingly influenced temple building, perhaps initially the appearance of traditional state temples less than that of smaller, rural shrines. Unfortunately, because of the lack of monuments, these changes cannot be demonstrated by the plans of Saite temples. One may only point to the development of the pronaos (see discussion in chapter 9), which seems to have taken another decisive step. This observation is verified by evidence of the far more developed pronaos of the Hibis temple (and the more shadowy pronaoi of Tell el-Balamun and Heliopolis).

The composite capital, which was fully developed during the later 30th Dynasty, was first formulated during the 26th Dynasty (see the discussion of columns in chapter 9). This flamboyant capital provided the new, ostentatious building form of the pronaos with the appropriate column type. The plans of the Abydos and El-Kâb temples, which can be restored to some degree, show a tendency to the square, centralized shape and suggest that the development of the later freestanding sanctuary with an ambulatory already was advanced. Other building elements typically found in 30th Dynasty architecture, such as the *wabet*, the roof staircase, and the ambulatory with the surrounding chapels, might have developed already in the 26th Dynasty.

For the concept of kingship of the Late Period, the nearly complete absence of colossal statues—until Nectanebo I and Ptolemaic times—is typical. Such monuments were memorials of an antiquated, divine kingship, which was replaced after the end of the New Kingdom by a more worldly rulership.[7] Such monuments did not belong to the repertoire of the influential Old Kingdom art the Saites intended to copy.

However, obelisks, which had also been absent from the repertoire for centuries, made their reappearance, apparently in connection with the rediscovery of hard stone carving under Psametik II (see the subsequent discussion of the buildings of his rule). Quite a number of obelisks of Psametik II and Apries are known, but none reached the colossal dimensions of those of the New Kingdom.

Beyond these admirable achievements of its own, the temple architecture of the 26th Dynasty paved the way for the architecture of the 30th Dynasty and the "Ptolemaic Style."[8]

The Building Methods of the Saite Period

Since practically no temple building of the Saites worth mentioning has survived, technical studies have to be content with observations of foundations. Some well-preserved remains of foundations of Saite temples grant an insight into the building methods of the 26th Dynasty. They exhibit a hitherto unknown aspiration for stability, which probably conforms with the inclination toward Old Kingdom architecture.[9] The foundation pit of the sanctuary area of the temple of Mendes (fig. 41) was 26.6 x 29.4 m wide and retained by a 2.6 m thick brick wall that was reinforced at strategic points with projections.[10] The foundations consisted of six courses of 1 m high limestone blocks that sat in the foundation pit in a 2.32 to 6.65 m thick sand fill. The amazing 11 m depth of the foundation is explained by the weight of the four, 7.8 m high granite naoi built on top. The foundation blocks were arranged so that their weight was equally distributed. In order to determine the position of the naoi from the beginning, their location was measured on each foundation course and marked by setting lines.

The foundation pits of the temple of Amasis at Athribis and of the Wadjet temple at Buto were also surrounded by brick walls and filled with sand.[11] In the latter, the aboveground masonry consisted of 2 to 3 m long limestone blocks, cased with quartzite slabs. These were attached with copper bands, pulled through drill holes, a method already used in the Middle Kingdom to join sarcophagus slabs.[12] In the Saite part of the Hibis temple at El-Kharga, the lateral joints of the wall blocks displayed *anathyrosis*.

The correction of the royal building cubit during the Saite Period is noteworthy.[13] The total length of 52.3 to 52.5 cm remained untouched but the subdivision was simplified. Whereas the old building cubit had seven palms of four fingers (i.e., 28 fingers), the new cubit had only six palms of four fingers (i.e., 24 fingers). It followed that the reformed palm now measured 8.75 cm and the finger 2.2 cm. We do not know why the old system, which had been used successfully for thousands of years, was suddenly altered.

Egyptian Architecture and the Mediterranean Countries during the Saite Period

The rule of the 26th Dynasty (664–525) coincides with the flowering of Greek overseas activity and the foundation of Greek settlements around the Mediterranean. Increasing international trade and the employment of Ionic and Carian mercenaries in Egypt after 620 brought Greeks and Egyptians into close contact and opened Egypt to scholarly visitors.[14] Quite naturally, a wave of Egyptian building ideas, elements, and techniques infiltrated the Greek world during the 26th Dynasty. This contact with an ancient, advanced civilization was of utmost importance for the Greeks, and the experience probably contributed to the emergence and development of monumental stone architecture in Greece. The enormous dimensions of the Ionic and western Greek temples built after 560, with their impressive concentration of columns, may indeed reflect a response to impressions obtained in Egypt.[15] Even the proportions of early Doric colonnades correspond to some degree to Egyptian examples, and the *entasis* of Doric columns has strikingly close parallels in the swelling of Egyptian papyrus columns. The enlargement of the central intercolumniation in Greek temples has also been derived from Egypt.

That early Greek architects also acquired engineering skills in Egypt is possible because they must have faced similar technical problems associated with building on a colossal scale.[16] Since lifting devices such as cranes were invented by the Greeks only at the end of the sixth century, earlier Greek temples could only have been built with the rudimentary Egyptian technology, using ramps, rollers, and sledges. The particularly solid foundations of Saite temples must have been an eye-opener for the still-inexperienced Greek builders. The method of filling foundation trenches of Greek temples with sand was an old Egyptian tradition.[17] The A-shaped square level with a plumb line used in Greece was *the* Egyptian leveling device attested since the 12th Dynasty. The *anathyrosis* also was frequently applied in Egyptian building since the Middle Kingdom. Wooden, stone, and metal dovetail cramps—so common in Greek architecture—had been used in Egyptian buildings since the Old Kingdom.[18]

Elements of Egyptian architecture and architectural decor had long before entered orientalizing art styles of cultures around the eastern Mediterranean. The expansion of the Saite empire further enhanced their diffusion in the seventh and sixth centuries. The cavetto molding was integrated into foreign architecture more than any other element. Monumental cavetto moldings topping tomb no. 50 of Salamis on Cyprus (ca. 600 B.C.) created a real Egyptian appearance.[19] Orientalizing cavetto moldings and lotus/palmette motives are common from the sixth century on in Carthaginian, Etruscan,[20] and Greek architecture in Italy, where they appear not only in stone but also in terracotta. Besides the Egyptianizing ante capitals and ornaments of the older Heraion of Paestum and other southern Italian Doric temples,[21] the *peripteral* Demeter temple "F" at Selinunt (ca. 530) must be mentioned.[22] The intercolumniations were closed by 4.5 m high screen walls with real gates at the temple facade and false doors coped with cavetto-like moldings at the other sides. A similarity with the Egyptian birth house is apparent, although their connection is conjectural. The motive of the volute is often combined with a ring of dropping leaves at the upper end of the shaft. Their resemblance to the Egyptian palm capital is astonishing. The oldest Ionic column in Egypt, found in the Apollo temple at Naucratis, is dated to 566.[23] The neck of the column was surrounded by two rows of dropping palm leaves, but the actual capital with the volutes is missing.

Certainly under Saite influence, bifacial Hathor-head capitals were introduced to Cyprus after the mid–sixth century.[24] Whether they were attached to polygonal faceted shafts and whether these shafts also came from Egypt is unknown. Hathor head capitals also entered Phoenician architecture.[25] At the Ionic treasuries of Klazomenai and Marssilia in Delphi, floral capitals that may reflect Egyptian palm capitals appear in the second half of the sixth century.[26] They display a ring of eighteen above one of twenty-two slender palm leaves raising vertically and curling outward and downward at the dropping tips.

Of great significance for Egyptian Late Period architecture was the creation about 600 of the composite capital in stone. It would appear that the invention of the Corinthian capital was also inspired by the Egyptian composite capital.[27] Its four lily-shaped corner volutes and the *acanthus* ring at the neck closely resemble Egyptian examples.

Single elements such as the sculptured frieze around the foot of the columns of the older (560) and younger (356) Artemision of Ephesos resemble the figure decoration of Egyptian papyrus column shafts.[28] Figure friezes around the foot of a column were later so much regarded an Egyptian feature that the *columnae caelatae* of the Roman Iseum were ornamented with this element.[29]

Occasionally the columns joined to the walls by buttress-like spurs of masonry in some Greek temples of the fifth to the third century have been traced back to similar forms in the Djoser complex at Saqqara (ca. 2620).[30] This derivation, however, must contend with the huge intervening span of time; H. Ricke, moreover, has stressed that these building forms have completely different histories of origin.[31]

Finally, the old Egyptian pyramid-shaped tomb type diffused since the eighth century over the Canaanite/Syrian and Anatolian area. This tomb type sur-

vived in Syria (Dana, Kapropera) until the sixth century A.D. The most spectacular successors were the step pyramid–like roof constructions of the Mausoleum of Halicarnassus (ca. 353–349) and the Lion Tomb of Cnidus (fourth century).

Greek and Near Eastern architects may also have improved construction methods from the Egyptian examples.[32] Block connections with dovetail-shaped cramps and the use of *anathyrosis*, for example, were common in Egyptian building techniques from the Old Kingdom on. The claw chisel, indispensable for working marble, also already was used in Egypt around 675. In Greek architecture, its use is attested only after 550.[33] However, the often proposed use of building ramps or the quarrying of building blocks by pounding was known worldwide and was even used by the Incas,[34] suggesting that such techniques developed independently.

Since the presence of Egyptian artists in Persia after 525 is well attested,[35] it is not surprising that not only Egyptian statues and stone vessels were found in Persia. As an example of a Persian commission to Egyptian artists, the greater-than-life-size statue of Darius I found at Susa must be mentioned. According to its dedication text, it was produced in Egypt,[36] and it shows a blending of Egyptian and Persian styles.

Between 521 and 484, architectural and decorative elements of Egyptian origin also appear in the buildings of Persepolis. Egyptian cavettos—even decorated with the winged sun disk—crown the doors of the palaces of Darius I and Xerxes at Persepolis (fig. 33).[37] These cavetto-topped doors are also depicted on the facade of the royal tombs of Naksh-i Rustam.[38] The colossal columns in the Apadana of Persepolis (ca. 518), which carry Egyptian palm-leaf capitals with attached papyrus buds, contribute to the cosmopolitan character of Achaemenid architecture.[39]

Figure 33.
Cavetto elements in the main hall of the palace of Darius at Persepolis (courtesy of the Oriental Institute, University of Chicago, no. 60709).

It seems that Egyptian architecture of the seventh to the fourth century influenced the building of neighboring countries, while receiving few new elements from abroad. One of the only known examples of Greek influence is found in the Ammoneion of the Siwa Oasis, which was constructed by Greek builders.[40] Ionic influence in the Egyptian homeland may have been found in the temple of Amasis at Mendes (570–526) with its four colossal naoi, which perhaps stood in an open sanctuary. This interior sanctuary court resembled the contemporary large open temples of Ionia, such as the Artemision of King Kroisos at Ephesos (ca. 560).[41]

The Buildings of the Saite Period

Psametik I, Wahibre (664–610)

At the beginning of the reign of Psametik I, involvements with the Assyrians may have lent priority to the building of strategically placed fortresses. Thanks to its geographic situation, Egypt could be attacked from Asia at very few places. The main threat came from the route along the Mediterranean coast of the Sinai. This route had to be protected by the powerful fortress of TELL EL-KEDUA, whose 10 m thick and probably 20 m high walls were fortified by fifteen towers. The second defense line farther inward was supported by the fortress DAPHNAE (modern Defaneh) at the Pelusian branch of the Nile, a 385 x 640 m enclosure, and a ward sitting on a 10 m high platform. The entrance through the Damietta branch of the Nile was barred by the *temenos* of Sheshonq III for Amun at TELL EL-BALAMUN. It was fortified under Psametik I with a 350 x 360 m wide and 12 m thick brick wall and a strong ward (plan II).[42]

The western border of the kingdom was protected by a fortress at MAREA (west of Alexandria). Literary and archaeological evidence also suggest that the founding of Naucratis as a military base might go back to ca. 620 B.C.[43]

The extraordinarily long reign of Psametik I also granted the country a fruitful period of peace, which encouraged temple building. Blocks with the name of Psametik I were found at so many sites that one can assume the king undertook a vast building program. The works were apparently centered around the capital SAIS.[44] In the nineteenth century enormous mounds at Sa el-Hagar still suggested an ancient capital and were identified with Sais. In a depression between two large, 25 m high debris mounds was a 500–700 x 700–900 m wide and 28(!) m thick brick enclosure with its front on the west. Whether this was the famous enclosure of Neith[45] or the royal palace is not known because no excavation was ever carried out. The mounds have been completely leveled.

This total loss of Sais deprives us of the most representative monuments of the 26th Dynasty. Their evaluation, therefore, depends completely on Egyptian inscriptions, the description of Herodotus (II.169–70, 175), and a few building elements found in the area itself or removed far away. The replacement of the New Kingdom temple of Neith by a sumptuous new building was probably a high-priority project for Psametik I and his successors, but only a few stray elements are left of this building.

Sais also contained a temple for Atum and the gods of Heliopolis. According to dedication inscriptions, a large quartzite sphinx dedicated to Atum, found in Alexandria, and a basalt column from Rosetta may have belonged to this building.[46] Since the column was only 35 cm thick and originally approximately 2 to 3 m high, it must have belonged to a smaller feature of the temple.

The Atum temple may have contained an intriguing structure of which only five slabs of green schist parapet or barrier walls are preserved. The 1.21 to 1.30 m high slabs are decorated on both sides, depicting Psametik I, Psametik II, and Nectanebo I officiating in front of deities. The juxtaposed rows of protective *uraei* and vultures on top of the slabs suggest a northern and southern series of barrier walls that apparently surrounded a cultic enclosure, perhaps for the celebration of the New Year's ritual. One slab is inscribed with the name of Psametik I (fig. 34).[47] The other slabs suggest an extension of the same structure under Psametik II and Nectanebo I (30th Dynasty).[48]

Ancient sources suggest that the temple complex of Neith incorporated an Osiris tomb called the "Mansion of the Bee," probably situated behind the temple house of Neith. According to Herodotus (II.169), the royal tombs were in front of the Neith temple. Outside the enclosure four more sanctuaries probably marked the four cardinal points: the *Mh-nt* in the north, the *Rs-nt* in the south, the "House of Ra" in the east, and the "House of Atum" in the west.

In the old temple-fortress of Amun at TELL EL-BALAMUN, Psametik I built a second, 22 x 50 m temple that had a 10 x 39 m front section (plan II).[49] The form and position of this part suggest a pronaos. The dimensions of the front section—similar to the pronaos of the main temple of Tell el-Balamun and to the pronaos of Nectanebo I at Hermopolis magna—suggest a double row of eight columns. If the front section was a pronaos, it would have been one of the rare early examples of pronaoi in Delta architecture.

The discovery of about thirty blocks of Psametik I in the walls retaining the sacred lake of TANIS attests that this site had a significant colonnaded building with fine relief decoration. The temple probably was destroyed by the Persians, and the stones were reused by Nectanebo I for the construction of the sacred lake.

Another temple may have been built under the Saites at HERMOPOLIS PARVA, the capital of the fifteenth nome, located 5 km south of modern Mansoura. The formidable Tell Naqûs near Tell el-Baqlieh bore evidence of the building until the beginning of the twentieth century.[50] Blocks with inscriptions of Psametik I, a sandstone naos of Apries, and a splendid, highly polished black granite vase of Amasis, both in the Egyptian Museum, Cairo, probably originated from this site.[51] The Thot temple was later enlarged or replaced under Nectanebo I.

At Nûb Taha, west of Tell el-Yahudiya, a part of a small granite naos for Atum was discovered. It may have originated in HELIOPOLIS.[52]

According to Herodotus (II.153), Psametik I added a temple for the Apis bull to the sanctuary of Ptah at MEMPHIS. The house of Apis stood to the south of the Ptah temple and contained a court that was "surrounded by a colonnade consisting of figures, twelve cubits high, rather than pillars." The court served—according to Strabo (*Geography*, 17.1.31)—for the run of the bull, which could also be observed by visitors through a window. To the west

Figure 34.
Green schist parapet wall from
the temple of Atum at Sais
inscribed under Psametik I
in the Brit. Mus., 20[800]
(courtesy of Brit. Mus.).

of this court was the actual temple with the stable of the sacred bull. Nothing was found of these buildings. To the south of the area of the suspected Apis temple, remains of the embalming house of the Apis bulls were preserved, a building that dates back to the reign of Sheshonq I.[53]

As suggested by a stela from the Serapeum, Psametik I also restored and equipped an existing Osiris-Apis temple, obviously a predecessor of the Serapeum in the cemetery of Saqqara.[54] We have, however, no archaeological evidence for the temple. Perhaps connected with this project was the construction under Psametik I of a cult chapel for the mothers of the Apis bulls, northeast of the Serapeum. The rather modest chapel was enlarged under Nectanebo II into a sizable sanctuary (see plans III–IV). It had an underground gallery with burial niches for the colossal sarcophagi of the cows, similar to those of the Serapeum.

Nitocris, divine consort of Amun, continued a tradition going back to the reign of Osorkon II of erecting small chapels for Osiris north of the Amun temple at KARNAK, where she built a chapel for Osiris with the title "The Lord of Life who gives Sed festivals." The small building was similar to the funerary chapels of the divine consorts at Medinet Habu and consisted of a pylon-like facade, a small court, and two cult chambers. The chapels, which served for a joint cult of Osiris and the divine consort,[55] later were integrated into the precinct of Amunra-Monthu by the 30th Dynasty enclosure wall. Access to the chapels from the south was maintained through separate stone gates through that wall.

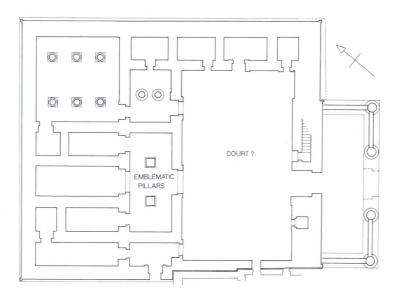

Figure 35.
Plan of the original temple of
Psametik I for Nekhbet at El-Kâb.

Figure 36. The temple of Psametik I for Nekhbet at El-Kâb seen from the
south, in the state of preservation in the early nineteenth century (*Description
I*, pl. 66).

The main temple of EL-KÂB (ancient Nekheb, Greek Eileithyiaspolis) was the Upper Egyptian crown sanctuary of the goddess Nekhbet, the Per-wer which played a large role at the coronation and Sed-festival ceremonies (plan XII). It represented the southern complement to the Lower Egyptian Wadjet temple of Buto, the Per-nu. Both temples were probably denoted by special building forms. Unfortunately, nothing is preserved at either site that would inform us about the appearance of the Upper Egyptian national shrine. Stone robbing before 1841 left only the foundations (figs. 35–36). One would perceive the temple as a new building of Psametik I because cartouches of the king and of Amasis appear in a crypt sunk into the foundations.[56] The existence of cartouches of Darius II may indicate that the decoration work dragged on into the Persian Period. The nearly square ground plan of the temple house of Psametik I reappears a hundred years later in the temple of Amasis (26th Dynasty) at Abydos, possibly suggesting a common planning characteristic of Saite temples. The subdivision in the interior was asymmetrical, with the entrance axis shifted more to the west (plan XII). A triple sanctuary was located in this axis, opening to a tranversal room, whose ceiling was carried by two pillars with the representation of the papyrus and the lily, the heraldic plants of Lower and Upper Egypt. One would assume that the roof of the sanctuary area surmounted the surrounding wings. In front of the broad room with the heraldic pillars was a large space that may have been built by Psametik I as a wide, open court. It was transformed under Hakoris (29th Dynasty) into a hypostyle hall. A small pylon stood in front. A four-column kiosk, built in the 26th Dynasty in front of the pylon, received inscriptions of Darius II.

To the west, the Nekhbet temple was adjoined to a smaller New Kingdom temple (of Thoth?), which was still in use in the 26th Dynasty.

Necho II, Wehem-ib-Re (610–595)

Psametik I was succeeded by his son Necho II. The young king also actively intervened in the affairs in the north and supported the crumbling Assyrian kingdom against the Neo-Babylonians.[57] On their march to the north in 609 the Egyptians were challenged by the Judaean army under King Josiah, who supported the emerging Neo-Babylonians. In the ensuing battle at Megiddo, Josiah perished (2 Chronicles 35:20–24) and Necho marched farther. The weakness of the Assyrians made Necho lord of Syria/Palestine and rival of Nebuchadnezzar II. Soon Necho's forces had to yield to Nebuchadnezzar's fierce offensive, and Necho had to content himself with fending off a direct attack on Egypt itself in 701. These struggles had strained Necho's resources so much that Egypt could not intervene when Nebuchadnezzar attacked the new Egyptian vassal Jehoiachin of Jerusalem in 597 and carried him and his treasures to Babylon (2 Chronicles 36:6–7).

To counter the permanent Asian menace, Necho skillfully created a dominant Egyptian fleet in the Mediterranean. In order to sail his ships from the Mediterranean through the Delta to the Red Sea ports, a canal was dug to connect the Bitter Lakes with the Red Sea.[58] This gigantic venture certainly occupied a huge army of workmen. Herodotus (II.158) reports that the project was abandoned unfinished after the loss of 120,000 lives and was later revived by Psametik II, Darius I, and Xerxes I. Herodotus (IV.42) also relates that Necho initiated the first successful circumnavigation of Africa, which was accomplished by hired Phoenician sailors.

The relatively small output of temple building during Necho's fifteen-year reign may be partially explained by the king's costly warfare and the development of an Egyptian navy. One may suspect, however, that some unfinished temple buildings of Necho were later completed and inscribed by Psametik II.

The reinforcement of the former Hyksos fortress of PITHOM at the eastern entrance to the Wadi Tumilat was probably part of the canal project. At the same time, construction was begun on an Atum temple, including the donation of colossal statues and a naos.

Works at the Neith temple at SAIS, inaugurated by Psametik I, continued as can be inferred from inscribed quartzite blocks found dislocated to Rosetta and Dîbi.[59] The location of Necho's tomb at Sais is supported by a scarab allegedly found there.[60] A quartzite block with the royal name was seen built into the mosque of TARRANEH (Therenutis), but no building of this period is known from the area.[61]

Psametik II, Neferibre (595–589)

Necho's son Psametik II skillfully continued the pacific policy against the Neo-Babylonians, restraining Nebuchadnezzar II from expanding his empire to the south. Considering Psametik's short reign of seven years, the number of temples carrying his name is so considerable that some of the buildings were probably begun by Necho II. Some temples consisted partially of granite and were distinguished by outstanding craftsmanship. This increased granite quarrying under Psametik II is also confirmed by a conspicuous number of royal cartouches on the rocks of the granite quarries at Aswan. Finally, one should mention the anthropoid hard stone sarcophagi of the Memphite cemeteries,[62] which due to their huge size and monumental character could be considered as architectural elements. Remains of granite obelisks and sphinxes of Psametik II were recently discovered in the sea in front of the Qait Bey fort of Alexandria.[63]

Under Psametik II, the construction of the Suez Canal seems to have reached such a state of completeness that the work could be commemorated by the erection of a larger-than-life-size statue of the king at the southern end of the canal. The approximately 5–6 m high statue, the head of which is preserved, cannot have stood alone but must have been part of a temple.[64]

During the reign of Psametik II, the previously tolerant attitude toward the southern neighbor Kush apparently changed. Perhaps in response to a Kushite intrusion into Upper Egypt, a punishing campaign was undertaken against King Aspelta in 593, which forced the Kushites to move their capital from Napata farther south to Meroe. Apparently as a result of these events, the details of which are unknown to us, depictions of Kushite rulers in sculpture and relief were destroyed in many places in Egypt.

The completion of the Neith temple at SAIS probably had priority but the temple has left few traces. A minor work of Psametik II was probably the completion and decoration of the green schist parapet walls of an unidentified structure (fig. 37) begun perhaps by Psametik I.[65] Also the royal tomb seems to have been—according to Herodotus (II.169)—in the precinct of Neith.

In 1842, R. Lepsius saw numerous blocks of a quartzite temple with representations of Psametik II and mainly of Apries in the village EL-NAHARIYA, 15 km south of Sais.[66] The blocks suggest another major temple, which was founded by Psametik II and continued under Apries. Nothing else is known about the site.

The Napoleonic expedition observed an extraordinary number of pharaonic building elements of granite and quartzite reused in modern buildings at EL-MAHALLA EL-KUBRA.[67] In 1828, Nestor l'Hôte counted over 120 granite columns built into the village mosques.[68] A 1.8 m long fragment of red granite with the name of Psametik II and a door lintel of Apries also was seen. An inscription on a fragment of an obelisk mentioned "Horus, Khenty-hedj, Great God, Lord of the Nome of the Bull."[69] Since El-Mahalla el-Kubra is equidistant from the sites of Sebennytos and the Iseum at Behbeit el-Hagar, one usually assumes that its monuments were protracted from one of these sites. Since granite relief blocks of Nectanebo II and Ptolemy II, typical for Sebennytos and the Iseum, are lacking at Mahalla, one can dismiss this assumption. The Saite blocks suggest an important sanctuary of the 26th Dynasty at El-Mahalla el-Kubra itself.

Under Psametik II a pair of more than 21.79 m high obelisks was erected in the temple of HELIOPOLIS on the occasion of his Sed festival. Augustus had one of the obelisks, which were probably thrown down by the Persians, brought to Rome in 10 B.C.[70] Possible remains of the pendant obelisk were recently fished out of the sea at the Qait Bey fort in Alexandria. Strabo visited and described the temple ruins in 31 B.C. (*Geography*, XVII.1.27–29). In front of the temple he saw a 30 m wide and 100 m long allée lined with sphinxes. Behind the allée were three pylons followed by the temple house, with "a noteworthy pronaos." Attached to the temple house's sides were high, flanking walls covered with reliefs.[71] Behind the pronaos was a hypostyle hall with several rows of high columns and then the sanctuary, which still contained the statue of an "irrational animal," perhaps a falcon-headed image of Reharakhte. Heliopolis was completely devastated in 525 by the Persians. Several obelisks that were burnt at the foot in order to topple them were still standing or lay on the ground.[72]

A block with the cartouches of Psametik II at ABYDOS points to the existence of a temple of Psametik II, that may have followed the tradition of the royal cult temples of Sethos I and Ramesses II. At an unknown spot at KARNAK a pair of 8 m high obelisks was erected.[73] A sandstone block with the representation of Psametik II in front of Khnum could originate from ELEPHANTINE and suggests building activities of the king in the old Khnum temple.[74]

Under Psametik II a kiosk was donated on PHILAE representing the oldest known monument on the island. It consisted of a double row of four columns, which were connected by screen walls. As a roof one may expect a flat rounded pediment.[75] Poor foundations and execution gave the structure the aspect of a provisional arrangement.[76] The building does not necessarily attest that a cult of Isis existed before the temple foundation under Amasis.

The kiosk construction may have been connected with Psametik's II campaign against the Kushites.

Psametik II was also the founder of the temple house of Hibis in the EL-KHARGA Oasis (figs. 38–40). Because of the oasis's administrative connection to Thebes, the temple was dedicated to the triad of Amun, Mut, and Khonsu, with substantial installations for the cult of Osiris. The 19.5 x 26 m temple was situated on the picturesque bank of an ancient lake that is now gone. Its decoration was only concluded under Darius I and II(?).[77]

Three sanctuaries in the rear of the temple open to the transversal hall of the table of offerings. The rear wall of the central shrine has a false door. To the side of the sanctuary is a chapel for the cult of the deified king. From small side chambers, staircases lead to the roof and into a sizable system of cult chambers for Osiris. A hypostyle hall with two-by-two papyrus capital columns follows in front. Its roof may have been raised to produce flat, lateral windows (fig. 58). Fear of the weight of this roof prevented the builders from trimming the column shafts to slender proportions. Instead, the shafts kept their thick, raw shape. The sculptors had begun, however, to chisel from one of the capitals sepals which were not part of traditional capitals—an important reference to the creation of new types of capitals occurring at that time. The single column put up as a repair in a rear chamber already has a developed composite capital. It dates, however, probably from the 30th Dynasty.[78]

Figure 37.
Green schist parapet wall from Sais, reinscribed under Psametik II, Vienna, ÄS 213 (courtesy of Inge Kitlitschka-Stempel, Kunsthistorisches Museum).

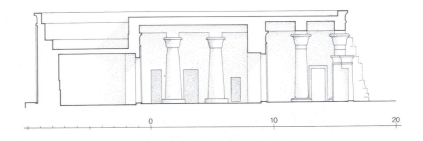

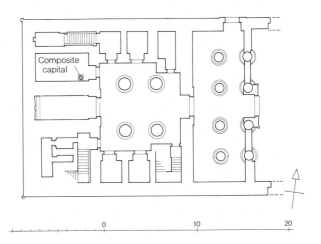

Composite
capital

Figure 38.
Reconstructed longitudinal
section and plan of the temple
of Psametik II for Amun at Hibis.

Figure 39.
Entrance into the hypostyle hall of
the temple of Psametik II for Amun at
Hibis with decoration of Darius I
(photo MMA, K6 23).

The front of the temple house consisted of a pronaos with four papyrus bundle columns and screen walls. During the construction of the pronaos, the side walls were extended for the addition of a court. This extension was, however, only carried out in the 30th Dynasty. The eight papyrus columns of the pronaos still show the New Kingdom type of open, bell-shaped capitals. Their bases are an early example for chamfering, so widespread in Ptolemaic-Roman times. Only the three central intercolumniations are open; the "windows" of the two lateral ones are filled with masonry. The screen walls rise high and have no lateral *torus*.

The temple was completely preserved until 1832. Thereafter the roof and other parts were taken down for the construction of an aluminum factory. Only excavations by The Metropolitan Museum of Art, New York, in 1910–1911 and restorations of the Egyptian Antiquities Service stopped the decline. At present, rising groundwater again threatens the temple, which can only be saved by transfer to higher ground. Despite the flaws inherent in a provincial temple, the Hibis temple remains—together with the Ammoneion of Siwa—the best-preserved and best-documented temple of the early Egyptian Late Period and is therefore a primary monument to the history of building.

Figure 40.
Hypostyle hall of the temple of Psametik II for Amun at Hibis (courtesy of MMA).

Apries, Khaaibre (589–567)

After the tragic early death of Psametik II, his young and politically inexperienced son Apries ascended to the throne. Even as the new king matured, his reign remained chaotic. Apries imprudently abandoned the peace politics of his predecessors. When the dreaded Neo-Babylonian ruler Nebuchadnezzar II marched against the rebelling Jerusalem and King Zedekia in 588, Apries daringly tried to stop him with the Egyptian army. Apries defeated the Cypriot fleet and conquered Sidon, but, beaten at the southern front, he could not prevent the fall of Jerusalem in 586. This second, more devastating, destruction of Jerusalem (the first one had occurred earlier in 597) triggered the Exile to Babylon and the flight of the surviving Jews to Egypt. The refugees were settled at the Egyptian border fortress of Daphnae. Threatened by the Medians, Nebuchadnezzar for the time being postponed a revenge campaign against Egypt.

The fate of Apries was sealed, however, not by the armies of Nebuchadnezzar but by a rather absurd episode. The troops of Apries suffered an embarrassing setback in 570 when, following an appeal for help by the Libyan ruler Adikran against Greek immigrants in Kyrene (Libya), they were totally defeated by the battle-hardened Greeks. This event prompted a military revolt in Egypt, headed by an army officer, Amasis. Apries apparently was forced to accept Amasis as a coruler, an agreement that lasted for only three years. After renewed conflicts in 567, Apries lost his life in the battle of Momemphis in the western Delta. Thereafter, the name of Apries was erased from his monuments and replaced by the name Amasis.

During sixteen peaceful years of Apries's rule, construction work mainly continued in the capital SAIS. Its "large and remarkable" palace is mentioned by Herodotus (II.163). Work at the Neith temple at Sais is attested by two quartzite blocks found in Rosetta. Several quartzite blocks found at other places also suggest a Sed-festival gate at Sais. Behind the Neith temple Apries also erected a building called the "House of the Bee," the tomb of Osiris,[79] which contained carefully worked, black basalt Hathor columns (fig. 261, left).[80] From their diameter of 38 to 41 cm one can calculate that the columns had a height of only 2.60 m. The highly polished columns show that the intercolumniations were not closed with screen walls. The "House of the Bee" was also distinguished by a pair of granite obelisks, slightly over 5 m high, which were later transported to the Iseum in Rome.[81] The tomb of King Apries at Sais is mentioned by Herodotus (II.169) as being "very near to the sanctuary, on the left of the entrance."[82]

In 1842, numerous quartzite blocks with the names of Psametik II and Apries were seen at EL-NAHARIYA, 15 km south of Sais. It was thought that the blocks had been brought from Sais.[83] However, there could have been another temple of the 26th Dynasty at this site.

At TANIS, the Anta temple built by Siamun was replaced by a new building (plan I). A kiosk with two-by-three columns was erected in front of the temple. Parts of the limestone paving in the kiosk were still preserved, as well as six granite palm columns of a height of 6.7 m that were reused from a no-longer-standing building of the Old Kingdom.[84]

Another project of Apries (and the corule with Amasis) was the new building of the Banebdjed temple, the ram-god of MENDES (Tell el-Rub'a). The Arab writer Subh el-A'sha still saw the ruin in the fifteenth century:

> The temple in the north of the town is ruined. The common people call it the temple of 'Ad. Remains of its walls and its roof are preserved to the present day. . . . Inside are huge cisterns of hard stone and with extraordinary inscriptions. . . . I saw there a hall of columns of hard stone made in one piece of about 10 cubits erected on a foundation of hard stone. . . . I saw gates there [naoi?], made of one piece of granite, nearly 10 cubits high, also on a foundation of granite.[85]

The gigantic remains of the temple were removed only in the nineteenth century. From the last remaining traces one can conclude that the central part of the Apries temple was 26.8 x 33.6 m wide and faced north. The foundations suggest that the total length of the temple was at least 100 m. One of four 7.8 m high granite naoi—probably mentioned by El-A'sha and dedicated to the "four souls of Banebdjed," Re, Geb, Shu, and Osiris—still stands (figs. 41–42). The naoi may have stood in an uncovered *hypaetral* sanctuary.[86] The inscriptions of the naoi show that they were usurped by Amasis, but they certainly date from the time of Apries.

Figure 41.
The naos of Apries on top of the partially missing foundations for the temple of Banebdjedet at Mendes (courtesy of Donald Hansen, New York)

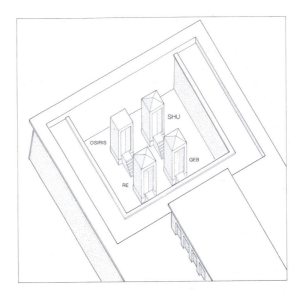

Figure 42.
Hypothetical reconstruction of
the sanctuary area of the temple of Banebdjedet at Mendes
with the four naoi.

Papyrus capitals and a splendid Hathor capital of red granite, now in the
Cairo Museum,[87] probably originate from a birth house located to the side of
the main temple. A sacred lake lay to the southeast, probably outside the
enclosure wall.

Apries also donated a quartzite naos for the sanctuary of Thoth of HERM-
OPOLIS PARVA (Bakliya, south of Mansura), which had been founded by
Psametik I and continued under Psametik II.[88] A limestone column of Apries
originates from a sanctuary in the necropolis in the northwest of ATHRIBIS
(Benha).[89] Quartzite sphinxes were—according to their inscriptions—erected
at HELIOPOLIS; two sphinxes reappeared in Alexandria.[90]

Royal building activities also may by suspected from the discovery of a few
inscribed blocks at Fuah, Ganâg, Hermopolis parva, and El-Mahalla el-Kubra,
but no details are known.

Apries carried out major building work in MEMPHIS, where the discovery
of blocks suggests building works in the Ptah temple. A special project was the
development of the fortress of Memphis into a representative palace. We do
not know whether an older palace that must have existed at Memphis was
crumbling, or whether the king intended to enhance his grip on access to
Upper Egypt. Also unknown is the percentage of older building parts incorporated into Apries's palace. A ramp led up to a 13 m high brick platform. Crossing a drawbridge, one reached the main gate, constructed of limestone blocks,
that was decorated with temple scenes copied from Old Kingdom models.[91]
The gate led to a 32 x 35 m wide central court, surrounded by private apartments. In the court stood 13 m high palm columns of limestone, which
shaped the portico for the actual throne room farther to the north. The roof of
the throne room was carried by 15 m high columns. A second gate, farther
east of the main gate, led through a long corridor directly into the reception
area. A massive tower in the southwest corner contained a staircase that led
to more living quarters at a higher level.

Numerous granite blocks, one of Apries and Amasis, were built into the Coptic monastery Deir el-Abjad (ca. A.D. 440). They could originate from an ancient Neshau, which is now buried under the monastery, or from the nearby complex of Triphis at ATHRIBIS (modern Wannina), where Petrie found a granite cavetto reused in the temple of Ptolemy IX at Athribis; the excavator believed it belonged to a temple of the 26th Dynasty.[92]

In the Thinite royal necropolis of ABYDOS, the tomb of king Djer (1st Dynasty), which was venerated as the tomb of Osiris, was repaired and a modest chapel was added.

In the Theban necropolis the chief stewards of the divine consorts, Ankhhor, Sheshonq, and Pedineith, erected in this period monumental funerary monuments.[93]

Amasis, Khnumibre (570–526)

Herodotus, who traveled in Egypt only eight years after the death of Amasis, informs us well about this king, one of the great personalities of the Late Period. Amasis's success in handling the complex situation in the country for forty-four years testifies to the political talent of this extraordinary leader.

After the former general had gained power in the civil war of 570–567, he made himself pharaoh and married Neith-aqer, a sister of the defeated predecessor, in order to strengthen his claim on the throne. Amasis was immediately confronted by two problems. One was the threat against Egypt first by the Assyrians and later by the Persians. As was to be expected, Nebuchadnezzar used the anarchic situation in Egypt as an opportunity to launch a revenge attack, invading Egypt in 568/567. Although his resources apparently did not permit a real conquest of the country, through this threatening gesture he reinforced the armistice with the new pharaoh. Amasis, however, succeeded in a countermove to conquer Cyprus, making use of the Egyptian fleet, which had been reinforced since Necho. The Babylonians were also checked in the north by the newly emerging Persians, relieving the pressure on distant Egypt. This balance of political forces granted Egypt forty years of peace, during which the king excelled as a lawmaker and reorganizer of the state finances. He finally glorified his reign which he had executed in the spirit of the Maat by the celebration of a Sed festival.

Egypt's internal peace was unsettled by serious tensions between the local population and Greek merchants and mercenaries, who now protected the country. Amasis reduced the pressure by checking the uncontrolled movement of mainly Greek foreigners in Egypt, at the same time granting them particular privileges in their trade post Naucratis, which had been founded earlier (ca. 620). At the same time, Amasis nourished close contacts with the Mediterranean Greek community, mainly with Polykrates, lord of Samos. His affiliation with the Greek world was shown by donations to the sanctuaries of Kyrene, Lindos, Samos, Delphi, and Sparta.

Friction with Greek mercenaries continued to smolder and finally led their commander, Phanes of Halikarnass, to defect to the Persian side. Phanes revealed the weak spots of the Egyptian border defenses to the Persians, a betrayal that had severe consequences. Amasis also alienated his own people.

His preference for foreigners and the taxation of the priesthood stamped Amasis as an atheist. The Egyptian opposition was probably propelled by Upper Egypt, which indeed seemed to have been neglected by Amasis, who confined his temple-building program to Lower Egypt. In the face of all these problems, Amasis became one of the great builder-kings of Egypt. During his last years Amasis was assisted by the minister of public works, Khnumibre, whose name, not coincidentally, corresponded to the second name of the king, and who was to survive his royal employer for many years.

The famous Lower Egyptian national sanctuary of BUTO (Tell el-Farâ'in) was honored by Amasis with a splendid new temple dedicated to the cobra-goddess Wadjet. Judging from the foundation pit, the temple was 31 x 65 m. The walls consisted of 2 to 3 m long limestone blocks cased with quartzite slabs, an exceptional method and combination of material. Even the roofing blocks were made of this extremely hard material. The temple was surrounded by a 20(!) m thick brick wall of 174 x 264 x 234 x 306 m, constructed over a Ramesside enclosure. Herodotus saw the temple still standing and reports:

> Buto contains a temple of Horus and Bastet and the temple of Wadjet, where the oracle is to be found, is quite big too; its gateway for instance, is ten fathoms in height (19.80 m). I will mention the most amazing thing I saw there: it was a temple within this precinct of Wadjet which is made out of a single block of stone (at least its sides were), with each wall forty cubits long and forty cubits high. Its roof was made out of another block of stone, with cornices measuring four cubits.
>
> So the temple was the most amazing thing I saw in this shrine, but the second most interesting thing was an island called Chemmis. The sanctuary in Buto is by a deep, wide lake, and the island is in this lake; it is said by the Egyptians to be a floating island. . . . Anyway on this island is a huge Horus temple, and three altars have been set up there as well. There are also a large number of palm-trees growing there, and plenty of other kinds of trees too, both fruit-trees and other sorts. (II.155–56)

The Wadjet temple was destroyed a hundred years later by the second Persian invasion in 343. As the excavation of 1965–68 revealed, its quartzite walls were carefully smashed into small pieces, probably to deal a blow to Egyptian nationalism.[94]

At MENDES, the construction and decoration of the temple begun under Apries for Banebdjed was certainly continuing, and the still-standing naos of Apries wears the cartouches of Amasis as well (fig. 41).

At BEHBEIT EL-HAGAR Amasis probably already constructed an Isis and Osiris temple, the Per-hebit, the "Festive House" that was later replaced by the famous Iseum of Nectanebo II, Ptolemy II, and Ptolemy III.

Following the tradition established by Amasis, the works at the Neith temple at SAIS were carried on, a building that has left no trace and is only known by Herodotus's description:

> He [Amasis] built, in the first place, such a wonderful gateway to the sanctuary of Neith at Sais, that he outdid everyone else by far, considering its height and dimensions, and the quantity and quality of its stone. Then he

also erected some huge statues and massive man-headed sphinx figures, and contributed to the repair of the sanctuary by having further blocks of stone taken there, some from the quarries of Memphis, but others, extraordinarily huge in size, from Elephantine, which is as much as twenty days' sailing from Sais. (II.175)

The gateway may represent a pronaos, which added a monumental front to the building begun by Psametik I. Apparently Amasis also thought the sanctuary of Neith built by Psametik I inadequate, for he donated that gigantic granite naos, much admired by Herodotus:

> But by far the most remarkable of his building works, to my mind, is a chamber hewn from a single block of stone that he brought from Elephantine. Transporting it took three years, and two thousand men (all from the pilot class) were asigned to the task. The external dimensions of this chamber are twenty-one cubits in length, fourteen cubits in width, and eight cubits in height; inside the single block of stone (as opposed to its external measurements) it is eighteen cubits and one pygon long, twelve cubits wide, and five cubits high. (II.175)

From the last sentence and larger numbers for the length than for the height, one can infer that the naos was not yet standing upright in the sanctuary but was lying on the ground in front of the pronaos. The reason was not only the grievances of the head engineer, mentioned by Herodotus, but mainly the fact that the 10 m high and over 7 m wide monolith could not pass the temple entrance. The builders probably planned to break through the rear wall of the temple but abandoned this project because the sacred tomb of Osiris stood there. The naos was broken up in the fourteenth century.

We do not know whether these works were connected with a Sed-festival building of Amasis, made of quartzite. Blocks from such a structure with Sed-festival decoration and texts were seen at Rosetta.[95]

Behind the Neith temple stood Apries's tomb of Osiris. This "House of the Bee" was the origin of a splendid sphinx of Basanit that later reached the Roman Iseum.[96]

Another important monument was certainly the funerary temple of Amasis, of which Herodotus says:

> In fact, although Amasis' tomb is further from the temple than the tombs of Apries and his ancestors it too is still within the courtyard of the sanctuary; his tomb is a huge stone colonnade lavishly decorated with, for instance, columns made to look like palm-trees. There are two doorways set into this colonnade, and behind these doors is the actual tomb. (II.169)

The burial of Amasis was at the time of Herodotus's visit, destroyed by order of Cambyses (Herodotus, III.16). The tomb of queen Nakhtes-Bastet-reru and her son Ahmose was, however, at Giza.[97]

Close to the marshes of Lake Menzaleh in the northeast Delta is NABESHA (Tell Fara'ûn, ancient Jemet, the capital of the nineteenth nome), with a Wadjet temple.[98] According to sculptural finds, the temple originated in the Middle and New Kingdoms. The existing, approximately 29 x 65 m temple was, however—according to the construction of the foundation pit—of the Late Period. The front part was perhaps a pronaos with four columns. In front of this temple, and at a right angle to it, Amasis erected another building. The 15 x 25 m structure was built of red granite blocks and may have been a birth house. During its excavation in 1886,[99] remains of the paving in the front area were still preserved, along with the foundations for a small entrance kiosk. The 4.5 m high rear wall of the granite naos was still standing on its quartzite base.

At ABU YASSIN, 3 km southeast of Horbeit, stood the tomb of the Kemwer, the sacred bulls of Horbeit. In 1937 the remains of probably twelve granite sarcophagi for the bulls were found. They were buried within a 20 x 30 brick m enclosure, which was probably connected with a funerary chapel. Some huge granite blocks carried "rather important inscriptions of the Saite period." They may well have dated to the reign of Amasis.[100]

ATHRIBIS (Tell Atrib near Benha) with its Khentikhety temple, was an important cult place of Osiris.[101] In the nineteenth century extensive ruins were preserved, which were, however, sold by the Antiquities Service before any scientific exploration could take place.[102] From sporadic finds and results of more recent excavations, we know that a Ramesside Khentikhety temple was especially patronized and enlarged in the 26th Dynasty.

In 1957–1958 the foundation pit of a 14 x 30 m Osiris temple was found and dated by foundation deposits to the reign of Amasis.[103] The front of the temple faced south and was enclosed by an entrance wing, perhaps a pylon or a pronaos. Remains of sphinxes suggest that a sphinx allée approached the temple from the south. In the area in front of the temple, about 120 wall blocks of the temple, some decorated, were found.

A roof fragment of a delicately dressed gray granite naos dedicated to Kem-wer, the Great Black Bull of Athribis, and another naos commissioned by Amasis were also found at Athribis. A splendid granite naos of Amasis in the Louvre (D 29), found at Alexandria but dedicated to Osiris, also must be mentioned here.[104] A temple wall restored from eight relief blocks in the Museum of Alexandria may originate from a Ptolemaic enlargement of the Osiris temple at Athribis.[105]

A stela of Amasis from the year 541 reports a devastating Nile flood causing damages at the dikes of MEMPHIS.[106] Perhaps because of the disaster, the temple house for Ptah was renewed. These works are attested by a block found reused in Cairo, which shows Amasis originally carved together with Apries.[107] Three quartzite and one granite blocks with Amasis's name were found in the area of the Ptah temple.[108]

Herodotus also reports (II.176) that Amasis built an "enormous and remarkable" Isis temple at Memphis. Two 3.4 m high quartzite doorjambs with representations of Amasis were found at Mitrahina (near the west end of the site), but no traces of the building were seen.[109] A dark granite naos dedicated to Neith also originates from Memphis.[110]

At the desert edge in front of the cemeteries of Saqqara, Amasis built the first temple for the guardian god of the necropolis, Anubis, the Anubieion. Massive terraced foundations suggest a building of considerable size and splendor. This temple was later incorporated into the large precinct of the Anu-bieion of Nectanebo I.

On the east bank of the Nile, somewhat south of Cairo opposite ISTABL 'ANTAR, remains of a temple were found in 1889, containing inscribed blocks and a colossal sandstone sphinx with the name of Amasis. Both temple and sphinx have vanished.[111]

Amasis resumed the old tradition of Sethos I and Ramesses II of building royal temples in the complex of Khentimentiu at ABYDOS. At the time of Petrie's excavation, remains of the 40 x 42 m foundations and the lowermost courses of the south and west walls were still preserved, containing reused blocks of Thutmosis III (fig. 43). The building consisted of a 2 m thick lime-stone enclosure surrounding a 29 x 32 m temple house. The entrance through the enclosure wall is lost, but a southwestern side entrance is pre-served. The main entrance into the temple house was set back in a niche with two columns, and probably was adorned with two obelisks, of which a frag-ment was excavated in the nearby village of Mensha.[112] Inside, a small hypo-style hall may have followed. Only the sanctuary, measuring 5 x 7 m, can be located in the interior. Here probably stood a granite naos and an altar. A frag-ment shows cartouches of both Apries and Amasis, dating the monument to the time of their coregency. The temple clearly differed from temples of the late New Kingdom and the preceding 25th Dynasty by the narrow ambula-tory, the lack of a colonnaded forecourt, and the entrance niche. Tendencies to a square ground plan can also be observed at the Saite temple of El-Kâb.

A small chapel of Osiris is attested at COPTOS. In the court north of the Great Hypostyle hall of KARNAK, a small chapel with four papyrus bundle columns with inscriptions from Nitocris (Meryt-Mut) to Ankhnes-Neferibre was built, the contemporary divine consorts of Amun.

Figure 43.
Plan of the temple of Amasis for Osiris at Abydos.

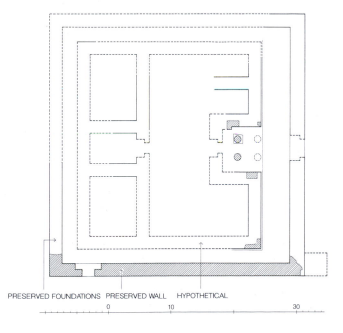

PRESERVED FOUNDATIONS   PRESERVED WALL   HYPOTHETICAL

0   10   30

From ELEPHANTINE comes a life-size basalt statue of Amasis, now in the Villa Albani-Torlonia in Rome.[113] The motive for the statue was certainly the continuation of the works of Psametik II. Several blocks of a rather large gate (height approximately 7.35 m) were recently discovered on Elephantine, which seems to have led through a brick enclosure wall, probably of the Satet temple. From the Satet temple, remains of six limestone columns and screen walls are preserved, suggesting a colonnade or kiosk.[114]

Amasis became, above all, the founder of the cult of Isis on PHILAE, perhaps as a side branch of the Osiris cult, which had a much older tradition on the island of Biggeh, west of Philae. On Philae, about 300 decorated blocks of a relatively modest temple of Amasis were found in the foundations of the Ptolemaic second pylon and hypostyle hall (fig. 44). The foundations were preserved under the court pavement of the temple of Ptolemy VI (plan XIV).[115] The Amasis building consisted of only three rooms along the axis, the last representing the sanctuary. The temple had the modest dimensions of 5.5 x 15.3 m. Amasis's temple probably was demolished under Ptolemy II, when the new temple was built directly behind the old structure.

In the ruins of the Roman station of 'AIN EL-MUFTELLA in the Bahariya Oasis were the remains of a Late Period cult area with four freestanding chapels of Amasis. The chapels are plain, architecturally insignificant structures. The condition of their wall decoration prevents an exact attribution to deities.[116]

The small and relatively unimportant Amun temple QASR EL-GHUEDA, in the El-Kharga Oasis, represents a similar, plain type (fig. 45). The appearance of the cartouches of Darius I was taken as proof of his patronage. One could suggest, however, that the temple's construction dates to the 26th Dynasty, a period in which other temples were also built in the oases. The 10.56 x 18.91 m temple house shows a pylon-like reinforcement at the front.[117] A hall of two-by-two columns follows, and behind is a transversal hall for the offering table. Three sanctuaries open to the transversal room. The largest shrine, in the north, had a 2.60 m wide vaulted sandstone ceiling. From the south, a staircase leads to the roof. The building is well preserved and is an important, if small, example of Saite architecture. A pronaos was added, probably under Ptolemy III.

Figure 44.
Plan of the chapel of Amasis for Isis on Philae under and behind the second pylon of the Ptolemaic temple.

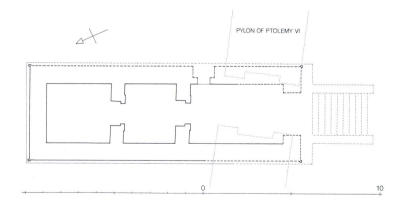

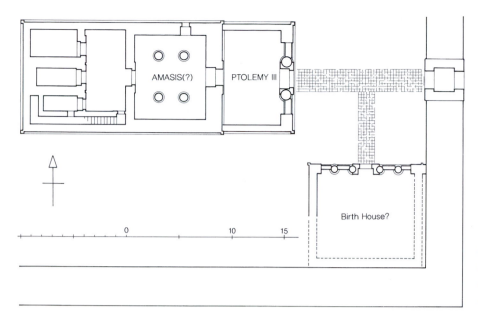

AMASIS(?)   PTOLEMY III

Birth House?

0   10   15

Figure 45.
Plan of the Saite and Ptolemaic
temple Qasr el-Ghueda in the
El-Kharga Oasis.

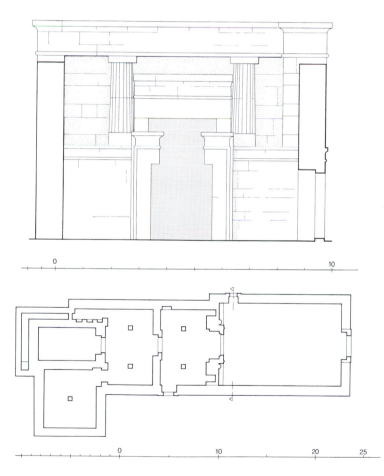

0   10

0   10   20   25

Figure 46.
Frontal elevation and plan of
the Amasis temple for Amun in
the Siwa Oasis.

Figure 47.
Actual state of the Amun temple of Amasis in the Siwa Oasis (courtesy of Anne Mininberg, New York).

The famous AMMONEION of the Siwa Oasis (Aghurmi) was built during the reign of Amasis.[118] Located on a spectacular limestone plateau in the west of the oasis was the palace of the local kinglets, who ruled the important caravan junction in the Egyptian western desert (figs. 46–47). The compound included the famous oracle temple, which the Persian army approaching from Thebes missed in 525 and which Alexander the Great visited in 331 as a pilgrim.

The Amun temple is relatively well preserved despite of now slowly crumbling rock on which it sits. Besides the Hibis temple in the El-Kharga Oasis, it is the only standing temple of the 26th Dynasty. The temple was built in Egyptian style and adorned with pure Egyptian decorations. Numerous details show, however, that Greek builders, probably from the Cyrene, were at work. The sanctuary comprised a sequence of four spatial units. A rectangular, deep forecourt was followed by two pillared halls, the roof of which was carried by two pillars. The first hall is a pronaos. The intercolumniations of its facade are, however, closed and depict a pronaos front in the form of two engaged Doric columns. These columns do not carry an architrave but directly support—against all building rules—the cavetto. The spacious sanctuary connects with an equally wide side room.

In addition to the Doric columns, the following features can be considered as foreign influence: the oversized, steep cavetto topping the temple; the vertical outer wall surfaces; the missing torus at the outside corners of the temple; the alternating heights of the block courses ("pseudo-isodomic"); the flat niche surrounding—without a cavetto—the central gate of the sanctuary; a lintel with downward-sloping lateral joints; and the rounded corbels for the support of the sanctuary roof.

The death of Amasis at the end of 526 spared the old king from seeing with his own eyes the humiliation of his country and his family in 525. Following tradition, he was buried in the royal necropolis of Sais and followed by his son Psametik III (526–525). The Persians took advantage of the situation. In the spring of 525, in the second regnal year of Psametik III, the Persian king Cambyses led his army, well informed and well prepared, against Egypt. In a bloody battle at Pelusium, in which Greek mercenaries vigorously fought on the Egyptian and Persian sides, the courageous but inexperienced Psametik III was defeated. Sais, with the palace of Amasis, was conquered and Heliopolis burned down.[119] Memphis was also taken after a siege, Psametik III and his family first were captured and humiliated, and later—after an attempt of agitation—killed. The temple treasures were plundered, the cult images abducted, and 6,000 Egyptian craftsmen were deported to build palaces in Persia.

Cambyses marched his army up the Nile as far as Elephantine, where he desecrated the sanctuaries.[120] His rushed attempt to reach Meroe by the desert route from Thebes was abandoned because of the hunger and thirst of his troops. Another army detachment was sent on an equally ill-considered mission from Thebes to Siwa and is said to have disappeared in the sands of the western desert.[121] Despite these embarrassing setbacks for Cambyses and the Persian army, Egypt remained continuously a Persian satrapy for 121 years, secured at strategic points by Persian garrisons.

The First Persian Domination
(27th Dynasty, 525–404 B.C.)

The attitude of the Persians against Egypt and its cults is controversial.[122] Reports on atrocities committed by the Persians under Cambyses are generally dismissed as anti-Persian propaganda by Egyptians and Greeks. The anti-Persian feeling was encouraged by the imposition of new taxes, mismanagement, disregard of local cults, and the dissimilarity of the foreign occupiers, who were unfamiliar with the country and overwhelmed by the problems of its administration. As a consequence, revolts broke out in 524, 519, and 486–484, with the result that the Persians intensified their grip on Egypt. About 460, Inaros, the Lybian chief of the Mareotis area (southwest of Alexandria), and Amyrtaios of Sais expelled the hated tax collectors.[123] In 460 the Persian satrap Achaemenes marched with a huge army to recover Egypt. In a fierce battle the Persians were defeated at Papremis (probably in the West Delta) and the satrap killed. However, the citadel of Memphis and other Persian garrisons remained in the hands of the Persians. After heavy struggles the Persians finally succeeded under the new satrap Megabyzus in restoring their power in 454. In the following years (450–440), the Greek historian Herodotus undertook his famous voyage to Egypt, which seems to have been calm during that period.

King Darius I (521–487) alone seems to have taken a more circumspect and conciliatory position toward Egypt and its cults, especially in regard to the Neith temple at Sais. In consequence, at least on a small scale the decoration of some temples could be continued.[124] In the El-Kharga Oasis, the decoration of the Amun temple of Psametik II at HIBIS was continued, and the cartouches of Darius I were inscribed on the small Saite temple of QASR EL-GHUEDA. The name of Darius I also appears on a granite block from BUSIRIS, the completely unexplored capital of the ninth Lower Egyptian Nome, suggesting that the Osiris temple of unknown date was restored. The name of Darius I also appears in the temple of Nekhbet at EL-KÂB.[125] Records of ancient expeditions to the quarries of the Wadi Hammamât suggest intensive mining of greenish graywacke. Some of the stone, which was much in demand for statue production, was probably shipped directly from the Red Sea to Persia.

The predecessor of the modern SUEZ CANAL, completed by Psametik II,[126] was of great importance to the Persians as a direct maritime connection to their homeland. Its maintenance was, therefore, also a Persian concern. Darius I and Xerxes I erected at least five stelae in four languages along the east bank of the canal, relating that ships could commute directly from the Nile to Persia.[127]

The 121-year Persian domination left minimal traces in Egyptian architecture, and even the number of stelae, stone sarcophagi, and other monuments in Egyptian style decreased significantly. This decrease in number did not affect quality, however, and the standard of private sculpture of the first Persian domination reached new heights. B. V. Bothmer claimed that "superb craftsmanship of the Late Period, equal in quality to the best of Egypt's past, but above and beyond that, is the lifelike expression of the face, which seems to reflect the vicissitudes suffered by the Egyptians during an alien domination."[128] Accordingly, even Udjahorresnet, an Egyptian supporter of the Persian regime, laments "the tremendous evil that ruled over the whole world, as it had never been seen before."

In 405 Amyrtaios (II) of Sais instigated a new uprising, which finally led to the liberation of Egypt. The rule of Amyrtaios entered history as the 28th Dynasty (404–399). The Persian army, which had gathered for a new attack, was torn by internal conflicts and could not reach Egypt again before 343 B.C.

5

THE 28TH TO 30TH DYNASTIES
(404–343 B.C.)

The Historical Background

Neither the expulsion of the Persian occupiers during the years 410–400 nor the subsequent return of local rule produced peace for the Egyptians.[1] The kings of the 29th and 30th Dynasties expended enormous energies in fending off attacks by the Persian army in 360/359 and 351.[2] Priority was given to the construction of gigantic brick enclosure walls to protect Egyptian sanctuaries from enemy invasion. Egyptian temples had traditionally been protected by enclosure walls, but the older fortifications were no longer sufficient to withstand the Persian assault. The new walls actually transformed the sanctuaries into real temple fortresses, as they are known from other first millennium cultures.[3] At the same time, the frontier fortresses built during the 26th Dynasty had to be renewed and strengthened.[4]

Above all, the short reigns of the first kings of the 29th Dynasty of altogether twenty to twenty-one years did not favor ambitious governmental programs of temple building. Only Hakoris (29th Dynasty), Nectanebo I, Teos, and Nectanebo II (30th Dynasty) undertook building campaigns with the aim of replacing all major Egyptian temples. The new buildings would be equipped with obelisks, granite shrines, and statues of the falcon king. Such an ambitious project, which could have been undertaken only by powerful rulers such as Ramesses the Great, proved to be beyond their abilities.

The ancient city of Sebennytos (modern Samannûd, in the center of the Delta) was of special interest to the Nectanebo kings, for it was the home and residential city of the royal family.[5] During the 30th Dynasty several temples were probably built there, as can be concluded from the appearance of four different ruined sites in the area.

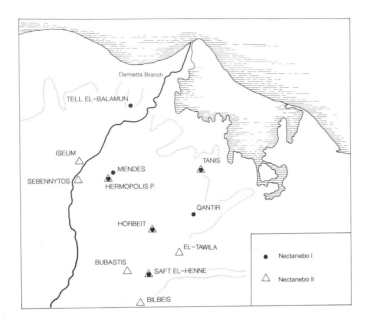

Figure 48.
Delta map with centers of
temple building of the 30th
Dynasty.

At least forty medium to large temples were built during the sixty years of
the 29th and 30th Dynasties. They are all more or less destroyed now, but to a
certain degree we can reconstruct the ground plans of several examples. The
distribution of the projects was remarkable because all known and suggested
temple projects in Lower Egypt, with the exception of Memphis, were concentrated in the northeast corner of the Delta (fig. 48). Because building projects
begun by the 30th Dynasty rulers were interrupted by the Persian invasion of
343 and only finished under the early Ptolemies, it is often difficult to credit
these buildings to one or the other.

Building Style and Architectural Form of
the 29th and 30th Dynasties

The furnishing of the old and new sanctuaries of the country with royal
images, in human shape or in the form of the sacred falcon, shows that the
kings of this period revived the ancient concept of the deified ruler. However,
no temples are known that were reserved solely for the cult of the ruler or that
followed the tradition of the "royal mortuary temples" of the New Kingdom.
Instead, the royal cult of the 30th Dynasty was attached to the cults of deities.
In the Ptolemaic Period this arrangement is clearly confirmed by the edict
of the priests' convention of Canopus in 238.[6] The decree orders that gilded
statues of the "beneficiary gods," that is, the ruling royal couple, should be
donated to temples throughout the country and carried in processions. This
attachment of the cult of the king to the temples of the gods may have given
an additional stimulus for the building of deities' temples. The royal cult
was specifically established in the birth houses, in which the young king was

identified with the son of the divine family.[7] The aspect of the birth house as scene of the royal cult would explain the remarkable development of these buildings from the 30th Dynasty on.

As early as 1887, Edouard Naville enthusiastically described the art of the 30th Dynasty:

> Looking at the monuments of the two Nectanebos, it is impossible not to be struck by the beauty of the workmanship as well as by the richness of the material employed. Egyptian art undergoes a new resurrection more complete than under the twenty-sixth dynasty. There is more vigour in the style than at the time of the Psammetichi; perhaps less delicacy than in the works of the Saite kings, but a decided tendency to revert to the stern beauty of the works of the great Pharaohs. The hieroglyphs engraved on the tablet and shrine of Saft, and on the cornices of Horbeit, are certainly among the most beautiful in Egypt.[8]

Naville also stresses that the kings of the 30th Dynasty apparently avoided usurpation of monuments and were driven by ambition to produce buildings of their own. Georg Steindorff, however, also remarks that despite the admirable work of sculptors, the hard stone reliefs of the temples of the Delta rarely achieve the quality of older work in limestone and sandstone.[9]

In 1960, Bernard V. Bothmer differentiated the classicistic archaizing tendencies of the 26th Dynasty from the archaistic tendencies of the sculptors of the 30th Dynasty.[10] In his opinion, for the 30th Dynasty "the Saite Period was the golden age, and from it they took their inspiration—adding new ideas and subtly changing and adapting the traditional."[11] Beyond admiring the technical achievements, archaeologists have defined stylistic characteristics of the relief and sculpture of the 30th Dynasty. The art of carving in hard granite and quartzite had declined during the century and a half following the end of the 26th Dynasty, but it was splendidly revived under Nectanebo I. The scale of 30th Dynasty stonework not only surpassed anything done in Saite times but also established a new tradition in Egypt that lasted far into the Ptolemaic Period. From the reign of Nectanebo I we have such major reliefs as a screen wall from Sais (fig. 60) and the naos of Saft el-Henne (fig. 62). Under Nectanebo II, entire temple walls made of granite were decorated with relief at Mendes, Behbeit el-Hagar (figs. 83–84), Sebennytos (fig. 86), and Bubastis. These reliefs are characterized by the strong modeling of the human body, creating a nearly three-dimensional volume. An accentuated tripartite division of the human torso (breast, ribs, belly) was to dominate the art of relief and sculpture into the Ptolemaic Period (figs. 84, 167).

This optical articulation of the body shape has parallels in Hellenistic relief modeling, but foreign influence can probably be ruled out. In spite of this stronger relief modeling, Egyptian temple relief of the 30th Dynasty does not break through the still-intact frontal surface and remains rigidly fixed in the two-dimensional grid of the temple walls.[12]

The evaluation of the buildings' stylistic features is much hampered by the loss of standing monuments, but one may elaborate on a few dominant features. A major aspect was a new monumentality manifesting the omnipotence of the deity and the invincibility of the system, crushing the individual. During the 30th Dynasty, numerous temples were surrounded by new enclosure walls of enormous dimensions, allowing one to conclude that the temple houses also should have displayed a similar monumentality. The homogeneous surfaces of the temple walls, now built of hard stone, amplified the impression of the physical weight of their mass and their indestructibility. In contrast to the white limestone walls of older temples, the monumental style was now enhanced by the contrast between the solemn black-gray and red-gray stone surfaces and the brilliantly lit surroundings emphasizing the cubic form of the building. No other stylistic means could have better expressed the intentions to revive the world of the Old Kingdom and the pharaonic kingship.

The enlargement of the pronaos in the 30th Dynasty, with its broad colonnaded front, disguised the block-shaped front with a sequence of brightly lit columns offset by dark intercolumniations. A real opening of the wall plane of the temple house or a visual relationship between the interior of the temple and the surrounding landscape was not intended, however. The stout shape of the 30th Dynasty columns still followed New Kingdom examples and did not have the slim proportions characteristic of the Ptolemaic style. The new articulation of the temple facade by an entrance kiosk or pronaos was supported by alternating column capitals. Significantly, the capital type is no longer selected for its symbolic value but becomes an expression of design, heralding an important step in the development of Egyptian architecture. Comparing the monotonous colonnades of the late Ramesside Khonsu temple (fig. 2) or of Sheshonq I at Karnak (fig. 8) with those of Edfu, Philae (figs. 195–196), or Kalabsha clearly shows that the original tendency toward orderly repetition and monotony is softened by induction of variety and structure.

It is rather improbable that creative connections with foreign countries developed during the relatively short period of the Nectanebo kings. All neighboring countries fell into Persian hands after 525 and were no longer capable of architectural achievement. Only the Ionian cities of western Anatolia undertook significant building projects during the fourth century. As discussed in chapter 4, Ionian architecture of this period may have been influenced by Egypt.

Building Methods of the 29th to 30th Dynasties

Well-tried pharaonic building methods saw few changes until the end of the New Kingdom. In the following centuries, however, changes and improvements occur in Egyptian building methods, partially because of contacts with the Greco-Roman world.[13] In the 30th Dynasty at the latest, setting smaller blocks in *isodomic* courses became routine. Tight joining of blocks, neglected for centuries, was rediscovered, and the archaic method of cutting oblique lateral joints abandoned.[14] Whereas oblique joints helped to reduce waste of stone material and transportation costs, the goal of the new ashlar masonry was time efficiency. The new technique of joining blocks did not not completely suppress oblique joints even in Ptolemaic times. The passion of the stonemasons to procure the utmost from the stone material was too deeply rooted.

During the building of the first pylon at Karnak under Nectanebo I(?), the old corner columns of the court of Sheshonk I were dismantled and reassembled. The study of these columns, which remained unfinished, permitted Uvo Hölscher to explain the methods of constructing columns with drums.[15]

Examinations of the 30th Dynasty temples of Elephantine undertaken by Ricke allow interesting insights into the building methods of the time. Nothing had changed since the 26th Dynasty in the construction of foundations. The foundation pit was still buttressed with plastered and whitewashed brick walls and filled with sand. The temple was not yet constructed on a continuous foundation platform as in Ptolemaic times; instead, its walls were placed on separate foundations, the compartments of which were filled with reused blocks. The foundation walls consisted of carefully laid sandstone blocks connected lengthwise by cramps.[16] The paving consisted of two heavy courses of well dressed blocks set between the feet of the aboveground walls.

The aboveground masonry was built of large, carefully joined sandstone blocks,[17] which were interlocked lengthwise by hard wooden cramps (fig. 49). The setting of blocks was prepared in the old tradition by scratching the alignment of the upper course into the top surface of the lower course. Flat bands, roughened to improve the adhesion of mortar, were outlined with scratched lines and appear on the top surfaces of the blocks. In the Hibis temple wrought iron shims were pushed into the lower *bedding joints* for leveling the blocks during the drying phase of the mortar.

The two towers of the unfinished first pylon at Karnak (probably 30th Dynasty) reveal important information about the construction sequence.[18] The pylons display a good example of the newly reintroduced ashlar masonry. However, the blocks were still set in pharaonic tradition with a rough front face, only to be dressed in the final phase. All essential setting lines are scratched into the block surfaces. The corner blocks still preserve the lines of the angle of inclination, as well as the notches on their top surface for stretching the cords. The corner blocks also show the rough shape of the corner torus with the engraved lines for the sculptors.

Figure 49.
Masonry of the 30th Dynasty at the first pylon of Karnak.

Figure 50. Limestone stela from Gabbari in the form of a kiosk with a flat, segmented pediment, Alexandria, 21763 (see Patrizio Pensabene, "Elementi architettonici di Alessandria e di altri siti egiziani," in *Repertorio d'arte dell'Egitto greco-roman*, serie C, vol. 3 [Rome, 1993], pl. 117[8]).

Figure 51. Ornament on a Hellenistic gold ring in the National Museum Athens in the form of an Egyptian kiosk with a flat, segmented pediment (after W. Weber, "Ein Hermes-Tempel des Kaisers Marcus," *Sitzungsberichte der Heidelberger Akademie der Wissenschaften* [1910]: 10–54).

Figure 52.
Hellenistic-pharaonic chapel facade (24863-4) and engaged papyrus-/palmette-bundle columns (3660 and 3664) in Alexandria.

FUNERAL CANOPY FROM THE UPPER CHAMBER OF THIS TOMB

An interesting method of surface treatment was observed on a column capital from the Hibis temple now in The Metropolitan Museum of Art.[19] The sculpted surface of the capital was covered with fine linen before the thin, final stucco layer and the paint were applied.

The wide dimensions of kiosks from the 29th–30th Dynasties onward required roof constructions of timber.[20] The stone architraves of several kiosks have preserved the sockets for the anchoring of wooden roofs. Some roofs were shaped as shallow barrel roofs. The combination of stone and timber for sacred buildings indicates an elementary change in the conception of Egyptian building.

The kiosk with a shallow barrel roof later entered Ptolemaic Alexandrian architecture (figs. 50–52) and was passed as a characteristic Egyptian building type down to Roman architecture.[21] These kiosks survive in depictions of Late Egyptian temples on Roman coins,[22] in the Nile mosaic of Preneste (Palestrina),[23] and as wooden coffins of the Roman Period with barrel-shaped roof constructions (fig. 53).[24]

During the 30th Dynasty, important sanctuaries were surrounded by huge brick enclosure walls that not only were considerably stronger than the older walls but also were built with improved techniques. To prevent damage from sagging, the walls were built in short separated sections. To eliminate cracks that open when brick masonry is drying, the bricks were laid not in wet mud mortar but in sand. To add more stability to the walls, the brick courses were laid not horizontally but sloping against the center of each wall section. In addition, the outside corners were often strengthened with stone casing.

The Buildings of the 28th to 30th Dynasties

Nepherites I, Nayf-aau-rud (398/397–392/391)

As can be seen from the discovery of two limestone relief blocks in TELL TMAI (Thmouis) and of a granite door frame at MENDES, during the short six-year

Figure 53.
Funeral canopy of Mentuem-saf from Thebes in the Royal Scottish Museum, Edinburgh, 1956.353 (after A. H. Rhind, *Thebes: Its Tombs and Their Tenants* [London, 1862], frontispiece).

reign of Nepherites I some probably modest projects were carried out. A high-quality basalt sphinx of Nepherites confirms, however, the continuation of high standards in sculpture.[25]

At the bank of the Nile in front of the Bubastide court of KARNAK, Nepherites I began a turning station for the bark of Amun (fig. 54). The unique building was completed under Psamuthis and Hakoris. The chapel was a resting place for the bark before its departure from Karnak and after its return from Luxor or the west bank. The chapel was built on the spot where the direction of the processional allée changed at 90 degrees. The front gate of the station in the west wall therefore had to be complemented by a second gate in the south wall. The building consisted of a front kiosk and an inner shrine, both of which were roofed with timber. The front architrave was an 8.25 m long wooden beam that carried—unique in Egyptian architecture—cavetto blocks of stone. The two antae piers of the shrine are decorated with the heraldic plants of Upper and Lower Egypt, the papyrus in the north and the lily in the south (fig. 55).[26]

Perhaps Nepherites I also began a birth house for Harpare, the divine child of Raittaui and Monthu in the complex of Amunra-Monthu at Karnak (fig. 56; plan IX). The building was directly attached to the Amunra-Monthu temple and not built at a right angle, as is typical for birth houses, but parallel to the axis of the main temple. A colonnaded court was added by Nectanebo I, and a gate was built or at least decorated under Ptolemy VI. The decoration of the birth house continued during the reign of Nectanebo II.

Nepherites I also built a huge *shena wab* south of the sacred lake at Karnak, replacing a predecessor of the 26th Dynasty. The structure is the largest known example of this building type.[27] A 45.5 x 55.5 m brick building rose above a platform 4.5 m high. A forecourt contained a slaughterhouse and a

Figure 54.
Reconstruction and plan of the bark turning station of the 29th Dynasty in front of the first pylon of Karnak.

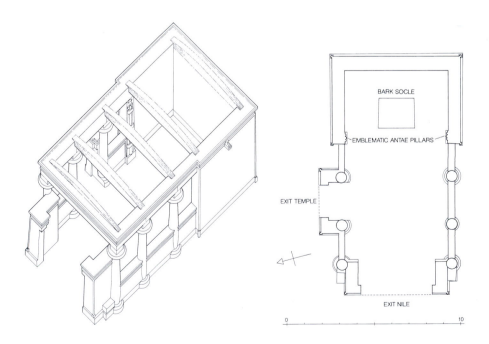

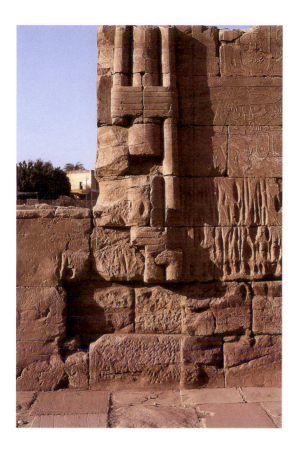

Figure 55.
Antae pier decorated with a papyrus-bundle column in the bark turning station of the 29th Dynasty in front of the first pylon of Karnak (photo A.O.).

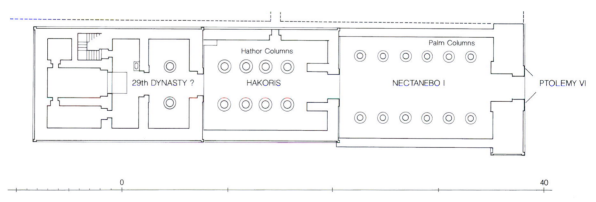

Figure 56. Plan of the birth house of the 29th Dynasty in the precinct of Amunra-Monthu at Karnak.

poultry den. A statue chapel followed a series of three chambers that probably served as magazines.

The tomb of Nepherites I was discovered at Mendes in 1992. It still contained an enormous limestone sarcophagus, but the burial itself had been completely devastated by the Persians in 342.[28]

Psamuthis (Psamut), Weser-Re setepen-Ptah (393)

In the reign of his successor Psamuthis, who was overthrown after a year by Hakoris, some small projects were carried out at Karnak. The decoration of the bark turning station of Nepherites I and of the *shena wab* was continued. A block from the *shena wab* bears the name of Psamuthis.[29]

Hakoris (Akoris, Heker), Maat-Khnum-Re setepen-Khnum (392/391–379/378)

The militarily distinguished King Hakoris conquered Cyprus (for the second time since Amasis) and repelled a renewed attack by the Persians in 383, pursuing them far into Asia. These military efforts did not prevent the king from building smaller temples, enlarging some Saite sanctuaries, and donating naoi, altars, and statues at numerous sites. One senses the ambitions that mark the political attempts of succeeding kings to revive Egypt's ancient splendor.

A quantity of limestone and black granite blocks with the names of Hakoris and Nectanebo I found at LETOPOLIS (Kôm Aushîm, northwest of Cairo) confirm that these kings rebuilt or enlarged the temple of the blind falcon deity Khenti-irti. According to a quarry inscription, blocks for the project were extracted at Tura in the years 393–388. A gray granite block of a cavetto topped by an uraeus frieze probably originates from a screen wall that may have belonged to a *wabet*, a roof chapel, or a pronaos. Other fragments belonged to a naos and a stela(?) with annals.[30] The site of the Khenti-irti temple disappeared in 1923 under modern houses, before excavations could take place.

A basalt sphinx of Hakoris found in Rome is dedicated to Ptah, Sokar, and Osiris and may have been paired with a similar sphinx of Nepherites in the older Serapeum of MEMPHIS.[31] A 2.08 m long limestone architrave with a beautifully written inscription of King Hakoris found in the monastery of Jeremias at Saqqara (south of the Unas causeway) mentions Hapi-Osiris and also suggests major construction works of the king at the Serapeum (fig. 63).[32]

Fragments of hard stone naoi of Hakoris were found at HERAKLEOPOLIS MAGNA (Ihnâsya el-Medîna) and in the White Monastery (Arabic Deir el-Abjad, church ca. A.D. 440). The latter may have been donated to the temple of ancient Neshau, the ruins of which are probably built over by the Deir el-Abjad. The name of the king is also attested from a block in the Monthu temple at MEDAMOUD.

At KARNAK a hypostyle hall of two-by-four columns was added to the birth house of Harpare begun by Nepherites I (at the east side of the Amunra-Monthu temple, plan IX). Reflecting the female aspects of a birth house, the columns carried Hathor capitals. The column shafts were smooth and their feet contracted (corresponding to the entasis of Greek columns) and decorated with papyrus "leaves." The interior of the building was provided with two spur walls which connected with the first pair of columns, similar to the hypostyle hall of the Hibis temple. The birth house was again enlarged by Nectanebo I, who added a colonnaded court and a pylon to the front.

In the temple of the primordial Amun at MEDINET HABU, the roof of the deteriorating ambulatory of Thutmosis III was supported by four fluted pillars.

Several small relief fragments of Hakoris from an unknown building were found at EL-TÔD.[33] They may indicate the beginning of reconstruction work in the sanctuary area of the Monthu temple.

Considering the nationalistic tendencies of the period, it seemed advantageous to expand the Upper Egyptian crown sanctuary of EL-KÂB (plan XII). The 260-year-old Saite building seems to have received a new forecourt with a pylon and three connecting chambers on the northeast side, which is almost identical to the layout of the older inner court behind. As a consequence, the inner court could be transformed into the hitherto missing hypostyle hall.[34] The middle axis was occupied, however, by a nave of higher papyrus columns, which towered over aisle columns of lesser height and unknown shape. The hall therefore had a clerestory lighting system in the New Kingdom tradition,[35] probably one of the last examples in Egypt. The type of hypostyle halls with a higher central nave had been replaced by halls with columns of equal height, which did not permit lighting through clerestory windows.

Three pairs of columns were still standing in 1798, when architects of the Napoleonic expedition drew a picture of the ruin.[36] Today the temple has been reduced to the lowest stone courses; some loose blocks also remain inscribed with the name of Hakoris.

On ELEPHANTINE the foundations of a temple of Hakoris were excavated in 1997; the results have not yet been published. Apparently a small intercolumniar gate was added between the columns of a Ramesside court of the Khnum temple.[37]

Although inscribed evidence is lacking, one would also like to date the first enlargement of the Saite Hibis temple at EL-KHARGA to the reign of Hakoris.[38] Instead of completing the colonnaded court that had been begun in the 26th Dynasty, the builders added a hypostyle hall in front of the pronaos, contrasting the common sequence of building parts (figs. 57–59). Its four-by-three, plumply proportioned columns have palm- and bell-shaped capitals (see diagram).

Different capital types in the same building part are common in buildings of the Ptolemaic-Roman Period but are unknown in New Kingdom architecture. We do not know when this type of arrangement first appeared, but the Hibis temple certainly was an early example. The alignment of the architraves is notable. In the nave, they follow the direction of the processional axis and accentuate the movement along the axis. In the aisles, the architraves lie at right angles to the axis and create a space that suggests pause and rest. Two spur walls lead inward, sustaining the longitudinal architraves of the nave. The new facade of the temple lacked a pylon, but—as is often the case in later Ptolemaic buildings—it was fronted by a plain wall with a central gate.

Hypostyle Hall of Hakoris, Amun Temple at Hibis

FRONT

b - a - a - b
b - b - b - b
b - a - a - b

BACK

a: Palm capitals
b: Bell-shaped capitals

Figure 57. View of the hypostyle hall of Hakoris in the Amun temple at Hibis (courtesy of MMA).

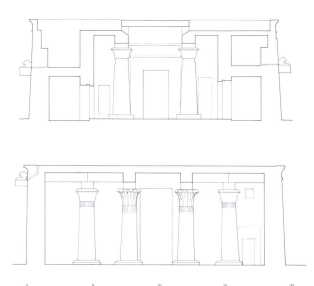

Figure 58. Sections of the hypostyle halls of Psametik II (*top*) and Hakoris in the Amun temple at Hibis (Herbert E. Winlock, *The Temple of Hibis in El Kharga Oasis* [New York, 1941], pls. 36, 40).

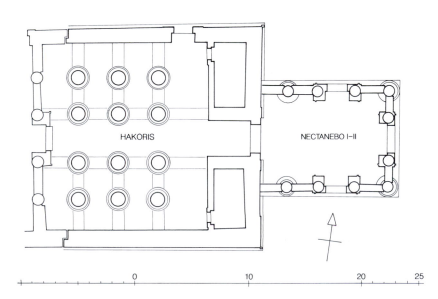

HAKORIS

NECTANEBO I-II

Figure 59.
Plan of the front part of the Amun temple at Hibis.

The hypostyle hall of the Hibis temple is the only partially surviving 29th Dynasty room, but the temple is only a modest provincial product and is not representative of contemporary sacred and residential architecture.

That the tomb of the king may have been at SAQAARA is suggested by his quarrying activities at Tura and an *ushabti* of Hakoris, found at Saqqara in 1922.[39]

Nectanebo I (Nakhtnebef), Kheperkare (379/378–361/360)

After Hakoris's death, his son Nepherites II succeeded him but was assassinated after a few months by general Nectanebo I, son of Djedhor of Sebennytos. This violent act at least provided Egypt with a capable ruler. During Nectanebo's eighteen-year reign the threat of a Persian invasion was constant. The armament to defend the Nile valley against an adversary superior by the number of his forces was the main priority of the new, military ruler.

Nectanebo passed his first test brilliantly. In 374/373 a 200,000-man army led by the Persian satrap Pharnabazus appeared at the northeast border of Egypt. Thanks to careful preparation, skillful strategy, and a punctual Nile flood, the Persians were outmaneuvered and compelled to make an embarrassing retreat.

Nectanebo's choice of the throne name Kheperkare, the name of the 12th Dynasty pharaoh Senwosret I, shows that Nectanebo saw himself at the outset of a new period, a revival of the country on the basis of Middle Kingdom tradition. Following ancient customs, temples received donations of property, primarily at Sais and Naucratis, Hermopolis magna, and Edfu (fig. 60). Statues of the king were donated to major sanctuaries, a practice that was later intensified by Nectanebo II (see fig. 82).[40] Since no significant temples had been built in Egypt for 150 years, a vigorous architectural manifestation was important. The invasion of Egypt and the repeated destruction of its temples by the Assyrians and Persians in 667/666, 661, and 525 demanded the construction of new and more effective enclosure walls. Consequently, all major Egyptian temples were walled in by enormous brick enclosures, which transformed the temple precincts into respectable fortresses. Only a military motivation would justify the disturbance inflicted to the temple precincts and their surrounding settlements by the construction activities. The walls were of the undulating type, built in alternating sections of concave and convex courses and probably crowned by crenellations.[41] Despite enormous military expenditures, Nectanebo I was one of the foremost temple builders of Late Period Egypt. The list of his building projects surpasses even those of Nectanebo II and the Roman emperor Augustus.[42]

At TELL EL-BALAMUN (El-Kom el-Ahmar), in the north at the Damietta branch of the Nile, the old temple citadel of Amun was rebuilt. The structure had been destroyed by the Persians in 525 (plan II).[43] The demolished enclosure of Psametik I was replaced by a larger, 25(!) m thick brick wall, as was the Ramesside Amun temple. The shape of the foundation pit suggests that the new temple had a 62 m wide and 74 m deep forecourt, followed by a 42 x 84 m temple house; 50 m northeast of the forecourt, a smaller temple, probably a birth house, was built at a right angle to the main building. The 34 x 48 m

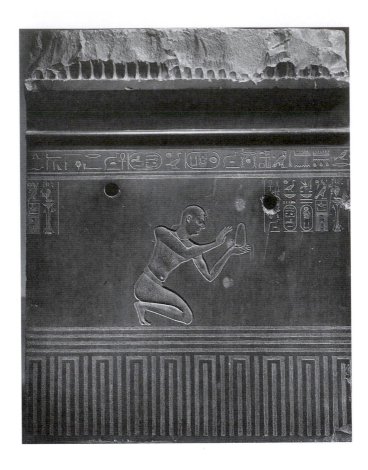

Figure 60.
Green schist parapet wall from Sais showing Nectanebo I with a bread offering, kneeling on the archaic motive of the palace facade, Brit. Mus., E 22 (courtesy of Brit. Mus.).

building was enhanced by a 52.5 m broad and 18 m deep pronaos. Of all pronaoi we know, only those of Akhmim and Hermopolis magna would have surpassed its dimensions. Probably eight columns would have formed the front of the structure, followed by at least one more row of columns inside. Because of the second Persian invasion the new temple remained unfinished, as may be inferred from the undecorated state of its granite naos, which was found in fragments. The temple was demolished down to the foundations during a military action, probably in late Ptolemaic times.

Under Nectanebo I a Khonsu-Neferhotep temple was added to the Amun temple at TANIS. The temple faced north, and its rear wall adjoined the third court of the Amun temple (plan I).[44] The location of foundation deposits suggests that the temple house was surrounded at the rear and along both long sides by a strong wall. The temple is completely destroyed.

Two more architecturally interesting entrance kiosks must be mentioned here, although they cannot be precisely dated.[45] The first one, in the Amun temple, stood behind the main entrance gate, built by Sheshonq III. The location of the kiosk *behind* the gate is unusual. Unfortunately, neither foundations nor column bases are left, and the connection with the gate remains unknown. There are remains, however, of four marvelous granite palm columns of the Old Kingdom. From the extraordinary height of the columns (10.8 m), one can conclude that the total height of the kiosk was about 14 m. Two more fragments suggest the existence of limestone papyrus columns, one inscribed with the name of Psusennes I, suggesting a 21st Dynasty date. However, since the temple house of Amun of that time was still far to the east, one would assume that the kiosk was built only in the 30th Dynasty, when the temple with its first pylon had grown in length.

The second kiosk (17 x 27.75 m) stood in front of the main gate of the complex of Mut/Anta (fig. 61). Its limestone palm columns, spaced at intervals of 4.55 m, stood on granite bases. The transversal span of 13 m could not have been roofed with stone.

Relief fragments with the names of Nectanebo I, Teos, and Nectanebo II, found in the area of QANTIR, suggest the presence of a temple of the 30th Dynasty that has not yet been located.[46]

According to its dedication, a small granite obelisk of Nectanebo I originated from the tomb of the Kem-wer, the sacred bulls at ABU YASSIN 3 km southeast of Horbeit (Pharbaetos). Under Nectanebo I, one of the sacred bulls was buried in a beautifully carved granite sarcophagus, parts of which are still preserved.[47]

Nectanebo I replaced a temple of Ramesses II at the old cult place for the falcon Sopdu, the lord of the eastern border, at SAFT EL-HENNE (Pi-Sopdu, Phacusa, 8 km southeast of Bubastis) with a new temple of 40 x 70 m. In 1884 E. Naville excavated its 5 m wide brick foundations and counted 142 basalt blocks from the temple's pavement.[48] The king dedicated a splendid granite naos to the sanctuary, decorated with a catalogue of deities. The completely preserved, black granite naos was broken in pieces by feebleminded treasure hunters in 1865 (fig. 62).[49]

A relief block of Nectanebo I was found at MUNAGAT EL-KUBRA (in the Wadi Tumilat). Building activities are also attested by relief blocks and a dark granite naos of the king found in the Saite temple of MENDES.[50]

Figure 61.
Plan of the kiosk of Nectanebo I(?), at the front of the temple of Anta at Tanis.

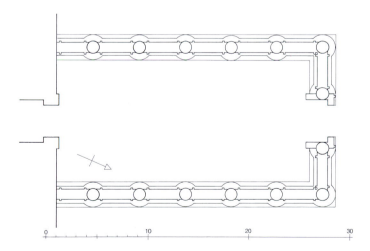

Figure 62.
The remains of the black granite naos of Nectanebo I for Sopdu at Saft el-Henne (Phacusa), Cairo, CG 70021.

Building works, which had been suspended during the first Persian Domination, were resumed in the Saite temples of Neith SAIS. A small granite naos dedicated to Neith of Sais and a column drum may have belonged to the Neith temple.[51] The unidentified structure of Psametik I and II (see figs. 34, 37) with green schist parapet walls, was either extended or completed. Three slabs apparently belonging to this structure and decorated by Nectanebo I were found in Alexandria, Rosetta, and Rome (fig. 60).[52]

Tell el-Baqlieh (Tell el-Naqûs, 5 km south of Mansoura) is the site of the ancient HERMOPOLIS PARVA. It was the capital of the fifteenth nome and was favored by the kings of the 30th Dynasty.[53] The location of the city's main temple, dedicated to Thoth, was indicated by a mound of huge red and black granite blocks, still visible in 1906. This material and two unfinished papyrus capitals, an inscribed block of Nectanebo I, and a statue of the same king point to an enlargement or replacement of the Saite temple. The 350 x 384 enclosure wall surrounding the sanctuary, like so many others, also may have been built during the reign of Nectanebo I. The well-known pair of granite lions in the Vatican, found in the Roman Iseum, carries a dedicatory inscription to Thoth and also may have come from here.[54]

Three quartzite slabs from ATHRIBIS (modern Benha) were probably screen walls of a chapel or kiosk called "House of the Seventy (protective demons of the embalmment)."[55] Since these demons were followers of Osiris, the chapel probably stood in the temple of Osiris at Athribis. Considerations of religious development date the chapel tentatively to the reign of Nectanebo I.

A slender Hathor capital column of limestone with the name of Nectanebo I seems also to originate from the Delta. The small dimensions suggest only a head-high kiosk, which was apparently dedicated to a female deity.[56]

We have no direct evidence, but we may assume that Nectanebo I founded a huge temple, the 260 x 300 m "Great Temenos" at the southern end of NAUCRATIS.[57] The brick enclosure, still 16 m high in 1884, has been leveled since. The main temple (in the axis of the Ptolemaic pylon) was apparently completed by Ptolemy I and Ptolemy II. Its scarce remains have never been examined. A big *shena wab* stood to the side of the main temple.

In the area of the temple of Ptah at MEMPHIS Flinders Petrie found a few poorly carved blocks of limestone, red granite, and quartzite with the name of Nectanebo I.[58] It was not possible to connect the blocks with a known structure.

In the cemetery of SAQQARA Nectanebo I built or enlarged the Serapeum, the mortuary complex for the deceased Apis bull, transformed in death into a "Apis-Osiris." The Serapeum was the most colossal tomb complex of ancient Egypt (fig. 63–64, plan III).[59] Because Apis bulls were buried here since the New Kingdom, an older temple is to be expected.

From the temple of Apis at Memphis, a 5 km sphinx allée was built through the fields to the tombs in the desert. The allée entered the Anubieion of Amasis at the desert edge and within its walls climbed the steep incline of the desert. The 20 m rise to the desert plateau was ascended by means of a staircase. The original number of the relatively small limestone sphinxes lining the allée must have been considerable. Mariette identified at least forty at Saqqara, Cairo, and Alexandria.[60] Both sides of the allée were flanked by brick walls, which did not, however, hold back the sand. As Strabo reports (*Geography*, XVII.1.32): "There is also a Serapeum at Memphis, in a place so very sandy that dunes of sand are heaped up by the winds; and by these some of the sphinxes which I saw were buried even to the head and others were half-visible. . . ."

Figure 63.
View of the entrance passage of the Serapeum at Saqqara with a sarcophagus lid abandoned by the transport workers (photo A.O.).

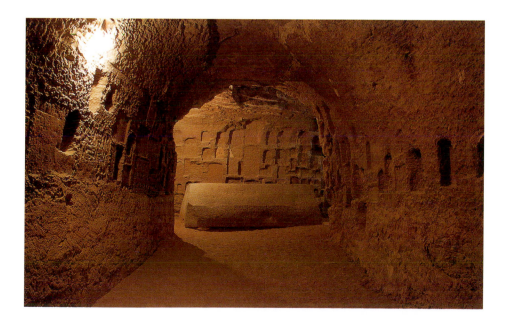

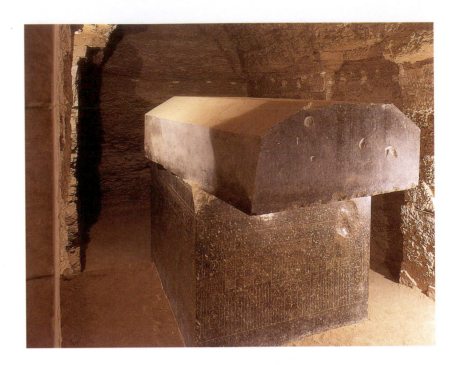

Figure 64.
Sarcophagus of an Apis bull
in the Serapeum of Saqqara
(photo A.O.).

The allée curved southward to a stone-paved dromos that led straight to the temple. The end of the sphinx allée and the dromos were flanked by Late Period funerary chapels and votive statues. Mariette excavated an Egyptian-style chapel at the dromos a chapel that contained a smaller-than-life-size limestone statue of an Apis bull.[61] To the chapel's side stood a small temple on a podium in Greek style with two Corinthian capitals *in antis*. In Ptolemaic times, an apse with eleven statues of Greek poets and philosophers was built opposite the juncture of the sphinx allée and the dromos.[62]

At the western end of the dromos, a triple gate led into the actual Serapeum. Aboveground, a 300 x 300 m enclosure encircled the area of the underground tombs and contained the funerary temple with another Apis cult image. Mariette's plan shows the temple surrounded on its north, east, and south sides by colonnades.

The temple stood on top of the entrance into a network of tomb galleries. Since the New Kingdom, sixty-four mummies of the Apis bulls were buried here. The earliest tombs consisted of single shafts. Since Ramesses II the bulls were placed in a community tomb. The tombs of the 26th and 30th Dynasty are arranged along a 350 m long, 3 m wide, and 5.5 m high central corridor, which gives access to lateral crypts with the sarcophagi (figs. 63–64). Some of the vaulted crypts began to be cased with limestone. The sarcophagi, mostly of red and black granite, measure on average 2.3 x 3.3 x 4 m and weigh up to 65 tons. Only a few are inscribed and decorated. Stelae, set into the walls near the entrance, are inscribed with precise dates and have become a cornerstone of Late Period chronology.[63] The main gallery was dug gradually as additional tombs were required, and was later supplied with more galleries.

At the north side of the complex was a temple of Hathor-Isis, perhaps of Nectanebo I, from which another road led to the catacombs of the mothers of the Apis-bulls, farther to the northeast.[64] Even the hitherto unidentified tomb of Nectanebo I could have been in the Memphite cemetery, perhaps east of the Serapeum.[65] The first tomb of Alexander the Great possibly was also located in this area; but probably under Ptolemy I, Alexander's body was removed to Alexandria.

At the desert edge of Saqqara, east of the Teti pyramid, are two brick precincts, the ANUBIEION in the north and the BUBASTEION south of it.[66] Not much remains of the original constructions, which probably date to King Amasis. Nectanebo I enlarged the enclosures to approximately 250 x 350 m each and built new temples. The approach to the Serapeum of Nectanebo I ascended through the better-explored Anubieion. This precinct was dedicated to Anubis, the dog-shaped lord of the necropolis.[67] Amasis had already built a small temple in the center part. Two more temples were added later north and south of the Amasis temple. All were standing—like the New Kingdom temples of Deir el-Bahari—on terraces.

The southern complex, the Bubasteion, was a sanctuary for Bastet/ Sakhmet and has been only poorly investigated. Its main temple stood above the steep bank of rock and is now razed to its brick foundations. A New Kingdom cliff cemetery beneath was used in Ptolemaic times for the burial of thousands of mummified cats.

The temple of Thoth at HERMOPOLIS MAGNA was, for unknown reasons, especially favored by Nectanebo I.[68] Apparently the people of Hermopolis had assisted Nectanebo at his coup against Nepherites II. The temple of Thoth was first distinguished during Nectanebo's fourth year by building a new temple for Nehemet-'away, the creator goddess and consort of Thoth. This 15.75 x 31.5 m building, which stood within the precinct of Thoth and at a right angle to the temple of Thoth, may have been a birth house for the god Neferhor. The front part of the temple was probably a pronaos with Hathor columns. A hypostyle hall followed and led into a triple shrine. The building was completed, after four years, in 371/370 B.C.

At the same time, the old pylon of Ramesses II that led into the complex of Thoth was enlarged by an *avant-porte*, called in Egyptology "Gate of the Sphinxes." In front of the gate stood obelisks, stelae, a pair of granite sphinxes, and two colossal statues of the king. Above all, the complex of Thoth was tremendously enlarged by the construction of a new, 15 m thick enclosure wall of 630 x 603 m (1200 x 1150 cubits). A new gate, 45 m in front of the Sphinx Gate, conducted through the new south wall, while three more gates pierced the east, west, and north walls.

In regnal year 8 of Nectanebo I, the New Kingdom temple of Thoth was demolished and work begun on a new 55 x 110 m temple with a huge pronaos (fig. 65). During the dismantling, two colossal baboon statues from the reign of Amenhotep III were cut apart and buried in the foundations of the new pronaos.

Whereas the main temple is now completely lost, we are better informed about the pronaos, because its columns and roof were still standing and were documented by several early travelers (fig. 66) before they were destroyed in

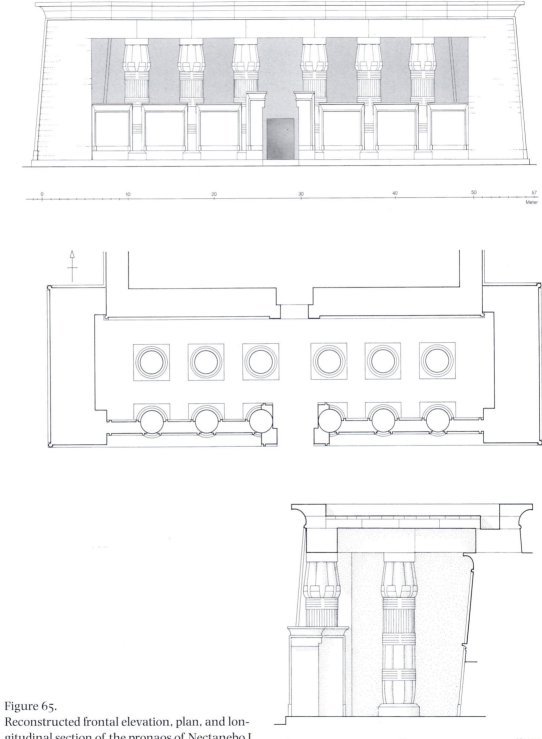

Figure 65.
Reconstructed frontal elevation, plan, and longitudinal section of the pronaos of Nectanebo I at Hermopolis magna.

about 1826.[69] In contrast to the three to four rows of columns in later pronaoi, this example had only two rows of six limestone papyrus-bundle columns (figs. 65–66).[70] The unvarying column type, the lack of composite capitals, the stocky column proportions (1:5.5), the top-heavy capitals, and the broad mass of the building gave the structure a ponderous, archaic quality.[71] Decoration work was continued under Nectanebo II but suspended after the Persian invasion in 343 and only resumed under Ptolemy I.

Under Nectanebo I, there seems to have been extensive building activity in the long-honored complex of Osiris at ABYDOS. The brick enclosure of Kom el-Sultan, which surrounded the sanctuary of Osiris, displays the undulating brick courses and the subdivision into single segments characteristic of the period. The 7 m thick, 240 x 314 m wall enclosed older buildings, including the temple of Amasis. Access to the complex was through a pylon built in the east wall. A new temple was built approximately 150 m west of the pylon. The temple matched in size (43 x 68 m) other late temples like Elephantine or Kom Ombo. The building was completely destroyed before Petrie started his excavations in 1902/1903. Only remains of a cartouche of Nectanebo I were found on a piece of a red granite naos.[72]

That the succeeding Ptolemies did not honor Abydos, which was one of the most eminent cult places of Upper Egypt, with a large new temple can only be explained by the existence of a monumental building of the 30th Dynasty which was thought to meet the demands.[73]

Nectanebo I also enlarged the temple of Hibis in the EL-KHARGA Oasis (figs. 67–70) by constructing a particularly elegant ten-column entrance kiosk in front of the hypostyle hall of Hakoris. This addition extended the overall length of the temple to 60 m. The 9.5 x 11.7 m kiosk was 9 m high and attached to the temple front of Hakoris (figs. 68–70). The architraves of the

Figure 66.
View of the remains of the pronaos of Nectanebo I at Hermopolis magna in 1798 (*Description* IV, pl. 51).

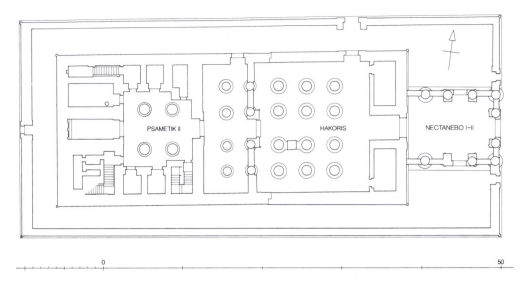

Figure 67. Plan of the Amun temple of Hibis in the 30th Dynasty.

Figure 68. The entrance kiosk of Nectanebo I at the Amun temple at Hibis seen from the south (photo MMA, K3 837).

long sides of the kiosk rested on top of the cavetto of the older temple front. The columns at the front and on the long sides were connected by screen walls with the main entrance in the temple axis and two lateral doors. Four types of capitals were used (see diagram).[74]

The program of capital types is clear. The open lotus in the east symbolizes sunrise. Papyrus is the plant of the northern lands, while the palm seems to represent the southern lands. For the two corners one had to compromise with composite types. The distribution of different capital types in the same building is one of the earliest known examples of this design technique.

The wide span of the kiosk required a timber roof, the construction of which can still be imagined from sockets in the entablature. Three 8.3 m long tie-beams supported a wooden ceiling that rested on the stone architrave behind the cavetto. A recess along the inner edge of the cavetto carried the beams of the probably shallow barrel roof.

The Hathor temple at DENDERA of the New Kingdom was also enlarged by Nectanebo I.[75] The origin of the Roman brick enclosure wall, which was 10 m thick and 280 x 280 m wide, probably goes back to his reign (plan VI). Furthermore, a small birth house for Isis was built behind the main temple (figs. 161, 184). As a result of later alterations of the birth house (Ptolemy VI Philometor, Ptolemy X Alexander I, Augustus), only the east wall of the Nectanebo building is preserved. In addition, a birth house for Hathor was built in front of the main temple. The 17 x 20 m building consisted of a triple shrine opening to a transversal hall. The central shrine and the facades of the two lateral shrines were faced with stone; the rest of the building consisted of brick. The cased walls were decorated under Nectanebo I. In the reign of Ptolemy II, the remaining interior walls were cased with stone and a staircase to the roof added. In the early Roman Imperial Period the front part of the birth house was demolished by the construction of a new court wall of the main temple.

The temple of Min of COPTOS was surrounded by a new enclosure wall and received a 2.18 m high naos of green graywacke with beautiful, slender proportions (fig. 71).[76]

Nectanebo I was also the first pharaoh to undertake extensive building operations at THEBES since the Kushites. The complexes of Amun at Karnak were surrounded by huge, 21 m high brick enclosure walls. Only the following four of the planned twelve gates of the complex of Amun were still built under Nectanebo I.

The gate of the Bubastide court was flanked by two colossal stone pylons, probably the largest ever built in ancient Egypt (figs. 6, 72). The 14.65 x 113 m towers would have reached a height of 38 to 40 m but remained unfinished (at 31.65 m). At the western front, four deep niches for the flagpoles are inserted. The pre-Ptolemaic date of the pylon is confirmed by inscriptions on sphinxes of Nectanebo I.[77]

In the last century, impressive remains of the brick construction ramps were still standing, but they are much reduced now. The west ends of the lateral colonnades of Sheshonq I, which were obstructing building work, were temporarily removed and replaced after the towers had reached a sufficient height. The new columns at the junctions were left unfinished and provide important information about Egyptian building methods.

Entrance Kiosk, Amun Temple of Hibis

FRONT (EAST)

b - a - a - b

NORTH   c   d   SOUTH

c   d

c   d

BACK (WEST)

a: Open lotus bundle capitals

b: Eight-stem, double-rowed, open papyrus-bundle capitals with palmettes

c: Open, bell-shaped papyrus capitals

d: Palm capitals

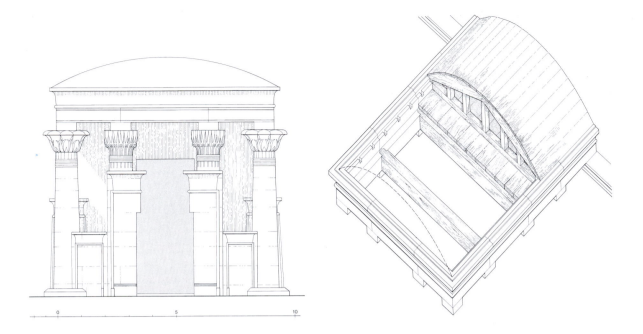

Figure 69. *(left)*
Reconstructed elevation of the facade of the entrance kiosk of Nectanebo I at the Amun temple at Hibis.

Figure 70. *(right)*
Suggested roof construction of the entrance kiosk of Nectanebo I at the Amun temple of Hibis.

The temple of Opet received a front gate of 6.52 m width (fig. 3). The decoration was continued under Ptolemy II and III. The gate is destroyed now. The 5.44 m wide gate in the north wall, near the temple of Ptah, may also belong to the period of Nectanebo I. The remaining gates were built by Nectanebo II and, after the second Persian domination, by the early Ptolemies.

The monumental east gate of the enclosure wall (Bab el-Malakha) was partially completed and inscribed under Nectanebo I (fig. 73). The huge gate was 13.40 m broad and 20.08 m high and had an avant-porte with double door wings. Some of the inscriptions were added under Ptolemy II.

The temple of Maat near the southern wall of the enclosure of Amunra-Monthu was enlarged with a 6 m wide gate (plan IX).

Side wings were added to the contra-temple that adjoined the eastern (rear) wall of the main Amun temple. A modest chapel was built into the southwest corner of the new enclosure wall. Only blocks of the interior rear wall are preserved depicting the front of a bark standing under a kiosk,[78] an unusual example of Late Egyptian relief depicting architecture.

A contra-chapel was added to the main temple of the precinct of Mut, and a large hypostyle hall with two-by-six columns was added to the unfinished birth house in the precinct of Amunra-Monthu (started by Hakoris, fig. 56). Normally one would have chosen—according to the purpose of the birth house—Hathor capitals. For unknown reasons, palm columns were used instead.

The temple of Amunra-Monthu, north of the main Amun temple, was surrounded by a separate wall.

A new Opet temple was planned or even begun between the temple of Khonsu and the great western enclosure wall. During the reign of Nectanebo I,

Figure 71.
Naos of Nectanebo I for Min of Coptos in
Cairo, CG70019 (Guenther Roeder, *Naos*
[Leipzig, 1914], pl. 15)

Figure 72. The unfinished first pylon of Nectanebo I(?) at the Amun temple at
Karnak (photo A.O.).

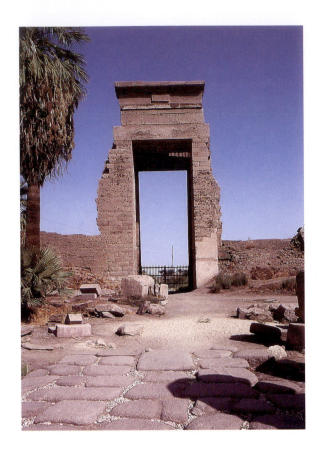

Figure 73. East gate of
Nectanebo II at Karnak seen
from west (photo A.O.).

a gate in that wall and a second gate east of it were completed (fig. 110). It is
not known how far the construction of the temple itself was carried out. The
building was completed in Ptolemaic times. Its square ground plan could,
however, be a creation of the 30th Dynasty.

The largest project in Thebes was the construction of a 5.7 m broad and 2
km long sphinx allée, connecting the two complexes of Karnak and LUXOR.
The road was flanked by about 700 human-headed sphinxes with small figures of the king between their paws.[79] A new forecourt was laid out in front of
the pylon of Ramesses II at Luxor, surrounded by a huge brick enclosure.

In MEDINET HABU the cartouches of the original Kushite(?) builder of the
entrance kiosk at the temple of the primordial Amun were replaced.[80] A gate
was built in the south, probably together with a new enclosure wall (plan X).

Blocks with cartouches of Hakoris and Nectanebo I found at EL-TÔD suggest that the replacement of the Middle Kingdom temple of Monthu began in
the 29th and 30th Dynasties. Due to the total destruction of the temple house,
we have no indications of the shape of the building and its association with
Ptolemaic additions.[81]

The huge enclosure wall of the temple of Monthu at ARMANT may also
have gone back to Nectanebo I. Remains of the brick wall were still seen by
Edmé François Jomard (1777–1862) but have completely disappeared since.[82]

In the ancient place Hefat, near MO'ALLA, Nectanebo I erected a temple dedicated to the falcon god Hemen. A relief block from the building was discovered when a canal was built in 1964 about 600 m to the north of the rock tombs of Mo'alla.[83] Excavations have never been carried out in the temple area.

EL-KÂB, the Upper Egyptian crown sanctuary, was honored by the addition of anentrance kiosk to the Ramesside pylon (plan XII). The kiosk's double row of five columns had Hathor capitals in accord with the female gender of the deity residing in the temple. The Hathor capitals sat on composite floral capitals. The precinct also received a new brick enclosure wall that included a gate placed in front of the Ramesside pylon (not included in plan XII). Probably also under Nectanebo I a birth house was constructed, focusing on the character of Nekhbet as a goddess of birth. The birth house was placed at a right angle to the axis of the main temple and stood in the court between the first and second pylons. At first the birth house was only a shrine surrounded by a pillared ambulatory; at an unknown date it was enlarged at the front by a hypostyle hall. The pillared front of the original building became the rear wall of the hypostyle hall. The front of the hypostyle hall apparently was closed.

Remains of a *shena wab* temple were found in the court between the outer brick enclosure wall and the first pylon (not depicted in plan XII). Like the birth house, the brick building stood at a right angle to the main temple axis.

Under Nectanebo I a small gate was built on ELEPHANTINE in the New Kingdom temple of Khnum.[84] The gate was inserted between two already standing columns. The rebuilding of the main temple was later undertaken by Nectanebo II.

Under Nectanebo a design was developed for the enlargement of the sanctuary of Isis on PHILAE, whose cult seemed to have gained importance. The kiosk of Nectanebo I now towers over the southern entrance staircase (figs. 74–78, plan XIV).[85] Recently, G. Haeny demonstrated that the kiosk was originally somewhat larger and stood at a different place. It was moved to its present location by Ptolemy XII to be combined with two obelisks.

The 7.6 x 11.5 m kiosk now stands on top of a flat platform and consists of a rectangle of four-by-six columns, which carry an interesting combination of Hathor and composite floral capitals. Sockets in the interior of the cavetto blocks show that the kiosk was covered by a timber roof, which probably had the shape of a shallow barrel vault. Shape and location suggest that the kiosk served in its second location as a bark station. Originally, however, it could have been the ambulatory of a birth house. Of its two obelisks, only the stump of the southwestern one remains standing upright.

The project of Nectanebo I also included a cult terrace at the south end of the island. It was later built over by the temple of Arsnouphis.

For the sanctuary of Isis, three courts were planned, enclosed by brick walls; their shape followed the irregular rock formation of the island. The main gate of the first court is lost. The eastern side entrance of the first court, called the "Philadelphos Gate," was decorated by Ptolemy II Philadelphos but already might have been built in the 30th Dynasty.

A monumental gate topped by a heavy cavetto leads into the second court and still exists today (figs. 79, 129). The gate opened to the main Isis temple,

Figure 74.
View of the kiosk of
Nectanebo I on Philae
(see H. G. Lyons, *A
Report on the Temples
of Philae* [Cairo, 1908],
pls. 3–4).

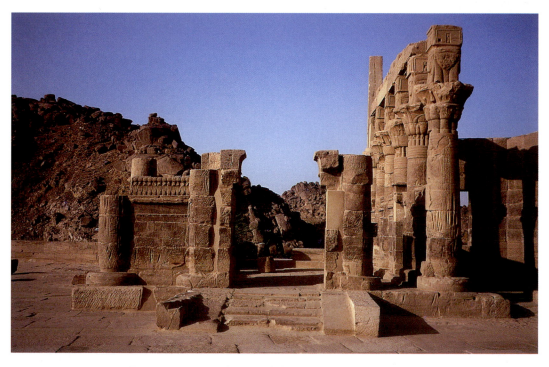

Figure 75. Frontal view of the kiosk of Nectanebo I on Philae (photo A.O.).

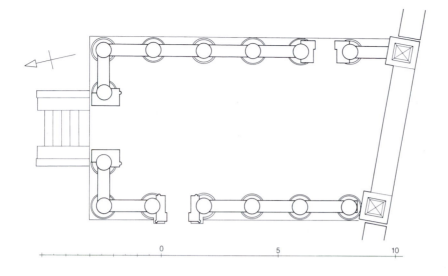

Figure 76.
Plan of the kiosk of
Nectanebo I on Philae.

Figure 77.
Reconstruction of a column pair of the kiosk
of Nectanebo I on Philae (E. Prisse d'Avennes,
Architecture, vol. 1 of *Atlas de l'art égyptien* [Paris,
1868–78], pl. I.47).

Figure 78.
Roof blocks with sockets for
the timber roof at the kiosk
of Nectanebo I on Philae
(photo A.O.).

seemingly the small shrine built by Amasis, which was later replaced by the
18 x 24 m temple of Ptolemy II (figs. 80–81).[86] Since the tiny size of the Amasis shrine does not harmonize with the huge dimensions of the Nectanebo
gate, one suspects that the temple "of Ptolemy II" was designed by or even
begun under Nectanebo I. An early date is supported by the pre-Ptolemaic
ground plan of the temple, which is square and has no freestanding sanctuary. The sanctuary was set against the rear wall of the temple house.
Three transversal rooms follow each other at the front. A *wabet*, now mostly
destroyed, stood east of the middle transversal room. The cavetto molding that
topped the light well in which the *wabet* stood is still preserved. A raised platform in the western part of the *wabet* area probably carried the kiosk. A series
of crypts were built into the external walls and in the foundations of the rear
part of the temple. Traces of two demolished roof chapels for the cult of Osiris
have been noted at the southeast corner of the roof.

A magnificent and completely preserved Ptolemaic birth house stands
at the western side of the court between the first and second pylon. The chapel
of the building, comprising two rooms, stands on a foundation, which separates the two rooms from the later ambulatory. A question is whether the
chapel was already begun in the 30th Dynasty.[87]

Teos (Tachos) (361/360–359/358)

Nectanebo I was succeeded by his son Teos. Persuaded by Greek advisers, and
taking advantage of the weak state of the Persian empire, the young king prepared an offensive against the Persians. To subsidize the enterprise, the politi-

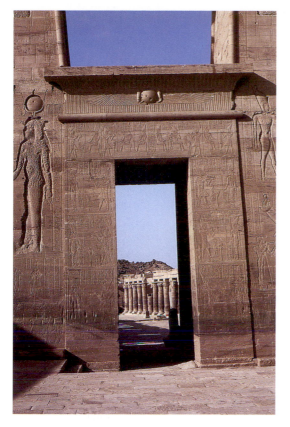

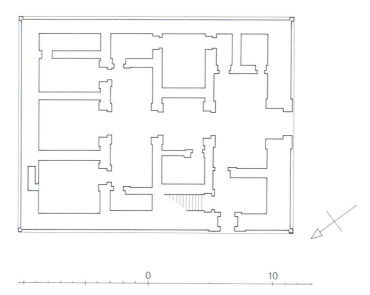

Figure 79. *(at left)*
Rear view of the gate of Nectanebo I at the Isis temple on Philae (photo A.O.).

Figure 80. *(top right)*
Plan of the temple house of Nectanebo I/Ptolemy II for Isis on Philae.

Figure 81.
The rear side of the temple house of Nectanebo I/Ptolemy II for Isis on Philae seen from the northwest (photo A.O.).

cally inexperienced ruler imposed heavy taxes on the temples and confiscated gold and silver from private hands. These unpopular measures had severe consequences for the king, who had already successfully reached Syria. His brother Tja-hap-imu, who was left behind as regent, plotted with the opposition. Tja-hap-imu persuaded his own son Nectanebo, who accompanied his uncle Teos as a commander, to rebel, and the troops indeed proclaimed Nectanebo as king (Nectanebo II). In a tactical move, Teos fled to the Persians, formally handed over Egypt to the Persians, and convinced them to appoint him as a Persian satrap. Teos died, however, during the march back to Egypt.

In Egypt, which was unaffected by these political machinations, some buildings begun under Nectanebo I were continued during the five regnal years of Teos.[88] A block with the name of Teos was found at Matariya (at Lake Menzaleh).[89] Fragments of especially fine relief are said to come from the area of Qantir (together with relief fragments of Nectanebo I and II),[90] and a block with Teos's name was recorded at Athribis.[91] Restoration work was carried out at the temple of Khonsu at Karnak. New buildings are not known, however, from the short reign.

Nectanebo II (Nakhtherheb) (359/358–342/341)

The Egyptian troops who had just removed Teos, and acclaimed Nectanebo, ironically soon turned against the new ruler because he allegedly favored Greek mercenaries. The army replaced him with a reactionary ruler of Mendes, whose name remains unknown. Thus the promising expedition against Persia collapsed in disgrace, and Nectanebo II hurried back to Egypt. Once in Egypt, he and his Greek mercenaries were trapped by the troops of the Mendesian contender in the fortress of Tanis. With the help of the Spartan commander Agesilaos, Nectanebo managed to break through, defeat his adversaries, and claim the kingship as Nectanebo II Nakhtherheb.

Still, the reign of the new king was overshadowed by the threat of a Persian invasion, and the mood of the inhabitants swayed between fear and hope for the strength of the defensive system. As usual for the period, Nectanebo hired more Athenians and Spartans as mercenaries. Under the Persian king Artaxerxes II (Ochus), his time seemed to have come. In 351/350 a huge Persian army appeared at the Egyptian frontier. However, the Persians were beaten for a second time and had to retreat, to the relief of the Egyptians and the entire Mediterranean world.

This tremendous defensive success earned Nectanebo II the reputation of a Horus falcon reincarnate.[92] In old pharaonic tradition, a royal cult for "Nectanebo the divine falcon" (pa bjk) was installed in the main sanctuaries of the country, as had already been done for his grandfather Nectanebo I (fig. 82).[93] During his relatively few peaceful regnal years, the king forced such an astonishing building program[94] that one has to understand it as an attempt to invoke the splendors of ancient Egypt and its gods and to secure a magic defense against the Asian menace. We know of at least six new temples in the Delta and even more new buildings or enlargements in Middle and Upper Egypt. In addition, chapels, obelisks, and naoi were donated to other temples, and numerous projects begun by his predecessors were completed. The build-

ing volume might be even greater, since numerous so-called Ptolemaic buildings were probably begun in the late 30th Dynasty.

According to Pliny the Elder (*Natural History*, XXXVI.9.14), a 35 m high, probably unfinished, or at least not erected, obelisk of a Nectanebo king was moved by Ptolemy II to Alexandria and later to Rome. One might assume that it was an obelisk of Nectanebo II at SAIS that could not be erected any more because of the Persian invasion. It was moved by the engineer Phoinix to Alexandria.[95]

Nectanebo II began the construction of a new temple for Isis and Osiris, the Iseum at BEHBEIT EL-HAGAR, at the Damietta branch of the Nile west of Mendes. The temple attracts special attention because it is the only temple ruin in the Delta of which substantial remains are left (figs. 83–85).[96] The temple has collapsed, and its tumbled blocks cover an area 80 m long and 50 to 60 m wide. Since a block was removed to Rome in the first century A.D.,[97] part of the destruction must have occurred in antiquity, probably caused by a strong earthquake. Ongoing stone robbing has reduced the pile considerably. Visitors on the site are thrilled, however, by the quality of the remaining wall reliefs and architectural elements and by the apparent possibility of reconstructing the temple. No such attempt, not even of an architectural survey, has ever been undertaken.

An 18 to 20 m thick brick wall of 241 x 362 m enclosed the temple. A processional allée flanked by sphinxes of Nectanebo II seemed to have connected the enclosure with a cult terrace in the west. The temple in the center of the

Figure 82.
Falcon image of Nectanebo II in MMA, Rogers Fund, 1934 (34.2.1) (courtesy of MMA).

Figure 83. Collapsed blocks of the Iseum of Nectanebo II at Behbeit el-Hagar.

Figure 84. Granite wall block of Nectanebo II from the Iseum in MMA, Rogers Fund, 1912 (12.182.4A), showing the king offering incense and a necklace to Osiris (courtesy of MMA).

enclosure faced west. The scholars of the Napoleonic expedition assumed that the Iseum formed a smaller prototype for the temple of Dendera at a scale of 5:7 with a pronaos of 18 x 30 m in the west. Parts of over 10 m high and 1.52 m thick columns with Hathor capitals are preserved.[98] The length of the ruin suggests the existence of more halls behind. The rear part of the temple (estimated as 40 m long and 25 m broad) contained a freestanding bark shrine of black granite, surrounded by the usual ambulatory with rows of secondary chapels.[99] The rear part of the temple seems to have been only 5 to 6 m high. Remains of small columns suggest the existence of a roof chapel. Instead of limestone, only granite, granodiorite, quartzite, and basalt were used.

The earliest cartouches on the wall blocks belong to Nectanebo II and were observed in the sanctuary area. Blocks west (in front) of the sanctuary area show exclusively cartouches of Ptolemy II. Blocks in the area of the pronaos/hypostyle hall and the cavetto of the temple facade carry cartouches of Ptolemy III. This sequence clearly shows the slow progression of the wall decoration.

The ancient SEBENNYTOS, a powerful city in the center of the Delta (modern Samannûd), was the home of the the kings of the 30th Dynasty. During their rule, a major temple for the creator god Onuris was built there, as can be concluded from numerous inscribed blocks at the site. The records on the location of the blocks are not quite precise, but they suggest a swampy area west of Samannûd, north of the railway station. No official excavation of the site is recorded. In 1911 about forty granite blocks were seen there. Two

Figure 85.
Gray granite wall block of Nectanebo II or Ptolemy II from the Iseum in MMA, Rogers Fund, 1912 (12.182.4C), showing the enthroned Osiris and traces of a goddess (Isis?) (courtesy of MMA).

showed the cartouche of Nectanebo II (fig. 86), others the names of Philippus Arrhidaeus, Alexander II, Ptolemy II, and Ptolemy XI Alexander II.[100] Inscriptions mention a granite pylon and a vestibule (Egyptian *rwt*). Remains of limestone foundations with blocks of granite, basalt, and quartzite were also preserved in the area. Fragments of granite palm capitals of 2 m in diameter also were seen. They must have belonged to palm columns, similar in height to the 10 m high Old Kingdom columns found at Tanis. Two schist naoi of Nectanebo II were also dedicated to Onuris-Shu.[101] All these elements point to a major new temple of the 30th Dynasty, completed and extended under the Ptolemies.

In antiquity, a legend had grown around the completion of the temple, the "Phersos," Egyptian Per-Shu. The god Onuris appeared in the king's dream, promising his assistance in the case that Nectanebo II would complete the decoration of the temple within 100 days. Since the king apparently could not achieve the god's demand, Onuris did not interfere when the Persians defeated Nectanebo.[102] The temple was described by El-Maqrizi (1364–1442) as still standing to its roof and still containing a series of royal statues and a large inscribed stela. Nevertheless, the "marvel of Egypt" was demolished in the fifteenth century.[103]

In 1828, Nestor l'Hôte still saw basalt and granite blocks of a temple of Nectanebo II in a mound outside the town.[104] The blocks could, however, have been brought from the main temple site.

Numerous limestone and granite blocks were found in front of the entrance to the 350 x 384 m enclosure of the temple of Thoth at HERMOPOLIS PARVA

Figure 86.
Diorite wall block of Nectanebo II from the temple of Onuris at Sebennytos in MMA, Rogers Fund, 1912 (12.182.4B), with a fecundity figure delivering a royal offering to Onuris-Shu (courtesy of MMA).

(Tell Baqliya, south of Mansoura). They may have belonged to a new temple of the 30th Dynasty, about which nothing else is known. Nectanebo II also dedicated a pair of approximately 4–4.5 m high black basalt obelisks for Thoth.[105] Two impressive, approximately 1.5 m high gray granite statues of baboons, dedicated by Nectanebo II, were found in the Iseum in Rome. Since baboons were the sacred animals of Thoth, and Delta temples were harvested by Roman statue collectors, one might assume that the two statues came from this temple of Thoth.[106]

The temple fortress of TANIS, in which Nectanebo II had just been besieged, was reinforced, and the old brick walls of Psusennes I were replaced by a stronger 370 x 430 m enclosure (plan I). The wall was not built in one piece but was segmented in protruding and receding sections, with gates in each of the four walls. The old portal of Sheshonq III served as the western gate. The eastern gate was built new under Ptolemy I—probably after being destroyed by the Persians in 443. For the newly installed cult of the Horus king, a temple was built in the southeastern corner of the precinct. The 26 x 62 m building faced east and apparently contained a 42 m wide pylon, with a huge entrance kiosk attached to it. A separate, monumental entrance in the enclosure wall emphasized the importance of the temple. Today, however, only the foundation pit is left.

E. Naville still saw fragments of an enormous granite ceiling block with the name of Nectanebo II at the site of the temple for the falcon god Hor-merty at HORBEIT (ancient Pharbaetus, west of Faqûs). The complete block was at least 8 m and might have covered a grand pronaos, that the king might have built in front of the main temple.[107]

In BUBASTIS, a new temple house was built for the lion goddess Bastet, enlarging the temple of Osorkon I and II considerably.[108] The probably square building of Nectanebo II measured approximately 50 x 50 m and either added to or replaced the innermost section of the old temple. Even the decorated walls of the temple consisted of red and black granite.[109] Fragments of basalt and dolerite suggest pavements of these rare materials. The temple facade was crowned by a cavetto and a 1.02 m high frieze of uraei, of which several blocks are preserved at the site.[110]

Six huge naoi for secondary deities were arranged in the area of the sanctuary, around the red granite naos of Bastet.[111] The main naos was not of the Late Period type, standing upright, but instead had the shape of a bark shrine and was accessible. It was approximately 1.7 x 3.6 m wide and 2.7 m high. All naoi could have stood in separate rooms. If they were assembled in a single room, it could not have been roofed over. The temple of Bastet would in that case have been another example for a *hypaetral* building, a temple type one has to suspect existed in the Delta (see fig. 42). Temple and town were so thoroughly destroyed by the Persians in 343 B.C. that the Ptolemies did not undertake restoration work in the area.

A 4 m long fragment of a granite pillar with the name of Nectanebo II probably originated from the ruins of TELL EL-AHMAR, 20 km northeast of Bubastis. The block was found by Naville at Tawila. A basalt capital was seen amid the remnants of a temple at Tell el-Ahmar, about which nothing is known.[112]

Red granite blocks of Nectanebo II were also found in neighboring SAFT EL-HENNE, ancient Pi-Sopdu, where Nectanebo I had begun a temple with an outstanding naos.[113] That the site was still important in Ptolemaic times is suggested by a stela of Ptolemy II. In the early Ptolemaic time, the work begun in the 30th Dynasty and interrupted by the Persian invasion of 343 may have been concluded.

In the border fortress of PITHOM (Tell el-Maskhuta) at the eastern exit of the Wadi Tumilat, an Atum and Re-Horakhty temple, built by the Ramessides and Necho, was enlarged by Nectanebo II. In 1883–84, Petrie still saw a large number of limestone blocks with relief of rare refinement. In 1914, Clédat rescued the last remaining fragments with the name of Nectanebo II from the lime kilns and sent them to the museum in Ismailia.[114]

Numerous granite and quartzite blocks with inscriptions of Nectanebo II were found in the mound beneath the modern town of BILBEIS (at the desert edge, 20 km southeast of Bubastis). Labib Habachi suggested that they came from Bubastis,[115] but they also could have belonged to a separate temple of Bastet at Bilbeis itself.

A granite door jamb found in Cairo in 1982 is inscribed with the name of Nectanebo II and refers to Ptah and Sakhmet, probably at MEMPHIS.[116]

Works begun under Nectanebo I in the Serapeum of SAQQARA were continued by Nectanebo II (plan III). To the east of and opposite the Serapeum of Nectanebo I, a terraced temple was built. The structure was reached by means of a broad staircase that led up from the Serapeum and was flanked by lion figures. Some limestone reliefs are preserved.[117] It was possibly the Horus temple (horus = "the king") mentioned in papyri. The temple was inadequately excavated by Mariette and requires a new study.

The royal sarcophagus was found reused in a mosque in Alexandria.[118] The discovery of an ushabti, being a part of the funerary equipment of the king, at Memphis suggests, however, that the tomb of Nectanebo II was at Saqqara. The tomb was never found, but one might suspect that it was not far from the previously mentioned Horus temple, near the Serapeum.[119] The Horus temple may, therefore, well have been the mortuary temple of Nectanebo II.

Another project was the extension of a cult and burial complex of sacred animals at the western slope of the Abusir promontory (plan IV). The complex was connected to the Serapeum by a 500 m long processional road. The sanctuary consisted of two brick enclosures. The larger, 56 x 95 m enclosure contained the access to the catacombs for baboons and falcons and a brick temple leaning against the cliff and facing west.

The road from the Serapeum entered this precinct from the south and reached, with a right-angle turn, the temple "A" for Osiris/Apis and Isis in the center of the precinct. The temple was a strong brick construction with two pylons followed by a square temple house. Parts of the building were cased with stone.[120] A now-destroyed entrance kiosk with palm columns was built in the court between the first and second pylons. The precinct also contained the catacombs of the falcons and baboons and perhaps two other, unexplored animal galleries. The decoration on the front of the cult chapel for the baboons, south of the main temple, depicted a kiosk. A row of four half-columns standing on square bases is preserved.[121] A separate, unexplored precinct in the north protected the entrance into the catacombs of the cows, the mothers of Apis. The tomb's access and interior and the monumental ramp entering the complex from the west still need exploration.

A group of limestone(?) blocks of Nectanebo II was discovered at Memphis built into a Roman bathing basin. Some blocks carry a torus and cavetto decorated with a frieze of cartouches.[122] The blocks may come from one of the king's buildings at Saqqara.

Nectanebo II also built a temple for Ptah-Sokar-Osiris at ABUSIR EL-MELEK, at the entrance into the Faiyum. Parts of walls with some relief blocks in position were seen beneath the local mosque.[123]

A granite naos was dedicated in the temple of Heryshef, the ram-headed lord of HERAKLEOPOLIS MAGNA (modern Ihnâsya el-Medîna), situated not far to the south of Abusir el-Melek.[124] The possibility that Nectanebo II added a pronaos to the small Amun temple at EL-HIBE has already been discussed in chapter 2 (see the buildings of Sheshonq I).

At HERMOPOLIS MAGNA, construction at the temple of Thoth, with its gigantic pronaos, was continued and the decoration begun. A dark, 2.52 m high granite naos dedicated by Nectanebo II to Thoth was found at the desert edge of TUNA EL-GEBEL, the necropolis of Hermopolis. It may have been taken from the temple of Thoth.[125] The king also dedicated red granite naoi to Osiris of ABYDOS.[126] Some blocks also suggest building work under Nectanebo II.

At COPTOS a chapel for the earth god Geb and Isis was built in the southwest corner of the main enclosure of Min.[127] Despite its modest size, the Geb temple played an important role and was repeatedly restored and slightly extended by Cleopatra VII, Augustus, Caligula, and Claudius.

It is possible that the temple house of the predominant Ptolemaic Haroeris and Heqat temple at QÛS was built during the 30th Dynasty (see the buildings of Ptolemy II and VIII). We have no evidence for it, however.

Following inscriptions on the walls of the bark shrine of Amun at KARNAK, Philippus Arrhidaeus was the founder of this shrine. One wonders, however, whether it was not Nectanebo II who initiated a large project to renew the central part of the Amun temple containing the temple of the Middle Kingdom and the bark shrine of the 18th Dynasty in front.[128] The project may have been carried out as follows.

At first, the decaying temple house of the 12th Dynasty was removed. Since buildings of the 18th Dynasty blocked access from the west, the innermost part of the new building, blocks for the bark shrine, had to be moved in from the east (figs. 87–88). The bark shrine had to be constructed first because the eastern sections of the temple house would have impeded access. The replacement of the bark shrine probably became necessary because the earlier shrine, built by Thutmosis III, may have been damaged by the Assyrians in 667/666, 661, or by the Persians in 525. Parts of the old shrine of Thutmosis III were buried in the foundations of Nectanebo's shrine.[129]

The new, 6.34 x 17.83 m shrine was 6.85 m high and consisted of two successive rooms, as had been the tradition during the New Kingdom. The level of the temple of the Middle Kingdom behind in the east was to be raised above

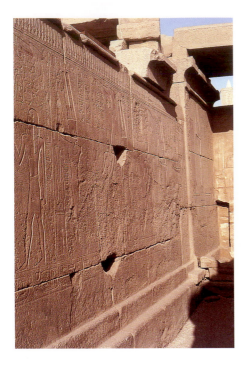

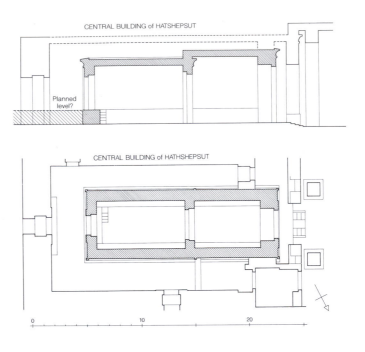

Figure 87. *(left)*
North wall of the central bark shrine of Amun at Karnak (photo A.O.)

Figure 88. *(right)*
Longitudinal section and plan of the central bark shrine of Amun at Karnak.

that of the bark shrine. The eastern door of the bark shrine was raised, therefore, under Nectanebo II to the new level and could be reached only by a flight of small steps. A wall step along the side walls of the shrine also shows the prepared higher level. Following contemporary temple design, an ambulatory with a row of chapels would have been placed behind the shrine. The Persian invasion of 343 probably terminated the project. Only the decoration of the sanctuary was completed under Philippus Arrhidaeus. Despite the careful design of the scenes, the quality of execution does not match the relief work of the 30th Dynasty.[130] The rebuilding of the Middle Kingdom temple was discontinued. One wonders why the Ptolemies, who built so much else at Karnak, did not revive the project but tolerated the vast construction gap between the sanctuary and the buildings in the east.

Possibly during the reign of Nectanebo II, the sanctuary of Khonspakhered outside the southeast corner of the complex of Amun, was enlarged. The dissimilar foundations suggest that an older triple shrine with a broad hall and a two-column hall was enlarged by the addition of a pronaos with two-by-four papyrus-bundle columns.[131] The shape of the forecourt with four pillars is uncertain.

Also under Nectanebo II, two *shena wab* buildings in brick were erected, one in the east of the complex of Mut and another one in the precinct of Amunra-Monthu.[132] Repairs were carried out at the temple of Khonsu, and the Amun temple at Medinet Habu received a sacred well.

A small temple with underground catacombs for the sacred Buchis bull was built at ARMANT.[133] The structure was located 150 m west of the main temple and was intended as an Upper Egyptian version of the Serapeum at Saqqara.

Except for the plain, undecorated catacombs with sandstone and granite sarcophagi, only a few column shafts with cartouches of Nectanebo II were preserved when the complex was excavated in 1931–1932. The origin of other columns with the name of Nectanebo II seen at Armant in 1931–1932 remains unknown.[134]

Several monuments of Nectanebo II are known from the Horus temple at EDFU. A monumental naos of quartz diorite ("syenite") still stands in the bark shrine of the Ptolemaic temple.[135] The 4.20 m high naos is topped by a pyramid-shaped roof (fig. 89). In front of the pylon and of the pronaos, two pairs of colossal gray granite falcons were found (fig. 90). Since they were unfinished and uninscribed, one could date them to the reign of Nectanebo II.

These monuments must have been added either to a still-standing temple of the New Kingdom/26th Dynasty or possibly to a temple of the 30th Dynasty. Blocks with the name Setepenre-mery-Amun (which could be either Alexander the Great, Philippus Arrhidaeus, or Ptolemy I) were found reused in the Ptolemaic court.[136] The existence of a new temple of Nectanebo II would clash, however, with the founding of the (now existing) new temple under Ptolemy III. For what reason should one have replaced the Nectanebo temple after 110 years? Is there the slight possibility that the "Ptolemaic" temple was already begun under Nectanebo II and left undecorated? Only study of the temple foundations and technical details would answer these questions.

At EL-KÂB the front part of the temple of Nekhbet was restored under Nectanebo II and provided with several pylons, and perhaps also with a birth house (plan XII). A small bark station was constructed east of the enclosure

Figure 89. *(left)*
The quartz diorite naos of Nectanebo II in the bark shrine of the Ptolemaic Horus temple at Edfu (photo of the situation before 1903).

Figure 90. *(right)*
Colossal falcon statues of Nectanebo II(?) in front of the pylon of the Horus temple at Edfu (photo A.O.).

wall. Numerous bark stations and small temples in the vicinity of El-Kâb suggest intense processional activities, similar to those of Thebes and other places.

For Khnum a new temple of considerable dimensions was built on ELEPHANTINE, replacing a predecessor of the 26th Dynasty. Some foundations of this temple are preserved and permit a hypothetical reconstruction of the plan of a 30th Dynasty temple.[137] The new 28.8 x 43.2 m building stood high above the Nile at the southeast corner of the island (fig. 91). The completely closed temple house—without a pronaos—was surrounded by an enclosure wall, which also incorporated a small forecourt.

The temple house contained, from east to west, a festival hall, a hall of the visiting gods, and an offering hall. The first two halls had four columns. A *wabet* was attached to the north side of the first hall. Three huge parallel shrines opened into the third hall. The larger central shrine belonged to Khnum, and the lateral ones probably to Satet and Anuket. The three shrines were probably surrounded by an ambulatory with a row of five chapels along the rear wall. The bark shrines and the ceiling of the entire temple were roofed with enormous granite beams weighing up to 25 to 30 metric tons. The sanctuary roof must have towered over the roof of the ambulatory because window slots were cut into the side of the ambulatory roof. The freestanding sanctuary part is another example of this promising building type. The sanctuaries were furnished with monolithic naoi, which remained unfinished, however. The interior and parts of the exterior of the temple were decorated under Nectanebo II. Some blocks show remains of gilding. The magnificent main portal, which is still standing today, was decorated under Philippus Arrhidaeus (figs. 94–95). Under Ptolemy VI(?) the temple was enlarged by the addition of a pronaos, and it was extended again in Roman times with a pylon and a monumental cult platform.

Two obelisk bases in front of the kiosk of Nectanebo I at the temple of Hibis at EL-KHARGA suggest the existence of a pair of sandstone(?) obelisks of considerable dimensions, which Winlock dated cautiously to the reign of Nectanebo II. A huge, 7.5 m wide and 11.4 m high gate (Winlock's "Great Gateway") was probably also added at that time as part of a new outer enclosure wall. The wall and gate are uninscribed but may well originate in the 30th Dynasty, the period noted for the construction of enclosure walls. A Ptolemaic(?) allée flanked by nine pairs of human-headed sphinxes connected the gate with a cult terrace for Amun at the banks of the lake of El-Kharga. Half of the gate is still standing, carrying Roman edicts of A.D. 60 and 68.[138]

As a result of interest in the oases that began in the 26th Dynasty, SIWA was honored with a new or enlarged temple at Umm Ubayda (fig. 92).[139] The temple was damaged by an earthquake in 1811, and the ruin was blown up in 1897 to provide building material for a police station. Only the remains of one wall of the sanctuary still stand. The temple stood some hundred meters southeast of the Ammonium and was attached to it by a processional road.

According to reports by early travelers, the temple was enclosed with a triple wall, the outermost of which measured 85–100 x 110–120 m. The walls enclosed priests' dwellings and perhaps the stable for the sacred ram of Amun. The temple house measured only 7.8 x 37.5 m and consisted of two or three antechambers with the 26.5 m long sanctuary behind. In front of the

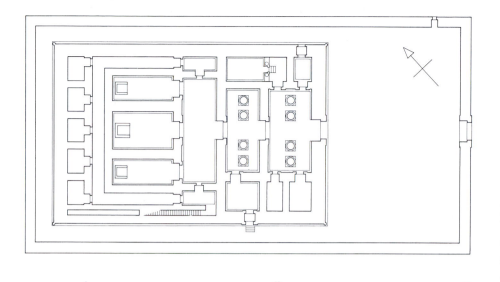

Figure 91.
Reconstruction plan of the temple of Nectanebo II for Khnum on Elephantine (after W. Niederberger, "Unter-suchungen im Bereich des späten Chnumtempels," *MDAIK* 46 [1990]: 189–93, and *MDAIK* 51 [1995]: 147–64).

Figure 92. View of the remains of the temple of Umm Ubayda at Siwa in 1820 (H. Minutoli, *Reise zum Tempel des Jupiter Ammon in der libischen Wüste und nach Ober-Aegypten in den Jahren 1820–21* [Berlin, 1824], pl. 7[2]).

facade stood an entrance kiosk, probably of Nectanebo II, with four columns at its front and four or more columns along its sides. Lateral entrances separated the second from the third columns. Fragments of approximately one meter thick "lotus" columns were mentioned by Cailliaud.[140] K. P. Kuhlmann assumed that Nectanebo II decorated an older, unfinished temple house, dating perhaps from the time of Amasis, and only added the kiosk. The building effort for this subsidiary sanctuary eclipsed that of the main temple, as if Umm Ubayda had been the main sanctuary at the time of Nectanebo II.

6

THE SECOND PERSIAN DOMINATION
AND THE MACEDONIAN DYNASTY
(343–304 B.C.)

In autumn 343, the Persian king Artaxerxes II (Ochus) appeared at Pelusium with a huge army.[1] Nectanebo II tried the same strategy that Nectanebo I had already exercised with great success in 373 and 351/350, namely, to delay the Persians at the entrance into the Delta marshes until they would be flushed away by the expected inundation. This time, the strategy had catastrophic consequences for Egypt. The Persians succeeded in penetrating into the Delta and cracking the defense chain by overpowering Pelusium. Thereafter, one Delta city after another fell, either by conquest or by betrayal of the mercenaries employed by Egypt, who tried to save their lives. Mendes, Heliopolis, and other cities and temples were destroyed—perhaps already for the second time since Cambyses's conquest in 525—and the walls of the most important cities pulled down. Nectanebo II surrendered Memphis and fled—perhaps too soon—to Upper Egypt. He died after a two-year exile in the south.

Egypt was punished severely for opposing Persian rule. Following Near Eastern practices, the ruling-class Egyptians were deported to Persia into banishment. As Cambyses had desecrated the royal tombs of Sais, Artaxerxes II ordered the destruction of the royal tombs of Mendes.[2] The libraries of the temples were confiscated but returned to the priest against ransom. For ten more years—from 343 to 332—Egypt was again a Persian satrapy under the governor Pherendates.

The Persians could not enjoy their conquest for long. In 338–336 Khabbash, who was perhaps Kushite, succeeded in liberating Egypt, including Memphis and the Delta, for a short time. It is obvious that no temple building was undertaken under such conditions. The unfinished building projects of Nectanebo II were only completed after the liberation from the Persians, mainly in early Ptolemaic times.

Alexander the Great (Alexander III of Macedonia) (332–323)

With the victory of Alexander the Great at Issos in the autumn of 333, the Persian Empire disintegrated and its domination of Egypt ended. After the conquest of Tyre and Gaza, which were heroically defended by the Persian garrisons, Alexander took Egypt without resistance in October 332. He marched through Pelusium to Memphis and was saluted as liberator and crowned in accordance with pharaonic tradition as "son of Nectanebo II." Egypt became part of Alexander's empire.

The establishment of a secure sea link between Egypt and Greece was of primary concern for the new government. For that purpose, the harbor city of Alexandria was founded on January 30, 331 B.C., and the Rhodian architect Deinokrates received the commission to plan the city.

Thereafter Alexander undertook his famous pilgrimage to the oracle Amun in Siwa, where he was probably greeted as the god's son and heir of the world domination. Alexander sacrificed in the temples of Heliopolis and Memphis and wished to be buried in the Ammoneion of Siwa, a request that was never executed. This appreciation for Egyptian cults was, however, not reflected in building activities, and the temples that were built or completed under his rule were few. The new regime primarily developed Alexandria.

A temple commissioned by Alexander for Isis at a canal in the eastern section of ALEXANDRIA was commemorated several times on coins of Trajan and Hadrian, where it is depicted as having a pylon, suggesting a temple in pharaonic architectural form.[3]

Limestone blocks found at ATHRIBIS originated from a hitherto unknown chapel of the time of Alexander. The decoration of the temple of Thoth built by Nectanebo I at HERMOPOLIS MAGNA was continued.[4] At KARNAK, the royal cult chapel in the age-old Akhmenu of Thutmosis III was restored for the new ruler, and a modest chapel for Khonsu donated.[5] The sanctuary of the temple of LUXOR received a new bark shrine of stone (fig. 93). The older shrine of Amenhotep III—perhaps of gilded wood—stood under four stone columns and was probably destroyed by the Persians.[6] The four columns, perhaps also damaged, were removed, and the architraves they had carried were laid directly on top of the side walls of the new shrine. Since these walls grew unusually high, the ceiling of the shrine was lowered, producing an inaccessible, empty chamber on top of the bark shrine. The shrine was not constructed with large granite blocks, as was the sanctuary of Philippus Arrhidaeus at Karnak, but with relatively small sandstone ashlar masonry, another reason for not dating the two sanctuaries to the same period (see chapter 5's discussion of the buildings of Nectanebo II).

The unpretentious temple of QASR EL-MEGYSBEH (Mesguesbeh) in the Bahariya Oasis also carries the name of Alexander.[7] The 7.30 x 9.40 m temple, dedicated to the unusual combination of Amun and Horus, has two rooms with incomplete decoration. The temple stood inside a brick enclosure, perhaps a military garrison, filled with four rows of narrow room units.

After Alexander's death in June 323, control of the empire passed to his mentally disabled half brother, Philippus III Arrhidaeus. Egypt was governed by Alexander's friend and commander Ptolemaios, son of Lagos, who was to

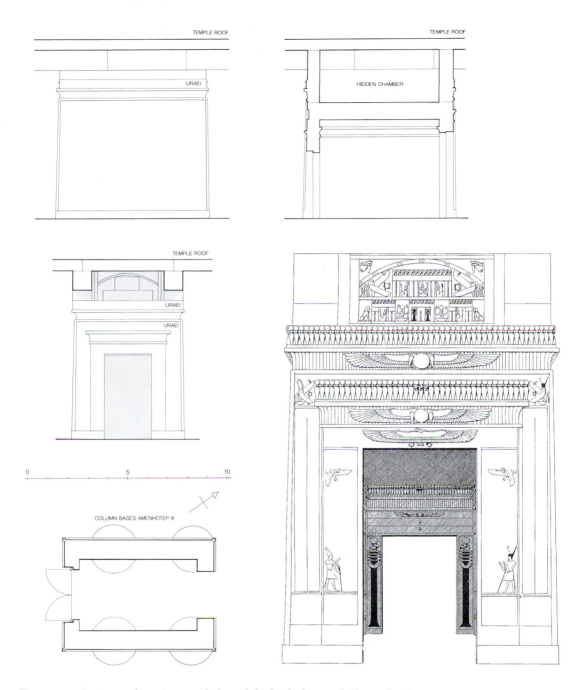

Figure 93. Sections, elevations, and plan of the bark shrine of Alexander the Great for Amun of Luxor (after R. A. Schwaller de Lubicz, *Le temple de l'homme: L'Apet sud à Louxor*, vol. 2 [Paris, 1957], pl. 86).

Figure 94.
View of the granite doorway
of Alexander IV for Khnum on
Elephantine (photo A.O.).

become king of Egypt as Ptolemy I Soter. Philippus Arrhidaeus was assassinated after a reign of six years; he never visited Egypt.

A foundation deposit at TÛKH EL-QARÂMÛS (between Bubastis and Tanis) suggests that an older temple of Sheshonq III was renewed or enlarged. A few cartouches with the name of Philippus suggest the continuation or completion of older building projects. His name is preserved on a door lintel from NÛB TAHA (in the southern Delta). Two granite cavetto blocks of the exterior walls of the temple of SEBENNYTOS are inscribed with the cartouches of Philippus. In HERMOPOLIS MAGNA, the decoration of the pronaos begun by Ptolemy I, was continued. At KARNAK, the decoration of the central sanctuary of Nectanebo II(?) was carried out and completed.

After Philippus's death, Alexander IV,[8] the young son of Alexander the Great and his Persian wife Roxana, became king of Egypt. He never saw Egypt

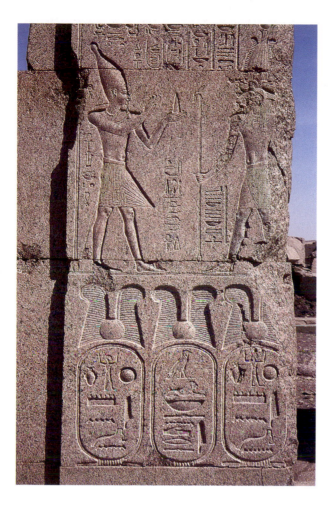

during his reign (316–304). The administration of Egypt was scarcely touched by the assassination of Alexander IV in 304 by Cassandros. Ptolemy I, who had been in power since 332, gained full independence.

Several relief blocks with the name of Alexander IV confirm that the decoration of the granite walls of the temple of Nectanebo II for Onuris-Shu at SEBENNYTOS, suspended since 343, was resumed.[9] The monumental granite gate of the temple of Khnum on ELEPHANTINE, built under Nectanebo II, also received relief decoration under Alexander IV (figs. 94–95).

Figure 95.
Detail of the doorway of Alexander IV for Khnum on Elephantine (photo A.O.).

7

THE PTOLEMAIC PERIOD
(323–31 B.C.)

The Historical Background

During the short Macedonian period that predates Ptolemaic rule (332–305), only a few selected holy sites were honored with royal attention. In most cases this consisted of the continued decoration of existing buildings. The start of independent Ptolemaic rule brought about a noticeable change. Temples were constructed at numerous sites and could only have been accomplished with royal initiative or funding. The appearance of a Ptolemaic cartouche on a building is not, however, proof of a royal commission. Private donors now also supported temple building.[1] Occasionally, construction work dragged on to the following reign and the building was inscribed with the name of the Ptolemy who concluded the work.

The economic prosperity of the country still permitted opulent temple building, and the Ptolemaic dynasty advanced this activity, despite its foreign origin and Greek orientation. Building in pharaonic tradition even flourished when huge funds had to be invested for the development of the capital Alexandria. Collecting, copying, and studying ancient texts was systematically carried out in the library of Alexandria, with the aim of cataloguing the complete ancient culture of the "host" country.[2] Following this tendency, priests in Egyptian sanctuaries gathered ancient religious texts and preserved them in stone on temple walls. These attempts from the Egyptian side cannot be explained as a pure passion for antiquarian collecting and preservation but rather as an attempt to counter the progressing Greek cults and ideas with the power of the established Egyptian cosmos.[3]

The Ptolemies and other Hellenistic rulers outside Egypt claimed heroic, godlike aspects, which were addressed by the placement of rulers' statues in Greek sanctuaries.[4] This specific Greek cult form led to the development of the building type of the Ptolemeion.[5] In Egypt, the Ptolemies and their queens were obliged to place their statues as cult images in the sanctuaries of pharaonic temples.[6] This cult form followed Egyptian tradition and differed considerably from the Hellenistic cult of the ruler. There is, however, no evidence in Egypt of typical Egyptian funerary cults and temples for the Ptolemaic kings.

About fifty medium-size and large temple buildings are known from the Ptolemaic Period, in addition to numerous gates, pylons, sanctuaries, colonnaded entrance buildings, and "smaller" projects. It is noteworthy that, except for the new temple for Anta at Tanis and the temple of Osiris at Taposiris magna, west of Alexandria, building activities were concentrated in Upper Egypt. This imbalance cannot be explained by the disappearance of Ptolemaic Delta monuments, because the destroyed Delta temples of the 26th and 30th Dynasties have left at least a few traces. Reasons for the decline of temple building in the Delta could be either the decreased importance of Egyptian cults in the area or a saturation of temple buildings caused by the heavy building activity of the 26th and 30th Dynasties. One would also suspect the intention to please the conservative population of Upper Egypt, which was a potential source of resistance against the Alexandrian government.

Formal and Stylistic Aspects of Ptolemaic Temple Architecture

We still know disappointingly little about architecture of the periods preceding the era of the Ptolemies, but we can at least grasp the results of the development of the previous 300 years. The so-called Ptolemaic style had its roots in the 26th Dynasty and was further developed in the 30th Dynasty. The progression was interrupted but not completely suppressed by the break of the Persian invasion, and architectural development experienced a splendid revival under Ptolemy II, as attested by a series of magnificent buildings. At that point a transformation of the temples of the Egyptian gods into sanctuaries built in the Greek style would have failed because of the resistance of the mighty Egyptian priesthood. The Ptolemies, therefore, sensibly accepted the continuation of the traditional, pharaonic style of building.

From the fourth and third centuries B.C. on, pharaonic architecture displayed new features.[7] Transformations in Egyptian architecture were usually generated by changes in ritual practices or a reassessment of kingship and the gods.[8] In this case, a new perception of architecture itself seems to have occurred (fig. 96). Sacred architecture from the Old to the New Kingdom was generally marked by cavelike, hollow spaces enclosed by planes or walls. The volume of cavities was balanced by a corresponding mass of masonry. This ancient concept resulted in an accumulation of huge blocks, which were sculpted into a building. In Ptolemaic structures, this building concept is replaced by construction with carefully prefabricated, individual stones, which were placed in regular courses of equal (isodomic) heights. The arrangement of headers and stretchers is so carefully observed that, for example, all rising joints sit precisely in one line. Bedding joints now run at the same level through the entire building, establishing the height of every building unit. This meticulous system of block layout radiates clarity and precision, metallic sharpness, or—in a negative sense—monotony and rigidity.[9]

Even the layout of the wall decoration became subjected to the regularized distribution of joints. One result was that some horizontal joints cut all human figures of one register at the same level, creating a certain static quality typical of Ptolemaic wall reliefs (fig. 164). The decoration programs of Ptolemaic temple walls therefore required careful preparation, with the help of sketches and drawings.[10] This new approach differed considerably from older decoration principles, which were marked by individual solutions, and—if necessary—improvisation.

Ptolemaic temples display a variety of interesting spatial configurations. The appearance of Ptolemaic temples was determined by the interplay between closed building volumes with heavy walls on one side and lofty colonnades or light membranes on the other side.

Seen from the outside, the temples of the Middle and New Kingdoms were relatively flat volumes emphasizing the horizontal dimension. Their differentiated, terraced roof heights reflected the height of the interior rooms beneath. In later buildings these stepped temple roofs were no longer visible from outside. From the temple of Ramesses III at Medinet Habu on, temple houses were marked by the growing height of exterior walls which prevented the viewer from understanding the interior configuration (figs. 97–98).[11] The temple's interior structure became a closed unit concealed by an equalizing enclosure wall. This high, surrounding parapet wall produced a courtlike open cult space on the rooftop that was securely shielded from the outside, offering a much wider range of cultic use than before.

The interior plan of a Ptolemaic temple was based on the idea of a freestanding bark shrine surrounded on three sides by an ambulatory with rows of chapels. The shrine's dimensions prevented the perception of an independent building standing within a wide space, instead crushing the visitor between the bark shrine and the surrounding chapels (fig. 99), perhaps an intended effect.

The plan of the temple house with a sanctuary encircled by layers of rooms or spaces enhanced the feeling of seclusion. This motive emphasizes

Figure 96.
Different concepts of wall masonry in the temple of Amenhotep III at Luxor *(left)* and the temple house of Augustus at Kalabsha.

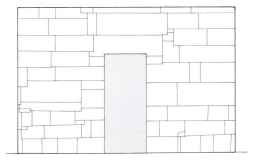

LUXOR TEMPLE

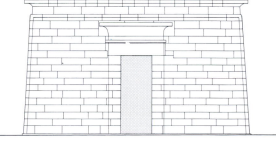

KALABSHA TEMPLE

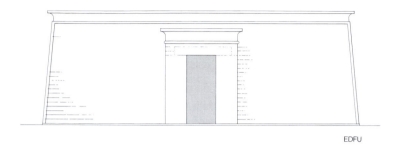

EDFU

KOM OMBO

Figure 97.
Facades of the temple houses of Ptolemy III at Edfu *(top)* and Ptolemy VI at Kom Ombo before the addition of the pronaoi.

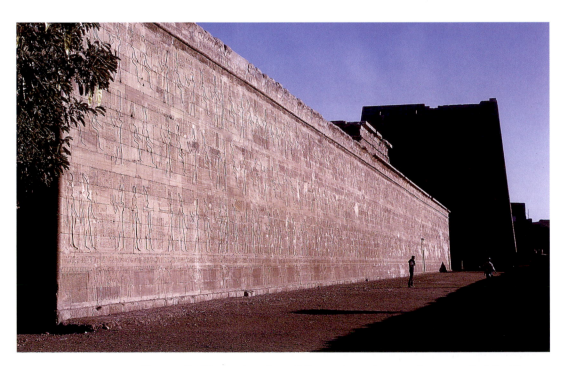

Figure 98. The vast surface of the western stone enclosure wall of the Horus temple at Edfu (photo A.B.).

the function of the temple as the dwelling of the divine. Whoever crossed over the threshold entered another world, as in churches of the Middle Ages, a *civitas dei*, the domain of the divine. Seclusion in Ptolemaic temples also was emphasized by the darkening of the entire temple, especially of the sanctuaries (fig. 99). This darkness was in contrast to the light conditions in the hypostyle halls of the New Kingdom, which were illuminated by sunlight entering through huge windows of the clerestory. The windowless hypostyle halls of the Late Period received light only when the gates were open. The fortresslike, defensive character of the temple house impressed the visitor also in the narrow corridor surrounding the long sides and the rear side of the building (fig. 98).

At the front, the temple's blocklike character is disguised by kiosks and pronaoi flooded in light (fig. 100). A real opening of the temple house was, however, not achieved because the columned structures were only added later to the closed temple facade. This new loosening of building forms was, however, not generated by aesthetic considerations but by functional requirements of the temple cult. The traditional seclusion of cultic proceedings still required hermetic isolation. However, the increase of cultic activities, with larger groups of laymen outside the sanctuaries, demanded that a representative cult stage be placed in front of the temple doors.

The pronaos embraced with its side walls and roof the front of the actual temple house. The autonomy of the temple house was, however, not negated

Figure 99.
The quality of space in the ambulatory of the Horus temple at Edfu (photo A.O.).

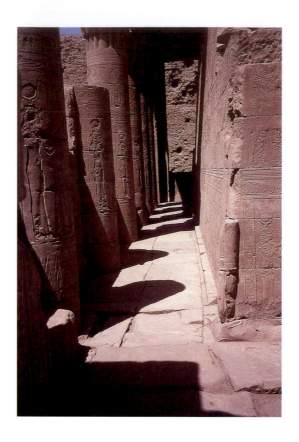

Figure 100.
The quality of space in the ambulatory of the birth house of Horus at Edfu (photo A.O.).

by the interlocking of two elements but even advanced because the front of the temple house penetrated deeply into the pronaos. An appealing connection of two contrasting spatial elements is also displayed by the birth houses of the Ptolemaic Period. A box-shaped, completely closed sanctuary is put under the protective roof of a colonnaded ambulatory, accentuating the formal autonomy of both buildings (fig. 100). Another example of the spatial organization of a Ptolemaic temple is the connection of court and temple house. In the New Kingdom, the court was added in front of the temple. Following the new concept, the temple house now stands within the court. The center of the forecourt is no longer an open space but is actually occupied by the temple house.

The combination of a colonnaded court with a pronaos was also carried out in a new way typical for Ptolemaic-Roman temple organization.[12] Whereas in the New Kingdom courts, rows of columns were attached directly to the temple house, in the Ptolemaic Period both elements were kept separate (see figs. 170, 176, 201).

Other changes concern the painting of the walls of the buildings. Many examples of traces of paint had survived until the early twentieth century but were damaged by human activity. In some color plates in the publications of the Napoleonic expedition,[13] R. Lepsius and D. Roberts display the contrast between the blazing colors of the original painted surfaces and the somber brown-gray of the stone that determines the buildings today. The palette of the temple of Ramesses III at Medinet Habu was distinguished by the reddish ochre-brown, yellow, lapis blue, green, and black in front of a dominating white background. The painters of the Ptolemaic Period returned to the basic color canon, the triad of dark blue, green, and red, but they added, as exotic accents, purple, pink, and gold. Especially eye-catching was the gilding of selected reliefs such as the huge head fetish of Hathor in the center of the rear wall of the temple at Dendera (fig. 164). The general impression of a Ptolemaic temple wall was that of a dense and strikingly colorful network of hieroglyphs and figures, which subdued the yellow color of the background.

The use of different capital types in the same building part or row of columns has a forerunner in the 30th Dynasty[14] but is a peculiarity of Ptolemaic temples. This innovation disturbed the hitherto accepted building rule, requiring that all capitals of a column row should be of the same type. The hitherto dominant uniformity has been replaced by variability. The deliberate intermingling of various capital types would have upset the Egyptian concept of order. Therefore, the mixture of different capitals followed certain rules. In a pronaos, for example, the principle of axial symmetry was retained. The distribution of types in the left half of the pronaos was mirrored by the right half. Therefore, along the center axis identical columns are placed on either side.[15] An entirely disconnected distribution of capital types is found only in the late Ptolemaic court of the temple of Edfu and in the early Roman courts of Philae and Kalabsha.

These and other characteristics of Ptolemaic architecture, especially of late Ptolemaic architecture, must be seen as baroque tendencies. As M. Lyttelton has pointed out, this development is closely connected with a similar phenomenon in the illusionist, stagelike Hellenistic architecture of Alexandria.[16] A representation of a house facade in the subterranean tomb of the Shatby cemetery, for example, is formed by six engaged Doric columns with a central entrance (fig. 101). Half-open windows are depicted between the engaged columns. Hellenistic illusionist architecture did not develop accidentally in Alexandria. Traditional Egyptian architecture contained illusionist or deceptive elements; dummy palaces and temples already distinguished the architec-

Figure 101.
Ptolemaic illusionist architecture in a rock tomb of the cemetery of Shatby at Alexandria (after Margaret Lyttelton, *Baroque Architecture in Classical Antiquity* [Ithaca, 1974], fig. 7).

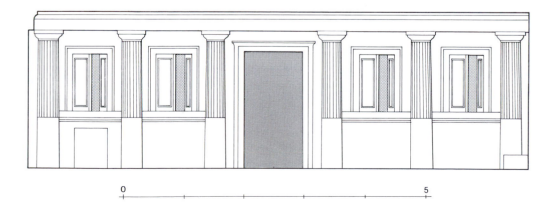

0   5

ture of the 3rd Dynasty.[17] The practice of depicting a columned kiosk on the facade of a building can be observed throughout the New Kingdom[18] and the Late Period (see fig. 26).

Amazingly, obelisks and colossal statues—with a few exceptions absent since the New Kingdom—made their reappearance in Ptolemaic architecture.[19] New obelisks were set up in front of the temples of Edfu and Philae, and old obelisks were moved from the destroyed temples of Heliopolis and reerected in Alexandria. Colossal Ptolemaic statues are known from Karnak, Naucratis,[20] and Rosetta.[21] In Alexandria, a number of colossal statues were recently discovered submerged in front of the Qait Bay fort.[22]

The development of architecture during the 300-year Ptolemaic era appears in three divisions. The early phase of Ptolemaic architecture comprises the reigns of Ptolemy I to Ptolemy V, that is, from 323 to 180 B.C. Building activity commences slowly during this phase and follows the architectural style of the 30th Dynasty. This dependence is not astonishing, since many unfinished 30th Dynasty buildings awaited completion. The same dependence on traditional prototypes determined the decoration of the temple walls. Under the first three Ptolemies, the plain and regular arrangement of figures and text differs so little from reliefs of the 30th Dynasty that dating by means of stylistic criteria alone is impossible.[23] The two gates of Ptolemy III, Euergetes at Karnak, the new temple houses of Deir el-Medine, Esna, and Edfu, the pronaos of El-Tôd, the small temple of Esna-North, and the Isis temple at Aswan belong to this period.

The middle period of temple building spans the reigns of Ptolemy VI to Ptolemy IX, the years 180 to 80 B.C. An increasing number of new temples defined the accomplished, classical Ptolemaic style. For example, a rigid structure and a dignified harmony characterize the pronaoi of Antaeopolis and Edfu, the hypostyle hall of the Isis temple on Philae, the pronaos of Medamoud, the birth house of Edfu, the temple house of Kom Ombo, and the temple of Dabod. Contemporary wall reliefs are characterized by a stronger play of light and shadow by means of their varying height of contour lines. A more pronounced concave contour of the waist and a more curvaceous line of the back of human figures induce more drama into the hitherto monotonous unvarying wall reliefs.[24]

The final phase begins under Ptolemy X (ca. 90 B.C.) and characterizes the buildings of Ptolemy XII Neos Dionysos and Cleopatra VII; it continues into the Augustan Period (A.D. 14). The architects of this period infuse a wealth of fantasy and creativity into the design of colonnaded structures, such as porticoes and kiosks with extraordinary roof constructions. This phase is further marked by strongly plastic capital types and widely spaced columns of uncommonly slender proportions. These means of architectural expression produce a bombastic, majestic effect, which can certainly be compared with similar tendencies in the contemporary Hellenistic architecture of Alexandria. Good examples of the late Ptolemaic style are the birth house of Armant and the pronaoi of Kom Ombo and Biggeh, followed in the Augustan Period by the pronaos and hypostyle hall of the Kalabsha temple and the kiosk of Philae. The overflowing forms of temple relief finally succeed in breaking open the hitherto intact surface structure of the temple walls (fig. 102).

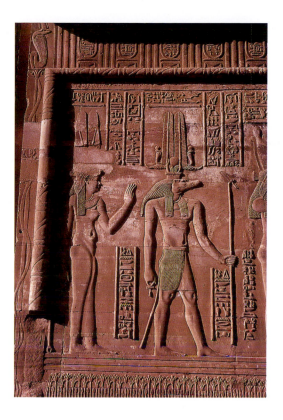

Egyptian Architecture and Foreign Countries during the Ptolemaic Period

The Ptolemaic rulers of Egypt finally accomplished the political aspirations of the pharaohs of the 25th, 29th, and 30th Dynasties, which was the creation of a powerful empire dominating the eastern Mediterranean. This international engagement enveloped Egypt in the turbulence of the Hellenistic world, facilitating a direct confrontation between Greek and Egyptian architecture. Within this configuration, pharaonic architecture maintains, of course, a strong and exemplary position. One has to admit, however, that the great and often dramatic progress in the field mainly affected architecture outside of Egypt, relegating pharaonic building to a more passive and observing role.

Greek buildings in Egypt could not evade, however, a typical pharaonic tinge. For example, in the third century B.C., a mortuary chapel was built on a cape of Stanley Bay (east of Alexandria) in the shape of an Egyptian kiosk with Doric columns. The exterior corners were formed by heart-shaped angle pillars, unknown in pharaonic architecture (fig. 103).[25] Single architectural elements (the cavetto, winged disk, the uraeus frieze, and sphinxes, specific column types and the segmentary pediment) also were added to Greek buildings in Alexandria and neighboring countries.[26]

The Egyptian cavetto had been used in Mediterranean countries for a long time. Its continued application in the Ptolemaic Period, for example, in Pales-

Figure 102.
Late Ptolemaic relief style in the pronaos of Kom Ombo (photo A.B.).

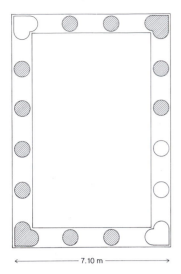

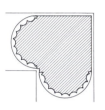

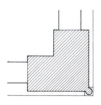

Figure 103.
Plan and detail of a heart-shaped corner column *(top and middle)* of a Hellenistic kiosk at a cape of Stanley Bay (east of Alexandria) in comparison with an Egyptian, L-shaped corner pillar.

7.10 m

tine and on Cyprus,[27] may therefore be the result of older local traditions, supported by a new wave of influences.

Greek acanthus decoration above the column base was probably indirectly inspired by the Egyptian concept of the lower-shaft floral decoration (figs. 153, 168, 173, 175). The motive seems to have spread from Alexandria across the Ptolemaic empire.[28] The so-called Nabataean column capital may ultimately have originated in Alexandria.[29] Screen walls of Egyptian type appear in the Rotunda, dedicated by the Ptolemaic queen Arsinoe II to the Great Gods of Samothrace.[30] The Egyptian building type of the freestanding gate with a pair of columns connected by an architrave (figs. 168–169)[31] may have contributed to the creation of Greek two-column monuments and finally the Roman triumphal arch.

How far Egyptian obelisks and stelae may have inspired the development of the spectacular storied stelae of Aksum in northern Ethiopia is another issue, which has not been studied in detail.[32]

This adaptation of Egyptian building elements coincided more generally with the emergence of a new stylistic sensitivity in architecture throughout the Hellenistic world. In Hellenistic and Egyptian architecture, more slender column shafts and wider intercolumniations not only altered the proportional balance of buildings but also created a new concept of space. The wider range of decorative elements in Egyptian temples and the greater variety in Hellenistic building herald the end of the more rigid traditional building in both cultures. A. W. Lawrence assumed that the widening contacts that characterize the Hellenistic age and the encounter with more flamboyant architectural forms of Egypt might even have contributed to the decline of the traditional, severe Doric proportions in the second century B.C.[33]

Building Methods of the Ptolemaic Period

One has to visualize the strange phenomenon in which, under the Ptolemies, temples in Greek and pharaonic styles were built in Egypt side by side. Both architectural forms had their own formal tradition and to some extent required different construction methods. Greek construction methods cannot be discussed here.[34]

During the Ptolemaic Period, the proven building methods of older times were obviously continued. For example, the descriptions of mythical temples recorded in Ptolemaic inscriptions still use the cubit. The ancient cubit measurements preserved in building inscriptions of the temple of Edfu record the dimensions of each room and permit a comparison with the actual building. J. Jacquet and P. Deleuze confirm that the recorded dimensions were carried out with insignificant variations of +/– 1 cm.[35] It is interesting to see that the architects occasionally deviated from the planned ideal because the wall texts needed more space than originally expected.[36] This does not mean that architecture was only built to accommodate wall surfaces for reliefs and inscriptions, but it indicates the importance of the wall decoration.

Foundation pits were still cased with brick and filled with sand. The oblique joints in masonry still occur occasionally, even after the success of the isodomic wall masonry. Isodomic masonry is typical for Greek building and was already used, for example, in the sixth century for the Doric temples of Sicily. In Egypt, considerably older examples suggest the possibility that this building method originated here.[37]

The quarrying methods used for hard stones such as granite and quartzite were essentially advanced by the use of a long series of wedges with metal shims. The development was also enhanced by the diffusion of iron tools and other technical improvements that helped to produce sharp edges of the stone and polished surfaces. Hard stones, which had been highly esteemed for temple building in previous periods, disappeared, however, from pharaonic (not from Greek) buildings in Egypt. From early Ptolemaic times on, temples were built of sandstone in Upper Egypt and Nubia and of limestone in Middle and Lower Egypt.

J.-C. Golvin and colleagues,[38] and more recently P. Zignani,[39] have pointed out important criteria for wall masonry of the period. One characteristic of Ptolemaic masonry is horizontal mortar grooves or rough recessed bands on the top surface of blocks, running parallel to the block alignment. In the Roman Period these bands are emphasized by sharply incised edges. Since the Middle Kingdom, Egyptian vertical joint faces show *anathyrosis* and vertical grooves for filling liquid mortar into the joints.[40] This method, at first used sporadically in the Middle and New Kingdoms, became standard in early Ptolemaic buildings.

Sculptors decorated temple walls with a pointillist method, following detailed model drawings. Without using a grid or guidelines, they began their work simultaneously at different parts of a wall, immediately cutting the details of the relief. More evidence for the rise of preparatory planning comes from the crypts of Dendera, which apparently were decorated before the roof blocks were set.[41] The required spotless wall surface was achieved by careful treatment of faces and joints and meticulous lever socket methods, which no longer require the filling of gaps with mortar and patch stones. Settling fissures in the masonry and the fracturing of edges was reduced by the insertion of wooden or metal shims or was prevented by continuous vertical separation joints.[42]

A detailed drawing of a column with a composite capital is engraved at a scale of 1:1 into the surface of a cavetto on the first pylon on Philae (Ptolemy V) (fig. 130).[43] The full-scale construction drawing apparently was used by the sculptor to transfer the measurements of the upward-diminishing radius of the column to the actual work piece. The discovery of a full-scale drawing engraved into a leveled plain is clear evidence that the Egyptian architects of the Late Period used the same drawing and construction methods still practiced in the tracing houses of medieval cathedrals.[44]

Pliny the Elder (*Natural History*, XXXVI.14.67) describes the water transport of an obelisk of a Nectanebo king by an engineer Phoinix at the time of Ptolemy II. This work was still carried out using ancient Egyptian methods:

> A canal was dug from the river Nile to the spot where the obelisk lay. Two broad vessels, loaded with blocks of similar stone a foot square—the volume of each amounting to double the size, and consequently double the weight

of the obelisk—were put [inside the vessels] beneath it [the obelisk]. The extremities of the obelisk remained supported by the opposite sides of the canal. The blocks of stone were removed and the vessels, being thus gradually lightened, received their burden.[45]

However, one may assume that Greek engineers introduced their new transport and lifting devices not only for Greek buildings in Egypt but that these modern methods finally also entered pharaonic building.[46]

The Buildings of the Ptolemies

Ptolemy I Soter (323–284 or 304–284)

Ptolemy, son of Lagos, ruled Egypt from 323, first as a governor for the family of Alexander. After the death of Alexander II/IV, in 306, he had himself crowned according to the ancient Egyptian ritual. All his successors followed this observance either for reasons of internal politics or because they felt themselves to be true followers of the pharaohs.[47] Despite their natural attachment to the Greek gods, all Ptolemies were attracted by the local cults and ceremonies, including Cleopatra VII, who committed suicide in full pharaonic regalia on a golden funerary bed (Plutarch, "Antony," 85.2–8). A special form of the cult of the Ptolemaic rulers and their queens was newly created after pharaonic and Greek models, closely linking the priesthood to the new dynasty.[48] Characteristic for Ptolemaic politics of religion were synods of priests. Representatives of major Egyptian cults met annually with the king to discuss religious and economic matters relating to the temples.

Following a suggestion made by the philosopher Demetrius of Phaleron to Ptolemy I, the cult of Sarapis was elevated to a kind of state cult.[49] The traditional, politically less desirable aspects of Sarapis as Apis bull and as Osiris, god of the dead, were modified in favor of the aspect of Sarapis as a god of the universe, as expressed by the anthropomorphic cult image of the new god.[50]

The Ptolemies' attachment to Egyptian cults was not prompted only by pious sentiment. The Ptolemies were primarily interested in the considerable tax revenues of the country, which supported their luxurious lifestyle and ambitious power game in the eastern Mediterranean. For that purpose, all measures to advance Egypt, its cults, and its economy had the main objective of increasing these revenues.

The reign of Ptolemy I was overshadowed by fights against the other Diadochs, wars that finally resulted in the acquisition of the Cyrenaica, Cyprus, and parts of Syria and laid the foundations for the Ptolemaic empire. After all, Ptolemy I commissioned building projects not only in Alexandria but also in the Nile valley. The development of Alexandria by the Rhodian architect Deinokrates[51] proceeded so well that the seat of government could be moved in 311 from Memphis to Alexandria. Work continued at the first temple of Sarapis, which perhaps had been already founded by Alexander the Great, on a hill of the district Rhakotis. The royal palace, the Sema with the tomb of Alexander, and the Museion with the famous library that became a center of

Greek scholarship were built. The Egyptian priest Manetho (ca. 305–285 B.C.), a counselor to the king and his successor Ptolemy II, wrote a history of the pharaonic kingdom in Greek.[52]

The frequent appearance of Ptolemy I's name on pharaonic monuments does not necessarily attest to significant new royal foundations but might only suggest repairs to earlier structures or the completion of unfinished buildings.

A significant new foundation in Upper Egypt was the Greek settlement of PTOLEMAIS HERMIOU,[53] which grew gradually into one of the largest cities of the Thebais.

The east gate of the enclosure wall of Nectanebo II at TANIS, which led to the Horus temple, was rebuilt (plan I). The original gate may have been destroyed by the Persians.

At TARRANEH (Therenutis), at the western edge of the Delta, a temple for Hathor-Thermuthis was built under Ptolemy I. The exterior decoration was only completed under Ptolemy II. This site was of special importance to the Ptolemies because it was the starting point of a caravan route to the Wadi Natrun, which had important natron and salt beds. The temple was found, destroyed down to the foundation trenches, in 1887/1888. The temple stood in a 53 x 59.4 m enclosure.[54] Unfortunately, no plan of the remains was made. At least a few surviving limestone blocks were rescued from the lime kiln,[55] and more blocks were found moved as far as Kom Abu Billo and Gireis. The 20 cm thickness of the blocks suggests a building of small dimensions. However, the extraordinary quality of the reliefs belong among the foremost examples of the art of the early Ptolemies. A Ptolemaic mortuary chapel for an unknown person with a pronaos *distyle in antis* was preserved in the nearby cemetery of Kom Abu Billo.[56]

Three basalt blocks of Ptolemy I and a small granite obelisk, found at NAU-CRATIS, may originate from an unfinished temple of the 30th Dynasty, completed by Ptolemy I and Ptolemy II. The temple, apparently in Egyptian style, probably stood within the "Great Temenos," a large brick enclosure.[57]

Under Ptolemy I, a new temple for the local crocodile god Soknebtunis was built at the place of an older predecessor at TEBTYNIS (Umm el-Breigât) at the southwestern Faiyum edge, apparently an indication of the earlier colonization of the Faiyum.[58] A 6.5 m wide, long processional road was paved with stone and approached the 60 x 120 m temple enclosure from the north. Two kiosks stood on this road, one 50 m in front of the temple, the second at a distance of 150 to 200 m. The road was flanked by sculptures of lions and sphinxes, as well as numerous cult buildings. At the temple entrance, which was formed by a pylon, stood a royal statue in pharaonic style, more lion sculptures and, nearby, a sacred tree. The temple was surrounded by a 3.5 m thick enclosure wall, which also enclosed priests' houses. According to the preliminary report, the rectangular temple house was "grandiose" and offered "important suggestions for the development of building methods in Egypt."[59] The temple itself was made of limestone and was surrounded by colonnades. The building was enlarged and completed under Ptolemy XII Neos Dionysos.

Under Ptolemy I at least three temples in Middle Egypt are attested by relief blocks. Several blocks with fine raised relief have come on the art market since 1955 and originate from a temple of Per-khefet, probably near Oxyrhynchos (modern El-Bahnasa).[60] Ptolemy I probably also built an important temple in the middle Egyptian SHARUNA (Kom el-Ahmar Sawâris on the east bank north of Minya), the decoration of which was completed under Ptolemy II. Eighteen blocks with remarkably fine reliefs were found by Smolenski in 1907; attempts to locate the building have so far failed.[61] A foundation deposit and the find of a fine relief block with a frieze of Hathor heads and cartouches of Ptolemy I suggest a temple for Hathor in CUSAE, the capital of the fourteenth nome.[62] Nothing is known about this temple, which has disappeared under the modern town of El-Qûsiya.

The necropolis of TUNA EL-GEBEL contained important animal cemeteries for the burial of mummified ibises, the sacred animals of Thoth, lord of the nearby town of Hermopolis magna. Several underground cult chapels cased with limestone blocks formed the entrance rooms into the ibis galleries. The rooms were up to 15 m long and contained cult niches with facades decorated in the shape of superimposed chapels carrying uraeus friezes.[63]

The Ptolemaic and Roman necropolis also included a variety of funerary chapels in the shape of small temples. The more elaborate examples (nos. 1–4, 10, and the tomb of Padykam) have an Egyptian pronaos at the front (*distyle* or *tetrastyle in antis*, fig. 104) with walled-up intercolumniations and small windows in the shape of chapel fronts. Some chapels are *prostyle* temples in the pure classical style (nos. 11 and 12) or represent houses in mixed pharaonic-Greek style (no. 21 and the "house of Isidora").[64]

Figure 104.
Facades of some Ptolemaic tomb chapels in the cemetery of Tuna el-Gebel (after Sami Gabra, *Rapport sur les fouilles d'Hermoupolis ouest* [Cairo, 1941]).

CHAPEL 5
IN CLASSICAL STYLE (UNPUBLISHED)

CHAPEL 4

CHAPEL 1

CHAPEL 10

The best-known structure is the mortuary chapel of Petosiris, the high priest of Hermopolis magna (ca. 300–285 B.C.). The pronaos of his chapel contains four columns, and the following hall is supported by four pillars. The wall decoration is a unique mixture of Egyptian elements rendered in Greek style, which is seen primarily in the costumes of the figures, their frontal views, and other iconographic details. An un-Egyptian excitement transforms the restrained flow of the Egyptian wall decoration into a turbulent torrent of undulating forms.[65]

In the same way as the preceding private tomb chapels of the Kushite Period had imitated contemporary temples with pylon-like fronts, the tomb chapels of the Ptolemaic Period depicted the open pronaos front of contemporaneous temples.

Ptolemy II Philadelphus (284–246)

On January 7, 282 B.C., after a coregency of two years, Soters's son Ptolemy II Philadelphus was crowned pharaoh. The joint reign of Ptolemy II and his sister-consort Arsinoe II was occupied with numerous wars in Syria, which finally led to the largest extension of the Ptolemaic empire.

Building activity again favored Alexandria. The imposing Pharos lighthouse, donated by Sostratos of Knidos, was completed around 280.[66] The 100 m giant consisted of a tall square tower, with slanting walls in the pharaonic tradition that carried a set-back, probably octagonal, upper tower with the actual lighting installation. The top was crowned by a bronze statue of Zeus-Soter.

Places outside Egypt also received splendid monuments, such as the sanctuary of the Great Gods of SAMOTHRACE, with a monumental propylon and the awe-inspiring rotunda of queen Arsinoe II, and the temple of Agathe-Tyche on DELOS.[67]

In the winter of 276/275, Ptolemy II celebrated the famous Ptolemaia festival in ALEXANDRIA with fabulous pageantry.[68] A Sed-festival gate dedicated at Medamoud might commemorate that occasion. Following Egyptian tradition, a pompous canopy of light material was erected for the festival, and a Dionysian-Osiride banquet was enacted in it. Haeny has shown that the tent was built in Egyptian style and had a kind of hypostyle hall with a raised central nave.[69] Based on these reconstructions, the building could be considered a formal link between Egyptian hypostyle halls and the later Roman basilica.

Ptolemy II supplied the Museion of Alexandria with a library which developed into the most important library of the Greek world. A huge obelisk of Nectanebo II(?) was moved from Sais, as described by Pliny the Elder (*Natural History*, XXXVI.14.67); in Sais, apparently, it had never been never raised and was lying on the ground. Once relocated, it was erected in the Arsinoeion of Alexandria to honor the queen Arsinoe II. Another prominent sanctuary for Arsinoe was built at the Cape Zephyrion (east of Alexandria), into which Berenike II donated her famous hair.

Ptolemy II performed his pharaonic role by personal attendance at the festival of the sacred ram of MENDES. His main interest, however, was the economy and the collection of taxes. The desire to increase revenues was assisted by a survey and inventory of the entire country. For similar reasons, Ptolemy II became one of the greatest founders of towns in Egyptian history. The fortress of PITHOM at the eastern end of the Wadi Tumilat was restored and supplied with a temple consecrated by Ptolemy II himself. This project was connected with the repair of the long-neglected "Suez" Canal, leading from Pithom in the Wadi Tumilat to the Red Sea. The canal project led to the foundation of the town of ARSINOE near modern Suez (Tell el-Qulzum) and the nearby fortress KLYSMA.

New harbor towns along the coast of the Red Sea supported the trade route to Arabia and India: BERENIKE (near the modern Eilath in the Gulf of Aqaba), MYOS HORMOS (north of Hurghada), PHILOTERAS (south of Safaga at the Wadi Gasus), LEUKOS LIMEN (Qûseir at the mouth of the Wadi Hammamat), BERENIKE TROGODYTIKE, PTOLEMAIS THERON (at Aqiq, south of Port Sudan), and ADULIS (on the Island of Massawa in Eritrea). An improved caravan route through the eastern desert from Berenike Tro-·godytike to Coptos promoted the rise of Coptos, which received a new temple for Min (see below).

At TANIS, a small chapel with a stela of the king and Queen Arsinoe II was built northwest of the main enclosure.

Everywhere in the country, temple building and temple decoration, left unfinished since the Persian dominion, were revived. Decoration work at ISEUM (Behbeit el-Hagar), which had started just before the Persian invasion of 343, was resumed. The decoration of the granite walls of the temple of Onuris-Shu at SEBENNYTOS was continued. A "high gate of granite" was added along with a *rwt*, which may have been a pylon or a hall.

At NAUCRATIS, Ptolemy II built a new, stone-cased pylon in the western enclosure wall of the "Great Temenos" (see the buildings of Ptolemy I Soter).[70] The pylon had the gigantic dimensions of 28 x 112 m and was furnished with an *avant-porte*.

Two complete, larger-than-life-size statues of Ptolemy II and his consort Arsinoe II were found in the gardens of Sallust in Rome,[71] masterworks of pharaonic-style sculpture. The statues are assumed to have originated in HELIOPOLIS.[72] Because the place was uninhabited since the total destruction by the Persians in 342,[73] a votive to Heliopolis is rather improbable. Another royal colossal statue is believed to originate from BUBASTIS.[74] At the Qait Bey fort off ALEXANDRIA, four bases and parts of 12 m high granite statues of a Ptolemaic king in pharaonic style and of the goddess Isis were recently pulled out of the sea. Their provenances are unknown.[75]

The Faiyum became the second focus of Ptolemaic economic activity, receiving thirty to forty new settlements intended to house the Macedonian-Greek veterans of the Ptolemaic army. With the help of canals and lifting devices, the governmental engineers Kleon and Theodorus secured the water supply for the new settlements and their fields at the desert edge of the oasis. With the help of dikes and drains, the surface of the Lake Moeris was lowered to dry up swamps. The old capital of the nome, KROKODILOPOLIS (pharaonic Shedet, modern Medinet el-Faiyum), was transformed into a modern Greek city with Greek institutions and temples and called after the queen Arsinoe II ARSINOE, a name later extended over the whole Arsinoitic nome. The big

Sobek temple in Shedet of the Middle and New Kingdom was probably also replaced by a new building under Ptolemy II. A limestone temple was built inside a 250 x 400 m brick enclosure wall 10 m wide. F. Petrie calculated that the temple measured approximately 150 x 200 m.[76] The pylon of the enclosure wall, built of limestone and granite was also enormous and partially standing in 1860. Petrie measured blocks of up to 2.3 x 7.6 m size that probably were door lintels. The area of the temple later fell into private hands and consequently was razed.

Ptolemy II also founded the Faiyum town of THEADELPHIA (modern Batn Ihrît), which received a modest sanctuary for Pnephoros. The temple house stood within a court with a well and a sacred tree. The temple house enclosed two consequent courts and a central chapel with three deep niches for the cult images in the shape of crocodiles. The main parts of the temple were of brick; only the gates and central chapel consisted of stone. Interesting paintings and graffite covered the walls. The temple—now completely destroyed—was found in 1912–1913, with much of its cultic equipment still in place, including an embalmed crocodile, lying on its processional stretcher. The temple's doors stood half-open.[77]

The temple of the local oracle deity Sokanobkonneus at BACCHIAS ('Umm el-'Atl, northeast of Karanis) also dates to the Ptolemaic Period. The 25 x 38 m brick temple contained three successive main rooms and numerous side chambers.[78]

The small triple-shrine sanctuary of Renenutet at MEDINET MADI (at the western edge of the Faiyum) originated in the late 12th Dynasty and was later enlarged by two subsequent pronaoi (figs. 105–106).[79] The outer pronaos measures 10.95 x 17.4 m and has four columns at the front, some, at least, with palmette capitals. Instead of an interior row of columns, an unusual dividing wall runs parallel to the facade and supports the roof. This frontal pronaos embraced an inner, smaller pronaos that was 11.7 m wide with two-by-two columns. The front of the Middle Kingdom temple was originally open, but since Ptolemaic pronaoi required a closed rear wall, the ancient facade

Figure 105.
Plan of the Early Ptolemaic extension of the temple of Renenutet at Medinet Madi.

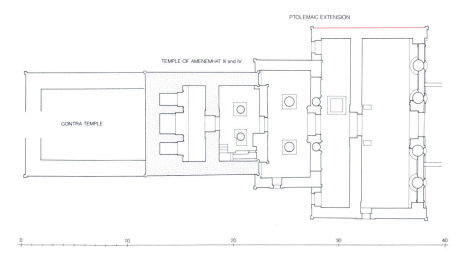

Figure 106.
View of the Early Ptolemaic pronaos and temple of Renenutet at Medinet Madi.

was sealed with a slightly protruding wall. The *distyle* front hall of the 12th Dynasty was transformed into an interior hall. Behind the rear wall of the 12th Dynasty temple, a well-preserved Ptolemaic contra-temple was discovered. All later elements remained undecorated, and the block surface left in bosses and no inscriptions reveal the builder's name. A date for the enlargement from the early Ptolemaic time to around Ptolemy VIII and IX has been suggested by the excavators.

From the temple front a processional road leads southward to a monumental, 7.5 m wide gate. 120 m beyond the gate, the road reaches a 8.2 x 11.4 m kiosk of unknown date.[80] Its two-by-four columns were found demolished with only the 3 m the high screen walls preserved.

At DENDERA the birth house erected by Nectanebo I, built mainly of brick, received an interior stone casing. Later, under Ptolemy VIII, the building was enlarged with a colonnaded kiosk.

In Upper Egypt, COPTOS was singled out by a new temple building, probably because of its special role as the starting or end point for a new caravan route to the Red Sea. A temple of the Middle and New Kingdom dedicated to Min, Hathor/Isis, and the divine infant Horus was replaced by an approximately 50 x 100 m temple standing on a high platform (fig. 107). Important elements of the older temple were built in the foundations. Unfortunately, nothing remains of the new temple, except a few parts of the high temple platform with two parallel staircases. The staircases suggest a double temple with two parallel axes, one for Min and a second for Hathor/Isis. In a unique architectural solution, the northern staircase rose between the columns of an entrance kiosk of

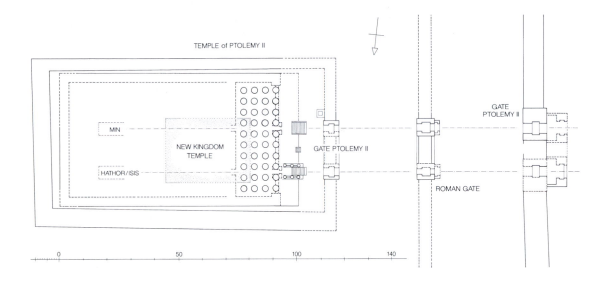

TEMPLE of PTOLEMY II

MIN

NEW KINGDOM
TEMPLE

HATHOR/ISIS

GATE PTOLEMY II

GATE
PTOLEMY II

ROMAN GATE

0   50   100   140

Ptolemy II.[81] Parts of Hathor capitals, probably originating from a pronaos, were still visible in 1893. According to Petrie, the capitals were two-thirds of the size of the capitals of Dendera, suggesting a column height of about 10 m. Their 2.28 m diameter and the 1.32 to 1.35 m height of the architraves help to reconstruct the layout of the suggested pronaos. The 50 m wide building probably had a front with ten Hathor columns, which must have been arranged—according to the two entrances—in three rows of two, four, and four columns, respectively. The question is whether the Hathor columns were restricted to the axis assigned to the Hathor/Isis cult or—for reasons of uniformity—occupied the whole front. The pronaos would have been three to four rows of columns deep, larger than that of the Hathor temple at Dendera. Columns of unknown type in the following hypostyle hall had a diameter of only 1.73 m and carried an architrave 1.05 m high. The columns themselves might have been 8 to 9 m high.

The temple stood within a system of three enclosure walls with double gates in the west (six doors altogether). The inner and outer enclosure walls, with their gates, might belong to the project of Ptolemy II. The northern gate of the outer enclosure was extended by a 12.30 m broad *avant-porte* with a doorway 5.20 m wide. We do not know whether the gates had pylon towers, perhaps of stone. The middle enclosure wall, with its double gate, seems to be Roman.

A "green basalt" naos of Ptolemy II with fine inscriptions was dedicated to the joint temple of the Great Horus Haroeris and the frog deity Heqat at QÛS (Apollinopolis parva). According to the (generally reliable) measurements of the Napoleonic architects, the naos would have had the unlikely dimensions of 8.75 m width, 8 m depth, and 20.8 m height.[82] Since monumental naoi were more common in the 30th Dynasty, one might suggest that an unfinished naos of Nectanebo II was inscribed under Ptolemy II. This assumption would raise the question of whether the affiliated temple—about which nothing is known—might also have been built during the 30th Dynasty.

Figure 107.
Hypothetical reconstruction plan of the temple of Ptolemy II for Min and Hathor/Isis at Coptos.

During the 12th to the 18th Dynasty, the temple of Monthu at MEDAMOUD grew into an important sanctuary, which was further extended under the Ramessides (plan VII). The temple later deteriorated and was only revived in Ptolemaic times, thanks to the chthonic-Osiride aspects of the cult of Monthu.[83] The building history of the sanctuary in Ptolemaic times seems to include at least two phases.[84] Under Ptolemy II and IV, the temple house of the New Kingdom was still used, but smaller buildings were erected in the south and southwest. At an unknown location, a Sed-festival gate (3.97 m wide and 6.85 m high) was built under Ptolemy II; it has been reconstructed from numerous blocks found reused in later constructions. The thickness was decorated with one of the latest representations of the ancient Sed-festival ceremonies.

The KARNAK temples were enclosed by huge brick walls in the 30th Dynasty. However, the stone gates of these walls were only built or decorated in Ptolemaic times. Inscriptions of Ptolemy II are found at the northern, main gate of the Mut enclosure.[85] The gigantic, 10.13 m wide and probably 16.6 m high gate was extended by an *avant-porte* 11.95 m wide. Both passages were closed with double-door wings. The gate terminated the sphinx allée of Nectanebo I connecting the Mut temple with the tenth pylon of the precinct of Amun. The *avant-porte* was flanked by the last two pairs of sphinxes of the road. In front of the gate the allée turned 90 degrees to the west in order to circumvent the northwest corner of the enclosure wall of Mut.

Historically significant was the designation of the tax revenues from Lower Nubia (Dodekaschoinos) to the Isis temple on PHILAE, contributing from the economic side to the rise of the cult of Isis. This designation probably occurred on the occasion of a military campaign, undertaken about 275, to intimidate bothersome bedouins and the Meroitic kingdom and to gain control over the gold sources and war elephants of Nubia. As a result of these events, the unfinished 30th Dynasty building projects on Philae were revived (plan XIV). Primarily the construction of the Isis temple was completed and the decoration work begun.[86]

Probably under Ptolemy II or perhaps already in the 30th Dynasty, the core building of the birth house was erected.[87] The birth house stood not at the usual right angle to the main temple but parallel to it, probably because of space problems.[88]

Ptolemy III Euergetes I (246–221)

After the death of Ptolemy II, his son Ptolemy III was crowned pharaoh. He and his queen, Berenike II, were primarily engaged in endless military struggles against the Seleucides, who also descended from the Macedonians. These campaigns were conducted as far away as Mesopotamia and finally secured Egyptian dominance over the empire of the Seleucides.

In Egypt, building projects in ALEXANDRIA were advanced. The older Serapeum, which might have been founded under Ptolemy I or even under Alexander the Great, was replaced by a new building on a rocky mound in the southwestern district of Rhakotis (fig. 108).[89] The building is now destroyed down to the foundation trenches, but they allow the reconstruction

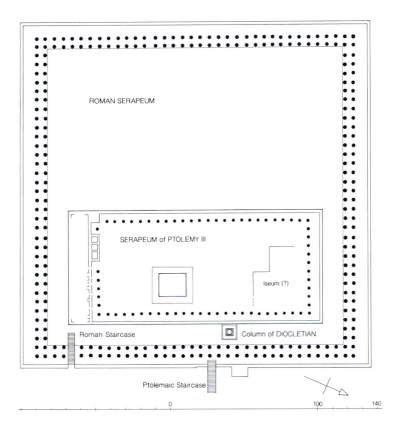

ROMAN SERAPEUM

SERAPEUM of PTOLEMY III

Iseum (?)

Roman Staircase

Column of DIOCLETIAN

Ptolemaic Staircase

0   100   140

of a 77 x 173.7 m wide temenos surrounded by interior colonnades.[90] A staircase led from the east side through a monumental propylon to the "Acropolis of Alexandria." The temple house, with its precious but bizarre sheathing of metal covers, seems to have stood in the northeastern corner.[91] The temple housed the famous statue of Serapis by Bryaxis, adapted after Phidias's statue of Zeus at Olympia. The statue was composed of different types of wood and metal. Obelisks and pharaonic statues emphasized the Egyptian background of the god. The inner court also contained the smaller temple of Isis and her son Harpokrates. Roman coins of the time of Trajan to Marcus Aurelius depict a temple on top of a double-stepped podium with a flat segmentary pediment carried by papyrus columns. The cult association of the male Serapis with Isis mater and the infant Harpokrates ("Horus the child") endowed the Isis temple with the aspect of a birth house. However, the overall plan of the temenos and remains of granite and marble columns strongly suggest that the Serapeum was not pharaonic but Greek.

In the older town of CANOPUS (15 km east of Alexandria, between Montaza and Abukir), Ptolemy III and Berenike II built another Serapeum.[92] The 80 x 80 m temple was furnished with numerous sculptures taken from pharaonic buildings of the Middle and New Kingdom. Gaining fame as an oracle place and a sanitarium, the temple transformed Canopus into an international pilgrimage center. Celebrated were its panegyries and boat proces-

Figure 108. Hypothetical reconstruction plan of the Serapeum of Ptolemy III at Alexandria with its Roman extension.

sions on the Canopic Canal flowing from Alexandria to Cape Zephyrion. Whether the situation of Canopus stimulated Roman architects to create "Canopic sites" is not known.[93] Until 1892, the ruins of Canopus were still extensive, but they were never properly explored.[94]

A Ptolemeion for Ptolemy III and Berenike II was built in front of the enclosure of Thoth at HERMOPOLIS MAGNA in Middle Egypt. The west-east-oriented, 66 x 122 m large court was surrounded by colonnades and contained the actual temple. Details of the temple inside the court, a relatively small *trikonch*-building, were probably classical. This Ptolemeion is the earliest known example of this specific temple type for the royal cult in Greek style.[95] The building type reemerged in the Caesareum at Alexandria and in the building program of Herod the Great in Palestine and spread over the Roman Empire.

A huge Ptolemaic temple stood at AKHMIM (Panopolis) with an enormous pronaos of Ptolemy IV (see the buildings of Ptolemy IV Philopator). It is rather improbable that the pronaos was built together with the temple house behind. One would rather suggest that the temple house was built under Ptolemy III, who had supported immense building programs in Upper Egypt. The Arab historian Ibn Gubayr still saw (ca. A.D. 1200) that "the interior of the temple consists of reception halls, small niches, entrances and exits, ramps, staircases, corridors and entrance openings, so that in it whole groups of people get lost; only by loud screaming can one lead one other's way." The temple was demolished in 1350. In the nineteenth century, debris of the Birba was still visible north of Akhmim.[96]

A small secondary temple of unknown function was built under Ptolemy III at MEDAMOUD southwest of the main temple. Its location and orientation suggest that it was a birth house (plan VII). Only foundation deposits and a sandstone altar of the building were preserved. Also a gate was erected in the forecourt of the New Kingdom main temple. From some preserved blocks, this rather modest gate was reconstructed in the Musée des Beaux-Arts in Lyon.[97]

A rather insignificant project was the addition of a pronaos to the Saite temple for Amun, Mut, and Khonsu at QASR EL-GHUEDA in the El-Kharga Oasis (figs. 45, 109). The pronaos, with its two columns, equaled the old temple house in width (10.56 m). Its depth of 6.62 m created a distance of 5.52 m between the front columns and the old facade, which could not be roofed without either interior columns or the use of timber.[98] The decoration was continued under Ptolemy IV Philopator and Ptolemy IX Soter II. In front of and to the south of the temple house stood another building with a four-column front, perhaps a birth house. Its interior structure is unknown. The sanctuary was probably also surrounded under Ptolemy III by a strong brick wall.

The temple of Hibis at EL-KHARGA was supplied with a *shena wab* with an entrance ramp conducting up to a small entrance kiosk in front of the actual building.

Under Ptolemy III the Opet temple at KARNAK, begun under Nectanebo I, was continued (figs. 110–111). The construction and decoration was concluded in the reign of Ptolemy VIII. Since it is not possible at present to differentiate between the three building phases the temple is discussed with the building program of Ptolemy VIII.

Figure 109.
View of the pronaos of
Ptolemy III in front of the
chapel of Amasis for Amun,
Mut, and Khonsu at Qasr
el-Ghueda.

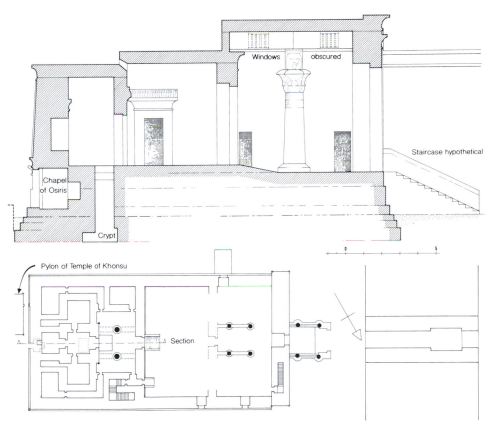

Figure 110. Longitudinal section and plan of the temple of Ptolemy III and
VIII for Opet at Karnak.

Figure 111.
The raised platform of the temple of Ptolemy III for Opet at Karnak (photo A.O.).

Figure 112.
The Bab el-Amara of Ptolemy III at the temple of Khonsu at Karnak (photo A.O.).

The temple of Khonsu at Karnak also received a monumental gate, the Bab el-Amara (fig. 112). The gate was completed but not the flanking pylon towers, which combined measured 70 m. They never rose above the foundations.[99] The 21(!) m high gate, with its harmonious proportions and splendid relief decoration, is certainly one of the most beautiful remaining buildings of Ptolemaic architecture. The 5.60 m wide and 14.32 m high passage could probably not be closed any more with wooden doors, requiring an *avant-porte*. A law court or "site of giving Maat" is mentioned in an inscription of the gate and may have met in the open, in front of the gate.

The building history of the Ptah temple at Karnak built by the Thutmosides is complex during the period following the New Kingdom. Under Ptolemy III, an entrance kiosk was added to a pylon-like gatehouse (fig. 113, plan VIII). The kiosk consisted of four slim columns with composite capitals and architraves that were bonded to the pylon. Whether they carried a wooden roof is not known; the small intercolumniations also would have permitted a stone roof. The gatehouse and the kiosk of Ptolemy III were partially inscribed under Ptolemy IV. The kiosk continued the extension of the processional approach that had begun in the 25th Dynasty; two more Ptolemaic gates were to follow.

The complex of Amunra-Monthu of KARNAK-NORTH was advanced (plan IX). The temple, with its back to the Amun temple, faced the distant sanc-

Figure 113.
The entrance kiosk of Ptolemy III at the temple of Ptah at Karnak (photo A.O.).

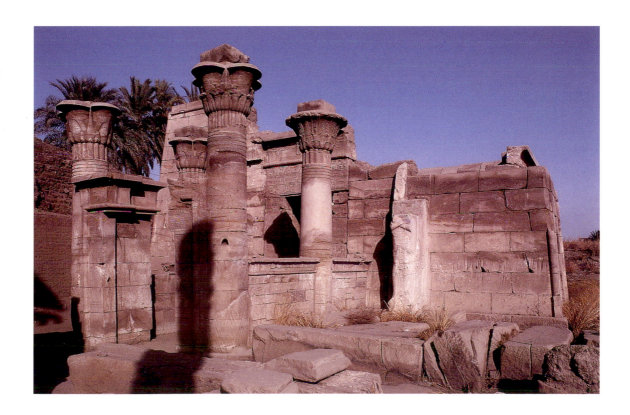

tuary of Monthu at Medamoud. This association was highlighted by a monumental rearrangement of the processional area north of the temple. The brick enclosure wall was perhaps begun in the 30th Dynasty. In the northern section of the wall the gigantic gate Bab el-'Abd was erected (plan IX, fig. 114). The 18.70(!) m high gate was extended by a 9.60 m wide *avant-porte*. The decoration of the gate was only completed under Ptolemy IV.[100]

This huge gate created a spectacular background for a 120 m long and 22 m wide processional approach, flanked on both sides by sphinxes and enclosed by a wall. At the midway point, outside the enclosure wall, the path of movement was halted by a group of three old, colossal statues (Amenhotep III and Sethos II), that faced toward Amunra-Monthu as he left his sanctuary. Still farther to the north, the allée approached a huge, 33 m long cult terrace that had a platform high above a canal, which probably connected the Nile with Medamoud.

The Napoleonic expedition recorded a small temple for Khnum built by Ptolemy III at the desert edge, opposite KÔM EL-DEIR, a few kilometers northwest of Esna ("Esna North") (figs. 115–116). The temple stood on an artificial terrace and faced the Nile which was some 500 m way. The temple contained a 10.45 x 20 m pronaos which embraced the temple house as if the pronaos

Figure 114.
The Bab el-'Abd of Ptolemy III at the precinct of Amunra-Monthu at Karnak.

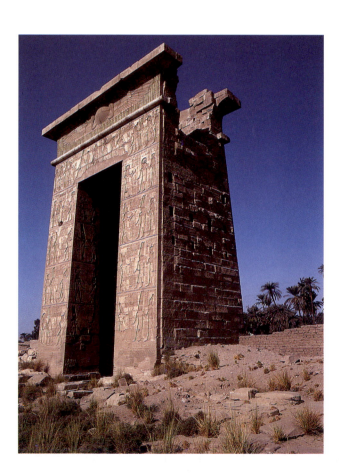

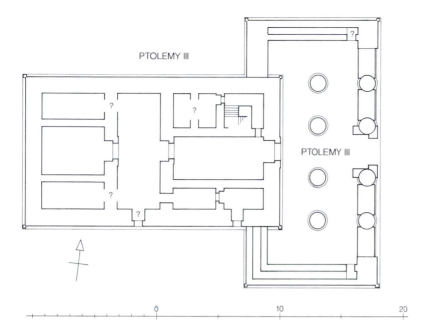

PTOLEMY III

PTOLEMY III

0   10   20

Figure 115.
Plan of the temple of Ptolemy
III at Kôm el-Deir (*Description*
I, pl. 88).

was added later. Both the pronaos and the temple were inscribed with the names of Ptolemy III. The two-by-four columns of the pronaos, which had composite capitals, carried two rows of transversal architraves. Narrow crypts were inserted into the side walls. A longitudinal room without columns followed the pronaos, corresponding to the hypostyle hall of larger temples. At its side were several chambers, the arrangement of which was probably not recorded correctly. The sanctuary faced a broad room that probably served as the offering room or hall for the visiting deities. The sanctuary seems to have offered access into two side chambers.

At some distance from the facade stood a cult terrace. Although the construction of the temple was poor, the structure was nearly completely preserved and still had lively painted decoration when it was destroyed by vandals around 1843.

On August 23, 237 B.C., Ptolemy III personally conducted the foundation ritual for a new Horus temple at EDFU, a project that was only completed ninety-five years later by Ptolemy VIII Euergetes II (see fig. 170). The building of Ptolemy III comprised only the actual 33.3 x 57.5 m wide temple house. Its relationship to an older project of the 30th Dynasty is unclear (see the buildings of Ptolemy VIII Euergetes II). Thanks to its completely preserved architecture, inscriptions, and decoration, the Horus temple is the best example of Ptolemaic temple building in Egypt. The new building not only answered needs of the cult of Horus but also combined as a kind of Pantheon all essential aspects of Egyptian religion. The architectural outcome resulting from such broad requirements is remarkably simple and reveals the work of experienced builders and designers. Building inscriptions above the wall dado of the interior rooms and on the inner enclosure wall contain an unusually substan-

Figure 116. The pronaos of Ptolemy III at Kôm el-Deir in 1816 (Jean Jacques Rifaud, *Voyages en Égypte, en Nubie et lieux circonvoisins* [Paris, 1830], pl. 149).

Figure 117. The facade of the *wabet* of the temple of Ptolemy III for Horus of Edfu (courtesy of MMA).

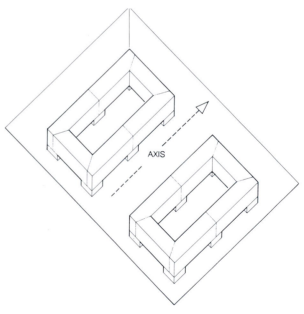

Figure 118. The arrangement of the architraves in the hypostyle hall of the temple of Ptolemy III for Horus of Edfu.

tial description of the temple rooms and their function. Taken together with numerous other inscriptions in the temple, they permit a complete reconstruction of the temple ceremonies.[101]

The bark shrine still contains the beautiful naos of Nectanebo II reused by Ptolemy III. The barks of Horus and Hathor stood in front of it under a wooden canopy. The bark shrine is surrounded on three sides by an ambulatory that includes thirteen chapels and their side chambers. The central chapel probably housed a falcon image in a wooden shrine. The ambulatory and the antechamber of the bark shrine receive minimal light from window slots, keeping the interior of the sanctuary rather dark (see fig. 99).

In the east wall of the transversal hall that leads into the ambulatory, a door opens into the *wabet*, the sanctuary used for the celebration of the merging of Horus with the sun disk (fig. 117). This well-preserved unit, close to the staircase leading to the roof, consists of an open light court and a cult chapel. The latter is elevated above the seemingly more profane court by a high step. The front of the chapel is "transparent," consisting of screen walls and two columns with magnificent composite capitals. The integration of the *wabet* complex into the overall plan of the temple, which facilitated circulation between the temple and its roof, represents a remarkable architectural design. The hall behind the hypostyle hall conducts to staircases on each side, which leads with flat steps to the temple roof. The western staircase reaches the roof in one straight flight, while the eastern one makes several 90 degree turns.

The front part of the temple house is occupied by the hypostyle hall with three-by-four columns with composite capitals. Their stocky shafts clearly retract at the foot indicating their descent from papyrus columns of the New Kingdom. The round column bases are beveled[102] and stand on square *plinths*. The disposition of architraves separates the two-by-three columns on the eastern and western sides of the hall and suggests that both column groups actually depict two separate colonnaded kiosks within a court (fig. 118). On the west side of the hypostyle hall are rooms for the preparation of sacred ointments and oils. Opposite, in the east wall, is the treasury for the cult implements, cloths, and jewelry for the cult images.

An elaborate and complex system of crypts is built into the thick exterior walls, arranged in three floors on top of each other.

A small temple for Isis was built at the southern edge of the newly founded town of ASWAN (Syene).[103] The temple may have been a station for the visit of Isis of Philae. The 15 x 19 m building was 7 m high. In the front part, an offering hall was supported by two square pillars with uniquely overhanging abaci (fig. 119). Two large side windows illuminate the room, in which an altar with a cavetto cornice is still preserved. The central sanctuary follows behind the offering hall. Its dimensions (4.5 x 7.41 m) surpass those of the sanctuary of Isis on Philae (4.2 x 5.25 m). A plump cavetto decorated with double-winged disks projects from the rear wall to protect symbolically the shrine, which stood in front. The sanctuary is flanked by two side chambers; the southern one was a secondary sanctuary with its own access from the front. The exterior and the roof of the small temple remained standing in bosses. The surrounding precinct has not been excavated and is now disgraced by a garbage dump, which even covers the temple entrance.

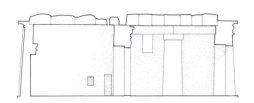

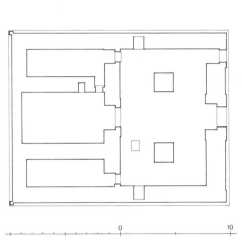

Figure 119. *(right)*
Longitudinal section and plan
of the temple of Ptolemy III
for Isis of Aswan.

Figure 120. *(bottom)*
Section and plan of the Ptole-
maic birth house of Isis of
Philae.

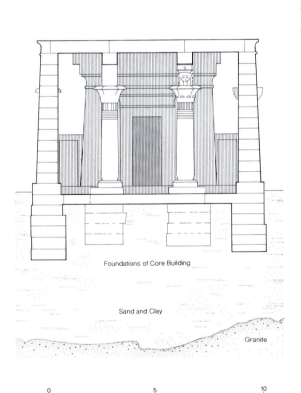

Foundations of Core Building

Sand and Clay

Granite

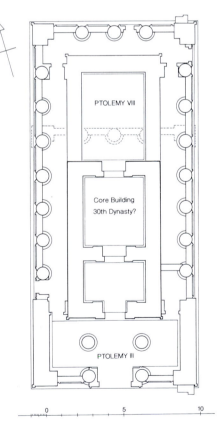

PTOLEMY VIII

Core Building
30th Dynasty?

PTOLEMY III

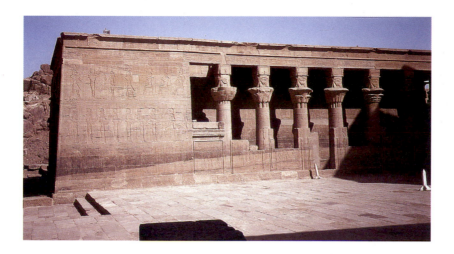

The cella of the birth house of the Isis temple on PHILAE was built during the 30th Dynasty or under Ptolemy II and consisted of only two rooms (figs. 120–121, plan XIV). Under Ptolemy III, the cella was enlarged with an ambu-latory.[104] The 6.7 m high ambulatory towered considerably over the original cella. The building was later extended by Ptolemy VIII.

Figure 121.
The birth house of Isis on Philae after the enlargement to the south under Ptolemy III (photo A.O.).

Ptolemy IV Philopator (221–205)

Ptolemy IV was crowned pharaoh in February 221 B.C. After a few years, he and his sister consort, Arsinoe III, were faced with enormous military chal-lenges from the expanding Antiochos III, who captured the Ptolemies' north-ern territory and whose army had already reached Gaza. On June 22, 217 B.C., Ptolemy overcame Antiochos in the spectacular battle of Raphia, in which both sides had fielded 70,000 soldiers and 100 elephants. The consequent invasion of Ptolemy IV into Syria ended successfully, and the victory was cele-brated with grandiose festivities in Memphis. Afterward, the pharaoh traveled by bark throughout the country, enjoying the adoration of his people and the priesthood. The following years of external—but not internal—peace were filled with sumptuous feasting and represented the culmination of the most glorious phase of Ptolemaic rule. One also has to remember the formidable Ptolemaic fleet anchored in the Mediterranean and the famous boat Ptolemy IV built for his voyages in Egypt and abroad, a "liner" furbished with fabulous comfort.[105]

A small step separated triumph from collapse. In the same year of 217, the discontented Delta population rose in rebellion, an uprising that was not put down until thirty-two years later. Despite the favor shown to Upper Egypt, this part of the kingdom also broke off in 207/206, with the rebel leaders[106] rul-ing the Thebais as "pharaohs" until 186. Through these events, Ptolemaic rule was restricted to Alexandria, and the foreign possessions and all building activities in Egypt were halted during the reign of Ptolemy IV and later.[107]

Before the rebellion, that is, between 221 and 207, some major building projects could be carried out. The sanctuary of Mut/Anta, which stood in the southwest, outside the main precinct of Amun at TANIS, was replaced by a new building (plan I). A 105 x 150 m enclosure wall, of unknown date, surrounded the temple. The main entrance in the enclosure, a brick pylon of Siamun, the founder of the temple, received a 17 x 27.75 m entrance kiosk with four-by-six limestone columns.[108] Deep limestone foundations suggest a solid stone temple of 33.2 x 53 m, but the plan of the temple can no longer be reconstructed. The foundation deposits date at least from the start of the construction to Ptolemy IV.

The temple of Min at AKHMIM (Panopolis), which was probably built under Ptolemy III, was embellished by a marvelous pronaos, the gigantic dimensions of which surpassed all other pronaoi in Upper Egypt.[109] The building, which was still standing in A.D. 1350, was described by several Arab writers (see the buildings of Ptolemy III Euergetes I), who clarify some basic points. According to the writers, the pronaos had forty columns, which may have been arranged in four rows of ten each. It had a width of 85 m, a depth of 30 m, and a height of 21 m. The huge stone slab of the roof was especially praised as creating a great impression.

North of the modern town of Akhmim, rubble mounds were still visible in the nineteenth century under the name Birba ("temple"), suggesting the site of the temple. One of several huge limestone blocks carried the cartouches of Ptolemy IV Philopator.[110] A palm capital was also seen, comparable to the palm columns of the nearby pronaos of Antaeopolis, built by Ptolemy VI.

The Arab writer Ad-Dimashqi (d. 1327) also describes a huge gate (or pylon?) with the double representation of the felling of enemies. Was the building identical with a gate seen in the last century, 30 m south of the temple ruin, and dated by an inscription to the reign of Trajan?

Remains of a text with cartouches of Ptolemy IV and Arsinoe III suggest, that the Anty temple of ANTAEOPOLIS was begun already under this king.[111] Since the evidence is meager, the Anty temple is examined in connection with the temple's pronaos, which was built under Ptolemy VI Philometor.

In the precinct of MEDAMOUD, the work on a birth house(?) begun under Ptolemy III was continued. A gate was constructed in front of the main temple of the New Kingdom. Blocks of the gate were found reused in the court of Ptolemy VIII and are now reconstructed in the Musée des Beaux-Arts in Lyon.[112] The gate was a rather modest passage, with a broken lintel and a height of about 4 m.

Building activity at KARNAK was insignificant and restricted to a brick Osiris tomb in the northeast corner of the precinct of Amun.[113] These enhancements of the Osiride aspects of Amun during the Ptolemaic period were a continuation of tendencies that began under Osorkon III and the 25th Dynasty.

Under Ptolemy IV, a new temple for Hathor was built in the rock bay of DEIR EL-MEDINE, replacing a building of the New Kingdom that had been damaged by the Persians and repaired by Ptolemy II and III. The new 15 x 24 m temple was built with its rear against the high cliffs and was surrounded by a brick enclosure wall (figs. 122–125). A cult terrace was constructed opposite the temple entrance, in the east wall of the enclosure.

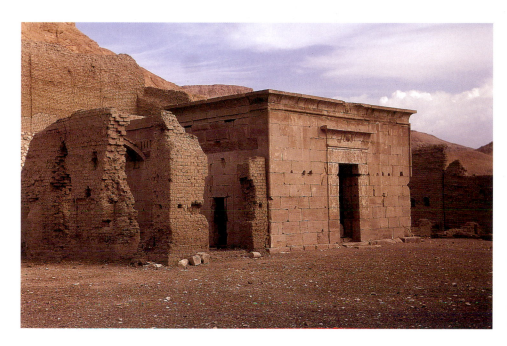

Figure 122.
The temple of Ptolemy IV
for Hathor of Deir el-Medine
seen from the southeast
(photo A.B.).

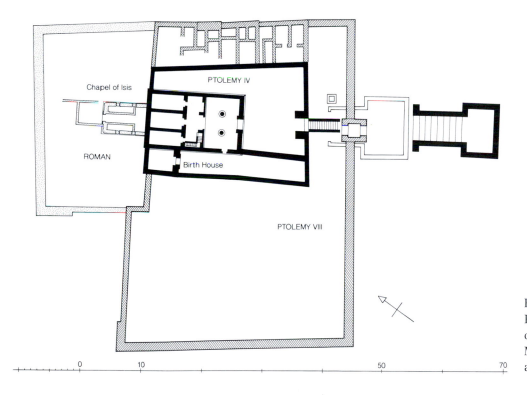

Figure 123.
Plan of the precinct
of Hathor of Deir el-
Medine in Ptolemaic
and Roman times.

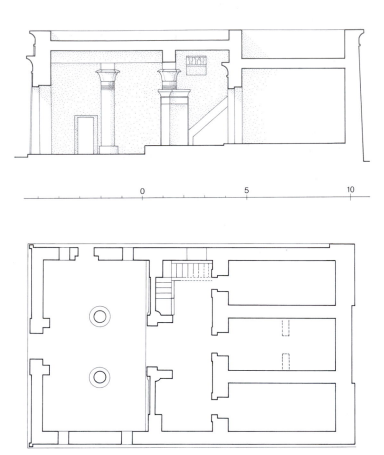

0   5   10

Figure 124.
Longitudinal section and plan
of the temple of Ptolemy IV
for Hathor of Deir el-Medine.

The plain exterior walls of the temple enclosed an interesting architectural arrangement that unites an entrance hall or forecourt with the facade of a pronaos.[114] The pronaos front rises on a step behind the entrance hall and has two columns with composite capitals *in antis*. On three sides the antae piers display engaged Hathor columns. Columns and piers are connected by screen walls. The broad room behind the columns and piers corresponds to an offering hall and includes the usual staircase to the temple roof. In the side wall above the staircase is a window with a fine stone grill composed of two miniature Hathor columns and a composite column.[115] Three parallel shrines open beyond the offering hall. The central room was dedicated to Hathor, and its entrance was accordingly decorated with a frieze of seven Hathor heads. One side chamber was dedicated to Osiris and the other to deities of the necropolis.

The renovation program of the temple precinct of Monthu at EL-TÔD, begun under the kings of the 30th Dynasty, was resumed under Ptolemy IV. The decoration of the temple walls was completed under Ptolemy XII.[116] The area of the sanctuary, the origins of which date to Senwosret I, had been replaced in the 30th Dynasty. Only the front wall survived and was integrated

into the new structure. Now, the front part of the temple also was leveled down to the foundation platform and replaced by a hypostyle hall and a pronaos of modest size (fig. 126). The Ptolemaic temple house is now so badly destroyed that one cannot see how much of the old ground plan was maintained, as was the case at Medamoud. Only half of the front of the 25 m wide and 10 m deep pronaos still stands. The pronaos had two rows of four columns, which probably carried composite capitals. The wide intercolumniations (5.5 m) suggest slender proportions and a light appearance of the building. Behind the pronaos stood a two-columned hall with side chambers. The decoration of the pronaos continued until the reign of Antoninus Pius. Twenty meters east of the temple, a sacred lake was begun but only completed in 88 B.C.

The old internal enclosure wall was replaced by a wider brick wall that also enclosed a bark station of Thutmosis III (plan XI). A huge, 11.60 m wide gate (A) offered access to the precinct. In front, a stone-paved allée flanked by fourteen pairs of sphinxes led north to an outer enclosure wall with the gate (P). A huge cult terrace with a wide access ramp was constructed in front of gate (P). It is remarkable that the axis of the Ptolemaic buildings abandoned that of the New Kingdom and returned to the axis of the Middle Kingdom temple, so that the bark station of Thutmosis III stood at an oblique angle to the Ptolemaic structure.

Figure 125.
Interior of the temple of Ptolemy IV for Hathor of Deir el-Medine (*Description* II, pl. 37).

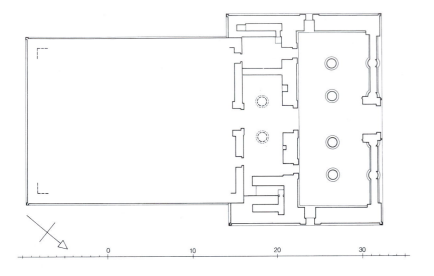

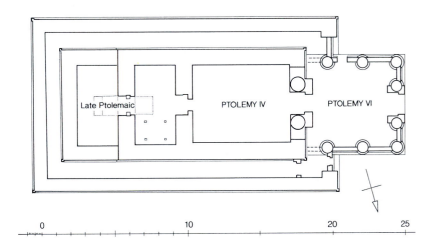

Figure 126. *(top)*
Detailed plan of the temple of
Monthu at El-Tôd.

Figure 127. *(bottom)*
Plan of the Ptolemaic temple
of Arsnouphis on Philae.

After only twenty-five years of work, the main building and decoration of the temple house of Ptolemy III at EDFU, was completed in 212.

According to a recent study, an Osiris tomb was built under Ptolemy IV on ELEPHANTINE. Single blocks exist, but there are no traces of the building itself.[117] The tomb may have stood north of the temple of Satet between a "House of Life" and a chapel of Imhotep.

A small temple for the Nubian lion god Arsnouphis was built under Ptolemy IV on PHILAE (figs. 127, 192, plan XIV). It stood at the southern end of the forecourt, on top of the remains of an older building. Considerable parts of the elaborately decorated walls were reconstructed in 1895/1896 by H. G. Lyons from blocks found in surrounding houses.[118] More blocks appeared when the temple was dismantled in 1972.

Psametik-Sa Neith Menkheperre (period of 207–186)

The temple of the ancient falcon god Hemen at ASFÛN EL-MATÂ'NA (10 km north of Esna) was probably extended under the rule of the Upper Egyptian rival kings of Ptolemy IV. The cartouches of King Psametik-sa-Neith Menkheperre were seen in 1905, on a temple wall under a high mound, occupied by a mosque. Unfortunately, no further excavation has taken place, and nothing else is known about the temple, which seems to have been of major importance from the Old Kingdom on.[119]

Ergamenes II (Arqamani, 218–200) and Adikhalamani (ca. 200–190)

The Kushite ruler Ergamenes II used the Upper Egyptian rebellion (207/206–187/186) to incorporate Lower Nubia and Aswan into his kingdom. He and his successor Adikhalamani, ruled at the same time as Ptolemy IV and Ptolemy V and appear as the builders of small chapels in former Ptolemaic territory at Dakka, Dabod, and Philae.[120] The projects were carried out with the help of the priesthood of Philae.

On PHILAE, the decoration of older buildings (birth house, temple of Arsnouphis) continued under Ergamenes II, who seemed to have particularly favored the cult of Isis. His cartouches were erased, however, after the reconquest of Upper Egypt by the Ptolemies and (posthumously) replaced with the names of Ptolemy IV by Ptolemy V.

At DABOD a Ramesside chapel was replaced by a 3.14 x 5.03 m chapel built by Adikhalamani, topped by the usual cavetto cornice. The chapel was dedicated to the favorite deities of the Meroites Amun and Isis. This shrine was enlarged under Ptolemy VI and became a real temple.

At DAKKA, a single-room chapel topped by a cavetto was built under Ergamenes II on a 5 x 6.8 m base (fig. 128). The chapel, dedicated to Thoth and Isis, later became the core of a relatively large Ptolemaic-Roman temple. The chapel underwent only small alterations during these additions and is still well preserved. The first alteration occurred under a succeeding Ptolemy, who built a gate with a broad hall and inscribed it with the names of Ptolemy II, III, and IV.[121]

Ptolemy V Epiphanes (205–180)

The premature death of Ptolemy IV and the ascent of his young son, Ptolemy V Epiphanes, had serious consequences for the ruling family in particular and for Egypt in general. For some time, the self-proclaimed guardians Sosibios and Agathokles succeeded in halting the collapse of the Ptolemaic empire, but the coast of Anatolia and Koilesyria, along with Tyros and Sidon, was lost.

After the brutal suppression of the Delta rebellion in 196, Epiphanes was crowned pharaoh in Memphis. The famous granite stela of Rosetta, which enabled Champollion to decipher Egyptian hieroglyphs, dates to that year.[122] The stela was found by Napoleonic troops in the fort Saint Julien at Rosetta and probably originally stood in the temple of Neith at Sais, confirming the restoration of Ptolemaic rule in the Delta.

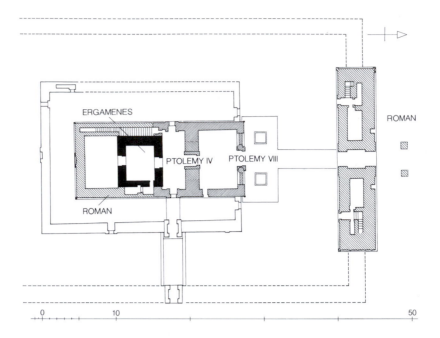

ERGAMENES

PTOLEMY IV   PTOLEMY VIII

ROMAN

ROMAN

0   10   50

Figure 128.
Plan of the Ptolemaic-Roman
temple for Isis of Dakka.

The government's financial difficulties and the rule of local opponents prevented new Ptolemaic building activity in Upper Egypt until 186.[123] After the restitution of Ptolemaic rule in 187/186, the entire royal family traveled to Upper Egypt and visited Philae. A few years later, in 180, Ptolemy V, who was only thirty years old, was assassinated by his generals. Most of the building projects begun by Ptolemy V could be completed only by his successors.

After the establishment of peace in the Delta, the temple of the lion deity Miysis (Mihos) of LEONTOPOLIS was rebuilt or restored. No traces of that building now remain.

For the occasion of his coronation at MEMPHIS in 196, Ptolemy V gave donations to the cults of the Memphite gods and for the restoration of the Apieion. Under Ptolemy V, a gateway was built connecting the Bubasteion with the Anubieion of Saqqara. A huge limestone block with images of the king and Anubis and a cavetto block with the name of Ptolemy V found in the Anubieion suggest that the central temple of Anubis built by Amasis was replaced by a prominent new building. Only the foundation platform now remains.[124]

Under Ptolemy V, a new temple was built for Khnum at ESNA. The temple was 19 m wide and probably 40 to 45 m long. The modest building grew to monumental dimensions during the early Roman Imperial Period with the addition of the famous pronaos. Only the facade of the Ptolemaic temple house at the back wall of the pronaos is still preserved; the actual temple itself has disappeared. The inside wall of the front of the temple house preserves traces of a small hypostyle hall with two columns and side chambers with a two-story side chamber (fig. 215). The latter probably contained an Osiris sanctuary, similar to the temples of Dendera, Edfu, and Philae. The decoration of the front of the temple was continued under Ptolemy VI; its interior, as can be seen at the inside wall of the front of the temple house, was never decorated.

In the nearby temple Pi-Khnum of Ptolemy III at Kôm el-Deir, the work was resumed on the unfinished decoration.

In the temple of Nekhbet at EL-KÂB, two blocks were found with the image of Ptolemy V. Since no building activities are known in the temple after Nectanebo II, the blocks might have belonged to restoration activities made necessary after damage suffered during the Upper Egyptian rebellion.

On PHILAE, the extension plans of Nectanebo I and Ptolemy II were also resumed. Certainly after 186, that is, in the last six years of Ptolemy V, the southern front part of the enclosure wall of Nectanebo I was taken down and replaced by a 20 m high (first) pylon, which incorporated the 180-year-old gate of Nectanebo I (fig. 129, plan XIV). The decoration of the pylon continued during the reigns of Ptolemy VI and XII. A side entrance through the west tower of the pylon leads directly to the birth house inside the court. The well-proportioned pylon is completely preserved up to the cavetto molding. A full-scale sketch of a column of the temple court was drawn on the cavetto of the pylon and used by the sculptors to transfer measurements to their work (fig. 130).

The staircase conducting from the south up to the temple platform was guarded by a pair of seated lions of archaic appearance, which might represent the Meroitic lion deity Arsnouphis.

In front of the eastern tower of the pylon, a 5.4 x 6.6 m chapel was built for the deified Imhotep (fig. 131).[125] Ptolemy V and his wife Cleopatra I dedicated the small sanctuary after the birth of their son, who later became Ptolemy VI. The decoration of the temple facade is representative of the harmonious layout of Ptolemaic wall decoration. The extension of the reliefs suggests that

Figure 129.
View of the pylon of Ptolemy V enclosing the gate of Nectanebo I on Philae (photo A.B.).

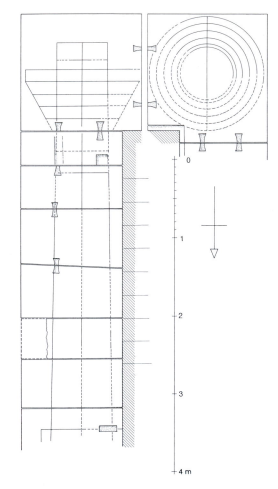

Figure 130.
Full-scale sketch for a column
on top of the first pylon of Philae (after Ludwig Borchardt,
"Altägyptische Werkzeichnungen," *ZÄS* 34 [1896]: pl. III).

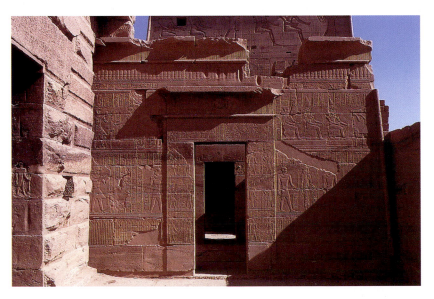

Figure 131.
The sanctuary of Ptolemy V
and Cleopatra I for Imhotep on
Philae (photo A.O.).

an entrance kiosk was planned, which would have transformed the facade into part of an interior room.

The small, unfinished Arsnouphis temple of Ptolemy IV was also extended and its decoration continued. The rear wall of the double-room sanctuary was opened in order to add a third chamber, which contained a granite naos (fig. 127).

Ptolemy VI Philometor (180–145)

Ptolemy VI, the son of Ptolemy V Epiphanes, ascended the throne as an underaged child, and his incompetent regents soon plunged the country into a renewed war against Syria. Their troops were beaten by Antiochus IV at Pelusium, the Delta was lost, and the young king Ptolemy VI was placed under the protectorate of the Seleucides. During a later campaign, Antiochus IV even conquered Memphis and was crowned coregent of Ptolemy VI. Under pressure from Rome, Antiochus IV was forced to retreat from Egypt, a country that was now engulfed in chaos under the triple rule of Ptolemy VI, his sister consort, Cleopatra II, and his younger brother Ptolemy VIII. The problems were increased by the hunger-inspired revolts of impoverished farmers in the Faiyum and the Thebais. In 164 Ptolemy VI was forced out of the country by Ptolemy VIII. Thereafter the rivals came to an agreement to divide the empire. Ptolemy VIII received Cyrene, and Ptolemy VI returned to Egypt. Despite these struggles, Ptolemy VI Philometor ruled the country as an unusually benefi-cent king until 145. Sanctuaries that had suffered war damage were repaired and new temples begun.

Ptolemy VI Philometor died in 145 B.C. near Antiochia in Syria, after fall-ing from a horse. This accident and the assassination of the son of Ptolemy VI finally opened the route to Alexandria and the throne for Ptolemy VIII Euer-getes II.

In the southern part of TANIS (called "Luxor" by the excavators), an older stone building of Apries was demolished in order to obtain building material for a new temple in the center of the city. The 200 x 300 m complex was ori-ented to the east and would have corresponded to the complex of Mut at Kar-nak—if one wishes to follow the impression gained from the general layout that Tanis was modeled on Thebes. The excavators assumed that the sanctu-ary was dedicated to Horus of Mesen.[126]

An intriguing architectural occurrence in the Delta was the construction of the Israelite temple at TELL EL-YAHUDIYA (17 km north of Heliopolis). After Antiochos IV sacked the temple of Jerusalem in 169–167 B.C., the Jewish high priest Onias and his followers fled to Egypt. Ptolemy VI allowed them to build a temple at a ruined ancient site. According to Josephus[127] and excava-tions of Petrie in 1905–6, the temple was located on a high acropolis and con-sisted of two elongated, successive forecourts ending with the actual temple house of 5.1 x 17.7 m. Petrie found Syrian-style battlements and Greek archi-tectural elements, reminding one of contemporary architecture in Israel.[128] In the year A.D. 71, Lupus, the prefect of Egypt, fearing that the Jewish revolt would spill over into Egypt, closed the temple of Onias, which soon afterward fell into decay.

Under Ptolemy VI, a large pronaos was erected in front of the temple of the falcon deity Anty (Antaios) at ANTAEOPOLIS (Qaw el-Kebir). Evidence consists of a Greek dedication text of Ptolemy VI and Cleopatra II on the central architrave of the pronaos.[129] Since the text mentions only the pronaos and Sir Gardner Wilkinson recorded another text with the name of Ptolemy IV, one might conclude that the pronaos was added to an existing, older temple house, built by Ptolemy IV.

The 85 x 260 m precinct, which faced northwest, was parallel to and dangerously close to the Nile, which was slowly changing its course. A 175 m long processional road led from a cult terrace in the north to the sanctuary. The allée passed a kiosk consisting of four by at least seven columns, apparently a bark station. The road then approached a monumental gate in the north wall of the enclosure. Some remaining architrave blocks (9.87 m long and weighing 43 tons) suggest the gigantic overall dimensions of the gate. The temple rose 85 m behind the gate in an open court (figs. 132–135). The elegant form of the pronaos can still be safely reconstructed thanks to the exact survey made by the Napoleonic expedition[130] and the Egyptian custom of linking the dimensions of a room to the diameter of its columns. The pronaos and the rest of the temple were washed away by the Nile between 1813 and 1821.

The pronaos contained three-by-six limestone palm columns. They were 11.625 m high (22 cubits 1 palm) and had a diameter of 2.325 m (4 cubits 3 palms), resulting in a proportion of 1:5. The column shafts, composed of twelve drums, were divided into three decoration registers by horizontal text bands. The dimensions of the pronaos can be calculated as 15.62 x 44.63 m.[131] The French expedition reconstructed seven gates in the front of the pronaos. The two outermost gates seem to be unnecessary, however, since the continuation of their path would have ended at the rear wall of the pronaos. The remaining five gates would have led to a central and four lateral bark shrines.[132] The four recipients of the cult assemblage around the god Anty are unknown. A row of five chapels arranged in a parallel line would not have allowed enough space for an ambulatory, an essential component of Ptolemaic temples. One may assume that the four secondary chapels were instead placed behind the pronaos. This arrangement would have left space for a central hypostyle hall with two rows of four columns.

Fifty-nine meters behind the facade of the temple, the limestone naos stood until 1813 in its original spot in the sanctuary. The carefully decorated naos was about 5 m high and topped by a steep pyramid-shaped roof.

The pronaos of Antaeopolis was a splendid example of classical Ptolemaic architecture. The conservative, harmonious forms and the uniformity of the palm columns gave the building an archaic severity that stressed the dynamic effect of vertical movement.

At the time of Nestor l'Hôte (1828–1839), a small chapel stood in the southeast corner of the brick enclosure of the Roman fortress of DIOSPOLIS PARVA (Hiw). Osiris was depicted in a niche at the rear wall.[133] The chapel was probably part of a larger Ptolemaic temple, the foundations of which were seen by Flinders Petrie in 1898–1899. Some relief blocks that had fallen into the foundation pit showed scenes of the king making offerings to Isis. A sandstone architrave preserved the name of Ptolemy VI.[134]

Figure 132.
View of the temple
of Ptolemy VI for
Anty of Antaeopolis
in 1798 (*Description
IV*, pl. 40).

Figure 133.
The temple of Ptolemy VI
for Anty of Antaeopolis
(computer reconstruction
by Barry Girsh).

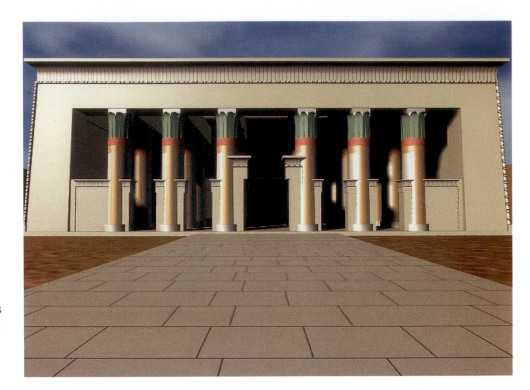

Figure 134.
Frontal view of the pronaos
of the temple of Ptolemy VI
for Anty of Antaeopolis
(computer reconstruction
by Barry Girsh).

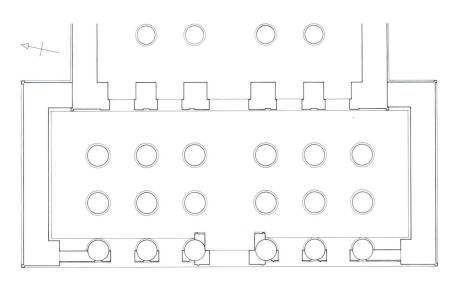

Figure 135.
Plan of the pronaos of
Ptolemy VI at the temple of
Anty of Antaeopolis.

At DENDERA, the birth house of Isis, located behind the Hathor temple, was extended by a porch of two-by-three central columns (figs. 161, 184). The front of the hall was later replaced with a row of four smaller columns. Because the lateral walls joined the corner columns with their lower parts, one may assume that the front parts of the side walls were open on top, producing, in an unusual way, the illusion that the building had a small pronaos. The birth house was later enlarged under Ptolemy X Alexander I and Augustus.

At KARNAK, the huge gate of the second pylon was restored. Its surface and decoration had sustained fire damage, probably when the wooden door wings were burned during the Upper Egyptian rebellion that took place under Ptolemy IV. Because wooden doors of such dimensions could be moved only with great efforts, and therefore were more symbolic, a smaller *avant-porte* was built into the door frame.

The temple of Ptah received a large new gate—probably along with the construction of a new brick enclosure. In the precinct of Mut, a small chapel was built (D),[135] and in the enclosure of Amunra-Monthu, a pylon was added to the 30th Dynasty birth house.

Relief blocks from ARMANT carry cartouches of Ptolemy VI Philometor and Ptolemy IX Soter II and attest to work during these reigns, probably in the main temple of Monthu.

At KOM OMBO, a new temple was started under Ptolemy VI (figs. 136–137, plan XIII). The building, which was to become a masterwork of Ptolemaic architecture, was conceived as a double temple with two processional axes, one leading to the sanctuary of Haroeris ("Horus the Elder," north) and the other to the sanctuary of Sobek (south). The building had a New Kingdom predecessor of which only a few elements remain.

Figure 136.
Plan of the temple for Haroeris and Sobek of Kom Ombo under Ptolemy VI.

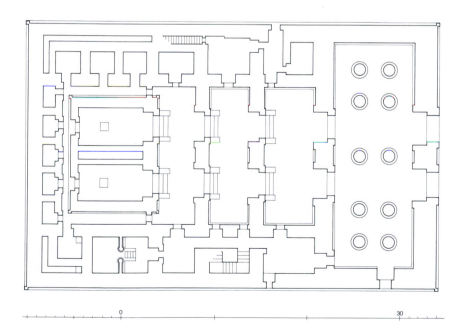

Figure 137.
The hypostyle hall of the temple of Ptolemy VI for Haroeris and Sobek of Kom Ombo seen from the south (photo A.O.).

The 28.5 x 44 m building had a double gate in its facade and two side entrances (fig. 97). The facade was in an unusual way crowned like a shrine by an uraeus frieze. An ambulatory surrounded the two main sanctuaries, which had black granite pedestals for the barks. Because the pedestals left no room for wooden statue shrines, the statues must have been housed in the barks or in the chambers behind the bark shrines. To the front, three broad rooms and a hypostyle hall follow each other. The rear wall of the innermost hall consisted of the facades of the two bark shrines and the entrances into the ambulatory, which had ten side chapels. The staircases to the roof were located at either end of the second hall. Similar to the arrangement in Edfu, the northern staircase was right-angled, the southern one straight. Side rooms branched off to either side of the first broad room and probably served for the production of ointments and other offerings. The large hypostyle hall that followed in front had two-by-five columns with open papyrus capitals.

As a result of the temple's orientation, the New Years' festival court, with its *wabet*, was located in the northern half of the temple. The relatively small unit is now completely destroyed. Numerous crypts were built into the exterior walls of the temple. Inside the separation wall of the two bark shrines, remains of three stories of crypts are visible, one below ground. The drainage system of the roof included lion-headed water spouts.[136]

The balanced proportions of the temple and the high quality of the masons' work reveal the high standard of Ptolemaic building. The partially sunk but mostly raised reliefs and the remains of their painted surfaces provide good examples of Ptolemaic surface articulation.

The decoration of the interior of the temple house was concluded under Ptolemy VIII Euergetes II, that of the exterior walls only under Nero and Vespasian.[137]

Another project of Ptolemy VI was the completion and decoration of the temple house of Khnum on ELEPHANTINE, which had been suspended since the 30th Dynasty; at the same time, a pronaos was added to the older structure (fig. 138). The unusually shallow pronaos had a double row of six columns, which supported a ceiling with astronomical decoration.[138] The forecourt was regarded as too narrow and therefore was extended to the east.

The 18th and 26th Dynasty Satet temple, which had probably been damaged by the Persians in 343 was, according to a building graffito in a foundation trench, taken down in 168 and a new temple begun in 164 under Ptolemy VI (fig. 138).[139] The 18.38 x 23.63 m (35 x 45 cubits) temple was built 30 m north of the Khnum temple, on a 2.7 m lower level. The half-preserved foundation platform helps to reconstruct the temple's plan. Despite a 180-year time difference, the new temple replicated, on a smaller scale, the Khnum temple. However, the first broad room was so small that its ceiling did not have to be supported by columns, and granite was used only for the frame of the main door. Crypts were hidden in the foundations of the sanctuaries. The Satet temple even underwent similar enlargements as the Khnum temple. Its similarity to the Khnum temple emphasizes not only the close connection of the two cults but also the slow development in temple building from the 30th Dynasty to the middle of the Ptolemaic Period.

Probably at the same time, a large detached kiosk was built in front of the temple. Only parts of the foundations and the granite lintels of the eastern and western doors are preserved.[140] The roofing of the 10 m wide kiosk would have been a considerable technical feat, even if timbers were used.

Figure 138.
Plans of the temples of Khnum *(bottom right)* and Satet *(bottom left)* on Elephantine.

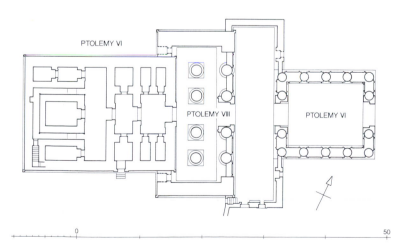

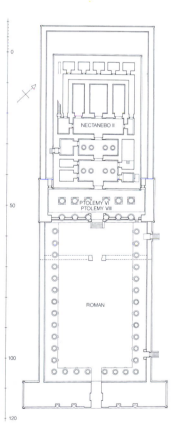

Perhaps in the last years of Ptolemy V, a new building project was designed for PHILAE, but extensive work could not have been undertaken in the few years between the end of the Upper Egyptian rebellion and the death of the king. However, construction work could have progressed after 180, under Ptolemy VI Philometor. The "Dodekaschoines-Stela" of the year 158, cut into the rock at the second pylon, attests that the building project was concluded by Ptolemy VI.[141]

The old, rather modest temple house of Nectanebo II or Ptolemy II became more impressive with the addition of a second, 13 m high inner pylon followed by a combination of a colonnaded interior court and a pronaos (figs. 139–140). From the outer court with the birth house, a staircase ramp climbed the bedrock up to the new pylon. Against all building tradition, the gate does not carry the usual cavetto cornice, and the two niches for the flagpoles, which traditionally are found on pylon facades, are located high up in the pylon's front. At the same time, the pylon forms the front part of an inner stone enclosure wall and an outer brick enclosure wall. Preserved parts of the stone wall reveal not only recesses and projections but also wave-shaped bedding joints. The undulating courses are stone duplicates of the similarly constructed 30th Dynasty brick walls. The combination of a colonnaded court and a pronaos behind the pylon is caused by the lack of space on the short granite outcrop. The deviation of the axis of the new pylon from that of the older temple is also a result of this problem, which produced complicated distortions in the building elements.

M.-A. Lancret of the Napoleonic expedition described the colorfully painted court and its ten columns:

> Today only one column is remarkably weathered; and in order to see the portico nearly as shining as it is presented by our illustration, one only has to wipe the dust and remove the debris which has accumulated. The colors are as one can see four, yellow, green, blue, and a more or less deep red. One could also add white. For white is not the color of the stone but applied with the brush.[142]

One could suspect the influence of Hellenistic architecture in the ease and elegance of the column proportions. However, the columns are so self-confidently conceived and shaped as a unified whole that potential foreign influence cannot have had great impact. The arrangement of the capitals displays an intricate configuration (see diagram).

The temple built by Ptolemy IV and V on PHILAE for Arsnouphis was enlarged under Ptolemy VI (or VIII?). An entrance kiosk with eight columns was built (fig. 127). Its roof must have been timbered and may have had a segmented pediment at the front.[143] Probably at the same time, the core building was surrounded by a corridor that connected at the front with the entrance kiosk. The corridor was decorated under Tiberius and probably carried a roof that rested on the old temple house of Arsnouphis. The easternmost intercolumniation of the kiosk of Ptolemy VI was opened on both sides to provide access to the ambulatory.

A small temple for Hathor was built under Ptolemy VI to the east and outside of the precinct of Isis (fig. 141).[144] The building contained a tiny pronaos

*Painted Court,
Isis Temple at Philae*

BACK

a - d - d - c
b - b - b - b
a - - - - - a

FRONT

a: Palm capitals
b: Four-stem, two-tiered papyrus capitals with palmettes in the spandrels
c: Open bell-shaped papyrus capitals
d: Single-stem, one-tiered, bell-shaped papyrus capitals with palmettes in the spandrels

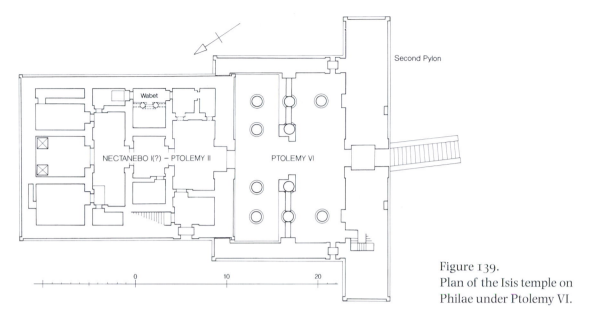

Second Pylon

Wabet

NECTANEBO I(?) – PTOLEMY II

PTOLEMY VI

0   10   20

Figure 139.
Plan of the Isis temple on
Philae under Ptolemy VI.

Figure 140.
Columns in the hypostyle hall of the
Isis temple on Philae built under
Ptolemy VI (David Roberts, *Egypt and
Nubia* [London, 1846], frontispiece).

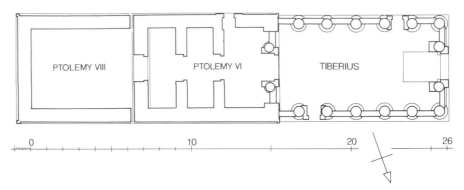

Figure 141.
Plan of the Ptolemaic/Roman temple for Hathor on Philae.

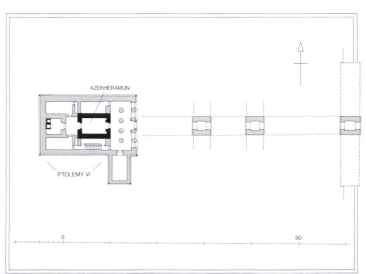

Figure 142.
Plan of the temple of
Ptolemy VI for Isis of Dabod.

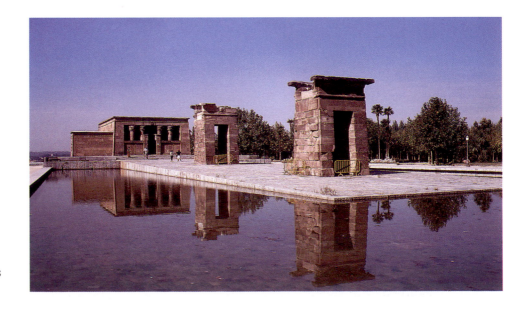

Figure 143.
The temple of Ptolemy VI for
Isis of Dabod, transferred in
1972 to the Parque de Rosales
in Madrid (photo A.B.).

with two columns and two broad rooms behind it. The location of the chapel, without a recognizable relationship to the approach to the main Isis temple or a connection to the Nile, is remarkable. The front of the temple, which had two columns *in antis*, was typical of the smaller temples of the Ptolemaic and Roman Periods, such as the temple of Arsnouphis on Philae and the temples of Taffeh, Dendur, and Dakka. The Hathor temple was considerably enlarged under Augustus.

Also under Ptolemy VI, the single-room chapel of the Meroitic king Adikhalamani at DABOD was extended on all four sides (figs. 142–143). The modest Amun temple was now rededicated to Isis of Philae. The facade of the temple house was a pronaos *tetrastyle in antis*. The composite capitals remained unfinished, while the decoration was slowly carried on until Augustus and Tiberius. A long processional approach connected a cult terrace at the Nile with the entrance gate of the enclosure wall. The broad, paved road passed through two further gates inside the enclosure and finally reached the temple house. These internal gates were probably freestanding, neither flanked by pylons nor connected to an enclosure. The pronaos collapsed in 1868 and was lost. The temple was removed in 1960–1961 as part of the dam rescue project and was rebuilt in 1972 in the Parque de Rosales near the royal palace of Madrid.[145]

Ptolemy VIII Euergetes II (164–163 and 145–116)

Ptolemy VIII, detested by the Romans as a weakling, was a complex character: cold-blooded assassin, clever politician, classicist, and benefactor of Egypt. After his return from exile in 145, he was crowned pharaoh in Memphis, but he was again expelled from Egypt in 132 by his sister consort, Cleopatra II (the widow of Ptolemy VI). In 127, he again brought Alexandria under his control and reconciled with the queen. In spite of his capricious political performance, Ptolemy VIII proved to be one of the most outstanding temple builders of the Ptolemaic Period. He died in 116 after an exceptionally long reign of fifty-four years, leaving the throne to the machinations of the two competing queens Cleopatra II and III.[146]

The impressive temple fortress of TAPOSIRIS MAGNA (Abusir, 45 km west of Alexandria), dedicated to Osiris, dominates a rocky mound with a vast view over the dark blue Mediterranean sea (fig. 144).[147] A pylon, with staircases in both towers, leads through the eastern part of the 84 x 84 m stone enclosure wall. Side entrances pierce the north and south walls. The 3.5 m thick enclosure wall includes the shallow recesses and projections that belong to the construction principles of brick walls, a late example of the old practice of translating brick into stone.[148]

The actual temple house that was inside the court is now lost, its place occupied by the ruins of a church. A spectacular, 2.55 m high granite naos dedicated by Amasis to Osiris of the Mariout, might originate from a Saite predecessor of the Taposiris temple.[149] A study of the architecture and date of the temple is still lacking, and an attribution to Ptolemy VIII is arbitrary. In the east, outside the remains of the town, a 17 m high lighthouse reflects the form of the Pharos tower in Alexandria.

Figure 144.
The pylon of the Ptolemaic temple of Taposiris magna (Abusir).

At DENDERA, a bark chapel was built for Hathor, situated west of the old Hathor temple. All that remains today are its access ramp and stone gate. The actual building behind them was made of brick and is now gone.[150]

Under Ptolemy VIII, a small 5.24 m high gate was built in COPTOS, at an unknown spot, perhaps in the southern part of the precinct. A few of its decorated blocks were preserved in the foundations of a later building (Augustan?) situated between the temple of Min and the sacred lake.[151]

Under Ptolemy VIII, a 9 m wide monumental gate was built in front of the Haroeris and Heqat temple at QÛS (Apollinopolis parva). The gate is now reduced to its lower block courses.[152] Since such gates were often erected in connection with a new temple, one might suspect that the temple house itself, which is now buried under the modern town, might also date to Ptolemy VIII. Judging from the size of the gate and a later western one, the temple should have had huge dimensions. In its sanctuary stood a naos of Ptolemy II.

The later building history of the Ptolemaic temple of Monthu at MEDA-MOUD is not yet quite clear (plan VII).[153] Reused blocks from buildings that belonged to the 25th and 26th Dynasty divine consorts of Amun and of Ptolemy II, III, and IV were discovered in the foundations of the court and pylon. They probably originally belonged to gates and chapels in the area of the later pronaos and court that fell victim to an enlargement of the temple under Ptolemy VIII.

A small birth house(?) had been built under Ptolemy III in the southwest part of the complex. Years after the Upper Egyptian rebellion (207/206 B.C.) during the reign of Ptolemy IV, Ptolemy VIII renewed the damaged(?) main temple (fig. 145). The ground plan shows that the renewal process differed from those at Dendera and Edfu. The old temple was not completely removed

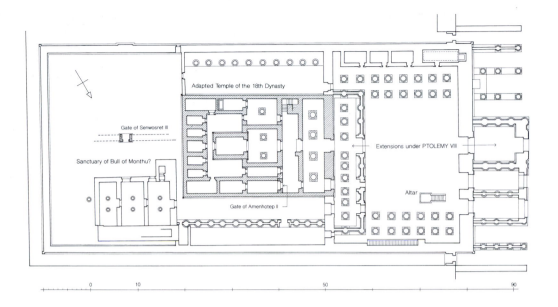

Figure 145.
Plan of the Ptolemaic temple
of Monthu at Medamoud
(see plan VII).

and replaced by a new building. Instead, the foundations, ground plan, and parts of the aboveground masonry were reverently retained, among them gates of Senwosret III and Amenhotep II. The 21 x 32 m temple house therefore displays a mixture of elements from the Middle and New Kingdom and Ptolemaic Periods. The layout of the rooms and the relationship between the room proportions and the thickness of the walls are reminiscent of earlier buildings. Typical for the Ptolemaic time is the freestanding sanctuary with a row of five chapels behind it as well as the chamfered edges of the columns of the hypo-style hall. Besides Monthu, his consort Raittaui and their son Harpokrates were adored here. The condition of the ruin does not allow specific rooms to be assigned to a particular deity.

Also under Ptolemy VIII, a 28.3 m wide and 5.7 m deep pronaos was added to the temple house, which was shifted asymmetrically to the north. The pronaos consisted of a double row of eleven, 7.6 m high columns. Since the pronaos accommodated three parallel entrance axes, the columns were arranged in groups of 2-2-3-4 (fig. 146). The first axis in the north passed along the side of the temple house and led to a western building complex, which allegedly was the area where the sacred bull of Monthu was kept. The middle axis gave access to a subsidiary shrine, while the southern axis led into the main sanctuary of Monthu.

The four columns flanking the central axis carried open, quatrefoil papyrus capitals; the nine other supports had closed papyrus capitals. The shape of some column shafts contradicted Ptolemaic style. Those of the inner row of columns were planed out. In the front row, only the two columns at the main entrance were carved with perfect bundles that had main and secondary stems reaching down to the foot. Of the nine other shafts, only the main stems reach down to the foot, whereas the secondary stems end planed out in the upper third. The columns with quatrefoil papyrus capitals not only included

Figure 146.
Columns of court and pronaos
of the temple of Monthu at
Medamoud (photo A.O.).

the usual cords around their necks but also have two more ties around the
shaft.[154] These irregularities impaired the uniformity of the facade as well as
the building behind it and were probably intended to diminish the contrast
between the older and the newly added elements of the temple.

The excavators assumed that the temple was enlarged with a colonnaded
court and pylon under Antoninus Pius. However, the block bonding between
the pronaos of Ptolemy VIII and a wall bonding to the northern enclosure
wall (fig. 147) and between the foundations of the pylon and the two Ptolemaic entrance kiosks (see below) prove that the pronaos, enclosure wall,
court, pylon, and kiosks were built as a unit under Ptolemy VIII. The decoration continued until late in the Roman Period.

A 20 x 35 m court was built in front of the pronaos and flanked on both
long sides by a double row of columns. The preserved lower parts of the
columns suggest composite types, probably corresponding to those of the
pronaos. The front of the court was closed by a 44 m wide and only 3 m thick
and probably not very high pylon. The front part of the court and the pylon
joined the brick enclosure of the New Kingdom, which was apparently still
standing.

Several kiosks or entrance porches were built against the front of the
pylon, with their scale reflecting the rank of the entrances. The main gate
received the largest kiosk, which must have been roofed with timber. The two
secondary gates in the north shared one smaller kiosk with two parallel axes.
Again, architectural uniformity was sacrificed to cultic requirements. The
space south of the center kiosk was occupied by a light canopy protecting a

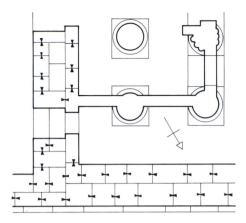

dais built against the pylon front. According to an inscription on the gate of Tiberius (see below), this installation served as a law court.

It is unknown whether the outer brick enclosure wall was also built under Ptolemy VIII. Since the main gate in this wall was erected under Tiberius (see chapter 8's discussion of the buildings of Tiberius), one would assume that the enclosure was built in Roman times. A secondary gate in the southwest seems to lead to Ptolemaic structures in the southwest corner of the court.

At KARNAK, the 30th Dynasty and early Ptolemaic building project of the Opet temple was resumed (figs. 110–111), a project that had produced only a gate in the main western enclosure wall of Amun and a small pylon in the planned forecourt. How much building work had been carried out before Ptolemy VIII is not yet clear. The Osiris crypt of the temple (see below) seems to go back to Ptolemy III. The main construction work and the decoration of the interior were carried out under Ptolemy VIII.

In close cultic affiliation to the temple of Khonsu, the temple of Opet created a stage for a cultic drama: Amun was thought to die in the form of Osiris, to enter the body of the mother goddess Opet-Nut, and to be reborn as Khonsu.[155] This motive of rebirth would actually identify the temple as the birth house of Khonsu.

The core building stands on a 1.9 m high, 19.6 x 22.7 m podium, which not only represents a primordial hill but also houses an underground tomb for Osiris and a birth chamber. From the court, a staircase ascended the platform. The ground plan of the temple is unusually tangled. The roof of the hypostyle hall is carried—appropriate to the goddess Opet—by composite capitals, with the added Hathor heads above composite capitals. The door lintels are adorned with uraeus friezes. Grids cover four large windows, placed directly beneath the ceiling. The central sanctuary consists of a square main room and a rear chamber with a niche for the cult image. The height of the podium, the raised proportions of the entire building, and the height of the doorways along the axis are remarkable features.

Since the end of the 20th Dynasty, the large royal "mortuary temples" of the New Kingdom in western Thebes were abandoned and exploited by stone

Figure 147.
The block bonding between the pronaos and a wall connecting to the northern enclosure of the temple of Monthu at Medamoud proves that pronaos, enclosure wall, and court were concurrent and the work of Ptolemy VIII.

robbers. Only the Hathor temple at Deir el-Medine and the temple of the primordial Amun of Medinet Habu were preserved as centers of the ancient cults. The Hathor temple at DEIR EL-MEDINE, built under Ptolemy IV, was provided with a new, monumental enclosure wall and a tiny birth house that leaned against the southern external wall (fig. 148). The decoration of the temple's interior continued.[156]

The temple of the primordial Amun of MEDINET HABU still enjoyed an esteemed reputation as a cult place related to that of Amun at Karnak. Ptolemy VIII apparently approved the restoration and embellishment of the sanctuary, which had last been renovated in the 26th and 30th Dynasties (plan X). The Kushite brick enclosure wall, which had been destroyed by numerous military actions, was rebuilt. The eastern section of the wall was converted into a pylon with a central entrance cased with sandstone. The front of the gate was embellished by an entrance kiosk with a pair of slender, widely spaced columns (figs. 149–150). Their composite, quatrefoil capitals still retain their original paint. The columns are 13.40 m high and have exceedingly slender proportions of 1:9 (diameter:total height). The 9 m intercolumniation could only have been bridged with timber. The kiosk was a masterpiece of Ptolemaic architecture.

At the same time, a small temple, the QASR EL-'AGUZ, was built southeast of Medinet Habu (fig. 151). The modest building was dedicated primarily to Thoth and the healer saint Imhotep but may have pursued aspects of the royal cult temples of the New Kingdom, creating a sanctuary for the cult of

Figure 148.
The precinct of Hathor at Deir el-Medine with the enclosure wall of Ptolemy VIII (photo Jan Roewer).

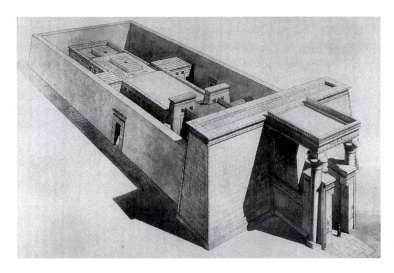

Figure 149.
Reconstruction of the portico of
Ptolemy VIII at Medinet Habu (Uvo
Hölscher, *The Temples of the Eighteenth
Dynasty* [Chicago, 1939], pl. 7).

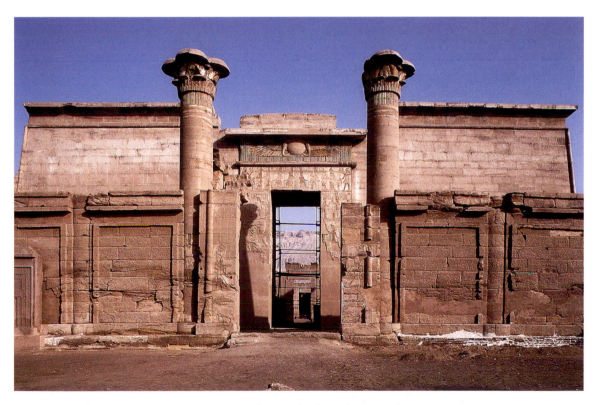

Figure 150. The portico of Ptolemy VIII at Medinet Habu from the east (photo A.O.).

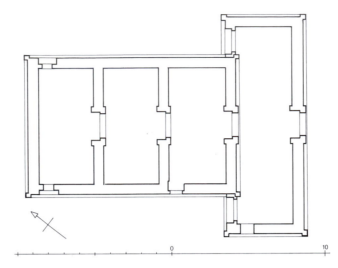

Figure 151.
Plan of the temple Qasr
el-ʿAguz of Ptolemy VIII at
Medinet Habu.

the Ptolemaic dynasty. The building has two sections. The front part consisted of a 14 m wide and perhaps 7 m high hall, similar to a pronaos but lacking columns. The hall was probably lit by means of large windows. The 8 x 13 m temple house lies behind the hall. The unadorned, box-shaped building was decorated only with a cavetto molding and contains, like the later temple of Kalabsha, three successive, broad rooms. The last room may have been the sanctuary, but side entrances lead directly to the exterior, an unusual arrangement for the most sacred part of the temple.[157] The temple was probably used as an oracle and a sanitarium.

A minor project was the transformation of the Amun sanctuary of the temple of Hatshepsut at DEIR EL-BAHARI into a chapel for the cult of Imhotep. For that purpose, the false door of the original room was removed from the rear wall and a deep rock chapel cut at its place. This work was certainly connected with the use of the temple as a sanitarium.

Under Ptolemy VIII, works were carried out at the Horus temple of EDFU, begun under Ptolemy III. For example, a roof kiosk was added and decorated. After a construction period of ninety-five years, the temple was inaugurated on September 9, 142 B.C. Ptolemy VIII and Cleopatra II attended the solemn ceremony of "presenting the house to its lord."[158]

The temple was regarded as inadequate, however, and on July 2, 140, the foundation stone for a great pronaos was laid (figs. 152–153). The addition, which was 34 m wide, 15.7 m deep, and 12.5 m high, was completed after sixteen years. The columns have chamfered bases, which sit on flat plinths above the pavement. Significant remains of paint invite a study of the color canon. Noteworthy is the layout of the column types, arranged in rows of three-by-six. In other pronaoi the sequence of capital types in the direction of the axis does not follow a recognizable pattern. Here the three rows of columns are linked by palm columns (b), which appear in all three rows, one behind the other (see diagram). A chapel for the purification of the priests was built into a left screen wall of the pronaos, a library for sacred papyri into the right one.

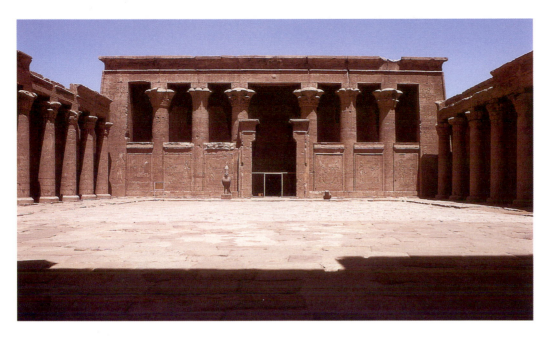

Figure 152.
The pronaos of
Ptolemy VIII at the
Horus temple at Edfu
seen from the south
(photo A.O.).

Figure 153.
The interior of the pronaos of
Ptolemy VIII at the Horus temple
at Edfu (photo A.O.).

A pair of monumental granite falcons that now sit in front of the pronaos probably belonged to the preceding 30th Dynasty temple.

After the year 124, a new birth house was built in the southwest corner of the enclosure, dedicated to the triad Horus, Hathor, and their son, the falcon-headed Harsomtus (Somtus) (figs. 154–155, 245). Three stairs lead to a podium on which a four-by-six column kiosk serves as an entry into the actual birth house. Its sanctuary is surrounded by an ambulatory. The high abaci of the composite capitals are decorated with Bes figures, a specific reference to the purpose of the building.[159] The decoration of the offering room and the addition of the entrance kiosk took place under Ptolemy IX Soter II.

These works still did not fulfill all the requirements of the cult. Plans were made for the construction of a colonnaded forecourt, a pylon, and a stone enclosure wall, and the digging of the foundation trenches had begun, when Ptolemy VIII died on June 28, 116 B.C.

At KOM OMBO, the architects of the Napoleonic expedition still found preserved the four Hathor columns and considerable parts of the walls of the birth house, with their splendid relief decoration of Ptolemy VIII (figs. 156–157, plan XIII). The building measured 18 x 23 m and was 9 m high. The plan was that of an ordinary temple with a room for visiting gods, an offering hall, and a sanctuary that was laterally isolated. The platform commonly found at birth houses existed, but the equally typical ambulatory, which was included in the birth houses of Ptolemy VIII at Philae and Edfu, was omitted.[160] Because of these peculiarities, the building resembled birth houses of the 30th Dynasty.

On ELEPHANTINE, a temple was built for the celebration of the rebirth of Osiris as the juvenile Khnum-Re. The temple probably stood north of the Nilometer and was connected with the Nile by a monumental staircase. Only about fifty disconnected blocks are preserved. The decoration was continued under Ptolemy IX Soter II, Ptolemy XII Neos Dionysos, and Tiberius.[161]

A pronaos with two-by-four columns was added to the nearby temple of Satet. Only the southern half of its foundation platform is now preserved. At the temple of Khnum, the building and decoration work begun under Ptolemy VI continued. The construction of the Khnum temple's pronaos was completed and the wall decoration begun (see fig. 138).

Following a royal visit to PHILAE in 115 B.C., the building activity begun by Ptolemy VI was resumed (fig. 192, plan XV). Two alterations transformed the forecourt of the Isis temple into a closed space. The east side was closed by a ten-column colonnade, which included five, two-story chambers. One room served as a laboratory for the sacred ointments, one was a priestly courtroom, and another was a library. The old birth house on the west side of the court was extended so that it reached the second pylon. The north wall of the birth house was removed and a new chapel added behind. For that purpose, the northern portico had to be shifted to the north and the resulting gap in the side porticoes closed with new columns (fig. 158). In addition, the terrace in front of the first pylon received a pair of 6.70 m high obelisks.[162]

Under Ptolemy VIII, a granite naos was dedicated to the main sanctuary of Isis and another in the northwestern side chapel.[163] A third naos of Ptolemy VIII was discovered in 1886, reused in a Coptic church. [164]

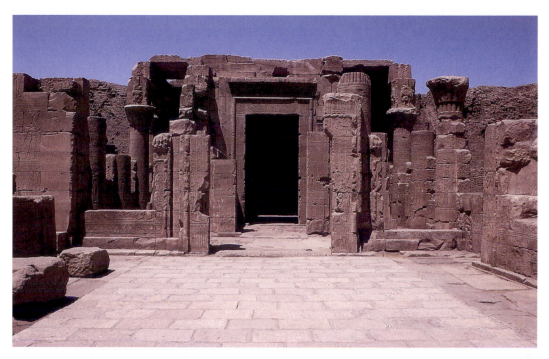

Figure 154.
Court and facade of
the birth house of
Ptolemy VIII for
Horus-Hathor-
Harsomtus of Edfu
(photo A.O.).

Figure 155.
End of the south side
of the birth house of
Ptolemy VIII for
Horus-Hathor-
Harsomtus of Edfu
(photo A.O.).

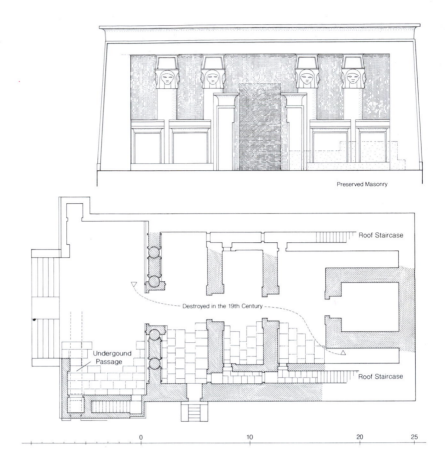

Preserved Masonry

Roof Staircase

Destroyed in the 19th Century

Undergound
Passage

Roof Staircase

0   10   20   25

Figure 156.
Reconstructed frontal elevation
and plan of the birth house of
Kom Ombo. Shaded areas on
plan recorded by the French
expedition.

The small temple that Ptolemy VI built for Hathor, north of the Isis temple,
was enlarged by means of a new sanctuary behind the original one, and the
temple enclosure wall was accordingly extended (fig. 141). The Arsnouphis
temple was enlarged in the same way, and the older granite naos was removed
into the addition. The cultic requirements that necessitated the enlargements
of these temples and of the birth house are not known (fig. 127).

The Thoth temple of Ergamenes II and Ptolemy VI at DAKKA (Pselchis)
was small. Under Ptolemy VIII the temple was enlarged by a pronaos that had
two front columns but no interior supports. Architraves over 6 m long bridged
the pronaos, however, and made more columns in the interior superfluous. At
the same time, the inner stone enclosure wall, which joined the front of the
pronaos, may have been built. A secondary doorway led through the stone
enclosure wall from the east directly into the interior of the temple. A comparison of the plans of Dabod and Dakka demonstrates how cultic requirements
and their architectural solutions differed from place to place. The temple of
Dakka was again enlarged in Roman times (fig. 128).

Ptolemy VIII also dedicated a 2.2 m high naos in the Isis temple at DABOD.
The naos was smashed in 1821 and carried away.

Figure 157.
The remains of the
facade of the birth
house of Ptolemy VIII
of Kom Ombo looking
north (photo A.O.).

Figure 158.
The birth house of
Isis on Philae after the
extension to the north
by three columns
under Ptolemy VIII
(photo A.O.).

Ptolemy IX Soter II, called Lathyros or Physkon
(116–107 and 88–80)

The fierce power struggle after the death of Ptolemy VIII led to a coregency of the "divine couple" Ptolemy IX, the son of Ptolemy VIII, and Cleopatra III, the daughter of Ptolemy VI. Soon the king traveled as a new pharaoh to Elephantine to perform the Festival of the Inundation. A few building projects document his—presumably politically motivated—interest in local cults.

An important project was the building of a new Triphis temple at ATHRIBIS (Wannina, south of Sohag) (plan V). The lioness goddess Triphis visited her consort Min in the "House of the Moon" in the neighboring Akhmim. Her temple complex is poorly explored and its shape rather obscure. The main, 39 x 45 m temple of the 26th Dynasty was set against the cliffs of the desert hills. The temple has only left a few traces in the bedrock. Under Ptolemy IX, the temple was either replaced by a new building or embellished with a huge 52.5 m wide stone pylon. At the same time, another, even bigger, stone pylon was built (10 x 70 m) in the northeast. The axis of that pylon is shifted so far that it seems to lead to a second, unexplored temple near the desert cliffs.

At KARNAK-NORTH, the embellishment of the forecourt of the temple of Amunra-Monthu, begun under Ptolemy III, was resumed (fig. 30). The decaying Kushite porch in front of the temple facade was taken down and replaced by a similar, new hall. The roof was carried by four rows of five columns, connected in the direction of the axis by screen walls. Because the two obelisks of Amenhotep III interrupted the alignment of the architraves, the roof between the second and third columns had to be left open. The main entrance into the 18th Dynasty temple of Amunra-Monthu was enhanced by a monumental gate in the old temple front.

Under Ptolemy IX Soter II, a small temple was built for Isis at EL-HILLA (Contralatopolis) on the east bank of the Nile opposite Esna (figs. 232–233).[165] The building history remains unclear because the temple was demolished in 1828. Several irregularities in the plan (shifting of the axis, different width of walls, wing chambers) suggest several building phases. The temple had a small pylon, about 10 m wide, with interior staircases. The modest temple house, with inscriptions of Ptolemy IX Soter II, was enlarged in Roman times by a pronaos.

The Ramesside rock chapel of Nekhbet-Hathor in the desert east of EL-KÂB was extended under Ptolemy IX Soter II and furbished with a front part that displays the originality of the Late Ptolemaic Period (fig. 159).[166] A monumental staircase ramp led to a 3.5 m high platform. The platform carried at the front a kiosklike structure of four-by-four columns with composite and floral capitals. The facade took the form of a kiosk with a front row of half-columns. The intercolumniations were closed, however. Unlike common kiosks, the building also had two rows of interior columns that carried a roof that was perhaps made of three parallel wooden barrel vaults with segmented pediments in front. An abundantly decorated and inscribed frontal gate was still recorded by Lepsius in 1843/1844 but is now destroyed. The rear wall of the kiosk, which was already gone at Lepsius's visit, may have matched the front wall.

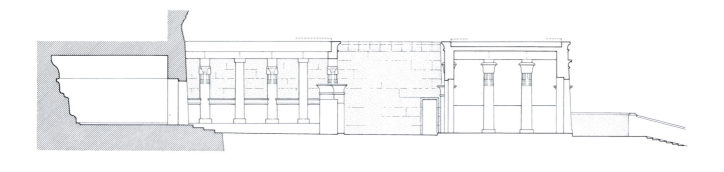

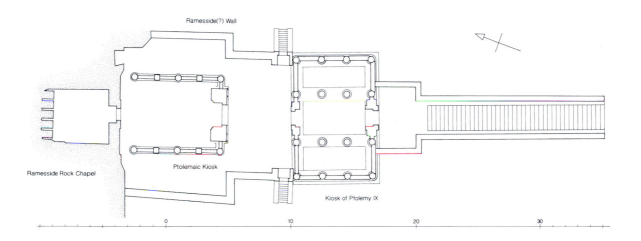

Ramesside(?) Wall

Ramesside Rock Chapel

Ptolemaic Kiosk

Kiosk of Ptolemy IX

0   10   20   30

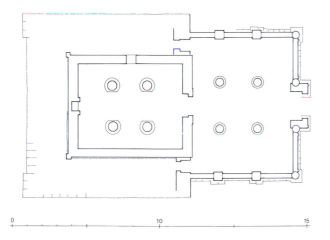

0   10   15

Figure 159.
Reconstructed longitudinal
section and plan of the *hemispeos* of
Ptolemy IX Soter II *(top and middle)* and
plan of the temple of Amenhotep III
at El-Kâb.

Behind the kiosk, the platform widened and touched the cliffs. This broader section was enclosed by a high enclosure wall, perhaps Ramesside, that was awkwardly attached to the rear corners of the front kiosk. Lateral gates behind the juncture opened to staircases that descended to the desert.

At the rear end of the platform stood another unusual kiosk with a small pylon. The long sides of the kiosk were formed by three columns alternating with pillars in between. The alternation between columns and pillars is innovative in Egyptian architecture,[167] and became a feature typical of early Christian architecture.[168] Columns and pillars probably carried Hathor capitals, and therefore the corners were formed not by the usual L-shaped corner pillars but by columns. The last architraves at the back of the kiosk secured the roof in the rock wall. Marks of the vaulted roof can still be seen on the rock facade behind. A huge Ramesside doorway opened into the rock cave. Five cult statues were chiseled out from the rear wall of the rock. This combination of a rock cave and terraced front building follows the old Upper Egyptian tradition of the temples of Mentuhotep (11th Dynasty) and Hatshepsut (18th Dynasty) at Deir el-Bahari.

Probably during the same period, the solitary desert chapel of Amenhotep III at El-Kâb received a pronaos or kiosk-like extension of which only the lower stone courses are preserved (fig. 159, bottom). The front of the nearly square building had four columns with half-open intercolumniations. The side walls were completely closed and structured by two engaged piers that produced the same pattern of alternating columns and piers described earlier. The wide roof span was reduced by two-by-two interior columns.

Figure 160.
The reconstructed Ptolemaic chapel of Kalabsha on Elephantine Island.

In EDFU, the construction and decoration of the huge stone enclosure wall of Ptolemy VIII continued. The birth house of the same king was further decorated and provided with a magnificent entrance kiosk. The birth house was surrounded by an ambulatory with four columns at the front and six on each side. The roof was made of timber.

The name of Ptolemy IX Soter II also appears on temple blocks at Coptos, on temple walls in the Hathor temple at Deir el-Medine, in the hypostyle hall of Kom Ombo, and in the Isis temple on Philae, suggesting that the decoration of older buildings was continued.

Probably under Ptolemy IX Soter II, an older sanctuary at KALABSHA was replaced by a small temple (fig. 160).[169] It was built on a stone platform that carried a 4 m thick enclosure wall with a monumental 7.2 m high front and a smaller lateral gate. A staircase from the Nile gave access to the platform. The building consisted of a pronaos *distyle in antis* with beautiful quatrefoil, four-tiered lily capitals. The sanctuary behind it was decorated under Ptolemy IX. The exterior walls and the gate were only completed in the early years of Augustus.[170] A small chapel not far to the north and outside the enclosure wall was perhaps built under Ptolemy V Epiphanes. Except for the latter chapel, the Ptolemaic constructions were demolished in the later years of Augustus and replaced by a new larger temple.[171]

Ptolemy X Alexander I (107–88)

After the death of Cleopatra II in 107, Cleopatra III and her brother Ptolemy X Alexander I expelled the surviving Ptolemy IX Soter II from Egypt. In 101 Cleopatra III died and Berenike III (daughter of Ptolemy IX and consort of Ptolemy X) became coregent with Ptolemy X. During renewed fights against the ousted Ptolemy IX, Ptolemy X was expelled by a military insurrection and killed in a sea battle at Cyprus in 88. During the years 91–88, a rebellion broke out in the south of Egypt, leading to severe destruction of monuments. In 88, Ptolemy IX Soter II returned after a nineteen-year exile in Cyprus, now controlling both Cyprus and Egypt. After his death in 81, his daughter and coregent Cleopatra Berenike III ascended the throne and took Ptolemy XI Alexander II, the son of Ptolemy X Alexander I, as her coregent and husband. Ungratefully, he murdered the old queen after eighteen days and was himself slain for that infamy by the furious crowds of Alexandria.

It is remarkable that public building work could be carried out under such circumstances. A few places in Upper Egypt managed to do so.

Sir Gardner Wilkinson mentions two small temples at SHEIKH FADL (opposite Oxyrhynchos), which seem to have been of Ptolemaic or Roman date but were destroyed around 1854.[172] He also records that:

> At Benoweét [BÂNAWÎT], to the W. of Marágha, are remains of a temple, with the name of Ptolemy Alexander [Ptolemy X Alexander I]; and at Basóna, about 1½ m. S. of Marágha, are some limestone blocks, one with the name of a Ptolemy or a Caesar; another of larger dimensions with the figure of a king (apparently a Ptolemy) offering to Khem, Isis, and other deities. The chief deity here and at Benoweét was probably Khem [Khnum].[173]

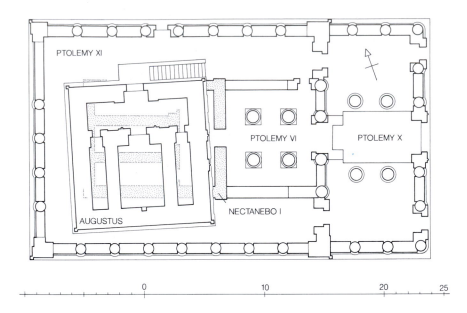

PTOLEMY XI

PTOLEMY VI

PTOLEMY X

NECTANEBO I

AUGUSTUS

0   10   20   25

Figure 161.
Plan of the Ptolemaic/Roman
birth house of Isis at Dendera.

At DENDERA, the Isis temple of Nectanebo I with a porch of Ptolemy VI was enlarged and became an imposing building (figs. 161, 184). The foundation platform was extended to total 20 x 25 m, and the two long sides and the back of the older building were surrounded by a colonnaded ambulatory. The ambulatory roof apparently rested on top of the core building. L-shaped pillars stood at the corners. The old facade of Ptolemy VI was removed and replaced by a new one of the same height as the ambulatory. The existing hall of Ptolemy VI towered over this ambulatory, probably creating an "old-fashioned" system of clerestory lighting.

In front of the temple was a forecourt surrounded by a parapet wall. In a second phase, this court was transformed into a porch with surrounding colonnades that joined the corner pillars of the ambulatory. The middle passage was a canopy of four freestanding columns. The side wings of the new colonnaded court can scarcely have been roofed because of the lack of an interior support.[174]

Under Ptolemy X Alexander I, the temple of Haroeris and Heqat at QÛS (Apollinopolis parva) received a huge western gate. With a front width of 10.33 m and a passage width of 4.41 m, it could well have been 18 m high. It carried on the 12.75 m broad top ledge of the 3.55 m high cavetto a dedicatory inscription in Greek. The giant gate stood at least until 1798 (fig. 162); 100 years later, stone robbers had reduced the marvelous building to a height of only 3.9 m.[175]

The Kushite entrance colonnade of the temple for the primordial Amun at MEDINET HABU was also transformed into a three-aisled hall by the addition of two lateral walls to the central column rows (plan X). In 1996, numerous relief blocks of the older Kushite construction were found built into the Ptolemaic foundations.[176]

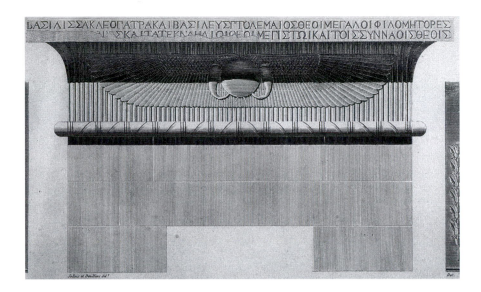

Also under Ptolemy X Alexander I, two side wings were attached to the old Amun temple of Thutmosis III at Medinet Habu. The small temple remained one of the few sanctuaries that received frequent additions but was never replaced by a major new building. The addition of building types over a long period resulted in a lack of aesthetic harmony, and the temple became an architectural pastiche. It is also remarkable that a cult terrace was never added to the east.

Figure 162.
The gate of Ptolemy X
Alexander I of the temple
of Haroeris and Heqat at
Apollinopolis parva (Qûs)
(*Description* IV, pl. 1).

Ptolemy XII Neos Dionysos, called Auletes (80–58, 55–51)

Following the horrendous incidents in the royal family after the death of Ptolemy IX, Ptolemy XII, the son of Ptolemy IX, was called to Egypt and crowned king in 76 B.C.[177] His reign was strained by pressure from Rome, which asserted its claim to the Egyptian throne through the testament of Ptolemy X Alexander I. Ptolemy XII prevented Rome from seizing inheritance only by payments of high "remunerations." This tribute was raised by tax increases that again drove the population to rebellion. In 58 B.C., Ptolemy XII was expelled from Egypt,[178] but he was reinstated in 55 B.C. with the help of Roman troops. Amazingly, in this second phase of the reign of Ptolemy XII, and despite disorder and poverty, some major buildings were erected in Upper Egypt.

The sanctuary of Triphis at ATHRIBIS (Wannina) was enlarged by a new, 45 x 78 m temple built of local limestone (fig. 163, plan V). The temple faced the southeast and stood at a right angle to the one or possibly two older temples. Dimensions, decoration, and inscriptions, but primarily the ground plan of the building, were unusual.[179] At the front was a pronaos of two-by-six columns.[180] Behind, a hypostyle hall followed, with a single row of six columns and small side chambers. Some parts of the temple were still preserved to the height of the roof. The pylon-like rear wall contained the two required stair-

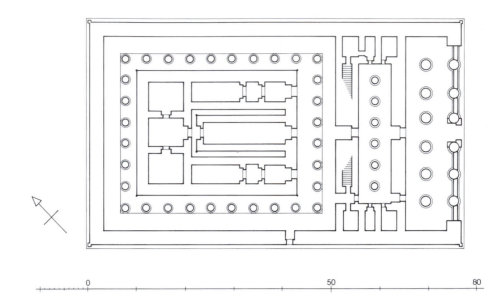

0   50   80

Figure 163.
Hypothetical reconstruction of the temple of Ptolemy XII Neos Dionysos, Auletes, for Triphis at Athribis (Wannina).

cases to the roof. The actual sanctuary area consisted of either a 32.6 x 36.2 m peripteral temple set inside an open court or an isolated temple house placed into a court surrounded by colonnades. Eight columns can be reconstructed on the short sides, as can ten on the long sides. The plan of the temple house had three longitudinal sections. The center one contained the bark sanctuary with a statue shrine behind it. The organization of the lateral branches and the location of their doorways are uncertain. Petrie suggested that an ambulatory surrounded the bark shrine, but there seems to be insufficient space. In the rear wall of the sanctuary, a door should have opened into the statue shrine.

It is difficult to explain the function and layout of the building without a proper excavation. Although L. Borchardt suggested that the structure might have been a birth house,[181] the layout of the interior and the dimensions, which are larger than those of the main temple, contradict this assertion and suggest an independent temple. Inscriptions indicate the existence of two temples at Athribis, the "House of Triphis" and the "House of the Moon," and the cult of more deities.

A small rock sanctuary of Asclepius, located halfway up the mountain may, according to Greek graffiti, also date to the reign of Ptolemy XII. The *speos* consists of two rock chambers with a cavelike cult niche. Remarkable is the building's facade which is decorated with two engaged palm columns supporting an architrave that once certainly carried a cavetto molding. A cavetto molding also crowns the central gate.[182]

At DENDERA, the Hathor temple of the 30th Dynasty(?) was replaced by a new temple. The construction lasted thirty-four years from 54 to 20 B.C. (figs. 164–167, plan VI).[183] The new building was to become one of the most acclaimed late Ptolemaic temples.[184] When Ptolemy XII died in 51 B.C., the temple was, after four years of building activity, still in its early stages, although it did contain some underground crypts. The main temple house was built during the twenty-one-year reign of his successor, Queen Cleopatra VII. At the time of her death in 30 B.C., the decoration work had just begun, covering the outer rear wall with a huge scene showing the queen and her son Caesarion (fig. 167). The goddess Hathor could take possession of her sanctuary in 30 B.C.

The new temple was a completely closed 35 x 59 m wide and 12.5 m high building with one front entrance and two side doors (fig. 164). The uniformity of the enormous wall surfaces was disrupted only by huge lion-headed water spouts, three along the side walls and two in the rear wall.

The 5.7 x 11.22 m bark shrine enclosed the four barks of Hathor, Horus of Edfu, Harsomtus, and Isis, which apparently were not enclosed by wooden shrines.[185] Along the surrounding ambulatory, eleven chapels served the cult of Hathor and her associates. Behind the bark shrine, the main chapel is embellished by a splendid, templelike facade topped by a cavetto with an uraeus frieze. Inside the chapel was an expensively decorated wooden naos that held the gilded, 2 m high seated cult image of Hathor. The naos stood in a niche of the rear wall. It is not known how the niche, 3 m above the pavement, could be reached.

Horus of Edfu, the consort of Hathor, enjoyed hospitality in a side chamber of the southwest corner. The other rooms served the cult of Hathor/Isis, Harsomtus, and Osiris.

In front of the bark shrine are two identical broad or transversal halls, first the hall of the divine ennead and in front the offering hall. From the offering hall, two staircases ascend to the temple roof. The building has a hypostyle

Figure 164.
Rear of the temple house of Ptolemy XII for Hathor of Dendera (photo A.O.).

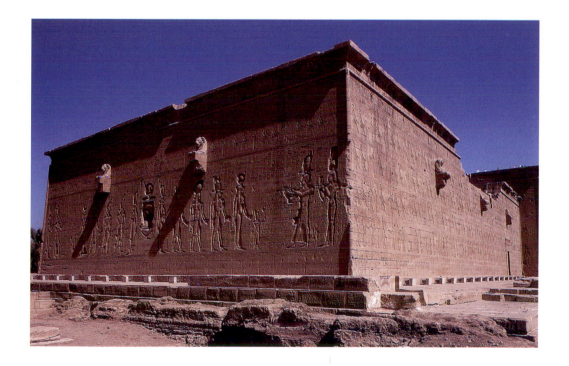

Figure 165.
View over the roof of the temple of Ptolemy XII for Hathor of Dendera (photo A.O.).

Figure 166.
Frontal view of the roof chapel of the temple of Ptolemy XII for Hathor of Dendera (photo A.O.).

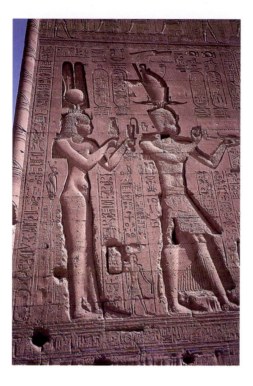

Figure 167.
Cleopatra VII Philopator and
Caesarion performing the
Hathor ritual, on the rear wall
of the Hathor temple at
Dendera (photo A.O.).

hall with two-by-three columns. Their composite capitals have Hathor heads
above. The bases and the lowermost drums of the shafts are of granite, the
upper parts of sandstone. The use of two different building stones in the same
column is unusual, as is the use of granite in a Ptolemaic temple. To the side of
the hypostyle hall is a room for storing cult objects and a laboratory for preparation of ointments. Two side doors led outside, the western one to the sacred
well.

The temple roof is structured in terraces because of the unequal ceiling
heights of the rooms below (fig. 165). The huge roofing slabs were originally
covered with thinner paving stones. Their surface was slightly inclined and
had channels to guide rainwater into the lion-headed water spouts that pierce
the outside walls.

The southwest corner of the roof still contains an elegant roof kiosk with
four Hathor columns on each side (fig. 166). Sockets in its architraves suggest
a barrel-shaped timber roof with a double hull and segmented pediment.[186]
Since the kiosk served to expose the cult images to the rays of the sun on New
Year's Day, roof windows must have been provided. In the floor of the chapel
one also notes the light well for the Horus chapel below, on the main floor. Sufficient light must have fallen through the ceiling of the roof chapel and penetrated into the room below.

Two sanctuaries for the celebration of the Osiris mysteries are concealed in
a kind of "mezzanine" floor northwest and northeast of the hypostyle hall.
Both sanctuaries have open courts, surrounded by a cavetto. From the rear
wall of the court, three doors lead into two succeeding chambers. On the

ceiling of the central room of the northeastern group a famous zodiac represented the cosmic aspects of the Osiris mysteries.[187]

A unique system of crypts, greatly surpassing those of other temples, is hidden in the mighty outside walls of the temple house. The elongated, narrow chambers and passages are decorated and inscribed and are arranged on three to four levels, directly above each other. The lowermost are laid deep within the temple foundations. Access was gained through trapdoors in the pavement and behind hidden sliding wall blocks.

At COPTOS, under Ptolemy XII Neos Dionysos, a south gate was built in the great enclosure wall of Nectanebo I(?), leading into the enclosure wall of Geb, located in the southwest corner of the main precinct. The inscriptions were completed under Caligula. The 6.1 m wide gate probably reached a height of 10 m.

At KARNAK decoration work on the first gate of the temple of Ptah continued (plan VIII). Farther behind, on the processional approach, a gate was erected in an unusual form that had only a few prototypes in the Egyptian history of architecture (fig. 168).[188] A doorway with a broken lintel was set between a pair of columns which were connected by an architrave.

The temple for Hathor at DEIR EL-MEDINE was surrounded by a new brick wall, which was much larger than its predecessor and is still standing today. A simple, 3.74 m wide stone gate in the southeast wall served as the main access. The old cult terrace was replaced by a new one placed directly in front of the gate.

At the Horus temple of EDFU, the extension project begun by Ptolemy VIII was resumed (figs. 169–176). The stone enclosure wall, begun under Ptolemy VIII, was completed and decorated. Under Ptolemy XII, the construction of the court and a massive, sophisticated pylon was advanced. The work was concluded and the building inaugurated on February 2, 70 B.C.

The towers of the pylon (figs. 169–173) were furnished with four, 40 m high flagpoles secured by a huge wooden anchor. Because no trees of such length existed, the flagpoles had to be made from several joined, imported trees. The doors were made of Lebanese cedar and installed in 57 B.C. According to the building inscription, they were 14.35 m high, 2.93 m wide, 31 cm thick, and sheathed with copper. The towers could be ascended by means of an interesting system of staircases, which were lit by slots in the walls. The staircases of Ptolemaic times are not straight, as are those of the New Kingdom, but turn at right angles. In the pylon of Edfu, they consist of forty-three landings with five to eight steps each.[189] At the level of the main door lintel, huge consoles protrude at the side of the gate from the front and rear of the pylon (fig. 173); they were probably meant to carry statues. Display of sculpture on the pylon itself is a rare feature.[190]

The paved court behind the pylon was surrounded by colonnades at the entrance side and along the two long sides (fig. 174). The column bases are chamfered and the lower ends of the shafts decorated with heavily carved papyrus leaves that cast hard shadows.

The text program of the court reveals an interesting feature. The festival calendars on the court walls and columns seem to be synchronized with the shadow cast by the pylon's cavetto molding. On December 21, for example, the

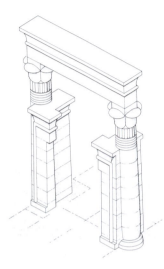

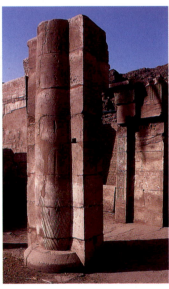

Figure 168.
Reconstruction *(top)* and remains of the gate of Ptolemy XII in front of the temple of Ptah at Karnak (photo A.O.).

Figure 169. Aerial view of the Horus temple of Edfu showing the final situation under Ptolemy XII (courtesy of Marilyn Bridges, New York).

Figure 171. Frontal view of the pylon of Ptolemy XII of the Horus temple at Edfu (photo A.O.).

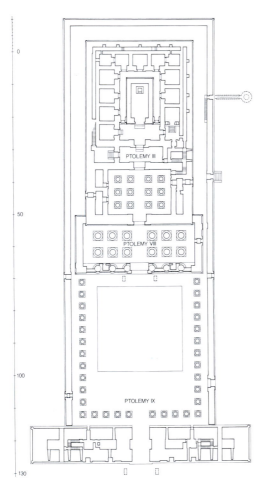

Figure 170. Plan of the Horus temple at Edfu under Ptolemy XII.

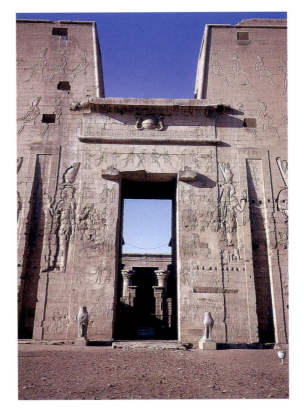

Figure 172. The gate of the pylon of Ptolemy XII of the Horus temple at Edfu with the granite falcon images (photo A.O.).

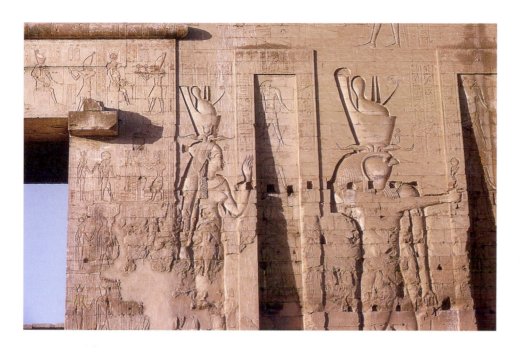

Figure 173.
Interaction of relief and
architecture at the pylon of
Ptolemy XII of the Horus
temple at Edfu (photo A.O.).

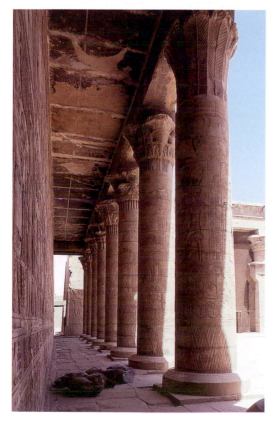

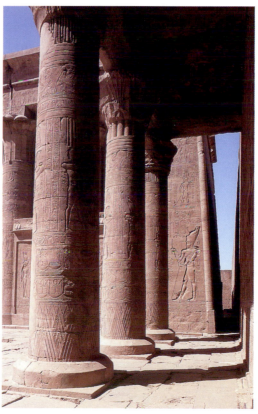

Figure 174. *(at left)*
The western colonnade
of the court of Ptolemy
XII in the Horus temple
at Edfu (photo A.O.).

Figure 175. *(at right)*
The detachment of
court colonnade and
pronaos in the Horus
temple at Edfu
(photo A.O.).

shadow reaches the tenth pair of columns; at the midsummer solstice on June 21, the pylon does not cast a shadow: it acts as a gigantic sundial![191] The decoration program of the court is dominated, however, by depictions of the festivities and offering ceremonies for Horus and his entourage.

The Ptolemaic court of Edfu also displays a new concept for joining architectural volumes (figs. 175–176). In the New Kingdom, court colonnades were attached directly to the temple facade. From now on, the colonnades terminated at some distance, freeing the front of the temple and isolating the temple house by means of an open space. The same principle was applied to the Roman courts of Kom Ombo and Kalabsha.

The temple area was enclosed, probably under Ptolemy XII and later Cleopatra VII, with a brick wall because a monumental gate in the entrance wall (south side) was built at that time. The gate was 9.38 m wide, with a 4.06 m wide passage.

Certainly because of Ombos's increasing importance as a trading post, the temple of KOM OMBO was particularly favored by Ptolemy XII (plan XIII). Following a revised plan for the temple precinct, a new monumental gate was built in the southwest corner of the complex; its passage was 15(!) m high. The gate allowed direct access from both the Nile and the land. The complex's 7 m thick brick enclosure wall respects the birth house of Ptolemy VIII Euergetes II and must therefore be later than Ptolemy VIII and probably date to the reign of Ptolemy XII.

The temple house of Ptolemy VI Philometor was embellished by a magnificent pronaos of 12 m high columns arranged in rows of three-by-five (figs. 189, 191). The column bases have heavily chamfered edges and stand on square plinths raised slightly above the pavement. The selection of capital types also uses two New Kingdom forms, the palm column and the Ramesside bell-shaped papyrus capital on a planed-out shaft. The distribution of capital types aspires to symmetry. The central row of columns (a-d-g) is flanked by pairs of matching capitals (b-b, e-e, h-h). The front row is particularly uniform. Similar to the later pronaos of Esna, the front row has four-tiered papyrus/palmette capitals; only their details differ. The casual wealth expressed by the details is well balanced by the ordered repose of the whole (see diagram).

Probably just before the arrival of the Napoleonic expedition, the two side walls of the pronaos were torn down so that the two front corners collapsed with the adjacent columns. The fallen architraves and capitals were still visible in 1850.[192] The ceiling, the splendid capitals, and other elements of the pronaos still show traces of blue, white, red, and black paint.

Probably during the reign of Ptolemy XII, the stone enclosure wall was built around the temple house, bonding to the new pronaos from the east. A row of seven chambers, facing the back of the temple house, is built against the rear part of the enclosure wall. The central chamber houses a staircase to the roof.

The construction of an elaborate fountain system in the north of the temple is not dated. Small crocodiles, sacred animals of Sobek, were probably kept there in a small stone basin.

The reason that a kiosk of Nectanebo I on PHILAE was dismantled and rebuilt at the southern tip of the island (figs. 74–78, 192, plan XIV) is un-

---

Pronaos, Temple of Kom Ombo

BACK

i - h - g - h - j
f - e - d - e - f
c - b - a - b - c

FRONT

a: Quatrefoil, four tiered papyrus/lily capital

b: Quatrefoil, five-story papyrus/lily capital

c: Single-stem, bell-shaped (capital destroyed)

d: Eight-stem papyrus/ palmette capital

e: Quatrefoil, two-tiered papyrus/palmette capital

f: Single-stem, bell-shaped papyrus capital

g: Single-stem, bell-shaped palmette/lotus capital

h: Quatrefoil, bell-shaped papyrus/palmette capital

i: Single-stem, bell-shaped palmette capital

j: Palm capital

certain. The decoration work on the first pylon and the court behind was continued.

West of the original, pre-dam Philae, and separated from it only by a hundred-meter-wide branch of the Nile, was the sacred island of BIGGEH (Bigga), the location of one of the sixteen mythical tombs of Osiris.[193] General access to the Abaton ("inaccessible") island and loud speaking were forbidden. In a cave believed to be the source of the inundation, the Nile god Hapy was thought to live, protected by a sacred snake. The rising and falling of the floods could therefore be easily related to the death and resurrection of Osiris. The statue of Isis of Philae frequently sailed to Biggeh to take part in the ceremonies conducted for her husband.

A monumental staircase ascended the terrace, which had a sanctuary that faced east.[194] An Augustan pylon in the enclosure wall led to the temple. Only the doorway is now preserved. Behind the doorway stood the temple itself, with a beautiful 13.69 m wide pronaos dating to Ptolemy XII (fig. 177). The pronaos probably had two rows of four columns. Today, enclosed in dense shrubbery, only the two middle columns of the facade stand upright, with remains of another column and three screen walls. Unfortunately, the details of the temple house are unknown. A granite altar of Ptolemy III found in the area points to the existence of an early Ptolemaic or 30th Dynasty temple. A colossal seated figure of Amenhotep II and a statue of Thutmosis III suggest an even older temple, which may be buried under the foundation platform. It is remarkable that no such early remains are known from the main island of Philae.

Under Ptolemy XII, the Isis temple at DABOD received a 1.94 m high granite naos, which was placed north of the older one of Ptolemy VIII. Both naoi were smashed in 1821. The naos of Ptolemy XII was restored in 1972 and transferred to Madrid with the temple.

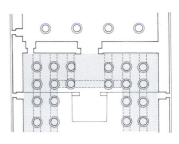

TEMPLE OF KHONSU, KARNAK

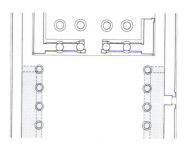

KALABSHA

Figure 176.
Different concepts of attaching court colonnades and temple houses in the New Kingdom (top) and the Late Period.

Cleopatra VII Philopator (51–30 B.C.)

After the death of Ptolemy XII, his nineteen-year-old daughter, the famous Cleopatra VII, ascended the throne. Immediately entangled in a power struggle with her brother Ptolemy XIII and his supporters, she was deposed in 48 B.C. Pompey's flight to Egypt after the lost war against Julius Caesar and Pompey's assassination by supporters of Ptolemy XIII brought Julius Caesar to Alexandria. He soon became involved in the internal fights that developed into the Alexandrine war. Early in 47, Ptolemy XIII was defeated and killed and Cleopatra VII reinstalled with her younger brother Ptolemy XIV. The ingenious queen soon won over the Egyptian priesthood by accepting her role as the "reborn Isis" and by maintaining their temple-building projects.

The construction and decoration of the temple house of DENDERA proceeded steadily, generating the famous relief at the rear wall of the temple that depicts the queen and her son Caesarion offering to Hathor (figs. 164, 184).

A bark station built at COPTOS, in the corner of the temple of Geb, was a humble building. However, its interior rear wall shows an unusual relief, a frontal view of a bark sitting in a bark shrine.[195]

Figure 177.
Remains of the pronaos of the
Osiris temple of Ptolemy XII on
Biggeh (photo A.O.).

Figure 178. (*at left*)
The birth house of Cleopatra VII at Armant before its
dismantling (photo Frith, ca. 1857).

Figure 179. (*above*)
The birth house of Cleopatra VII at Armant (computer
reconstruction by Barry Girsh).

Participants in the Napoleonic expedition and other early artists and photographers[196] documented the birth house of ARMANT before its demolition in 1861–1862.[197] The birth house was located not in front of the main temple and at a right angle to its axis but behind the temple of Monthu with its entrance to the southwest (figs. 178–180). Thirty-one meters distant from the birth house to the southeast was the sacred lake, with a wide staircase ascending directly to the birth house.[198]

The birth house may have been built in three phases. The oldest part, the core building, contained three chambers, with a false door against the wall of the second room. The sanctuary was surrounded by a colonnaded ambulatory with L-shaped corner pillars. The roof beams of the ambulatory rested on top of the sanctuary. Seven columns stood on the long sides, two or three at the rear side of the ambulatory.

In a second phase, a high entrance kiosk was added to the birth house. The entablature of the kiosk was carried by four columns along the two sides, and by six columns at the front. The rear part of the architraves rested on top of the older temple facade.

In a final phase, a second kiosk, with the amazing height of 16.55 m, was added to the front of the first one. Two columns on the long sides and four at the front carried the entablature, which must have been roofed by a shallow timber vault. The columns were remarkably slim (ratio 1:9). The height of the abaci shows that they were intended to be carved into Bes figures. The capitals and parts of the decoration of the kiosk remained unfinished. Cartouches of Cleopatra VII and her son Ptolemy XV Caesarion date parts of the decoration to their joint rule in the years 44–30 B.C. The construction of the core could have started under Ptolemy XII Neos Dionysos.

Figure 180.
The birth house of Cleopatra VIII at Armant (computer reconstruction by Barry Girsh).

The birth house was one of the last important Ptolemaic buildings, and its luxuriant decoration represented an excellent example of the baroque style of their architecture. The daring roof construction of the entrance kiosks, the play of light and shadows at the capitals, and the effect of the huge, window-like openings that created beautiful connections between interior and the exterior spaces must have been stunning.

8

THE ROMAN PERIOD
(31 B.C.—A.D. 385)

The Historical Background

On September 2, 31 B.C., Augustus defeated Cleopatra and Marc Antony's fleet at Actium, near modern Preveza at the northwestern coast of Greece. The victor pursued the unfortunate couple to Egypt, where they committed suicide in August 30 B.C. With the slaying of the last surviving Ptolemy, the seventeen-year-old Ptolemy XV Caesarion, the Ptolemaic dynasty ended, and Egypt became the personal estate of Augustus and his successors, governed by a personal prefect of the emperor.

At the beginning of Roman rule, quite naturally, military and secular building projects prevailed over temple building. As everywhere in the Roman Empire, forts were built at strategic points. As in all North African and Near Eastern provinces under Roman control, new foundations as well as ancient towns were provided with baths, theaters, hippodromes, triumphal arches, colonnaded roads, gates, forums, and basilicas.[1]

As a sign of continuing creativity, special building forms developed in Egypt and were exported to other parts of the empire. They include the *tetrastylon*, a honorific four-column monument,[2] and the *komasterion*, a hall used for the organization of processions. The *caesareum* was developed from the Ptolemeion and became the prototype for other sanctuaries built by Herod the Great and others for imperial cults.

One of the first political measures taken by Augustus was the confiscation of the huge temple properties and, typical for the Roman sense of order, the incorporation of the diverse priesthoods into a single, Alexandria-based central administration. These measures certainly secured the predominance of Greco-Roman cults and made building activity dependent on the authorities in Alexandria.

Nevertheless, about forty temples and chapels in pharaonic style are known to have been built under Roman rule, most of them south of the Faiyum. Roman-style temples were restricted to Alexandria and a few other towns, and they cannot be discussed here. Apparently, ancient Egyptian religion gave way to Greco-Roman cults in that part of Egypt. All preserved temples of the Roman Period are either small or extensions of already existing earlier buildings, such as the pronaoi of Dendera and Esna; no new large temples were built.[3]

However, Roman temple building considerably exceeded Ptolemaic building in the western oases of El-Kharga and El-Dakhla, as was shown by the discovery of a dozen stone and many more brick temples.[4]

Pharaonic Temples in the Roman Period

Egyptian temple architecture in the Roman Period proceeds without a conspicuous stylistic break from Late Ptolemaic architecture. Subtle changes can be detected, however, that are characterized by simplification. This tendency is partially a result of the replacement of builders who emerged from diverse local Egyptian traditions by government architects who identified themselves with the unity of the Roman state. The main reason for the new, Augustan austerity was, however, the politically motivated elimination of the exotic and "decadent" ways of the late Ptolemies, mainly of Cleopatra and Marc Antony.

Instead of developing the exuberant creations of the Late Ptolemaic era, builders returned to the more austere pre-Ptolemaic building forms. For example, architects of the new regime rejected most of the flamboyant late Ptolemaic quatrefoil capital forms and created plain, bell-shaped capital types, tightly arranged in a grid of floral patterns.[5] Even the new capital types were not new inventions, but were developed from basic existing types.

A corresponding constraint was achieved by reducing the number of building types and standardizing the prevailing temple plans. New, local building types could only develop in distant areas with dynamic building activity like the Faiyum, Nubia, and the western oases.

Occasionally buildings in Roman style occur within the enclosure wall of a pure Egyptian-style temple, such as the small temple for Serapis and Isis at the Luxor temple or the temple for Augustus and the gate of Diocletian on Philae. After a few generations of Roman occupation, a clear separation between pharaonic and classical styles was no longer strictly followed, especially in the hinterland. For example, the walls of the temples of Karanis and Medinet Madi are shaped in a *rustica* pattern and the kiosk with Ionic columns in front of the Neronic south temple of Karanis stand on a platform with an Egyptian cavetto. An acceptance of classical conceptions of space can be observed in the design of the temple forecourt on Philae, where the rigid axial organization of Egyptian tradition was loosened up in a baroque manner, allowing an oblique view of the temple facade. Even in Alexandria, Roman architecture was heavily tinted by pharaonic elements (figs. 181, 268).

A peripheral but interesting phenomenon is the appearance of Nabataean temples on the Sinai peninsula. At QASR GHEIT, on the desert route between El-Qantarah and Pelusium, a completely preserved Nabataean sanctuary was

Figure 181.
View of the vestibule of the second-century tomb of Kom el-Shukâfa (photo Anna-Marie Kellen).

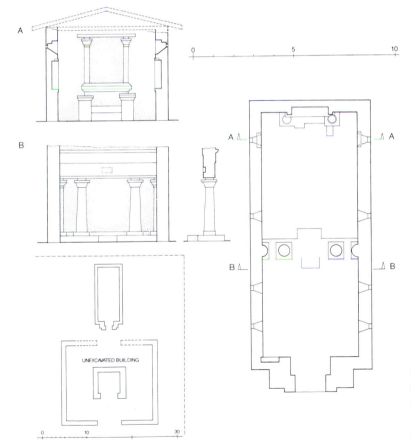

Figure 182.
Sections and plans of the Nabataean temple of Qasr Gheit (after J. Clédat, "Fouilles à Qasr-Gheit," *ASAE* 12 [1912]: 145–68).

discovered in 1912. Only parts of one of two buildings were excavated and showed the use of pharaonic building elements (fig. 182).[6]

During the long Roman rule, the spiritual resources of Egyptian temple building were consumed, and structural and formal principles would have required a new directive. The lack of theological and political motivation, combined with economic problems, prevented this new orientation. From around A.D. 180 onward, Egyptian architecture stagnated and declined.

Building Methods of the Roman Period

Typical Roman building features such as the use of *orthostates*, *rustica* masonry, monolithic column shafts, or cast (cement) walls were restricted in Egypt to Roman-style buildings. The construction methods of contemporary pharaonic buildings were not much different from those used earlier. Large-format blocks, blocks with complicated shapes, and ordinary wall blocks were still dressed during or after setting.[7] Following an old tradition, guiding lines for the succeeding courses were scratched onto the top surface of the foundation course. From the lowest to the uppermost course, the setting line was repeatedly constructed and scratched into the blocks in order to guarantee the proper angle for the slanting wall surface.

Wall blocks arrived in a roughly square shape in *bosses*, mostly with a carved mason's mark. First the bedding joint was dressed flat, then the block was turned over and the four top edges cut along previously scratched lines. By viewing above the upper edge of the L-shaped builder's square, one could check the level of the edges and remove the remainder with the pointed chisel. Thereafter, the vertical joints were cut and their right angle checked again with the builder's square. Joints were cut to produce *anathyrosis*. Thereafter, the bosses along the lower and the two vertical front edges were roughly chiseled off. The back side and the outer, invisible faces of foundation blocks also remained rough.

Moving and setting of blocks was carried out with the help of rollers and levers, which were inserted into carefully cut lever sockets. Pairs of lever sockets tended to be carved in the top surface for levering blocks parallel to the alignment. For movement from the front, lever sockets were cut into the upper surface of the front boss.[8] In general, runner blocks had one cramp, while headers had two, often also in a transversal direction. Except for the smooth, 4 to 25 cm wide bands along the edges, the joints were left rough and slightly sunk; a pointed chisel was used for this work. In order to pour in liquid mortar, funnel-shaped grooves with a semicircular section were cut into the joining face of already set blocks. Some joints were so well cut that they were scarcely discernible on the finished wall. The mortar in the bedding and touching joints was made from pink gypsum.

The removal of the upper edge of the front bosses along the setting line was the final procedure after a course of blocks had been set. At the same time, on the top surface of each course, parallel, rough plaster bands were chiseled to allow tighter adherence of the mortar. In Roman masonry, these grooves are clearly defined and sharply cut.

The most advanced achievements of Roman engineering, for example, cranes or the giant wooden wheel for lifting heavy weights, probably entered Egyptian construction sites during the Roman Period.[9] Other examples were the amazingly simple wood and rope devices that were used to lower the obelisks sent overseas by the Romans.[10]

Metrology

As is to be expected in a country with strong traditions, the pharaonic cubit measuring system was still used in Roman times, at least for pharaonic buildings.[11] The design was still organized with the help of a grid, which was also

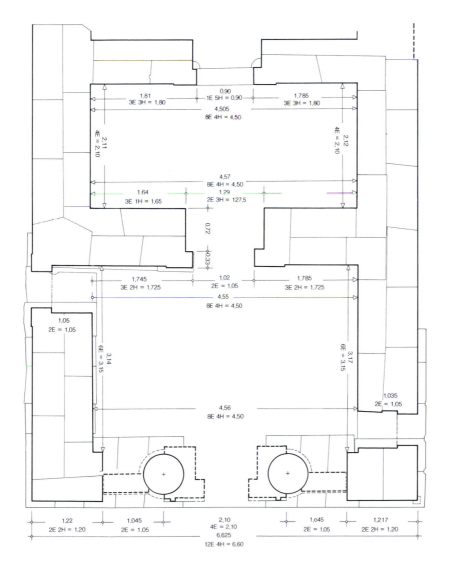

Figure 183.
Metrology of the plan of the Augustan temple of Dendur. Ancient project: E = cubit, H = palm. Modern state: plain numbers.

probably based on cubit measurements.[12] A good example is the temple of Dendur, for which all main measurements can be expressed in cubits and palms (7.5 cm) (fig. 183). The question remains as to whether Egyptian architects of the Late Period added a module system to the cubit calculation. Based on the importance of proportional systems in contemporary Hellenistic and Meroitic architecture, F. W. Hinkel suggested that the traditional rigid cubit measurement was gradually replaced by a more flexible module application.[13] Hinkel assumes that the module was defined as one-sixteenth of the total width of a building. The ground plan would be formed from a sequence of several harmonic rectangles, which had the proportion of 8:5. In an upright position, such a rectangle would establish the outline of the planned building's facade.[14]

The Buildings of the Roman Period

Augustus (30 B.C. to A.D. 14)

Augustus recommended himself to the Egyptians as a legitimate heir to the pharaohs and soon continued the Ptolemaic tradition of sponsoring monumental state buildings. He extended his building policy "to transfigure Rome, a city of brick into a city of marble," to Egypt, enacting a vigorous temple-building program that, of course, used sandstone instead of marble. As clever politicians, the Romans never promoted the Roman building style for Egyptian temples. Herod the Great, who was inspired by Augustus to undertake a similar architectural building program, did not hesitate to use the internationally dominant Roman style for buildings in his territory.[15]

The Caesareum of ALEXANDRIA, begun by Cleopatra VII and Julius Caesar, was completed by the architect Pontius. In 13–12 B.C. it was embellished by the addition of two obelisks of Thutmosis III, which were removed from the ruins of Heliopolis.[16]

The construction and decoration work in the Hathor temple of DENDERA had proceeded so well during the reign of Cleopatra VII that the temple could be handed over to the goddess in the first year of the emperor's reign, in 30 B.C. In addition, the birth house of Hathor-Isis, situated behind the main temple, was altered (figs. 161, 184). The core of the building of Nectanebo I was replaced with a new sanctuary, located behind the additions of Ptolemy VI and of Ptolemy X Alexander (plan VI). No attempt was made to integrate the older building. Only a false door at the eastern exterior wall reminds one of the original sanctuary. The new orientation of the building rotated the temple face from east to north, a change that facilitated access from the main temple in the north.

The new sanctuary consisted of a broad room with three parallel shrines. The entrance into the center shrine is decorated with an ornate chapel facade. In order to match the level of the Hathor temple, the new building was erected on a high platform. A temporary access staircase led up at the side of the platform. The roofing slabs were not positioned—as usual—beneath the level of the cavetto molding but on top of it, and would probably have been hidden by

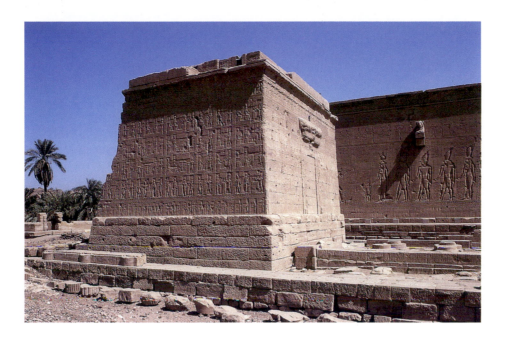

a parapet wall. The project remained unfinished. Since the new building was on a much higher level than the surrounding Ptolemaic colonnades, one may assume that there were plans to raise all older structures accordingly. The east gate in the enclosure wall of the Hathor precinct was also added in the time of Augustus or Tiberius.

Under Augustus, a small temple was built for Isis at EL-QAL'A, 1 km north of the temple of Min at Coptos (fig. 185).[17] Despite its small size, (16 x 24 m) the temple contains all the room units familiar from larger temples. The main sanctuary opens into the room of the visiting gods. An ambulatory around the sanctuary connects to two side chapels and to the *wabet* located in the southwest corner. In front of the main sanctuary are the offering hall with side chambers for offerings and cultic cloths and a broad vestibule without columns. The rear parts of the temple are still standing and are surrounded by modern houses. An unusual feature is a second, transversal axis with a wide entrance that leads to the secondary sanctuary. This chapel seems, in accordance with the character of Isis, to have been a birth house.

A temple for Mut, Isis, and several other deities was built at SHANHOUR, between Qûs and Luxor (fig. 186).[18] At the beginning, the 13.5 x 18.8 m temple was relatively modest, containing two antechambers, a *wabet*, a staircase to the roof, and an ambulatory surrounding the sanctuary. A contra-chapel was attached to the external rear wall. The small temple, which still stands today, was enlarged under Trajan.

Probably also in Augustan times, as a last Egyptian temple in the Theban area, the temple of DEIR EL-SHELOUIT was built 3 km southwest of Medinet Habu (fig. 187).[19] A 16.8 m broad and 12.9 m deep temple house was erected inside a large, 58 x 81.5 m brick enclosure wall with a stone gate in the east.

Figure 184.
The birth house of Augustus for Isis at Dendera, seen from the south (photo A.O.).

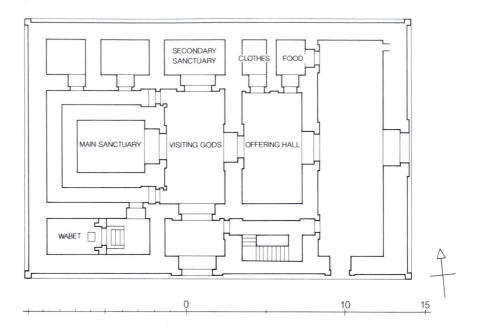

Figure 185.
Plan of the temple of Augustus
for Isis, Nephthys, Haroeris,
and Harpokrates at El-Qal'a,
Coptos.

In contrast to the similarly dimensioned temple of El-Qal'a, the builders did
not replicate a complete temple on a smaller scale. Instead, they reduced the
layout to a rather large shrine surrounded by an ambulatory with three side
chambers on the north and south. The usual rear row of chapels (in the west)
is lacking. A staircase in the southeast leads to the roof, and a *wabet* is
attached in the northwest. The gate and roof of the sanctuary and the light
well of the *wabet* are topped by an uraeus frieze. The front of the *wabet* probably consisted of two columns. The center of the exterior rear wall shows a
false door.

Sebakhîn removed the surrounding brick buildings within the enclosure
wall and exposed the originally invisible, deep foundations that today are lifting the building to an odd view. A dividing wall with an Augustan gate in the
center of the court, still seen by early travelers, was also removed. Inscriptions
on the first gate mention the names of Galba, Otho, Vespasian, and Domitian;
inscriptions in the interior include Trajan, Hadrian, and Antoninus Pius. The
nearly square ground plan, which is reminiscent of the temple Claudius built
for Harendotes on Philae (see fig. 217) makes one wonder whether the architects of Deir el-Shelouit originally intended to build a pronaos.

The temple of KOM OMBO, which had just been enlarged with a gate and a
pronaos by Ptolemy XII Neos Dionysos, was again extended under Augustus
(figs. 188, 191, plan XIII). The temple was surrounded by a 3 m thick stone
enclosure wall, which included a rectangular, colonnaded court at the front of
the temple. The southwest corner of the new forecourt obstructed the view
from the entrance gate of Ptolemy XII to the facade of the main temple.[20]
Access to the court was provided by a 14.5 m wide and approximately 15.75 m
high double gate in the west wall (figs. 189–190). This impressive building

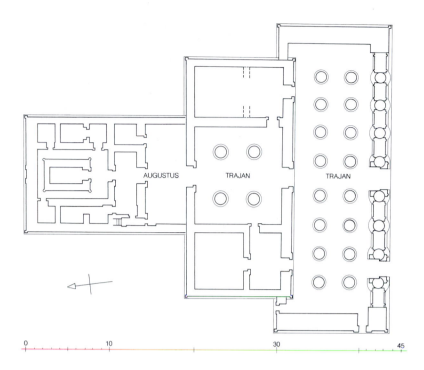

AUGUSTUS   TRAJAN   TRAJAN

0   10   30   45

Figure 186.
Plan of the temple of
Augustus for Mut and Isis
at Shanhour.

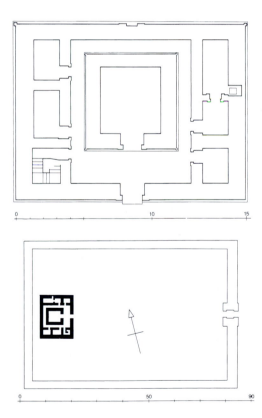

0   10   15

0   50   90

Figure 187.
Plans of the Augustan temple
of Deir el-Shelouit.

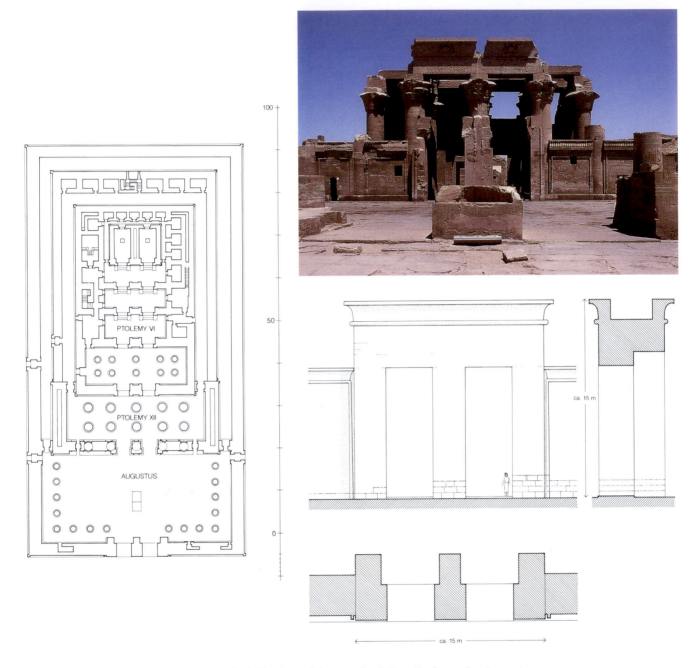

Figure 188. *(at left)* Plan of the temple of Kom Ombo under Augustus.

Figure 189. *(top right)* Remains of the Augustan double gate in front of the pronaos of Ptolemy XII at Kom Ombo (photo A.O.).

Figure 190. *(bottom right)* Reconstruction of the Augustan double gate of the temple of Kom Ombo.

could be climbed through a staircase in the wall.[21] The court was surrounded in the south, west, and north by colonnades (fig. 191). The western colonnade was divided in two by the double gate. The north and south colonnades ended before reaching the pronaos. This partition of the court colonnades into two branches on an L-shaped ground plan corresponds to the arrangement in the courts of Edfu and Kalabsha (figs. 175–176) and follows a special Ptolemaic-Roman design principle. A huge stone altar stood in the center of the court.[22] On both sides of the altar are small basins of unknown purpose, originally closed by a lid or grill.

On ELEPHANTINE, the Ptolemaic forecourt of the Khnum temple was finished with the addition of a huge, 47 m broad pylon and a cult terrace, both towering high above the Nile. The side colonnades of the court joined the pylon, which therefore must have been planned or begun at the same time as the construction of the colonnades (fig. 138).

The advancement of the cults of female deities was continued with building projects for Isis on PHILAE (fig. 192, plan XIV). The most impressive building of the period was the huge kiosk, which was, until recently, ascribed to Trajan.[23] G. Haeny has convincingly suggested Augustus.[24] The 15 x 20 m kiosk is 15.85 m high and was probably meant to shelter the bark of Isis at the eastern banks of the island (figs. 193–194). The four-by-five columns all carry different, lavishly structured composite capitals that are topped by 2.10 m high piers. These were intended to be sculpted into Bes pillars, similar to the examples found in the birth houses of Philae, Armant, and Dendera. This work was never completed, however, along with the decoration of the cavetto moldings, screen walls, and gates. Sockets in the architraves suggest that the timber roof was completed. Three 12.50 m long, probably triangulated trusses, which were inserted into a ledge at the back of the stone architrave, carried

Figure 191.
View of the Augustan court of the temple of Kom Ombo seen from the northeast (photo A.O.).

Figure 192.
Aerial view of the island of
Philae (courtesy of Marilyn
Bridges).

the slightly vaulted roof. The ceiling was attached to the underside of the
trusses. The building represents another example of the unusual combination
of wood and stone in the same structure.

The kiosk fascinates the viewer with its simple shape, huge dimensions,
and splendid column capitals. Inside, he experiences a perception of space dis-
torted by the missing ceiling. Above, huge openings, contained by the columns and their architraves, enhance the visual continuity into the exterior
space dominated by the blue sky. Below, the screen walls define an interior
space.

Under Augustus, the area in front of the first pylon of Philae was shaped. A
20 x 90 m trapezoidal court was enclosed by a 42 m long eastern and a 77 m
long western colonnade. The court contracts slightly to the south (figs.
195–196, plan XIV).[25] The capitals of the colonnades display a great variety of
types, and the column bases stand on unusually high plinths. The relatively
shallow colonnades do not really define the court as an enclosed space but
promote spatial continuity and movement from the temple facade in the
north to the kiosk of Nectanebo I in the south. P. Gilbert compared the irregular spatial organization to Hellenistic squares surrounded by colonnades.[26]
Gilbert also saw a Hellenistic influence in the unorthodox configuration of the
buildings on Philae.[27] H. Jaritz showed that several architectural features of
the western colonnade related to the temple of Osiris that stood opposite Philae on Biggeh Island.[28] He even suggests that the western colonnade of Philae
provided a kind of pronaos for the distant temple of Osiris. One has to remem-

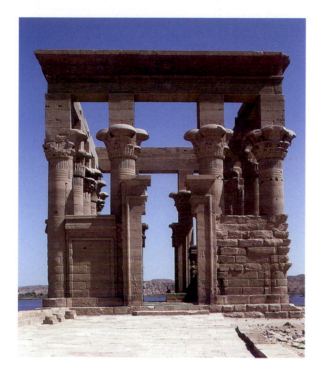

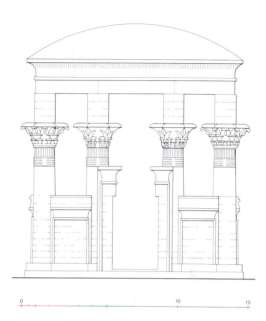

ber, however, that spatial planning and the distribution of buildings on Philae were restricted by the topographical conditions of the small rocky island.

A small temple for Augustus was built on PHILAE by the prefect Rubrius Barbarus in 13–2 B.C.; it was one of the first Roman-style buildings in the East (fig. 192, plan XIV).[29] The temple was a 10 x 16.8 m *prostyle* in Corinthian-Doric order standing on a podium. The pediment was carried by four granite columns with Corinthian capitals.[30] They were sculpted from diorite, a hard material, rarely used in architecture. The temple faces northeast to receive arriving boat traffic but turns its back on the Isis temple.

Contemporaneously with the extension of Philae, the temple of Osiris on BIGGEH Island received a pylon. The central gate is still standing.

Augustus's patronage of the cult of Isis also included architectural enlargements of the Nubian temples. Building activity in this area allowed the Roman government to announce its presence at the borders of Meroe.

The small Isis temple at DABOD built by Ergamenes II, Adikhalamani, and Ptolemy VI was extended by means of three gates and a corresponding temenos wall. This extension placed the modest sanctuary inside a monumental setting (figs. 142–143).[31]

A small kiosk was built on an imposing plateau, north of the Roman fortress of QERTASSI, 40 km south of Philae (figs. 197–198). The kiosk offered shelter to Isis of Philae on her annual voyage through her Nubian province. The building has five columns on the long sides and four on the short sides, with gates on the north, south, and west. The columns flanking the gates carried Hathor capitals, referring to Isis. The remaining capitals were composite.

Figure 193. *(left)*
The Augustan(?) kiosk on Philae seen from the west (photo A.B.).

Figure 194. *(right)*
Reconstructed elevation of the Augustan(?) kiosk on Philae.

Figure 195. *(top)* The Augustan forecourt of the Isis temple on Philae looking south (photo A.O.).

Figure 196. *(bottom)* The Augustan forecourt of the Isis temple on Philae looking north (photo A.O.).

Figure 197.
View of the kiosk of
Qertassi (photo A.O.).

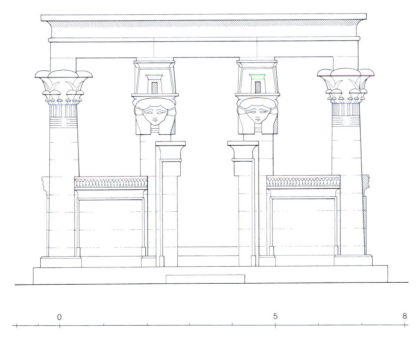

Figure 198.
Reconstructed elevation
of the kiosk of Qertassi.

0   5   8

The roof construction is amazing. The architraves supported not a timber roof but sandstone slabs that rested on the architraves of the long sides. The slabs measured 7 m, probably the maximum length possible for sandstone slabs. Wooden roof beams were probably not used because of the lack of timber in this arid area. The intercolumniations were closed against the wind with wooden shutters or grills, as can be seen from sockets. Inside, the kiosk was four steps higher than outside. Due to its elegant shape and spectacular location, the kiosk was a jewel of Lower Nubia. According to G. Roeder, it dates to Augustan or early Roman times.[32]

At TAFFEH (or Taifa, ancient Taphis, north of Kalabsha), three temples for Isis were built in Augustan times (figs. 199–200, left).[33] The larger southern temple consisted of a square sanctuary similar to the Meroitic chapels of Dabod and Dakka. It was subsequently enlarged by a pronaos, perhaps still under Augustus. The pronaos is an uncustomary square with three rows of two columns. The front columns of the pronaos had disappeared before Frederik Ludwig Norden recorded the temple in 1738. The 10 x 14 m building was enclosed by means of a stone wall with a small pylon in front. The remaining parts were destroyed between 1860 and 1880, without further study having taken place.

The smaller, 6.5 x 8 m Isis temple in the north was possibly also built in Augustan times and, like a birth house, stood at a right angle to the south (main?) temple. The north temple had a ground plan similar to the pronaos of the southern temple. The two-by-three columns carried fine palmette/lily and palmette/papyrus capitals. Some details of the open facade are surprising. The two front columns are formed by square pillars with engaged columns on the four sides. In the third or fourth century A.D., the facade underwent considerable alterations. The right screen wall was replaced by a secondary entrance. This side door and the central entrance received elaborate lintels decorated with several cavetto cornices and uraeus friezes. Both lintels were reused from other structures. Parts of the frontal intercolumniations were walled up. The rear wall of the interior has a statue niche, as does the Dendur temple. The collapsed temple was only rediscovered during the Nubian salvage campaign and presented to the Rijksmuseum van Oudheden in Leiden, where it has been a highlight of the exhibition since 1978.

At an unknown, late Roman date, a third, small chapel was built in a wadi 400 m southwest of Taffeh (fig. 200, right).[34] The modest building, a desert station for the traveling cult image of Isis of Taffeh, is remarkable only because of its flamboyant facade. The door frame depicts the front of a colonnaded kiosk with an uraeus frieze, set under a larger colonnaded kiosk with a cavetto. A third cavetto and uraeus frieze follow on top of the building. A corresponding abundance of entablature elements at the northern temple of Taffeh is dated into the third or fourth century A.D.

The temple of the Nubian sun god Mandulis and Isis of KALABSHA (ancient Talmis) was especially enriched under Augustus. Initially, the unfinished decoration of the late Ptolemaic temple and its 7.20 m high front gate was completed.[35] In the later years of Augustus, these buildings were replaced by a large new temple (figs. 201–203). A towering cult terrace was built above the Nile and connected by a causeway to the huge pylon of the temple.

Figure 199.
View of the south temple of Taffeh in 1816 (Jean Jacques Rifaud, *Voyages en Égypte, en Nubie et lieux circonvoisins* [Paris, 1830], pl. 159).

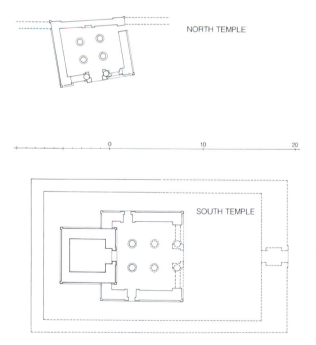

NORTH TEMPLE

0   10   20

SOUTH TEMPLE

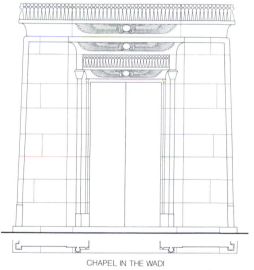

CHAPEL IN THE WADI

Figure 200.
Plans of the north and south temples of Taffeh *(left)* and reconstructed facade of the chapel in the wadi (H. Ricke, *Ausgrabungen von Khor-Dehmit bis Bet el-Wali* [Chicago, 1967], fig. 42).

Figure 201.
Frontal view of the pronaos of the later Augustan temple of Mandulis and Isis of Kalabsha (photo A.O.).

Figure 202.
Northern colonnade of the court of the temple of Kalabsha (photo A.B.).

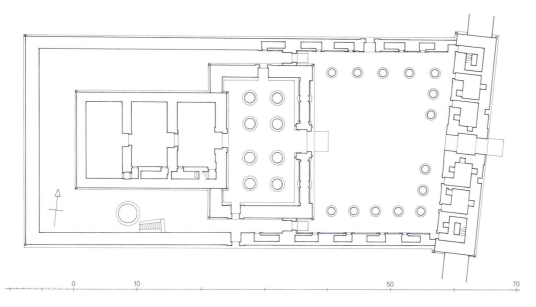

Figure 203.
Plan of the Augustan
temple of Kalabsha.

The 34 m broad pylon is not parallel to the temple facade but shifted 6 degrees off its axis to the southeast, producing considerable distortion in the otherwise regular building. The court behind the pylon was surrounded by colonnades along the pylon side and the two long sides. These extraordinarily slim columns carried composite capitals. As was the case in the courts of Edfu and Kom Ombo, the side porticoes are not connected with the temple. A splendid 24.35 x 16.32 m wide and 12.20 m high pronaos gives entrance to the court. The composite capitals of the three-by-four columns exhibit a distinct pattern (see diagram).

An offering hall, a visiting god's hall, and a sanctuary, which follow behind the pronaos, have ample dimensions but lack the usual side chambers. The cultic function of the temple perhaps yielded to the propagandist qualities. Inscriptions and reliefs remained unfinished. The pronaos is clearly separated from the rear part of the temple, as is the pylon from the court walls. The four separate units of temple house, pronaos, court, and pylon were, therefore, built after each other but certainly within the reign of Augustus. An architectural survey in 1961 yielded precise measurements and a system of proportions suggesting a grid that combined ground plan and elevations in a single design.[36] The slender column proportions and the wide intercolumniations suggest a new sense of form and space that was perhaps influenced by Roman architecture. The 12 m high enclosure wall was built of brick except for the stone socle. The bedding joints of the stone socle undulated and offer a good example of building features borrowed from 30th Dynasty brick walls. In the southwest corner of the complex stood a small birth house–like kiosk, surrounded by four-by-five columns; the kiosk remained unfinished (fig. 247). In 1962, the temple was taken down and rebuilt together with the kiosk of Qertassi and the Ramesside rock temple of Bet el-Wali on an island just south of the new Aswan High Dam.

Pronaos, Augustan Temple of Mandulis and Isis at Kalabsha

BACK

f - e - e - f

d - c - c - d

b - a - a - b

FRONT

a: Quatrefoil, five-story lily capital

b: Quatrefoil, two-tiered papyrus/palmette capital

c: Damaged quatrefoil, multistory lily/papyrus capital

e: Damaged quatrefoil, lily/(damaged) capital

f: Palmette/papyrus capital

About 15 B.C., the Roman governor Petronius built a small temple at DEN-DUR (ancient Tuzis) for Isis, Osiris, and two brothers (Pediese and Pahor), who became local heroes.[37] A 30 m wide cult terrace overlooked the Nile (figs. 204–206). Behind it stood a monumental stone gate. From the gate, two flanking walls ran around the temple and isolated the structure from the cult terrace and the Nile. The 6.55 x 13 m temple house is a modest but well-executed *distyle in antis*. The two front columns carry composite capitals. An offering hall and a sanctuary with a statue niche follow behind; the decoration of the interior remained unfinished. A crypt was built into the rear wall. A rock chamber in the cliffs behind may have represented the tomb of Pediese and Pahor, who were said to have drowned in the Nile. In 1963, the gate and temple were taken down as part of the Nubian salvage campaign. In recognition of the American contribution to the campaign, the gate and temple were presented to the United States and in 1978 rebuilt in The Metropolitan Museum of Art, New York.

Farther to the south, the small Ptolemaic Thoth temple at DAKKA was transformed into a temple fortress. The temple was surrounded by a 270 x 444 m stone wall with an entrance building along the Nile (fig. 128). A 24.31 m broad and 11.62 m high pylon was built. From the pylon, a 55 m long processional approach led to a cult terrace at the Nile, into which numerous blocks of Hatshepsut and Thutmosis III were inserted which were brought from the New Kingdom site of Quban on the opposite side of the river. A new inner stone enclosure wall was connected to the pylon. The small temple of Ergamenes II and Ptolemy VIII was enlarged at the two long sides. Its rear wall was opened to allow for the addition of a new sanctuary with a granite naos. The temple collapsed in 1908–1909 and was rebuilt by A. Barsanti. In 1961 the temple was transferred to the area of Wadi el-Sebu'a.

The Roman presence was also manifested at the southern border at MAHARRAQA (Hiera Sykaminos) by an interesting, unusual temple building (fig. 207). This temple, dedicated to Isis and Serapis, cannot be securely dated because it was neither completed nor inscribed. However, since temple building in Nubia declined after the reign of Augustus, one might date the Maharraqa temple to this period. The temple was a 13.56 x 15.69 m wide building consisting of an interior court surrounded on three sides by colonnades. The slightly wider southern colonnade was separated from the other two by screen walls and was accessible from the court by means of a central door. The main entrance was placed in the wall that faced the Nile, with two secondary doors on the other sides. The exterior walls were topped by cavettos, and the corners were accentuated by vertical tori. The structure does not represent the forecourt of a larger, unfinished project but is a complete building. Although one must admit that all building elements are Egyptian, the plan of the building has no parallels in Egyptian architecture and might be foreign. The spiral staircase that leads from one of the corners of the court to the roof is unparalleled in pharaonic building.[38]

'AIN AMUR, a well at the northern desert route between El-Kharga and El-Dakhla, generated in Roman times a caravansary. A stone enclosure wall with an 80 m side length was built there along with a small Amun temple. H. E. Winlock suggested a late Ptolemaic–early Roman date (fig. 208).[39] The tem-

Figure 204.
Old view of the Augustan
temple of Dendur
(courtesy of MMA).

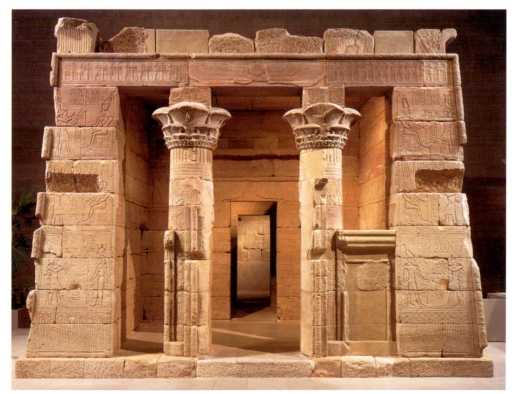

Figure 205.
Facade of the temple
house of Dendur (photo
P. Lachenauer, courtesy
of MMA).

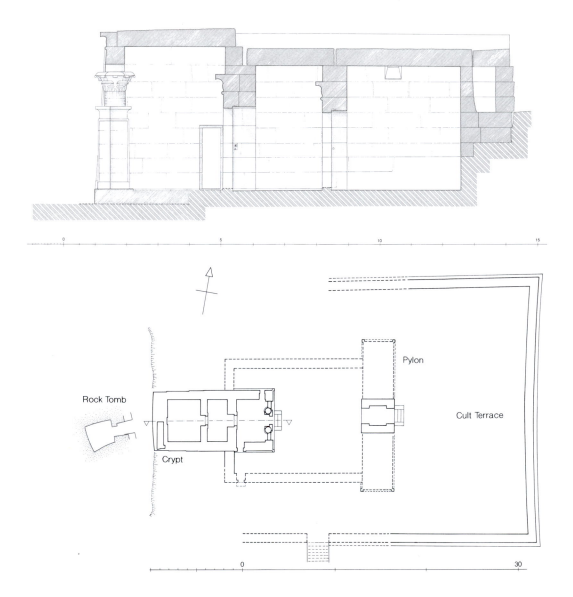

Figure 206.
Longitudinal section and
plan of the Augustan temple
of Dendur.

ple was a modest but strong stone construction of 8.9 x 15.7 m, apparently
with an entrance kiosk, two antechambers, and a sanctuary. The wall decoration is largely destroyed.

An Augustan sandstone temple dedicated to Amun "the Victorious" was
discovered in 1981 at 'AIN BIRBIJEH ('Ain Birbiya) in the El-Dakhla Oasis and
has since been restored.[40] The originally 10 x 13 m building contained a broad
room with a sanctuary, a side chamber, and a staircase to the roof. The temple
was later enlarged by means of two front rooms with side chambers. Still later,
a pronaos with a four-column facade was added at the front and a contra-
chapel against the rear wall. The temple stood within a 21 x 42 m enclosure
wall, the gate of which was inscribed with a dedication to Augustus.

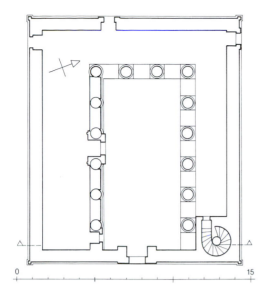

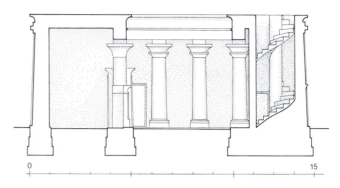

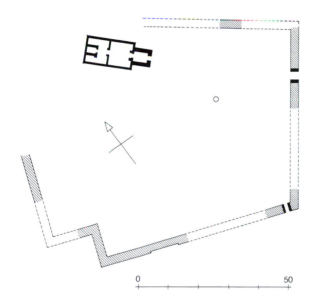

Figure 207. *(top)*
Plan and section of the Roman temple
of Maharraqa.

Figure 208. *(at left)*
Plan of the early Roman sanctuary
of 'Ain Amur.

The reign of Augustus marked an important phase of temple building not only in Egypt but elsewhere in the Roman Empire. The incorporation of Egypt, with its extraordinarily ancient culture, into the Empire also initiated an early tendency toward "Egyptomania." Augustus himself contributed to this trend by bringing two obelisks from Egypt to Rome. The obelisk of Ramesses II from Heliopolis was erected in 10 B.C. as a victory monument in the Circus Maximus (since 1589 on the Piazza del Popolo). Another obelisk, that of Psametik II from Heliopolis, was reerected as the gnomon of Augustus's giant sundial on the Campus Martius. About 15 B.C., the senator Epulo Gaius Cestius built a pyramid at the Porta Ostiensis for his tomb; a second pyramid (lost today), the Meta Romuli, was built at the Vatican.

Tiberius (A.D. 14–37)

After the death of Augustus (August 29, A.D. 14), the unchanging prosperity of Egypt permitted the emperor Tiberius to continue the temple-building program. It is difficult to establish whether during Tiberius's twenty-three year reign new temples were built or only unfinished Augustan projects completed.

According to a dedication inscription,[41] the famous pronaos of DENDERA was dedicated to Hathor under Tiberius (figs. 209–212). The structure measures 26.03 x 43.00 m and is 17.20 m high. An 8 m long architrave spans the central intercolumniation.[42] The towering cavetto, built from one course, and the massive volume of the corner tori cast heavy shadows and articulate the edges of the magnificent facade. The four-by-six, 14.3 m high columns of the pronaos are topped by quadruple Hathor heads.[43] The majestic capitals occupy one-third of the column height and accentuate their fetishlike character. The shafts are profusely decorated with scenes, and their straight bases stand on flat plinths. The paint, still preserved in the nineteenth century, was dominated by the blue of the Hathor head's wig (fig. 261). The narrow interior of the pronaos is stacked with eighteen columns, whose 2 m high architraves are arranged parallel to the axis of the temple. The floor of the hypostyle hall reached the outside court level. Since tradition ruled that the processional approach should gradually descend from the inside to the outside, the builders had to lower the floor of the central nave of the pronaos to obtain the required progression of floor levels.

At MEDAMOUD, the huge Tiberius gate was erected in front of the Ptolemaic pylon (plan VII). It was 11 m wide and 8.8 m deep and probably formed part of the 130 x 164 m wide Ptolemaic brick enclosure wall.[44] A 132 m long road, flanked by seventeen pairs of human-headed sphinxes, connected the gate with a huge cult terrace in the west.

The small Hathor temple on PHILAE, built by Ptolemy VI east of the Isis temple, was considerably enlarged under Tiberius (fig. 141, plan XIV).[45] A kiosk with fourteen Hathor-headed columns was added to the front of the pronaos. The roof was timbered. A cult terrace was built at the back of the temple from where the cult statue could overlook the Nile. Since the terrace was placed at the back of the temple, the cult statue had to be carried around to the entrance at the front.

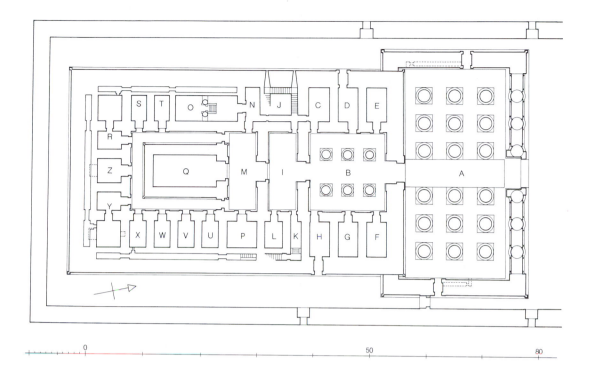

0   50   80

Figure 209. *(top)*
Plan of the Hathor
temple at Dendera
under Tiberius.

Figure 210. *(bottom)*
Pronaos of Tiberius
for Hathor of Dendera
(photo A.O.).

Figure 211. *(top)*
The pronaos of Tiberius for Hathor
of Dendera (photo A.O.).

Figure 212. *(bottom)*
The interior of the pronaos of
Tiberius for Hathor of Dendera
(photo A.O.).

Caligula (A.D. 37–41)

Under Caligula, the Forum Julium in Alexandria was dismantled and an obelisk, erected there under Augustus, moved to Rome. This uninscribed obelisk stood in the Circus Vaticanus until 1586, when Domenico Fontana transported it to St. Peter's square. Caligula, who favored the cults of Isis and Serapis, is considered the builder of the first Iseum Campese.[46] Since the temple burned down in A.D. 80 and was replaced by a new building under Domitian, nothing is known about the older temple.

Building activity in Egypt was minimal. Two gates at the southern approach of the Geb temple complex of COPTOS carry the names of Caligula, and a third carries that of Claudius; the latter was still standing in 1910.[47] One might suspect that all three gates were built together with the temple of El-Qal'a under Augustus/Tiberius and only inscribed later.

Claudius (A.D. 41–54)

The temple of Khnum at ESNA, built under Ptolemy V, was enlarged with a huge pronaos in Roman times (figs. 213–216). Despite the cartouches of Claudius, which occupy prominent parts of the temple walls,[48] it is not certain that he was the actual builder. The pronaos measures 20.2 x 37.36 m and is 14.98 m high. Four rows of six, 12 m high columns with composite capitals carry the roof. The column bases are not chamfered and do not stand on the usual plinths. A symmetrical grouping of capital types is found only at the front of the pronaos (see diagram). The differences are slight and barely noticeable. The capitals of the inner columns are not arranged according to a discernible system. The capitals are mostly variations of the palmette motif on a bell-shaped papyrus capital, creating a uniform view (fig. 216). The reason-

> *Pronaos, Temple of Khnum at Esna*
>
> c - b - a - a - b - c
>
> ---
>
> a: Quatrefoil, two-tiered papyrus/palmette capital
>
> b: Quatrefoil, two-tiered palmette capital
>
> c: Quatrefoil, three-tiered palmette capital

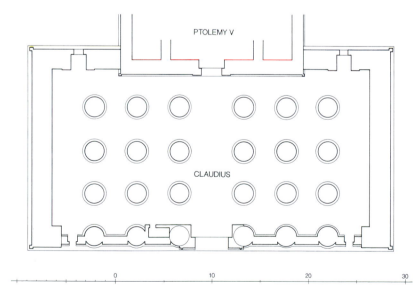

Figure 213.
Plan of the pronaos of Claudius for Khnum of Esna.

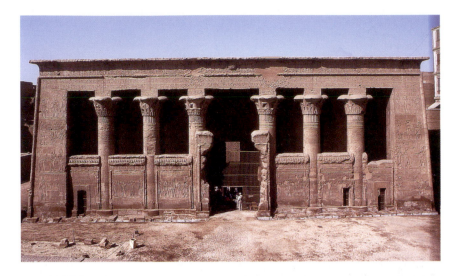

Figure 214. *(top)*
Frontal view of the pronaos of
Claudius for Khnum of Esna
(photo A.O.).

Figure 215. *(bottom)*
Rear side of the pronaos of
Claudius for Khnum of Esna
showing remains of the temple
house of Ptolemy V.

ably fine sculpting of the details cannot hide the fact that the flat floral elements adhere to the surface, indicating a loss in plasticity in the carving of column capitals.

Probably also under Claudius, a temple for Harendotes was built on PHILAE (fig. 217, plan XIV). The temple stood on a platform, located west of the Isis temple.[49] A central staircase led up to the temple. The unusual, square plan (14.5 x 14.7 m) was probably dictated by the nearness of the edge of the island. The front of the *tetrastyle in antis* faced east and consisted of four columns with papyrus/palmette capitals.[50] The foundation shows that a second row of columns did not exist. The hall was covered with 4.5 m long architraves running east to west. A square sanctuary, surrounded by an ambulatory

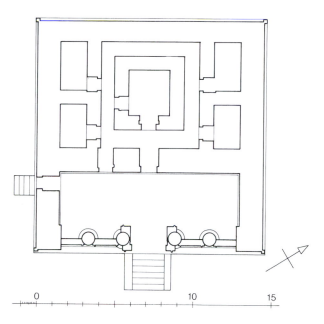

and four wing chambers, followed directly behind the pronaos. The temple was taken down in Byzantine times to the foundation platform and the stones used for building a church nearby.

Figure 216. *(left)*
Palmette capitals of the pronaos of Claudius for Khnum of Esna (photo J. P. Sebah).

Figure 217. *(right)*
Plan of the temple of Claudius for Harendotes on Philae.

Nero (A.D. 54–68)

In A.D. 66, a brawl between Greeks and Jews in Alexandria degenerated into a rebellion. During its suppression by Roman troops, nearly all Alexandrine Jews were slain, allegedly 50,000 individuals.[51] It seems a wonder that temples could be built under such conditions.

In the Faiyum city of KARANIS, the (larger) "South Temple" was dedicated to the crocodile deities Pnepheros and Petesukhos (figs. 218–219). The 17 x 23.6 m temple was built on top of the remains of an older, probably Ptolemaic structure. The door lintel carries a dedicatory inscription of the time of Nero (A.D. 59–60).[52] The building contains a narrow, deep court with small, vaulted side chambers and a roof staircase. Another small room with two vaulted side niches follows behind. The small sanctuary houses a central platform for the shrine with the cult images, side chambers, and another staircase.

This temple, its northern neighbor, and the temple of Dionysias in the Faiyum represent a local temple type that may have developed from Ptolemaic examples at the Faiyum cities of Bacchias, Tebtynis, and Theadelphia. The large number of tiny chambers with many corners, the platform for the shrine of the cult image, and the deep wall niches for crocodile images are characteristic. These elements seem to reflect local cultic practices of an originally non-Egyptian population.

The buildings also show the gradual infiltration of Roman building elements into Egyptian architecture. The exterior temple walls display Roman rustica masonry. The hard gray limestone of the lower block courses and the gate contrasted with the soft, yellow limestone of the upper courses. Directly in front of the temple house stood a 10.20 x 13.50 m kiosk with four-by-seven Ionic(!) columns on a socle with an Egyptian cavetto molding. The (timber) roof may have been barrel-shaped or gabled. (The "North Temple" is discussed with the building projects of Marcus Aurelius and Lucius Verus.)

Two completely destroyed temples located within a vast brick enclosure wall of the town of DÎMEH (Soknoupaiou Nesos, on the west bank of the Birkat Qarûn lake) may also date from this time. One temple, probably that of Sobek, was rectangular, built of stone, and measured 17.2 x 18.8 m; the second temple was of brick. A long, stone-paved processional approach led from the precinct to the lake. Parts of the brick enclosure wall still rise to an impressive height.

A rather large temple for Sobek stands in the ruins of the military settlement of DIONYSIAS (Qasr Qarûn) at the end of the Birkat Qarûn lake. The 19 x 28 m temple, built of hard limestone, is well preserved to the cavetto molding and roof (figs. 220–221). The date of the temple is uncertain, although similarities with the two temples of Karanis suggest a corresponding date. The remote location and the lack of inscriptions may explain why the temple was measured only by E. F. Jomard in 1799. Since the survey was carried out when the temple was still half buried in sand, serious errors occurred.[53]

The exterior walls are of fortresslike height with a small entrance in the front and at one side. In the interior, three halls of remarkable height (6.5 m) follow each other and are flanked by the usual side chambers and staircases. Jomard measured roofing beams 7 m long. The sanctuary, placed in the third hall, consists of three parallel shrines, two of which are deep enough to accommodate long, crocodile-shaped cult images.

An unusual number of chambers and crypts occupies a mezzanine floor and rooftop. A remarkable feature is a roof chapel directly above the sanctuary. Like a *wabet*, the chapel consists of an open forecourt and a chamber with a pair of columns at the front.

An unconventional pronaos was built against the facade of the temple. The central part consisted of a porch with three-by-four columns. The innermost row of columns is formed by engaged columns built against the temple facade.

A 300 m long processional allée led to a kiosk. The square building had four columns on each side and was 10 m wide and 9 m long. The roof might have been of timber. The date of the kiosk is unknown.

Other kiosks in the Faiyum area are known, but since they lack inscriptions and have not been studied they can only be roughly dated to the "Ptolemaic-Roman" Period. Two kiosks were found in front of the temple of TEBTYNIS (Umm el-Breigat).[54] The limestone kiosk closer to the temple is considered "Ptolemaic." Another, now half-destroyed kiosk stood 150 to 200 m in front along a processional approach. A third half-destroyed kiosk was found in front of the temple of MEDINET MADI.[55]

Three small chapels were built in the time of Nero, at TEHNA EL-GEBEL (ancient Akoris).[56] At the same time, a small rock temple of Ramesses II at the

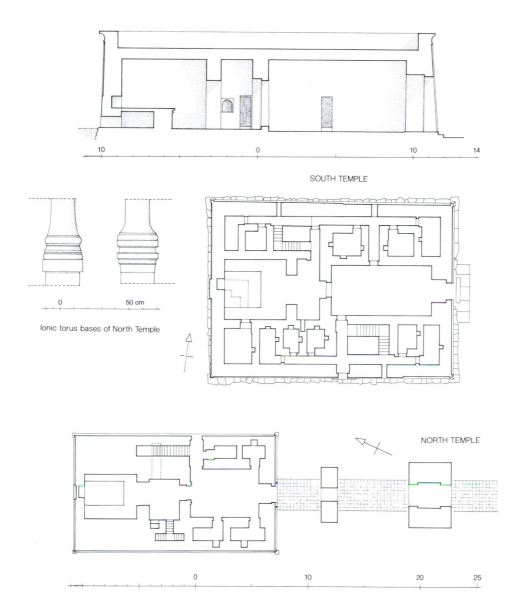

SOUTH TEMPLE

Ionic torus bases of North Temple

0   50 cm

NORTH TEMPLE

0   10   20   25

western slope of the mountain was enlarged. The Ramesside temple of four axially arranged rooms received a 9.5 x 20 m hypostyle hall with two-by-four columns that probably had Hathor-head capitals.[57] In front of the temple, a sequence of three wide forecourts was built, surrounded by colonnades with Ionic columns. Massive gates along the processional approach connected the courts.

When Tiberius had the stone enclosure wall of the temple of DENDERA built, the wall cut into the birth house of Nectanebo I, which protruded into the court (plan VI). The birth house was replaced by a new building, perhaps under Nero (figs. 222–223). Although the dedication inscription refers to

Figure 218.
Section and plan of the South Temple *(top)* and plan of the North Temple of the Roman Period at Karanis with a torus base from the outside corners of the North Temple.

Figure 219. *(top)*
Frontal view of the South
temple of Karanis.

Figure 220. *(bottom)*
Frontal view of the Roman
temple of Sobek at Dionysias
(photo A.O.).

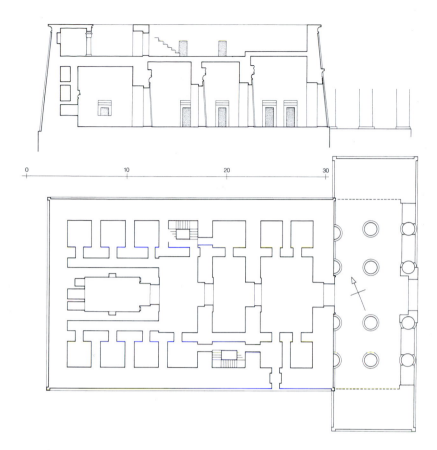

Trajan, Nero is depicted in the pronaos of the Hathor temple, offering the model of a birth house.[58] The particularly well-designed ground plan of the birth house follows Ptolemaic models. The core building contains a sequence of three rooms. Two corridors that isolate the large sanctuary are notable. These passages are too narrow to be used and must have been added for symbolic and optical effect. The rear wall of the sanctuary is dominated by an enormous false door that is framed by a double cavetto molding on slender columns and topped by an uraeus frieze.[59] A cult niche high up in the wall corresponds to the location of the statue niche in the sanctuary of the main temple.

The birth house was surrounded by an ambulatory. The composite capitals of the columns carry high pillars with Bes figures. The frontal ambulatory extends by the addition of three columns into a kind of kiosk, with the front corners formed by L-shaped pillars. The kiosk had a timbered roof that somehow must have connected to the stone structure of the birth house. The previously mentioned relief of Nero depicts a segmented pediment with a huge sun disk. This merging of the ambulatory with a kiosk is a novelty. At older birth houses, a court was attached as a separate structure (see figs. 245–246).

Under Nero, the temple of DEIR EL-HAGAR at the western boundary of the El-Dakhla Oasis was built for the Theban triad (figs. 224–225). The temple stood inside a 41 x 78.5 m enclosure wall with a small gate and a processional

Figure 221.
Preliminary longitudinal section and plan of the Roman temple of Sobek at Dionysias.

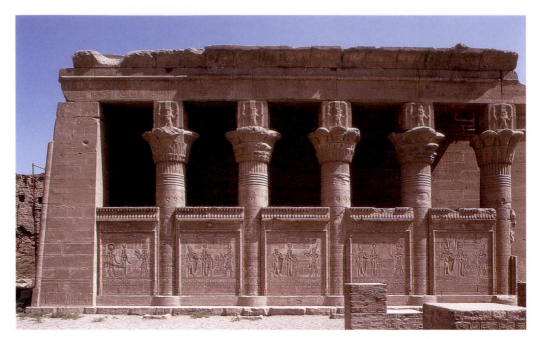

Figure 222.
The southern ambulatory of the later birth house of Nero(?) for Hathor of Dendera decorated under Trajan and Hadrian (photo A.O.).

Figure 223.
Interior view of the later birth house of Nero(?) of Hathor at Dendera with the false door in the sanctuary (photo A.O.).

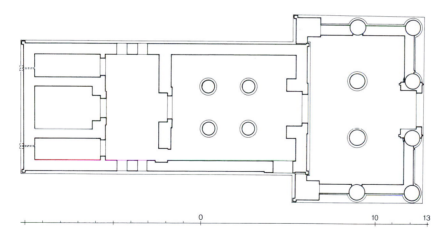

Figure 224. *(top)*
The remains of the temple of
Nero at Deir el-Hagar before
the excavation.

Figure 225. *(bottom)*
Plan of the temple of Nero at
Deir el-Hagar.

0   10   13

approach flanked by colonnades. The temple imitated the ground plan of the great state temples but without an ambulatory. The 7.30 x 16.2 m sandstone building contained a central sanctuary with two side chapels, which face a common offering room. A small hypostyle hall with four pillars stood in front. Two engaged piers supported the architraves. Under Titus, an entrance kiosk was added that consisted of a double row of four columns. The roof of the temple collapsed after 1822 and was recently restored.

Vespasian (A.D. 69–79)

Vespasian's relationship with Egypt was overshadowed by fights over increasing taxes. A momentous event was the dispatching of his son Titus, with Egyptian reinforcement troops, for the siege and destruction of the temple of Jerusalem in A.D. 70. The resulting problems with the Alexandrine Jewish community led to the preemptive destruction of the Jewish temple of Onias at Tell el-Yahudiya in A.D. 73. The relationship between the emperor and the Egyptian population was much improved when Titus, wearing an Egyptian diadem, attended the consecration of a new Apis bull at Memphis. In 1984, a Roman fortress was excavated at NAG' EL-HAGAR, on the east bank north of Aswan. Between column fragments and other reused elements, some relief blocks show Emperor Vespasian. The source of the material is not known.[60]

Domitian (A.D. 81–96)

Despite Domitian's inclination to Egyptian cults in Rome, his fifteen-year rule produced few buildings in Egypt. Soon after his accession, however, he rebuilt the famous Iseum Campese in ROME, which had burned down in the year A.D. 80, under Titus (fig. 226).[61] The huge, 67 x 228 m sanctuary in Roman style consisted of two components, which were separated by a transversal court that could be entered from both ends through mighty gates. The southern component was probably the Serapeum, a wide *exedra* with colonnades, today covered by San Stefano del Cacco. A deep hall or court was attached to the vertex of the exedra. The northern component was the Iseum, a rectangular temenos with a long processional approach that led to the actual temple house, the foundations of which are preserved behind the apse of the church Santa Maria sopra Minerva.

The combination of an elongated rectangle with an exedra and a deep hall was repeated in the Forum of Trajan and the temple of Serapis in Hadrian's villa at Tivoli. These layouts anticipate the arrangement of the nave, transept, and apse of the Christian basilica.[62]

The temple included at least seven, but probably more, obelisks.[63] The *columnae caelatae*, 9.5 m high, gray granite columns, were found at the site of the Iseum and were similar to the columns of the Artemision of Ephesos, sculpted with figure friezes imitating decorated Egyptian columns.[64] The statues, of which several splendid examples have survived, were original Egyptian or Egyptianizing.[65]

Domitian also restored the famous Iseum of BENEVENTO and supplied it with two granite obelisks.[66]

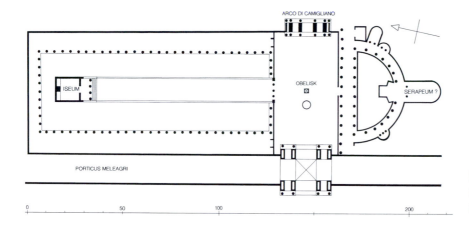

ARCO DI CAMIGLIANO

ISEUM

OBELISK

SERAPEUM ?

PORTICUS MELEAGRI

0   50   100   200

Figure 226.
Reconstructed plan of the Iseum
Campese of Domitian at Rome.

Figure 227.
Rear side of the (north) gate of Domitian
at the precinct for Hathor of Dendera
(photo A.O.).

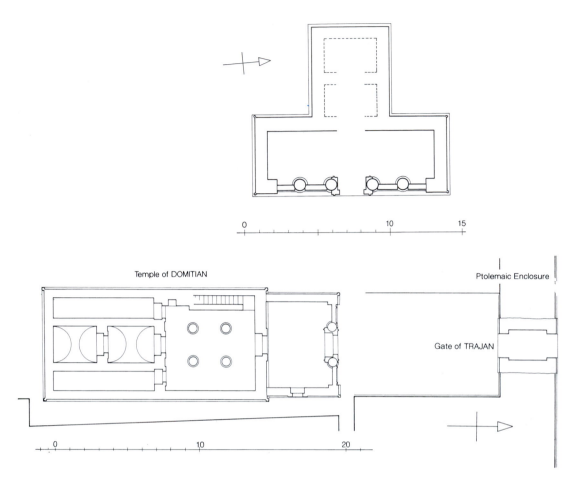

Temple of DOMITIAN

Ptolemaic Enclosure

Gate of TRAJAN

Figure 228. *(top)*
Plan of the temple of Domitian for Khnum, Satet, and Anuket at Aswan.

Figure 229. *(bottom)*
Plan of the temple of Domitian for Isis/Serapis/Horus at Qasr Dush.

In Egypt a small temple in Egyptian style was built at HERMOPOLIS MAGNA, in the complex of the creator goddess Nehemet-'awy, the consort of Thoth. Some blocks and column fragments have survived.[67]

In the time of Domitian, a gate was built in the north wall of the temple of DENDERA (fig. 227). The huge, 10.10 m high gate was closed by means of a single door.[68] The remains of a temple inscribed by Domitian were discovered in 1906, at KOM EL-RESRÂS (Reseiris) on the west bank of the Nile, 5 km south of Silsileh. No excavations were undertaken.[69]

In ASWAN a small temple was built for the triad of Khnum, Satet, and Anuket (fig. 228). The temple stood in the southern part of the town, with its back to the Nile. The columns carried composite capitals. The building and its four-column pronaos were completed under Nerva. The building was destroyed at the beginning of the nineteenth century, leaving only the front of the pronaos and some foundations.[70]

Under Domitian, the Ptolemaic(?) fortress at QASR EL-DUSH (ancient Kysis), at the southern end of the El-Kharga Oasis, was honored by a temple that was dedicated not to Amun, as were the older temples in the oasis, but to the "younger" gods Isis, Serapis, and Horus (fig. 229).[71] The 7.55 x 15.32 m stone temple house had a hypostyle hall with two-by-two slender columns. A two-partitioned sanctuary followed with two elongated side wings. The sanctuary and side wings were covered with vaults. Later a pronaos with two front columns was added, probably covered with a timber roof.

Nerva (A.D. 96–98)

Except for a 14 x 19.5 m temple at DIOSPOLIS PARVA (Hiw) no building is known from the emperor's short reign.[72] The temple was probably dedicated to the local Hathor and stood close to an older, Ptolemaic temple. Both temples were later incorporated into a Roman fort. A stone-paved processional road approached the Roman temple from the north.

Trajan (A.D. 98–117)

The originally friendly disposition of the emperor to Alexandria was impaired when the Jewish community, agitated by messianic prophecies, rose against Romans and Greeks in Egypt in 115. This rebellion raged on in the form of guerrilla warfare to the end of Trajan's reign. The bloodshed resulted in the death of half a million people, most of them Hellenized Jews. War damages to buildings were observed up to Hermopolis parva.

At AKHMIM (Panopolis), one of several huge blocks found in front of the Ptolemaic temple of Min carried a dedicatory inscription of Trajan dating to the year A.D. 109. The 7 m long block seems to have been the lintel of a 5 m wide doorway, suggesting a 15(!) m high gate (see chapter 6's discussions of the buildings of Ptolemy III Euergetes I and Ptolemy IV Philopator).[73]

Probably under Trajan, the Augustan temple of SHANHOUR for Mut, Isis, and several other deities was considerably extended (fig. 186).[74] The small Augustan temple house was enlarged with an addition to the front, with side wings that protruded on both sides far beyond the facade of the old temple house. The central part of the addition comprised a hypostyle hall of four columns. Later, but probably during the same reign, a monumental pronaos was added to the front. A depth of three rows of columns and a width of eight columns can be reconstructed. The pronaos was 28 m wide and 13.8 m deep. The pronaos is destroyed now to the lowest courses of blocks.

At the fortress of QASR EL-DUSH in the El-Kharga Oasis, an outer forecourt was built in front of the enclosure wall, with a brick pylon and a stone gate. This court was part of Domitian's temple of Isis, Serapis, and Horus within the enclosure wall. The gate carried Trajan's dedication inscription of the year 116. North of the gate was a wide cult terrace.

Hadrian (A.D. 117–138)

Emperor Hadrian, Empress Sabina, and a huge entourage traveled to Egypt in 130–131 and stayed for ten months. The journey included a lion hunt in the western desert and a visit to the statues of Memnon of Amenhotep III on the west bank of Thebes.

As a noble gesture, the emperor donated a new library to ALEXANDRIA. The Serapeum, which had been heavily damaged during the rebellion of

114/115, was magnificently restored. The originally smaller temenos was surrounded by a new, square enclosure wall that extended the temple complex to 237 x 237 m. This extension required huge substructures for the platform above the original temple mound (see fig. 108). The Serapeum was reached by means of a monumental, hundred-step staircase, leading to a colonnaded propylon. The new temenos was surrounded on all sides by double colonnades. This ground plan corresponded to that of a Caesareum. Egyptian elements (columns, etc.) were no longer used. The new temple of Serapis inside the court was, following the architectural style of Hadrian's time, domed (cf. the Pantheon in Rome). With its high elevation, platform, surrounding colonnades, and isolated temple, the Serapeum can be compared to Herod's temple of Jerusalem. Following orders of Theodosius I, the magnificent building was demolished in 391. Under the Mamelouks, numerous architectural elements and parts of obelisks and colossal statues were recovered and submerged as a breakwater in the sea near the Pharos.[75]

In Middle Egypt, near modern Sheikh Abâde, Emperor Hadrian founded the Roman town of ANTINOUPOLIS, in memory of Antinous, who drowned in 130 in the Nile. The walled 1,100 x 1,800 m town was located at the western end of a new desert route to the Red Sea town of Berenike, which was intended to facilitate trade with Arabia, India, and China. The imperial town was supplied with splendid buildings, all in the classical style.[76]

In the hard-stone quarries of the MONS CLAUDIANUS, a small and modest temple was built for the cult of Serapis in the years A.D. 117–119. The plain sanctuary had a tetrastyle porch with Ionic columns. The building is much damaged now.[77]

In 124, a small Roman-style temple for the "Zeus Helios, the grand Serapis," and for Isis, was built in the court of Nectanebo I in front of the LUXOR temple. The 8 x 12 m building was a peripteral temple with four-by-five columns carrying a gabled roof. The sandstone gate was topped with an Egyptian cavetto with a winged sun disk. The walls and column shafts consisted of burned brick, and the roof was certainly of timber.[78]

The temple of Monthu at ARMANT was enlarged at the front under Hadrian, probably by a huge pronaos. Lepsius saw parts of 2.10–2.40 m thick columns with the cartouches of Hadrian still in situ standing on their bases. Columns of such a diameter would have been 15–17 m high. Judging from the foundations, which at Lepsius's time were exploited as quarries, the building must have been exceptionally vast and splendid.[79] Today nothing is left.

On PHILAE the huge "Gate of Hadrian" was constructed, west of the second pylon of the Isis temple. Since the gate became the carrier of the Abaton decree[80] and the decoration addresses Osiris, it must have been used by the procession of Isis on her way to the Osiris tomb on Biggeh Island. The staircase leading down to the Nile was torn away by the river, as was a towering entrance kiosk at the Nile front of the gate. This kiosk was attached to the pylon-like front of the Gate of Hadrian. A roofed entrance passage east of the gate leads to the subsidiary door of the Isis temple.[81]

Another foundation of the time may have been the temple for the local triad Tutu, Neith, and Tapsais at ISMANT EL-KHARAB (ancient Kellis) in the

El-Dakhla Oasis.[82] The 150 x 170 m enclosure wall contained the main temple. A colonnaded processional approach to the temple terminated at a 6 m wide entrance porch of brick columns. The stone temple behind was dated by the excavators as "Hadrian or Antoninus Pius." An original one-chamber chapel was enlarged several times at the front and a contra-chapel with an entrance kiosk was added behind. Some walls of the building are still preserved under the sand.

Characteristic for the merging of styles during this period is a 32 m long brick temple at the side and parallel with the stone temple. It consists of an elongated court and a hall covered with a 4.8 m wide vault. The walls show a colorful dado in Roman style combined with Egyptian temple decoration higher up.[83]

At TIVOLI in Italy, Emperor Hadrian built his famous, grand villa, which was one of the most impressive foundations of his time. Between many diverse structures, it contained a "Canopus"—following the basic layout of the Iseum Campese. The emperor also showed his interest in Egyptian cults by dedicating temples to Isis at Petra and Samaria.[84]

Antoninus Pius (A.D. 138–161)

The reign of Emperor Antoninus Pius was the last productive phase of Roman Egypt, which generated not only the famous Faiyum portraits[85] but also several superior building projects. ALEXANDRIA received a huge hippodrome with the "Sun and Moon Gates."

In the second century, probably under Antoninus Pius, a temple was built in pure Roman style in the center of the acropolis-like city mountain of TEHNA EL-GEBEL (Akoris). It was possibly dedicated to Serapis. Only the temple podium and parts of the four front columns remain.

At DENDERA, the precinct of Hathor received an eastern side gate, which led directly to the birth house of Isis.

A huge, 8.75 x 42 m entrance kiosk was designed under Antoninus Pius for the temple of the primordial Amun at MEDINET HABU (figs. 230–231, plan X).[86] Unfortunately, the great project remained only half completed. The building had a single row of eight, 13.4 m high columns, incorporating the central column pair of the Ptolemaic entrance kiosk (fig. 150). The screen walls had the enormous thickness of 2.80 m, producing unfamiliar corner solutions. Because of the dimensions, the entablature, cavetto, and roof of the 15 m high building would, if finished, be constructed of timber.[87]

A 26 x 41 m wide court was begun in front of the kiosk, paved with sandstone slabs and surrounded by a 4.5 m high stone wall topped with a cavetto. The court had its main access from the east and two secondary gates along the lateral axis. The court resembled the Roman court at Kom Ombo, but its low enclosure walls would certainly not have been able to carry the roof of colonnades.

At ARMANT a stone gate was built as part of an unidentified building, 150 m west of the main temple.

The small Isis chapel of EL-HILLA (Contralatopolis) on the east bank of the Nile, south-southeast of Esna, was enlarged under Antoninus Pius (figs.

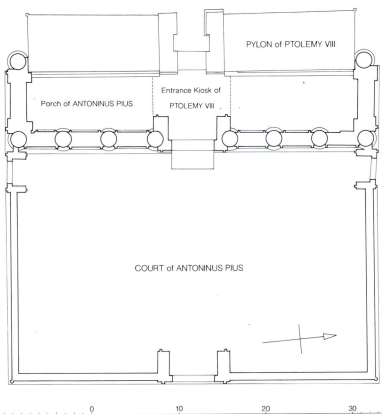

PYLON of PTOLEMY VIII

Porch of ANTONINUS PIUS

Entrance Kiosk of
PTOLEMY VIII

COURT of ANTONINUS PIUS

0   10   20   30

Figure 230.
Reconstruction of the unfinished pronaos of Antoninus
Pius at Medinet Habu (Uvo
Hölscher, *The Temples of the
Eighteenth Dynasty* [Chicago,
1939], fig. 51).

Figure 231.
Plan of the court and unfinished pronaos of Antoninus
Pius at Medinet Habu.

212–233).[88] The old pylon front was extended with a 7.28 x 13.51 m pronaos, which contained two rows of four, nearly 7 m high sandstone columns with palm and composite capitals and Hathor-head capitals in the center (see diagram). The temple of El-Hilla was taken down in 1828 to obtain building material for a government building.

A small temple for the local gazelle goddess Anuket was built under Antoninus Pius at KOMMIR (Kom Meir), 12 km south of Esna.[89] The temple was discovered in 1941 but not completely excavated. It consisted of a temple house, fronted by a 24 m broad pronaos. The 14.5 x 19.8 m temple house contained two transversal rooms (offering room and room for the visiting gods). The middle chapel, with two statue chambers, faced the inner transversal room. A staircase led through the masonry of the west wall to the roof.

On the east bank of the lake of El-Kharga, two small temples were built at NADÛRA (fig. 234), possibly as peripheral stations for Amun of Hibis. The larger temple (Nadura A) was enclosed by a brick wall with a sandstone gate in the west and a subsidiary gate in the north wall. The temple had an 8.17 x 11.45 m pronaos with four front columns, which are now destroyed. The roof must have been of wood.[91] The 12.6 m deep temple house followed behind the pronaos. The freestanding sanctuary followed behind a room that was either an open court or a closed space roofed by either two or four columns. Since the front of the temple house and the rear wall of the pronaos were constructed as a unit, both parts must have been built at the same time.

In the WESTERN OASES, protective sand and reduced human activity have preserved several temples of the second or third century A.D. Without proper excavations, these mostly uninscribed temples can be only approximately dated and are only hypothetically attributed here to the period of Antoninus Pius. Several similar features suggest that these temples form a group. Their elongated ground plan, with a typical succession of small chambers, is remarkable. The series starts with a larger anteroom, which has benches along the walls.[90] Because the brick walls were too fragile to carry a longitudinal barrel vault, the room must have been either open or covered with a timber roof.

The second, smaller temple (Nadura B) had a 5 x 10 m pronaos with two front columns, which should have been followed by two more columns inside the pronaos. The pronaos fronted the temple house with three small chambers.

The Amun temple of QASR 'AIN EL-ZAIJAN in the El-Kharga Oasis was renewed under Antoninus Pius according to the dedication inscription on the lintel (figs. 235–236). The originally Ptolemaic temple of 7.22 x 13.56 m stood in a well-preserved, 26 x 68 m brick enclosure wall with a front pylon. The temple house consisted of a hypostyle hall and an offering room with a cult niche.

A small temple is located west of the main temple of QASR EL-DUSH (fig. 235). It was built of brick and had three vaulted rooms. Another brick temple stood near the Roman castle of EL-DEIR (fig. 235).

The "Doric" temple of BELÂD EL-RÛM in the Siwa Oasis also represented the sametemple type (fig. 235). The temple still existed in 1869 but was destroyed soon after.[92] It probably was a 25 m long building containing three,

---

Pronaos, Isis Chapel of El-Hilla

BACK

b - c - c - b
b - a - a - b

FRONT

a: Hathor capital
b: Eight-stem, two-tiered papyrus/palmette capital
c: Palm capital

Figure 232. View of the pronaos of Antoninus Pius at the Isis temple at El-Hilla (Contralatopolis) (*Description* I, pl. 90).

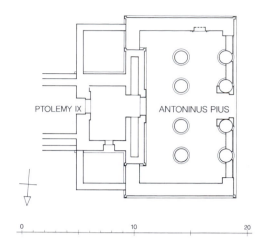

Figure 233. Plan of the pronaos of Antoninus Pius at the Isis temple at El-Hilla (Contralatopolis).

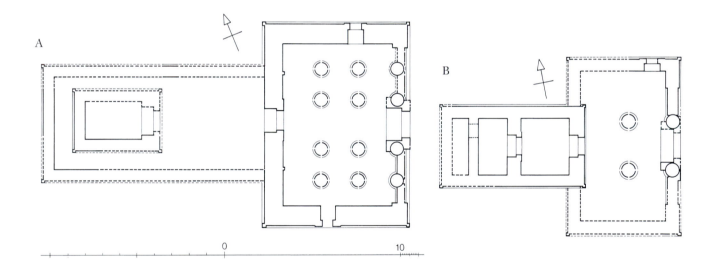

Figure 234. Plan of the two temples A and B of Antoninus Pius at Nadûra.

Near EL-DEIR

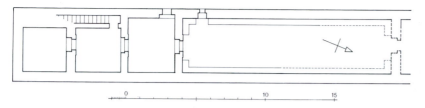

QASR 'AIN EL-ZAIJAN

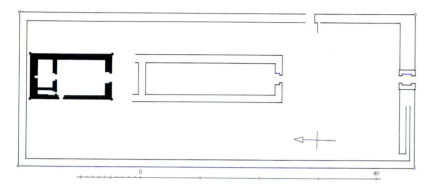

Near QASR DUSH

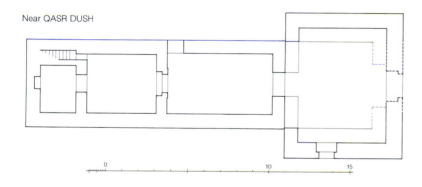

Figure 235.
Plans of the late Roman temples near
El-Deir, at Qasr 'Ain el-Zaijan, near
Qasr Dush, and at Belâd el-Rûm.

BELAD EL-RUM

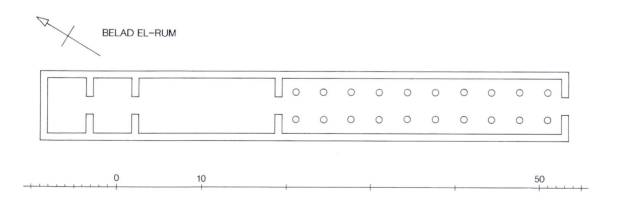

Figure 236.
Gate of the temple Qasr 'Ain el-Zaijan.

6.5 m broad rooms. The rooms followed behind a 34 m long court, which was flanked by 6 m high colonnades with Doric columns.[93]

Numerous smaller mortuary chapels in the oases of the western desert probably also originated from the first to second century A.D. Most are built with carefully dressed blocks. They reflect local, predominantly Roman styles but were occasionally decorated with an Egyptian cavetto.[94]

Marcus Aurelius (A.D. 161–180) and Lucius Verus (A.D. 161–169)

The reign of Marcus Aurelius in Egypt was interrupted in 172 by a rebellion of local troops led by the priest Isodoros. The rebellion did not have much effect on communal prosperity, as demonstrated by building projects in the hinterland.

The "North Temple" of the Faiyum city of KARANIS (fig. 218) was probably dedicated to the local crocodile god Soknopaios, perhaps in conjunction with other deities. The excavators dated the temple to the time between the first and third century,[95] but the pitiful conditions of the country in the third century certainly would have prevented temple building. One therefore would think of an earlier, more prosperous period, possibly that of Marcus Aurelius. The well-preserved Egyptian-style temple faces south. In front of the temple stood two gates with stone jambs. The 10.61 x 18.05 m temple house was built of limestone blocks arranged in undulating courses. The outer corners have tori standing on Ionic(!) column bases. The interior of the temple contains a small court, a sanctuary, and small side chambers. A cult niche is set into the exterior of the rear wall. The North Temple belongs to the same temple type as the South Temple of Karanis and the temple of Dionysias.

The Ptolemaic temple of ASFÛN EL-MATÂ'NA was enlarged with a pronaos under Marcus Aurelius and Commodus. In 1986, some inscribed blocks were discovered reused in a mosque.[96]

Commodus (A.D. 180–192)

The name of Commodus is preserved only on some relief blocks from the Horus temple at TAHTA (Hut-tyt, northwest of Sohag).[97]

Septimius Severus (A.D. 193–211)

Emperor Septimius Severus visited Alexandria in 199–200 and dedicated a temple to the goddess Cybele, baths, a gymnasium, and a pantheon. As a curiosity, one should mention the restoration of the then famous "singing" statues of Memnon at Thebes, the colossal statues of Amenhotep III at Thebes. Their acoustic phenomenon was silenced forever by this work.

Caracalla (A.D. 198–217)

The inhabitants of Alexandria ridiculed Emperor Caracalla, who in 215 came to Egypt and took horrible revenge. The situation in Egypt did not permit new building projects. Caracalla's famous baths in Rome contained a Serapeum.

Diocletian (A.D. 284–305)

The third century brought disaster to Egypt.[98] The short reigns of emperors in faraway Rome led to delayed recognition and confused governmental structures. Epidemics, looting, and the decline of the irrigation system followed, worsened by the 247/248 invasions of the Blemyes in Upper Egypt. The population of Alexandria shrunk to a third and the Faiyum town of Karanis was half ruined between 235 and 250. Pressure on ancient Egyptian religion increased through contact with Greek philosophy, Judaism, and the gradual rise of Christianity. These conditions, combined with the lack of government funding, led to an abandonment of most pharaonic temples from the middle of the third century.[99] The only emperor who ruled for a longer time and tried to halt the decline was Diocletian. Through persecutions of those who opposed the worship of the emperor, he tried to curb the spread of Christianity in Egypt. One of the few nonmilitary monuments of his reign is the so-called Pompey's column (which has no connection with Pompeius) in the Serapeum of Alexandria. About A.D. 302, this 28.7 m high granite monument was dedicated by the Alexandrines to thank the emperor for sparing the city after a rebellion.

The temple of LUXOR was transformed into a fortress.[100] The architects skillfully incorporated the temple into a fort using the pylon of Ramesses II as the main entrance. The second hypostyle hall of the old temple was converted into a traditional Roman sanctuary (*sacellum*). A *ciborium* with four columns sheltered a throne or an altar that stood in front of an apse in the rear wall. The walls were painted with frescoes depicting the march of Roman soldiers and horsemen.[101] The rear part of the temple was blocked.

In A.D. 296, the main entrance of the island of PHILAE shifted from the south tip to the north, to the temple of Augustus, which was adorned with a triple gate (fig. 192, plan XIV).[102] The gate was in Roman style but reflected with its heavy cornices, pilaster, and window framing pharaonic architecture.

Constantine the Great (A.D. 306–337)

The recognition of Christianity by Constantine the Great in 323 did not pacify Egypt. Power struggles between Christian factions and the misuse of their earthly power only increased the chaos.

In A.D. 330, imperial engineers succeeded in lowering the 32 m obelisk of Thutmosis III at KARNAK. It remained stranded in Alexandria because no ship could carry the giant to Constantinople. In A.D. 356, Constantius' engineers managed to move the 455 metric ton monolith to Rome and erect it in the Circus Maximus. The obelisk was toppled by the East Goths and broken into three pieces. In 1588, the fragments were reassembled and reerected in the Piazza San Giovanni in Laterano. Either about A.D. 330 or under the reign of Theodosius I, a second obelisk at KARNAK, the western obelisk of Thutmosis III at the seventh pylon, was removed and brought to Constantinople and erected in the hippodrome, in 391. This is the last known relocation of an obelisk in antiquity.[103]

Theodosius I (A.D. 379–395)

The recognition of Christianity was followed by forced Christianization under Theodosius. The official abolition of non-Christian cults encouraged gangs of monks to terrorize followers of the traditional "pagan" faith and to destroy their temples.[104] This wave of persecution peaked in 391/392 with the destruction of the Serapeum and its famous library. The Egyptian temples were either converted into churches or demolished for their building stone, such as granite column shafts and column capitals.

Remnants of the ancient religion could resist longer in Upper Egypt than in the north, and the cult of Isis survived on the remote island of Philae until 535/537.

The architectural history of the Egyptian Late Period and its adaptation by Roman architects terminated before the beginning of the third century A.D. During the long period from A.D. 180 to 430, no noteworthy religious architecture was produced in Egypt. It was the east Roman emperor Theodosius II (408–450) who created conditions that enabled the emergence of a fresh and different Christian architecture in Egypt (cathedral of Hermopolis, ca. 430–440; Deir el-Abyad, ca. 440; St. Menas at Abu Mîna, ca. 490). This new architecture developed in Egypt from the middle of the fifth century on, and combined features of late Roman architecture from the Levant with elements that recalled pharaonic buildings.[105] At that point, however, the spiritual sources of pharaonic architecture had deteriorated to the point that they could no longer influence new developments. This does not mean that early Christian church building in Egypt was completely unaffected by pharaonic tradition. A careful analysis by Peter Grossmann shows that inclined exterior walls and flat roofs of Egyptian churches are typical Egyptian phenomena. The Egyptian cavetto was frequently used in church building (without the horizontal torus); and the cube-shaped head pieces on top of the columns of Egyptian churches are repeating the shape of pharaonic columns with capitals, adding a Hathor head or Bes figure to a composite capital. In some multi-aisled churches, the outer colonnades surround the raised central part on all four sides, similar to the design of the festival hall of Thutmosis III at Karnak. Since hypostyle halls were no longer built in the Late Period, it is deceptive, however, to reflect on such a connection between New Kingdom–period and Christian-period architecture.

PART II

CHARACTERISTICS OF
THE ARCHITECTURE
OF THE LATE PERIOD

9

SACRED BUILDING FORMS
OF THE LATE PERIOD

Wabet

The beginning of the New Year was celebrated in Egyptian temples with grand ceremonies. The cult image of the lord or mistress of the temple was placed under the roof of the *wabet*, the "pure hall," a structure resembling a throne canopy with two columns at the front (fig. 237). The *wabet* dominated a small open court. There, festive offerings took place to which all the other cult images of the temples were assembled.

Examples of a *wabet* and a New Year's Court are well preserved in the temples of Edfu and Dendera,[1] while traces of several more are visible in other temples. The court could be entered by means of two doorways, one that led from the hall of the visiting gods and one from the staircase to the roof. This staircase was used to carry the cult images from the New Year's Court to the roof chapel, where the statues were exposed to the bright sunlight.

Predecessors of the *wabet* and a New Year's Court are found in the solar courts of New Kingdom royal cult temples. These structures already included the *wabet*'s main architectural features, such as the open altar court connected to a rear chapel and a staircase to the roof.[2] Similar spatial elements in Egyptian-style Kushite temples may represent the transitory phase between the New Kingdom solar courts and the lost examples of the Saite Period (fig. 31).

Pronaos

The pronaos is a colonnaded hall added to the front of the temple. Main formal differences between a pronaos and the similar hypostyle hall appear in

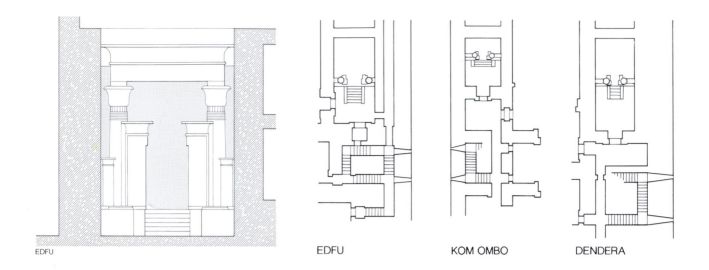

EDFU   EDFU   KOM OMBO   DENDERA

Figure 237.
The building type of the *wabet*
as represented in the temples of
Edfu, Kom Ombo, and Dendera
(see fig. 117).

the design of the facade, of the roof, and of the attachment of the pronaos to the temple house. The front of a hypostyle hall is normally completely closed, while that of the pronaos is formed by columns *in antis* that are connected by screen walls. The roof of the pronaos is on one level, while those of the New Kingdom halls have a towering central nave. Whereas hypostyle halls were integral parts of the temple house, pronaoi clearly express their independence. The side walls of the pronaos do not continue those of the temple house but enclose the corners of the temple from the side (see figs. 203, 209, 215, 228). Whereas hypostyle halls reach their culmination during the New Kingdom, pronaoi dominate later Egyptian architecture.

Both building types had extremely long periods of development. Whereas plain hypostyle halls with columns of equal height can be found in all periods of Egyptian history, hypostyle halls with a higher central nave developed during the 18th Dynasty and flourished in the 19th and 20th Dynasties.[3] The pronaos begins with the Djoser complex of the 3rd Dynasty. The facades of two dummy palaces in the Djoser complex, termed *maison du nord* and *maison du sud*, were shaped as representations of pronaoi, with four columns connected by screen walls (fig. 238). Later monumental successors were the colonnaded halls of the valley temples of the 5th and 6th Dynasties (fig. 238). The front columns of these halls had no screen walls. Similar colonnaded halls with an open front occur during the 18th Dynasty in the temples built by Amenhotep III at Luxor and Soleb and during the 19th Dynasty in the rock temple of Sethos I in the Wadi Mija (Kanais) and the temple of Ramesses II at Herakleopolis magna (Ihnâsya el-Medîna).

The temple of Psametik II at Hibis includes an early example of a true pronaos with screen walls between the front columns (fig. 239).[4] The tendency to increase the depth of the pronaos is apparent. Whereas early examples had two rows of columns, the great pronaoi of the Roman Period have as many as four rows (see table 1).

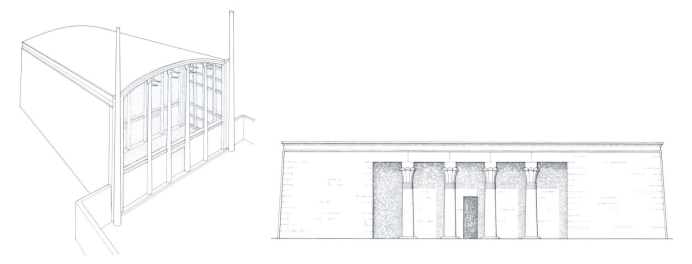

Figure 238. Reconstruction of the prototype for the so-called Southern Palace in the Djoser complex at Saqqara *(left)* (after Ricke, *BemerkungenAR* I, pl. 4) and reconstruction of the front of the valley temple of Sahura.

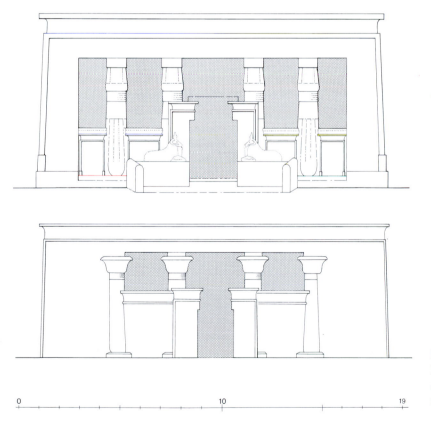

0   10   19

Figure 239.
Reconstructed frontal views of the pronaoi of El-Hibe (30th Dynasty?) *(top)* and the temple of Hibis (Psametik II).

Table 1. Chronological List of Major Pronaoi

	Width	Height	Depth
HIBIS (Psametik II) 2 x 4 columns	18.65 m	7.40 m	6.38 m
HERMOPOLIS MAGNA (Nectanebo I–II) 2 x 6 columns	57.75 m	18.375 m	21.00 m
AKHMIM (lost) (Ptolemy IV?) 4 x 10 columns	ca. 86.00 m	ca. 26 m	ca. 30.00 m
ANTAEOPOLIS (lost) (Ptolemy VI) 3 x 6 columns	45.30 m	15.25 m	ca. 19 m
ELEPHANTINE Temple of Khnum (Ptolemy VI?) 2 x 6 columns	36.75 m	13.65 m	13.13 m
EDFU (Ptolemy VIII) 3 x 6 columns	40.55 m	15.674 m	18.705 m
KOM OMBO (Ptolemy XII) 3 x 5 columns	ca. 40 m	ca. 14 m	ca. 17 m
DENDERA (Augustus/Tiberius) 4 x 6 columns	43.00 m	17.20 or 18.05(?) m	26.03 m
ESNA (Claudius) 4 x 6 columns	37.36 m	14.98 m	20.2 m

The spacing of columns is crucial and does not follow a simple square grid of invariable squares (fig. 240). The central nave is, like that of hypostyle halls, considerably wider than the side aisles, and the intercolumniations of the side aisles are slightly longer in the direction of the temple axis. The distance between the innermost row of columns and the rear wall is narrower, and that between the last lateral row and the side walls wider than the average.

Stylistic changes are suggested by the alignment of the architraves (fig. 241). In the New Kingdom examples and the pronaoi of Hermopolis magna and El-Hibe, the alignment of the architraves of the central nave follows the axis of the temple. The architraves of the lateral aisles, however, are aligned at a right angle to the axis and parallel to the pronaos front. In the later pronaoi of Kom Ombo, Edfu, Esna, Dendera, and Antaeopolis, all architraves (except those at the facade) are aligned parallel to the temple axis.

Considering the function of the pronaos, one wonders why some temples had one from the outset, while others only had one added later and still others never received one. S. Cauville's and D. Kurth's studies of the decoration program of the pronaos of Edfu have revealed that this pronaos was used as a

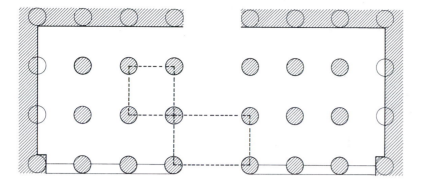

Figure 240.
Schematic drawing of the layout of columns and walls in the Ptolemaic pronaos of Edfu. The columns partially or completely hidden by the walls do not exist but suggest the concept of spacing.

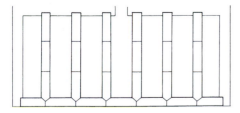

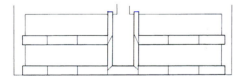

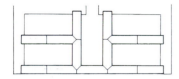

LUXOR, AMENHOTEP III

EL−HIBE, SHESHONQ I

HERMOPOLIS, NECTANEBO I

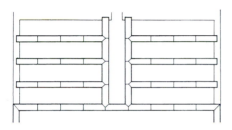

EDFU, PTOLEMY VIII

Figure 241.
The development of the alignment of architraves in pronaoi from the New Kingdom (top) to the Ptolemaic Period.

reception hall for all the deities who were, from the local point of view, significant representatives of all parts of the country. Thus the pronaos generated a "theological unification of Egypt."[5] According to a complex scheme, the columns of the Edfu pronaos were attributed not only to selected local deities but also to their major theological counterparts in other parts of the country. The addition of a pronaos, therefore, bestowed on the temple national, even cosmic, significance, an aspect beautifully displayed by the astronomical scenes of the ceiling at Edfu and in other pronaoi. Due to the character of the pronaos of Edfu as a "pantheon," the profuse selection of different capital types may reflect the multitude of gods and cults found in Egypt.

Entrance Porches and Kiosks

Besides the pronaos, three other colonnaded structures became characteristic components of late Egyptian temples: entrance porches, kiosks, and entrance kiosks (fig. 242).[6] All three have forerunners in New Kingdom architecture, but they developed and significantly transformed mainly during the Late Period.

Entrance porches were built against the front of a building (fig. 243). They generally consist of two to four parallel rows of columns, which are often connected in the direction of the temple axis by screen walls. This partition created a central nave and four parallel and often disconnected side aisles. The entrance porches originated during the New Kingdom and are most prominently represented by the temple-palaces of the Amarna Period.[7] These porches stood on platforms and were open from three sides but had no screen walls. The porches of the 25th Dynasty were parterre, and their rows of columns were connected by screen walls (fig. 243). Under Taharqa, the main gates of several major Theban temples received such porches.

Porches were used for different purposes. One objective was to offer shade to participants in processions, assembled at the temple gate. The demand for

Figure 242.
The three related types of (A) entrance buildings (Amunre/ Monthu, Karnak), (B) entrance kiosk (Hibis), and (C) freestanding kiosk (Philae).

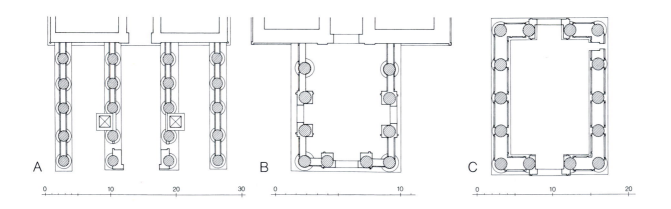

A

B

C

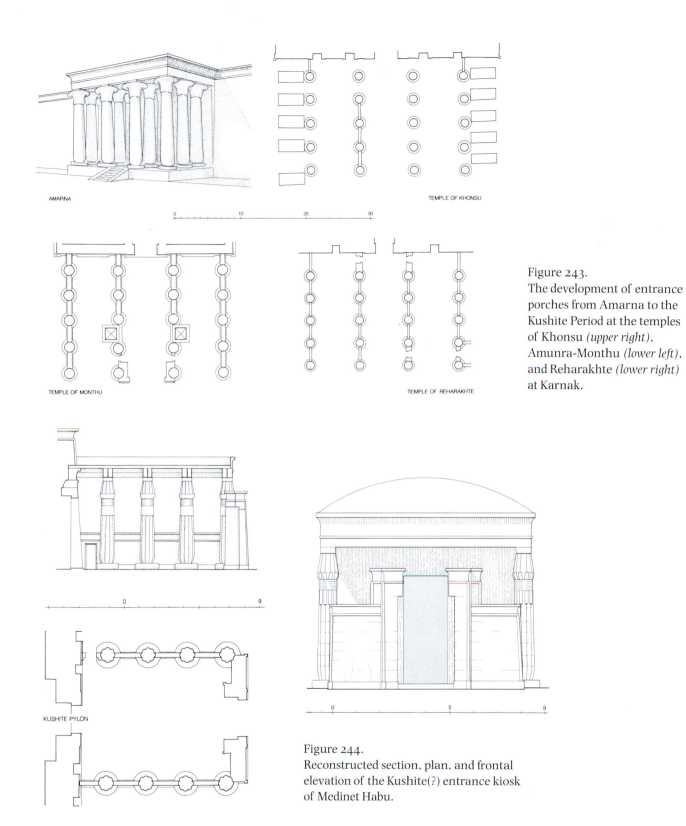

AMARNA

TEMPLE OF KHONSU

0   10   20   30

TEMPLE OF MONTHU

TEMPLE OF REHARAKHTE

Figure 243.
The development of entrance
porches from Amarna to the
Kushite Period at the temples
of Khonsu *(upper right)*,
Amunra-Monthu *(lower left)*,
and Reharakhte *(lower right)*
at Karnak.

0   9

KUSHITE PYLON

0   5   9

Figure 244.
Reconstructed section, plan, and frontal
elevation of the Kushite(?) entrance kiosk
of Medinet Habu.

porches at temples seems not to have existed before the 25th Dynasty, because of the composition of processions. It seems that in earlier times, the procession consisted only of priests who escorted the bark from the interior of the temple outside. In the Late Period, however, laymen assembled in front of the gate and joined the procession outside the temple. These shelters seem to have been forerunners of the Greco-Roman *komasterion*. Porches at temple gates were also localities for the administration of justice and waiting areas for petitioners who asked for an oracle, consulted with priests, or delivered votives.

Kiosks were freestanding canopies consisting of columns connected by screen walls.[8] The screen walls of kiosks are interrupted by doorways not only in the axis of the processional path but also at right angles to it. The main doorways carried a broken lintel; the subsidiary doorways were often cut directly through the screen walls and had no framing device. Forerunners of kiosks were certainly the temporary wooden canopies for the royal throne that are frequently represented in wall paintings from the Middle Kingdom on.[9] In the 12th Dynasty, canopies with a sacral function were converted from wood into stone using pillars in place of columns.[10] These shrines certainly sheltered the divine bark or a cult image. Bark stations of the New Kingdom were normally, though not always,[11] positioned at a right angle to the processional road, while the late kiosks stood directly in the middle of the road. The stone kiosk with columns appears for the first time in the reign of Amenhotep III along, with several other new building elements.[12] This building type may have been transmitted from the New Kingdom to the Late Period via now-lost kiosks in the Ramesside residences of Memphis and Qantir.

More than a dozen good examples are known from Kushite and Meroitic architecture at Gebel Barkal, Kawa, Naqaʿ, and Meroe. They at first followed Egyptian tradition but later converted under the influence of Roman architecture into local forms. The most spectacular Kushite kiosk was built in the forecourt of Karnak under Taharqa. The formidable Augustan kiosk on Philae represents a later phase of development and marks the peak of Egyptian kiosk construction.

The entrance kiosk is not detached but is built against the gate of a temple. Whereas entrance porches were built mainly for more profane purposes, the entrance kiosk was reserved mainly for the divine bark. Forerunners again appear in the architecture of the late 18th Dynasty.[13] The entrance kiosk also reappeared in Kushite times, as suggested by the example at Medinet Habu (fig. 244). Later examples are the huge entrance kiosks of Ptolemy VIII at Medamoud and Medinet Habu and, finally, the magnificent porch at the birth house of Cleopatra VII of Armant.

As pointed out earlier, the kiosk translates an originally wooden structure into stone and belongs to the category of *fictive* or *dummy architecture*. This change in materials did not, however, always result in four-sided buildings. In some cases, only the frontal view of a kiosk or entrance kiosk was projected against a plain, completely closed temple facade. Formerly freestanding columns became engaged half-columns. This building or decoration form had its forerunner in the dummy facades of the Ramesside rock temples of Nubia.[14] The increasing use of dummy facades enhanced the development of engaged half-columns or semidetached columns in Late Period architecture.[15]

In contrast to the mainly functional purpose of half-columns in later European architecture (to support arches and vaults), the Egyptian half-columns were not load-bearing but were part of the symbolic facade decoration.

Birth Houses

A temple type frequently encountered in Late Period sacred precincts is the birth house.[16] This temple form was thought to be so typical of Egyptian architecture that in 1867, a fine, full-scale birth house was built for the world exhibition in Paris. Following plans of A. Mariette, the reconstruction combined features of the birth houses of Philae, Kom Ombo, and Edfu (fig. 245).[17]

In the birth house (Arabic *mammisi*), the birth of a juvenile god was celebrated in the form of a mystery drama or nativity play that identified the young deity with the rising sun. The celebration of the divine birth therefore

Figure 245.
The development of birth houses from the 30th Dynasty to the Roman Period.

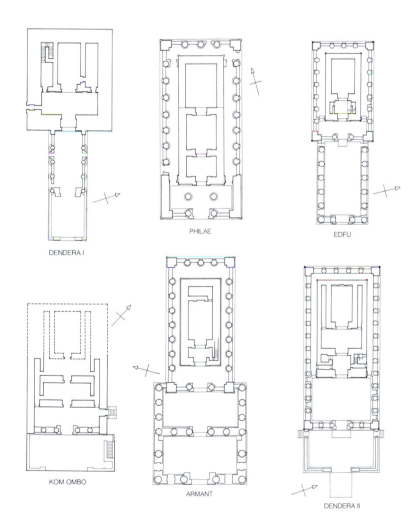

DENDERA I

PHILAE

EDFU

KOM OMBO

ARMANT

DENDERA II

assumed "cosmic dimensions."[18] The concept of the infant god and the daily rebirth of the sun encouraged an equation between the young king and the eternal renewal of kingship. The birth house could therefore be understood in the wider sense as a royal cult chapel.

Simple (but lost) forerunners of this temple type seem to have existed since the Ramesside Period.[19] They were not restricted to the temples of female deities but, a place for the royal cult, also were attached to temples of male gods, for example, Horus of Edfu, Sobek and Haroeris of Kom Ombo, and Monthu of Armant. Birth houses occupy a special location within a temple precinct, standing laterally in front of the temple facade with the entrance facing the axis of the main temple.

Birth houses attained their familiar architectural form only during the Ptolemaic and Roman Periods (fig. 246). The examples of the 30th Dynasty were small chapels, which consisted only of a shrine with an antechamber and a staircase to the roof, which may have been used for rituals. The antechamber was so broad that the sanctuary could be flanked by side rooms or corridors. Similar to the sanctuaries of the royal cult temples of the New Kingdom, the rear wall of the sanctuary was filled by a false door.

From the Ptolemaic Period on, these small buildings were surrounded on all sides by an ambulatory with columns connected by screen walls (fig. 245).

Figure 246.
The birth houses of Nectanebo I *(lower left)*, the Christian church, and the birth house of Nero *(behind)* at Dendera (photo A.B.).

The floral capitals of the columns perhaps referred to the papyrus swamps of Khemmis, where Horus was thought to have been born and hidden from Seth (Herodotus, II.156). As a symbol of the feminine aspect of the building, the floral capitals were topped with pillars decorated with Hathor faces (Philae) or figures of Bes, the protector of childbirth (Dendera and Armant). The roof construction of the larger birth houses is noteworthy. The roofs of the ambulatory were higher than that of the actual sanctuary in the center, creating a sunken area on the roof surface. This basin collected rainwater that required a complicated drainage system.[20]

Ptolemaic and Roman birth houses formally resemble a Greek *peripteros* (fig. 247), except at the corners, which were formed not by columns but by L-shaped pillars.[21] A colonnaded facade of a birth house with engaged Hathor columns is represented on the front of a chapel of the 25th Dynasty at Karnak that may have had aspects of a birth house (fig. 26).

Smaller birth houses could also be extended by means of a colonnaded kiosk or a forecourt, such as Dendera I, Armant, and Edfu. These enlargements became necessary because of increasing cultic activities. The great number of processions and their participants in the Ptolemaic Period required more sacred space.[22]

Borchardt explained the form of a birth house sheltered by an ambulatory as a depiction in stone of a primitive birth tent or hut.[23] One should not forget, however, that the birth house was not instantaneously created with an ambulatory but was the outcome of a long development that started with much simpler forerunners.

About two dozen birth houses are attested, although not all of them have been preserved, most in Upper Egypt (see table 2).

Figure 247.
The birth house of the Augustan temple of Kalabsha, exceptional for being a true *peripteros*.

Table 2. Birth Houses of the Late Period

Ruler	Birth House
Ramesses II	Ramesseum (blocks reused at Medinet Habu)
	Karnak, temple of Khonspakhered, complex of Mut
Osorkon I	Bubastis, Mihos temple
Taharqa	Karnak, sanctuary of the divine consorts in the complex of Amunra-Monthu
	Karnak, temple of Khonspakhered, complex of Mut
	Luxor, chapel of Hathor
Kushite(?)	Karnak Harpare temple, complex of Amunra-Monthu
Amasis(?)	Mendes, destroyed building
Hakoris	Karnak, temple of Harpare, complex of Amunra-Monthu
Nectanebo I	Tell el-Balamun, destroyed building
	Hermopolis magna (Nehemet-'away)
	Dendera I, birth house of Harsomtus
	El-Kâb, birth house
	Kom Ombo, birth house of Khons-Hor and Panebtauwy
	Philae, birth house of Horus
Ptolemy III	Serapeum Alexandria, temple of Isis and Harpokrates
	Qasr el-Ghueda, uninscribed building
	Medamoud, birth house of Harpare
	Philae, birth house of Horus
Ptolemy VIII	Temple of Opet, Karnak
	Deir el-Medine, birth house
	Edfu, birth house of Harsomtus
	Kom Ombo (enlargement)
	Philae, birth house of Horus (enlargement)
Ptolemy XII(?)/ Cleopatra VII	Armant, birth house of Harpare
Augustus	Kalabsha, uninscribed kiosk
Nero-Trajan	Dendera II, birth house of Harsomtus

Cult Terraces

Egyptian cult images frequently left their temple precinct and visited a terrace located some distance from the temple gate (figs. 248–250).[24] Since these terraces frequently tower over a canal or the banks of the Nile, they were misinterpreted as a landing station or a quay. Access to the water was, however, neither required nor always possible.[25] These terraces communicated primarily with the temple and were separated from the river by a parapet. Only occasionally was the terrace flanked by staircases or ramps that descended to the water (fig. 248); these may have been used to load the divine barks onto ships. Tomb paintings of the early 19th Dynasty suggest that the cult images were placed on the terrace in order to view their territory or salute another, visiting

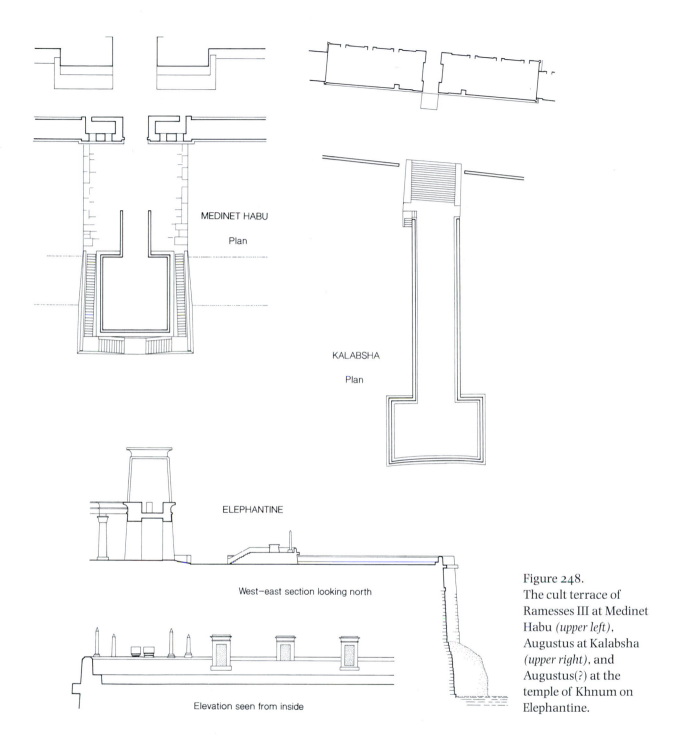

MEDINET HABU

Plan

KALABSHA

Plan

ELEPHANTINE

West–east section looking north

Elevation seen from inside

Figure 248.
The cult terrace of
Ramesses III at Medinet
Habu *(upper left)*,
Augustus at Kalabsha
(upper right), and
Augustus(?) at the
temple of Khnum on
Elephantine.

Figure 249.
The Augustan(?) cult
terrace at the temple of
Khnum on Elephantine
as reconstructed by
Horst Jaritz (photo A.O.).

Figure 250.
The cult terrace in front of the Augustan temple of Kalabsha (photo A.O.).

god.[26] Cult terraces (see table 3) are known from Ramesside temples, but they increased in number during the Ptolemaic and Roman Periods.[27] It is remarkable that no such terraces are known from temples north of the Faiyum. The reason may lie in different Lower Egyptian cult practices.

The terraces were elevated and accessible—similar to monumental altars—from the side of the temple by a ramp. The three exterior sides of the terrace curved inward for stability of the masonry. A low, chamfered parapet wall sits on a projecting ledge. The connection between temple and terrace was provided by a stone-paved processional approach, ideally flanked by sphinxes. The lower end of the ramp was occasionally adorned with an additional pair of small sphinxes. Sometimes the podium carried a pair of obelisks, which flanked the socle for the bark. Numerous small obelisks, shrines, and altars stood on the parapet of the terrace of the temple of Khnum on Elephantine (fig. 249), erected as votives by donors who hoped to participate in the rituals. The parapet of the terraces at the temples of Isis and Hathor and at the Roman kiosk on Philae involved pillars that supported a roof or sunshade and converted the terraces into kiosks. The transformation of terraces into pillared

Table 3. Examples of Cult Terraces

Ruler	Temple Site
Ramesses II	Karnak in front of the first pylon Wadi el-Sebu'a
Ramesses III	Medinet Habu, royal mortuary temple
26th to 30th Dynasty	Karnak, temple of Amunra-Monthu
Nectanebo I– Early Ptolemaic	Philae, Isis temple
Ptolemy III(?)	Qasr el-Ghueda, Amun temple
Ptolemy IV and VIII	Deir el-Medine, Hathor temple Tôd, Month temple
Ptolemy VI(?)	Dabod, Isis temple
Augustus	Elephantine, Khnum temple Philae, kiosk of "Trajan" Dendur, Isis temple Kalabsha, Mandulis temple
Tiberius	Medamoud, Month temple
"Roman"	Philae, Hathor temple Esna, Khnum temple Dendera "North building"

kiosks suggests that cult terraces occasionally became the nucleus for the development of a juxtaposed contra-temple. Now and then these are found at a certain distance from the main temple—as, for example, at the temple Umm Ubayda, opposite the Ammoneion of Siwa.

H. Jaritz has shown that the terrace of the temple of Khnum on Elephantine also allowed religious societies to assemble and to participate in ceremonies from "outside the ritual frontiers" of the temple.[28]

Columns

Pillars with square, rectangular, or octagonal sections dominated temple architecture of the Old and Middle Kingdoms. Their large, unstructured surfaces and the precise contrasts of light and shade endowed pillared structures with a serene, monumental quality. During the 5th Dynasty, columns with floral capitals emerged. Their animated forms and colorful paint contrasted with the linear, geometrical forms of the surrounding building masses and helped to balance the monumental power of these buildings. After the New Kingdom, the column supplanted the pillar in most cases. The plants chosen to lend their form to columns were palm, papyrus, lotus, and lily, all delicate organisms that seem scarcely suited to carry heavy loads. It was, rather, their symbolic quality that prompted their acceptance in architecture. It is futile, therefore, to search for prototypes in "natural" material (for example supports made of real papyrus bundles); the real link between the actual plant and the stone column was the wood support. Representations in tombs from the Old Kingdom onward show wooden columns of the aforementioned floral types being used in secular buildings.

The symbolic meaning of floral columns is to some degree obvious; one may assume that the represented plants were so closely connected with regions of the country or certain cult places that their appearance in columns would have been understood as a reference to these locations. A remarkable feature is the supremacy of the Lower Egyptian emblematic plants (papyrus, lotus, and palm) over the Upper Egyptian lily, which remained a rarely used column form.

The palm, papyrus, and lotus columns assumed standardized shapes during the Old and Middle Kingdoms. Late Period examples display slight alterations, such as the lowered neck binding along the shaft or the elongation of the proportions.

The palm column, dominant since the Old Kingdom, was still esteemed in the Late Period. At Tanis, Old Kingdom palm columns were reused under Osorkon II, and Taharqa embellished the temple of Kawa with new palm columns. Huge palm columns adorned the palace of Apries in Memphis, and Herodotus saw palm columns in the funerary chapel of Amasis at Sais.[29] Later specimens appear in the temples of the 30th Dynasty, the Ptolemies, and the Romans. The slender, elegant Old Kingdom form was—not to its advantage—in the Late Period modified to a plump barrel shape. The lowering of the neck coils exposed the upper end of the stem, which is denoted by three bands of dentils as representing a palm tree (fig. 251). A pair of date fruits rises from every second branch. Palm capitals at Edfu and on Philae add sculpted dates. The famous banquet tent of Ptolemy II in Alexandria was also adorned with wooden palm columns.[30]

Whereas closed papyrus bundle capitals disappear, with a few exceptions, from the late building repertoire, the open papyrus capital of the New Kingdom became the source of new creations of the Late Period. In the Amarna Period bell-shaped capitals already were subdivided into four stems, diverging from the principle of a single papyrus plant (fig. 252).[31] The bell-shaped capitals of Psametik II in the temple at Hibis were covered with a garland of eight vigorously modeled papyrus blossoms (fig. 40). Another transitional form, this one found at Hibis, possibly dates to the 30th Dynasty: papyrus capitals were encircled by a wreath of alternating papyrus and lily blossoms (fig. 259).

The closed papyrus columns of the pronaos of Nectanebo I at Hermopolis magna, rare surviving representatives of an old column type, display interesting innovations (fig. 253). Their shafts were formed from eight rounded (not triangular) papyrus stems and banded with five cords not only at the neck but also twice farther down the shaft.

This triple division of the column shaft was anticipated by bundle columns in rock tombs at Amarna[32] and by Ramesside column shafts with tripartite

Figure 251.
Two palm capitals of the Augustan court on Philae.

decoration. The lowest section was covered by the foot leaves of the papyrus, the middle with figural scenes, and the top with secondary stalks. However, these three sections were not yet separated by actual bands.[33] The vertical flow of lines therefore still dominates, whereas the columns of Hermopolis magna emphasize the horizontal.

When transformed into a stone column capital, the lotus blossom displays two different phases of flowering, either the completely closed or the half-opened calyx. The closed variation was used on either the single stem or on the more complicated bundle or cluster column. Both variations were known in the Old and Middle Kingdoms. The lotus-bundle column, which had been used only rarely in any period of Egyptian architecture, also remained a rarity in late building and was finally abandoned. The single-stem type is represented in late architecture by two fine limestone columns from the palace of Apries in Memphis.[34] The petals are strongly modeled on four sides of the capitals, with a blossom rising in between the petals. On each side, a bundle of three smaller blossoms seems to be pulled through the neck bands. A Ptolemaic example stands in the northern portico of the birth house on Philae (fig. 254). A wreath of eight lotus leaves with three blossoms seems to grow from the necking, and above are sixteen sepals of closed lotus blossoms.

The open lotus calyx variation, which is known from the Old Kingdom on from paintings and reliefs, was mainly used on wooden columns.[35] Some rare stone examples are found from the 30th Dynasty on. A pair of peculiar-look-

Figure 252. *(bottom left)* Capital of a papyrus-bundle column from a kiosk of Amarna (from Rainer Hanke, *Amarna-Reliefs aus Hermopolis* [Hildesheim, 1978], fig. 24).

Figure 253. *(bottom right)* Reconstruction of a papyrus-bundle column of the pronaos of Nectanebo I at Hermopolis magna.

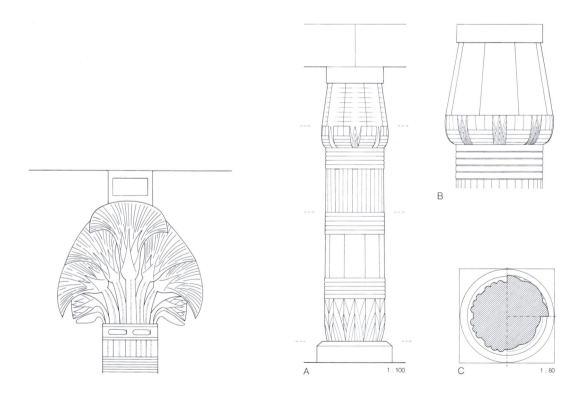

ing capitals with a wreath of sixteen open lotus blossoms graced the entrance kiosk of Nectanebo I at Hibis (figs. 68–70). Their stalks are pulled through the neck bands together with the stalks of thirty-two smaller lotus blossoms. Complicated compositions of Hathor and two-tiered lotus calyx capitals are found in the east and north halls of the birth house of Philae (fig. 254). A quatrefoil capital in the Ptolemaic court of Edfu shows four tiers of open lotus blossoms diminishing downward in size.[36]

The motive of open or closed lotus blossoms is frequently applied in relief to bell-shaped capitals.

The Egyptian lily was apparently not a botanical species but rather an artistic creation. Characteristic were the spiral sepals with a red "tear" spinning from their underside. As can be concluded from wall paintings in Theban tombs, lily capitals were first used for wooden canopy columns in the late 18th Dynasty.[37] Construction sketches of capitals from about 675 B.C.[38] and the use of the lily motive on composite capitals from the sixth century B.C. on show that lily capitals must have existed in stone from the time of the 26th Dynasty. Quatrefoil, multitiered lily capitals were used on Philae (fig. 255).[39] Composite stone capitals occasionally add lily motives to papyrus and lotus blossoms, gradually developing a new plant capital type, an artificial papyrus/lotus lily.

Figure 254.
Closed and open lotus-bundle capitals with a raised, unfinished abacus at the Ptolemaic birth house on Philae.

Figure 255.
Quatrefoil, three-, and five-story lily capitals of the Augustan court on Philae.

Similar to the development of papyrus capitals, a trend away from the organic to invented forms can be noticed.

No connection exists between the palm capital and the capital decorated with the motive of the palmette, a plant that does not exist in nature. A fan-shaped, pinnated blossom emerges from lancet-shaped sepals (fig. 256). The inflorescence is rounded on top and can be deeply sunk between surrounding blossoms or can protrude visibly; it can be two-tiered or swordlike and elongated. The raised sepals are never curled, deviating in that detail from the similar representation of the lily. The shape of the palmette differs from similar floral motives that appear in ceiling paintings of the Middle Kingdom, in Cretan vase painting, and in ancient oriental motives of the tree of life. Exact parallels are the palmette toppings of Attic funerary stelae of the fifth century.[40] Egyptian capitals with palmette motives apparently developed during the creative 26th Dynasty (ca. 590) but spread from the 30th Dynasty on. Bell-shaped capitals covered by a network of artificially intertwined palmettes are favored in the Roman Period. Palmettes were easily combined with papyrus motives but generally occur alone.

The canon of wood and stone column types seems to have been completed by the beginning of the New Kingdom. A new type appears, however, in the

late 18th Dynasty. In wall paintings of Theban tombs one notices for the first time composite columns, as opposed to composite capitals.[41] A single column carries up to four capitals of different types sitting on top of each other, forming a disconnected stack of papyrus, lotus, and lily types.[42] That these peculiar creations were not imaginary paintings but existed in reality is suggested by several three-dimensional representations found on objects placed in the tomb of Tutankhamun (fig. 257)[43] and by limestone column fragments from Amarna.[44]

More unconventional stone columns and capitals were developed in the architecture of the Amarna Period: a sixteen-stem papyrus-bundle column, structured by four ring bands and decorated with a wreath of suspended ducks, and a column decorated with vine arbor[45] are the first columns that carry composite capitals.[46] Like many novelties of the period, these innovations had no immediate, long-lasting impact and were abandoned by Ramesside builders.

The next addition to the column repertoire can be observed 700 years later during the reign of Psametik II. Fragments of capitals found in the tomb of Neferibre-sa-Neith at Saqqara were decorated on the wide overhanging lip with unusual floral motives (fig. 258). The overhanging molding of the capital was ornamented with triangular petals, from which bundles of palmette-like plants rose. Other innovations of the period have been discussed previously in connection with the development of the papyrus capital (fig. 259).[47]

Figure 256.
A single-, double-, and multi-story palmette capital of the Augustan court on Philae.

Figure 257.
Fan handle in the shape of a composite column from the tomb of Tutankhamun, in the Egyptian Museum, Cairo (courtesy of MMA).

The rarity of surviving 26th Dynasty monuments probably obscures the actual stage when column capitals developed. Only the greater number of preserved monuments from the 30th Dynasty on discloses the change that had taken place since the 26th Dynasty.[48] The papyrus, lotus, palmette, and lily capitals were no longer stacked on top of each other as was done on 18th Dynasty composite columns. Motives of different plants were united on the same composite capital.[49] The pure bell shape, which was the basis of the composite capital, was no longer ornamented with shallow floral elements; the floral parts now protrude distinctly, creating intense effects of light and shade.

The combination of papyrus, lotus, and lily, which are the main emblematic plants of the two lands on the same capital, may be meaningful and represent the unification of Egypt.[50] In addition, the widening of the traditional, rigid canon now offered ample possibilities for the creation of new types. The new forms can hardly be classified consistently[51] but their basic elements can be defined (fig. 260). Floral elements were attached to bell-shaped capital cores with simple quatrefoil or eightfold cross sections. Diminishing in size from the top down, the capitals were organized into two to five tiers. Empty spots between the petals were occasionally filled with representations of vine leaves, date twigs, or grain ears. Rarely, the lower part of the capital was entwined with a wreath of Greek acanthus leaves (in the Augustan forecourt of Philae). The multitude of details seems confusing because of the increased schematism and distance from nature. The plants' identity was clarified, however, by bright painting following a specific color canon. Palm branches and papyrus plants were green with red striped petals. Lilies and palmettes were red with blue sepals and stems. Not all capitals were composite in the sense that of combining different plant forms, since some repeated the same plant in successive tiers. The more schematic forms of floral motives used on Ptolemaic capitals occasionally reverted to more naturalistic forms during the Roman Period.

The larger number of components on the capitals is also reflected by the greater segmentation of the shaft. The bundles of plants were tied up beneath the neck of the column by five to six cords. This necking originally surrounded a small section at the upper end of the shaft. From the 26th Dynasty, the cords were shifted downward, so that the single plant stalks became visible. They consisted of four or eight main stalks with eight or sixteen smaller stalks in between. The lower part of the shaft is never structured, and its plain surface covered with decorations and inscriptions.[52] The foot of the column shaft ends without the contraction typical of older papyrus columns, enhancing the tendency to guide the eye upward along the shaft. The foot of the shaft is decorated with pointed, sharply cut papyrus leaves. The base, which is round, high, and chamfered along the upper edge, rests on a square, flat plinth. The addition of square plinths has no tradition in Egyptian building and suggests the influence of Hellenistic buildings.[53]

In temples of the Late Period, different column types could, in contrast to building practices of the New Kingdom, be juxtaposed in the same row or building section. This richness of forms was augmented by lively coloring and activated a baroque-like movement in the hitherto static calmness of Egyptian colonnades.

Figure 258. *(top left)*
Fragment of a floral capital from the tomb of Neferibre-sa-Neith at Saqqara from the period of Psametik II (after E. Drioton and J.-P. Lauer, "Les tombes jumelées de Neferi-brê-sa-Neith et de Ouahibrê-men," *ASAE* 51 [1951]: pl. 16).

Figure 259. *(top right)*
Bell-shaped capital with floral ornamentation of the time of Psametik II at Hibis (courtesy of MMA).

Figure 260. *(bottom)*
Basic forms, structure, and decoration of composite capitals.

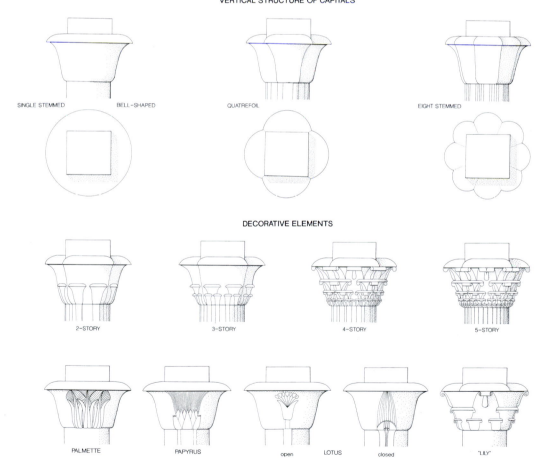

VERTICAL STRUCTURE OF CAPITALS

SINGLE STEMMED   BELL-SHAPED   QUATREFOIL   EIGHT STEMMED

DECORATIVE ELEMENTS

2-STORY   3-STORY   4-STORY   5-STORY

PALMETTE   PAPYRUS   open   LOTUS   closed   "LILY"

The increase of temples dedicated to female deities in the Late Period and the development of birth houses gave new impetus to the use of Hathor-head columns and pillars. This ancient, fetishlike element appeared in stone for the first time during the New Kingdom.[54] In the Late Period, some modifications are noticeable. The original form of double-faced Hathor columns or pillars was replaced by types with four faces (figs. 261–262).[55] The columns were also amplified[56] by an element in the shape of a chapel (wrongly called a *sistrum* sound box) placed on top of the fourfold Hathor heads. The element of the Hathor head crowned with a chapel was occasionally placed on top of a floral capital producing a composite column.[57] Whereas in the New Kingdom the Hathor head consumed half of the column height, the capital was reduced to a third of the total height from the 26th Dynasty on.

Figure 261.
Basalt Hathor-head column of Apries *(left)*, Cairo, 22/12/20/2 (photo by Anna-Marie Kellen, with kind permission by the Egytian Musem, Cairo); Hathor-head column of the pronaos of Tiberius at Dendera *(right)* (*Description* IV, pl. 12).

At the birth house of Armant and the Roman kiosk on Philae, only the floral capitals were completed, while the towering abacus blocks for the Hathor capital were left rough. Sometimes the high abacus blocks were decorated not with Hathor heads but with heads or figures of Bes, the protector demon of childbirth (fig. 263).[58] Unusual combinations appear in a temple of Taharqa at Gebel Barkal, where a Hathor capital is raised above a Bes pillar.[59] An extraordinary creation was a two-sided Bes figure that covers the total height of the pillar;[60] it bears a similarity to the royal statue pillars of the Middle and New Kingdoms.

Egyptianizing Hathor capitals were also appreciated abroad and began spreading about 1200 B.C., as a result of the expansion of the cult of Astarte-Hathor-Isis over the entire Mediterranean.[61] In the early first millennium, Hathor capitals were introduced into Cypriote and Phoenician architecture. From there, they reached Carthage. Hathor capitals were finally used in the imperial temples of Isis and other Egyptian deities in Rome, Pergamon, and Leptis magna. There they were—complying with the style of the period—juxtaposed with lotus blossoms and uraei as well as with elements of Corinthian architecture.

The Hathor head and the Bes figure are the only figural components found on Egyptian columns, contrasting strongly with the generous use of figural capitals, for example, in eleventh- and twelfth-century Europe.[62]

Figure 262.
Fourfold Hathor capitals at the Ptolemaic roof chapel of Dendera *(left)* and a composition of a floral capital with a fourfold Hathor capital carrying a chapel at the Ptolemaic birth house on Philae *(right)*.

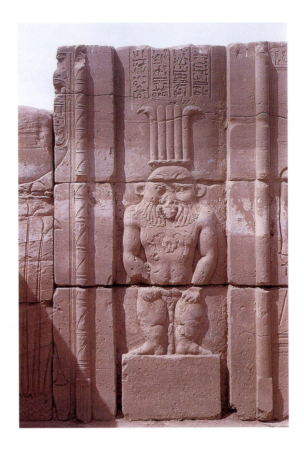

Figure 263.
Bes figure at a column shaft of the Ptolemaic porch in front of the first pylon of the Mut temple at Karnak (photo A.B.).

During the New Kingdom, sandstone or limestone was used for columns. The 26th to the 30th Dynasty saw a return to the hard stones of Old Kingdom tradition. Papyrus-bundle columns, Hathor columns, and columns with composite capitals were preferably sculpted in granite or even basalt. It is noteworthy that Late Period hard stone columns were not built from blocks, as were limestone and sandstone columns, but were monolithic. This practice also followed the Old Kingdom ideal.[63] From Ptolemaic times on, hard stone was confined mainly to buildings in the Greek style.

Screen Walls

The lower part of the intercolumniations of kiosks, pronaoi, and birth houses were closed by screen walls,[64] resulting in a building form that became a trademark of late Egyptian architecture (fig. 264). These intercolumnar dividers probably originate with wooden, portable blinds that were used to subdivide interior rooms of temples according to cultic requirements. Screen walls were already depicted in the 3rd Dynasty Djoser complex as mat hangings between slender wooden supports (fig. 238). In the New Kingdom, intercolumniations between pillars of bark stations were regularly closed by shallow parapet walls

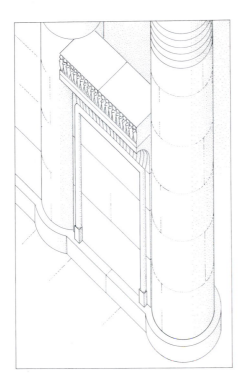
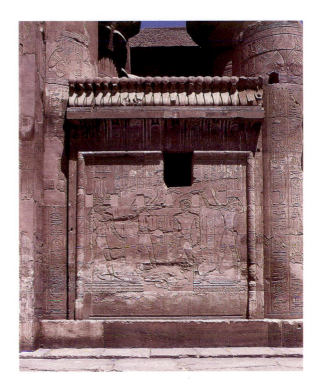

with rounded or chamfered tops. These walls did not reach the height of later screen walls and were not visual dividers.

The royal throne canopy of Amenhotep III and the podium sun altars of Akhnaton were surrounded by this new element. Screen walls divide the halls of rock tombs at Amarna.[65] From the Kushite Period on, intercolumniations of kiosks were closed with screen walls. These walls are attached to the column shaft and display the protruding center part of the column shaft. The screen walls were generally only half as thick as the columns; sometimes they were even thinner and formed from a single slab. The front face was always topped by a cavetto, whereas the interior was not articulated. According to their protective function, screen walls were ideally surmounted by an uraeus frieze. The rectangular, upright front of the wall offered a welcome surface for decoration and inscription with subjects concerning the exterior of a temple such as purification scenes.

The frequent use of half-open intercolumniations in temples of the Late Period was a new development for architecture that generally avoided windows. As a compromise, screen walls both opened wall planes to light and air and granted the interior of the building adequate seclusion.

Figure 264.
Schematic representation of a screen wall *(left)* and an example from the Ptolemaic pronaos of Kom Ombo (photo A.O.).

Broken-Door Lintels

During the 18th Dynasty (under Amenhotep II), the first examples of the broken-lintel doorway appear, an element that enjoyed increasing appreciation

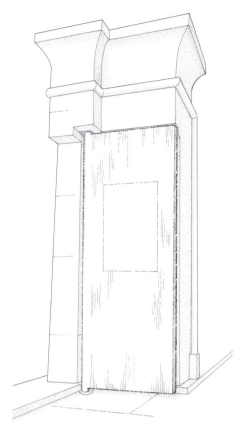

Figure 265. *(left)*
Broken-door lintel with a
quatrefoil papyrus/palmette
capital in the Ptolemaic
Hathor temple at Deir el-
Medine.

Figure 266. *(right)*
The hanging of a wooden
door leaf in a broken-door
lintel.

and became a trademark of the architecture of the Amarna Period. The construction of doorways with broken lintels is simple but ingenious (fig. 265). The doorjambs carry the two ends of the lintel, which protrude far over the passageway and contain the upper pivots for the door under their shoulders, certainly strengthening the stability of the door leaf (fig. 266). The screen walls, topped with cavettos, turn inward at the reveals.

The broken-door lintel was certainly invented to allow easier passage for processions carrying towering barks and standards. Enhanced light within the temple was another advantage. Open lintels were of special interest to the builders of Amarna temples because the rays of Aton could more easily reach the processions.[66] In Late Period architecture we frequently find broken lintels at the doorways of porches and kiosks, at the pronaos and the *avant-porte*.

The broken-door lintel was also common in Alexandria and seems to have influenced the development of the hollow pediment of Hellenistic architecture in Petra, Asia Minor, Northern Africa, and Italy.[67]

IO

CONCLUDING REMARKS

Stylistic Developments and the Formation of Types

Despite the generally held assumption that Egyptian architecture is unchanging and stable, the study of the 1,300 years of Late Egyptian temple building clearly shows conspicuous functional and stylistic alterations.[1] In general, they came to pass slowly and imperceptibly over long periods of time, gaining sudden impetus from specific events. These more active phases of development were closely connected with changes in other areas, primarily with the appearance of powerful rulers who bolstered their new government programs by reviving temple building. Taharqa, Psametik I, Amasis, Nectanebo I, Ptolemy I, and Augustus instantly come to mind.

The observation that practically all building elements and aspects of Late Period structures were anticipated in some form during earlier periods is typical for architectural development in general.[2] However, their fresh selection, combination, and variation generated innovative alterations. As in other periods of Egyptian building, several aspects hamper a conspicuous display of stylistic transformation. The main underlying reason is the authoritative, unchangeable structure of Egyptian architecture, which easily absorbed cultural changes. This retrospectivism could restrict but not totally suppress stylistic development, for new cultic demands and new concepts of architecture generated stylistic changes within architectural structure.

The architecture of the Late Period is, on the one hand, distinguished by the development of prominent new building types such as the entrance porch, kiosk, *wabet*, pronaos, and cult terrace. One has to realize, however, that the ground plan of the main temples also developed and changed. The most basic Late Period temple type originated during the late New Kingdom and is represented by the temple of Khonsu at Karnak (figs. 1–2) and probably by the lost temples of the Third Intermediate Period.

During the 25th Dynasty, a slight variation arose from this central type and led to the design of temples like that of Khonspakhered at Karnak and those at Tabo, Kawa, and Sanam. The 25th Dynasty was also the time during which entrance porches and kiosks were added to extant temples.

The redesigning of temple facades gained more impetus during the 26th Dynasty, with the development of the monumental pronaos and the invention of new floral capital types, which provided the new columned halls with the appropriate building elements. The loss of most of the temples of the 26th Dynasty allows only a vague picture of these buildings. The temples seem to have had compact, square ground plans and contained sanctuaries large enough to house monumental naoi. The use of exotic, colored, hard stones for temple walls, door frames, and columns certainly enriched temple building with a special quality, which can no longer be envisaged.

The developed form of a Late Period temple materializes for us with the 30th Dynasty sanctuaries of Satet and Khnum on Elephantine. More information is offered by the slightly later Ptolemaic temples of Dendera, Edfu, Kom Ombo, and Medamoud. As is the case with older Egyptian temples, these buildings are marked by a linear sequence of spaces. This succession is reflected in elevation by the increase of the ceiling heights from the sanctuary out. Correspondingly, the ground plane lowers from the sanctuary to the temple front, and consequently, the temple grows in size from the inside out. The plan of the temple ideally includes six spatial components:

1. The sanctuary area, which is the dwelling place of the gods. An ambulatory with chapels for the guest gods encircles a central, dominant bark shrine. The inner sanctum is built behind the bark shrine, against the center of the rear wall. Whereas the central location of the bark shrine required an axial movement of festive processions of the main bark, the U-shaped stringing of chapels along an ambulatory supports the circular path of movement to and from the subsidiary shrines.

2. The anteroom of the sanctuary area was the assembly point for the guest gods awaiting the departure of the bark procession from the central bark shrine. At this point the paths from the sanctuary to the temple exit crosses those of the entrances into the ambulatory and the *wabet*.

3. The hall of the offering table was the dining hall in which the cult images were nourished with offerings. At the same point, the axial path through the temple crossed that of the lateral processional staircases to the roof.

4. At the start of the ceremonial procession, the cult images make their first "public" appearance in the hypostyle hall. The direction of movement is underlined by the linear arrangement of the monumental columns of the central aisle. The hypostyle hall is flanked by rooms that are functionally related to the areas behind it and that are connected with the production and storage of offerings, ointments, and cult implements. Side exits to the water supplied by sacred fountains create a third lateral axis.

5. The function of the pronaos as a symbolic space for uniting the gods of the two lands is reflected by the great number of columns. This multiplication of forms favors the consecration of special columns to certain gods depicted on the column shaft. The distribution of these gods follows

a complicated system of religious and geographic associations.[3] The front opening to sunlight and air accentuates the accessibility of the pronaos to the gods of the country.

The linear arrangement of spatial units of these temples is superimposed by a second principle, the circular arrangement of subsidiary rooms around the dominant center. Each extension of the temple to the front (by a pronaos or court) also added a new ring of walls—like an onion skin—around the temple house. In contrast to the New Kingdom, the Late Period temple grows not only in length but also in width (fig. 267). This concept has its roots in the desire to isolate and protect the sanctuary with as many walls as possible. At the same time, this layout assisted the increasing processional activities of the Late Period temples. Of course, not all temples display this principle.[4] On the other hand, ring-shaped plans were not a new innovation, as some examples appeared during the 18th Dynasty.[5]

It is quite clear that this sumptuous organization of temple rooms could only be realized in a large building. Medium-sized temples could only accommodate a more basic and modest version of this ideal and lacked forecourts, pronaoi, or hypostyle halls. In such cases, these more embryonic ground plans comprise the sanctuary area and one or two antechambers, which seem to combine the function of the offering hall, the hall of the visiting gods, and the hypostyle hall. This combination of a sanctuary with one or two ante-

Figure 267.
Temples enlarged during the late New Kingdom by additions along the axis *(left)* and by enveloping spaces in the Late Period *(right)*.

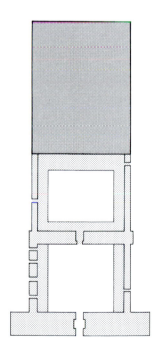

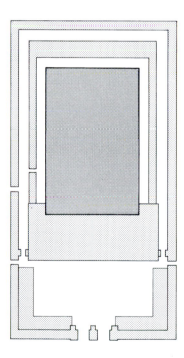

MEDINET HABU

KOM OMBO

chambers is found in the chapel of Amasis on Philae, at Qasr el-ʿAguz, Kalab-sha, and Qasr el-Ghueda, in the chapel of Hathor on Philae, and at ʿAin Amur, Deir el-Hagar, and Nadura A. As a substitute for an actual pronaos, the temple facade is occasionally shaped as a *distyle in antis*. Examples of this arrange-ment are found in the temples of Arsnouphis and of Hathor on Philae and the temple of Dendur. Other single- or double-room chapels were later enlarged with a distinct pronaos (the temples of Qasr el-Ghueda, Deir el-Hagar, Dakka, and Dabod—and most ambitious of all, the temple of Kalabsha).

Archaistic Tendencies

The period from 1070 to the end of Roman rule was an unending sequence of foreign invasions, rebellions against foreign dominance, and interior power struggles interrupted by only short periods of peace. These brief productive periods sufficed, as demonstrated in the preceding chapters, to bring to bloom Egyptian architecture and prevent the disruption of tradition. It was certainly the external peril that continually motivated Egyptians to create monumental architectural manifestations of the Egyptian state as a kind of self-defense.

New temples achieved under such conditions were, according to building inscriptions, considered to be manifestations of mythical, imaginary forerun-ners. The Egyptians even visualized these imaginary or fictitious primordial temples and described them with exact measurements.[6] Only a precise replica of the primordial prototype could fully accomplish its purpose. Knowing in a few cases the new building, its actual predecessor, and the fictitious descrip-tion of the prototype, one realizes, however, that the new buildings did not really duplicate the primordial prototype.[7] The description of the mythical prototypes was even composed artificially in order to justify the new build-ings. This fixation on the past, or more precisely on a fictitious memory of a mythical past, is a historistic phenomenon also known from other aging cul-tures. As a rule, the concept represents an attempt to master the fear of transi-tioness and ruin.[8]

Completely different and rather peculiar possibilities for adhering to the past were found in the usurpation and spoliation of earlier monuments. The practice of filling foundations and wall cores with reused temple blocks and elements was a tradition that went back to the Middle Kingdom.[9] Later, the rulers of the Hyksos Period inscribed their names onto monuments built by the preceding rulers of the 12th Dynasty, and Ramesses II had old royal sculp-ture reinscribed and recut to update portrait features. This spoliation suggests beyond pure practical considerations the objective to transfer the powers inherent in old monuments into the new construction.[10]

A new way to capture the past was pursued during the Ptolemaic Period. Obelisks, sphinxes, statues, and columns were transported from pharaonic temples to Alexandria, but without necessarily changing the inscriptions or hiding their origins. The combination of unrelated elements certainly displays a motive, and the reused monuments became a point of reference to the gov-ernmental program of the Ptolemaic rulers. The Romans followed the same pattern. In the Augustan temple of Kalabsha, even blocks of its Augustan predecessor were reused. More conspicuous was the gathering in Rome and Constantinople not only of Greek statuary but also of Egyptian obelisks, sphinxes, and statues. This activity was certainly generated by the Roman government's policy of visually demonstrating its claim to global domination. Spoliation of pharaonic and Roman building elements also continued in medieval Islamic architecture of Cairo[11] and even has close parallels in early European church building.[12]

Divinities Distinguished by New Temples

The distribution of Egyptian temples changed considerably over the millennia, depending on various religious and political factors. Ruling families naturally bestowed their gifts on the temples and gods of their hometowns and capital cities. The rivalry between Thebes, Memphis, and Tanis, between Sais, Sebennytos, and Bubastis, and later between Alexandria and the rest of the country certainly affected the distribution of building projects.

But other, less obvious factors also produced changes. In the earlier periods of Egyptian temple building, temples for male gods such as Amun, Horus, Monthu, Ptah, Osiris, Reharakhte, and finally Aton prevailed, followed in the Late Period by the cult of the male god Sarapis. In the Late Period one can clearly observe a hitherto unexplained shift to temples for female deities such as Opet, Bastet, Hathor, Isis, Neith, and Triphis.[13] This emphasis on the sanctuaries of goddesses is clearly reflected in the distribution of building projects in the country, apparently bypassing the traditional centers of temple building. Examples are given in Nubia, where practically all newly built Isis temples were erected not at the place of Ramesside building activity but at new sites. Somehow connected with the preference for female deities is the appreciation of youthful gods such as Harsomtus, Harpokrates, Harpare, and Khonspakhered, whose cult generated the temple type of the birth house.

Patrons and Builders

As in most early and in some later cultures, Egyptian architecture was state architecture and was closely attached to the governmental system, perhaps much closer than the other arts. Architecture therefore submits to totalitarian authority, which secures its power and immortality in stone. Such a rigid system granted architects less latitude for individual innovation than was granted, for example, to Greek or medieval European architects. However, Egyptian architects cannot be dismissed as henchmen of a royal ideology, for ideology was certainly manipulated by the same architects who defined the rules for building.

As in older periods of temple building, pharaonic architects remain largely anonymous. We hear only about the "overseer of work" or the "royal master builder" and other officials who now and then mention in their biographies that they built a specific monument.[14] They do not clarify their role in the planning or construction of the monument, details that would most interest us. They boast sporadically and in general terms of the professional execution of an important assignment but never rejoice or boast about their achievement. They considered their share in building a temple to be a small contribution to a royal donation to the gods. This devotion differs considerably from the attitude of architects of later periods.

Several lists of many generations of "royal overseers of the works" from the Persian period are preserved in the graywacke quarries of the Wadi Hammamat.[15] They lack details about the builders and their activities, but at least they display professional self-esteem and an awareness of traditions of their trade, an attitude that certainly contributed to the continuity of building in times of political instability. The planning of a temple must have been rather intricate because not only aspects of building technique but also cultic requirements and the wall decoration had to be considered.

Such projects cannot be conceived without written or visual references. We would expect that detailed explanations of projects were supported by sketches, but no traces of such documents have survived. Building inscriptions in the temples of Edfu and Dendera might echo such documents. The details of these descriptions surpass by far the brief and general records of New Kingdom building inscriptions, which exhaust themselves in praising the splendor and magnitude of a new temple. Judging from preserved books such as the "Arrival of Ra in His Mes-nekhet-Palace" or the "Sacred Book of the Primitive Times of the Gods," these descriptions of Ptolemaic temples were filled with religious material, including, for example, the mythological background of the temple. The predominance of religious content in Egyptian building descriptions suggests, however, that temple planning was left not to pragmatic "overseers of the works" but to priests. The appearance of special literature by architects writing about their buildings is a phenomenon that is encountered in Greco-Roman architecture.[16]

In ideal cases the capacities of a creative designer and a "overseer of the works" were united in the same person, comparable to the famous medieval abbot Suger (1081–1151), who wrote two works in which he explained the new abbey church of St.-Denis. Names of numerous Greek architects who erected buildings in the Greek style are recorded from the Ptolemaic period on: for example, Deinocrates, who planned and began the construction of Alexandria.[17]

Egyptian Late Period Architecture and Western Architecture

Hellenistic Alexandrine architecture, enriched with pharaonic elements and ideas, contributed considerably to the development of baroque style in Roman building.[18] It would be misleading, of course, to claim for ancient Egypt the mainstream of this long and complex branch of architectural development. Only a few shadowy pharaonic building ideas may have survived in Western architecture, currents that can be more sensed than sighted. This exchange occurred primarily via Alexandria and the North African and oriental provinces.

More consequential than the direct adoption of single elements was the conceptual influencing of the Roman perception of building. The attachment of Roman architects to Egyptian architecture might be rooted in a hidden affinity for related building concepts. It may have been the precise, geometrical structure of Egyptian building, reflecting a well-ordered cosmos, that intrigued the Romans, for Roman architecture was dominated by similar rigid principles of order.[19] Therefore, one may not be surprised that, in contrast, Greek architects made much less use of Egyptian architecture. Their temples were conceived as animated organisms,[20] and the organization of a Greek temenos was not regulated by rigid mathematical rules but instead reflected the particular topography surrounding the sanctuary and its rich historical background.

Along with the transfer of pharaonic building concepts and elements to Roman architecture went other adaptations in Roman building. For example, the Egyptian style merged with classical decorative elements in the catacombs of Kom el-Shukafa in Alexandria to form a peculiar hybrid. There the Roman corner pilasters carry papyrus-bundle capitals, and the coping molding of the Egyptian cavetto is decorated with a chevron pattern (fig. 268).[21]

Probably due to the growing appreciation of ancient Egyptian cults[22] and their artistic distinctness, pharaonic building elements also spread from Alexandria to Roman architecture outside Egypt's borders. Egyptian architectural elements appear in the contemporary Roman-based architecture of Palestine and Transjordan, including the tomb of Zechariah in Jerusalem (ca. 25 B.C.), the towerlike "altars" in Lebanon (first century B.C. or A.D.), the Nabatean rock architecture of Petra (first century B.C. to second century A.D.)[23] and at Medain Saleh (ancient Egra) in neighboring Saudi Arabia (first

Figure 268.
Pilaster capitals in the second-century tomb of Kom el-Shukafa.

to second century A.D.). In Rome, Pergamon, Benevent, and numerous other places temples for Serapis and Isis were built in an essentially Roman style but were enhanced with Egyptian accents.[24] Even the ancient palm capital survived in Roman architecture.[25] Egyptian motives such as Nile scenes also prospered in southern Italian wall painting, which depended heavily on Alexandrine prototypes, for example, at Pompeii.

Another root of Egyptian tendencies originates in the early "Egyptomania" of imperial Rome. Roman emperors, travelers, and officials visited and admired Egyptian monuments in Egypt and re-created a kind of miniature Egypt at home. As a result, at least four huge and over forty "smaller" obelisks were transported in risky expeditions across the Mediterranean and reerected in Roman hippodromes or in one case on a sundial.[26] Funerary monuments were built in pyramid shape, and pleasure parks received canopic grottoes.[27] Even Egyptian stone material such as porphyry, granite, graywacke ("basalt"),[28] and gneiss ranked so high that the tedious quarrying and transport of even gigantic column shafts from the Mons Claudianus and the Mons porphyrites were undertaken.[29]

Whereas Egyptian relics in Roman architecture have previously been studied,[30] their last shadowy descendants in the architecture of the early Christian period and the Middle Ages are less established. One can sense, however, that the distinct organization and rigid axial alignment of an Egyptian temple are still reflected in Christian church building. Even the progression of forecourt–pronaos–hypostyle hall–sanctuary is to some extent paralleled by the sequence of atrium–westwork–nave–choir with the altar found in churches.

The ancient Egyptian building concept of the divine or royal canopy as a symbol of heaven and a shelter for the statue shrine or enthroned king may have entered church building through Roman, especially east Roman, architecture.[31] The concept of the architectural canopy resurfaces in the cross-shaped basilica. This building type also appears at a smaller scale in the form of the ciborium, the colonnaded baldachin with a heavy roof that shelters an altar above a saint's tomb.[32] The old question of whether Egyptian hypostyle halls with basilica-like clerestory lighting influenced Roman, and consequently early Christian, basilicas, is, however, currently denied.[33]

The elevation of the Holy of Holies in churches above the surrounding base plane was the expression of similar basic building ideas in pharaonic as well as in Western architecture. In Egypt, the sanctuary was raised on a symbolic "primordial mound," which was thought to shelter the cave of the creator god. Similarly, the floor level of the medieval altar often rises considerably due to an underground crypt with a saint's tomb.[34] The assemblage of chapels of visiting or minor gods around the shrine of the lord of the Egyptian temple has an amazing analogy in Christian churches since the sixth century in the ring-shaped crypts and radiating chapels of the ambulatory along the apse.[35]

The type of the intercolumnar slab seems to survive in the choir screen walls of Byzantine and Western churches. Some Christian screen walls were profusely decorated, framed by columns, and even carried an obviously Egyptian cavetto (fig. 269).[36] Without number are the examples of palm leaf capitals in early Christian churches that suspiciously resemble Egyptian palm leaf

capitals.[37] The entrance porches and kiosks of late Egyptian temples were later—according to Greco-Roman cult practices—transformed into the *komasterion* for the grouping of the participants in processions. They reappear in medieval church building, in the shape of an atrium in front of the west facade[38] or the gate canopies (*protiro*) of Romanesque churches in northern Italy.[39] They can also be traced to the *Galilee* narthex of northern Romanesque and Gothic churches.

Another pharaonic architectural element that may have been an inspiration to Hellenistic, Roman, and consequently medieval architects is the visual emphasis on the portal.[40] The theatrical role of church portals in the Middle Ages, not only as the background for processions but also as a place of judgment and completion of treaties, has its forerunners in the "site of giving Maat" that was attached to Egyptian temple gates.[41] The custom of adorning temple gates with lion figures (fig. 129) can be traced back to the valley temple of Khephren of the 4th Dynasty and the 12th Dynasty story of Sinuhe, who says, "My forehead touched the ground between the sphinxes, and the royal children stood in the gateway to meet me."[42] Corresponding pairs of lions carry the gate canopy of Italian Romanesque church portals, which were situated "inter duos leones" (fig. 270).

Figure 269.
Screen wall in the church of Santa Maria Assunta at Torcello/Veneto, ca. 1008 (after Gianna Suitner-Nicolini, *Romanisches Venetien* [Würzburg, 1994], pl. 15).

Figure 270.
The gate canopy of the
church of San Ciriaco in
Ancona (thirteenth century).

To pursue the intricate ways of development and spreading of these features from ancient Egypt or other Near Eastern cultures into European architecture must be left to art historians of the late Antique and Christian periods.[43]

Ancient adaptations of Egyptian architectural elements were founded on natural exchange and development and differed from Egyptianizing tendencies in modern history.[44] These more recent architectural manifestations of "Egyptomania" from the early eighteenth century to the 1930s did not grow out of the latest Egyptian examples of building but were artificially designed after a scholarly study of ancient Egypt. Single elements considered to be typical were selected from different periods of Egyptian history and blended into an idealized and imaginary Egyptian style of the "Egyptian Revival." The latest, rather eccentric outgrowths of "Egyptomania" are the pyramid-shaped mansion of Jim Onan in Wadsworth, Illinois (1989), or the cartoon-like Luxor Hotel in Las Vegas (Veldon Simpson, 1993). In contrast, examples such as the famous glass pyramid of Ieoh Ming Pei in the court of the Louvre in Paris (1989) could be respected as a true outgrowth of pharaonic building ideals.

APPENDIX: LIST OF LATE PERIOD TEMPLES

The following list only contains sacred buildings in Egyptian style. Single naoi, statues, and so forth, are not included.

"Unexplored building" = Building known only from stray blocks. Location most often unknown.
* = Building substantially preserved.
+ = Building recorded but destroyed in modern times.

Temple Buildings of the 21st Dynasty

PINODJEM I (1071–1033)
Karnak
*Completion of temple of Khonsu
*Sphinx allée, bark basin

PSUSENNES I Aakheperre setepenamun (1040–992)
Tanis
Amun temple and enclosure wall

SIAMUN Netjerkheperre setepenamun (979–960)
Tanis
Amun temple enlarged, court, pylon
Temple of Anta

Memphis
Royal cult chapel

Temple Buildings of the 22nd Dynasty

SHESHONQ I Hedjkheperre setepenre (945–924)
Tanis
Amun temple continuation
Tell Balala
Unexplored building
Memphis
Monumental gate
El-Hibe
*Amun temple
Karnak
*Forecourt and gate of Amun temple

OSORKON I Sekhemkheperre setepenre (924–889)
Bubastis
New temple of Bastet
Extension of temple of Atum
Memphis
Chapel for Bastet and Horus
Atfih
Extension of Hathor temple

OSORKON II Usimare setepenamun (874–850)
Tanis
Two forecourts of Amun temple
East temple, "Mansion of Millions of Years"

Bubastis
    Hypostyle hall with Sed-festival gate, granite
        naos, propylon
    Mihos temple
Leontopolis
    Mihos temple
Pithom
    New temples for Atum, Shu, Tefnut,
        Reharakhte, and the Theban Triade
Karnak
    Small chapel

SHESHONQ III Usimare setepenre/Amun (825–773)
    Tanis
        Gate at Amun temple
    Tell el-Balamun
        Forecourts of Amun temple with two huge
            pylons
    Tell Umm Harb
        New Thoth temple (Mesdet)
    Tukh el-Qaramus
        Unexplored temple
    Mendes
        Unexplored building
    Kom el-Hisn
        Unexplored building
    El-Bindarîa
        Unexplored building

OSORKON III Usermaatre setepen-Amun (777–749)
    Karnak
        *Chapel of Osiris Heka-djed

SHESHONQ V (former IV) Aakheperre (767–730)
    Tanis
        Temple for Amun, Mut, and Khonsu

Temple Buildings of the Kushite Period in Egypt

SHABAKA Neferkare (716–702)
    Memphis
        Chapel and porches
    Abydos
        Unexplored building
    Karnak
        Gold house
        *Sed-festival gate at temple of Ptah
        Two Osiris chapels

Luxor
    Entrance porch at Ramesside pylon
Medinet Habu
    *Extension of the Amun temple
Esna
    Unexplored building
Edfu
    Sed-festival gate(?)

SHABITKU Djedkaure (702–690)
    Memphis
        Unexplored building
    Karnak
        *Extension of chapel of Osiris-Heka-djet
        Chapel at the Sacred Lake

TAHARQA Nefertem-khu-Re (690–664)
    Memphis
        Restoration of Amun temple
    Karnak
        Kiosk in the first court
        Temple at the Sacred Lake
        *Two gates at the temple of Ptah
        Entrance porch of temple of Khonsu
        *Entrance porch at east gate
        *Chapel of Osiris Nebankh
        *Chapel of Osiris-Ptah-Nebankh
    Amunra-Monthu complex (Karnak)
        Entrance porch
        Chapel(?) on podium
        Extension of temple of Harpare and Raittaui
        Temple of the Divine Consorts
    Mut complex (Karnak)
        Conversion of temple of Mut
        Entrance porch
        *Conversion of Khonspakhered temple
    Luxor
        Chapel of Hathor(?)
    Deir el-Bahari
        *Temple of Hatshepsut: entrance kiosk
    Edfu
        Sed-festival gate
    Qasr Ibrim
        Brick temple
    Buhen
        Enlargement of South Temple
    Semna-West
        Small brick temple

Temple Buildings of the 26th Dynasty

PSAMETIK I Wahibre (664–610)
- Sais
  - Neith temple
  - Atum temple
- Tell el-Balamun
  - Second Amun temple
- Tanis
  - Columned building
- Hermopolis parva
  - New Thoth temple
- Memphis
  - Apis temple
- Karnak
  - Osiris chapel
- El-Kâb
  - New Nekhbet temple (date?)

NECHO II Wehem-ib-Re (610–595)
- Pithom
  - Atum temple
- Sais
  - Neith temple: decoration
- Tarraneh (Therenutis)
  - Unexplored building

PSAMETIK II Neferibre (595–589)
- Sais
  - Neith temple: continuation
- El-Nahariya
  - Unexplored building
- El-Mahalla el-Kubra
  - Unexplored building
- Heliopolis
  - Pair of obelisks and other buildings
- Abydos
  - Royal cult temple(?)
- Karnak
  - Pair of obelisks
- Elephantine
  - Works in the old Khnum temple
- Philae
  - Kiosk
- El-Kharga/Hibis
  - *Amun temple

APRIES Khaaibre (589–570)
- Tanis
  - Extension of Anta temple
- El-Nahariya
  - Unexplored quartzite building
- Mendes
  - New Banebdjedet temple
- Sais
  - Neith temple: continuation Sed-festival gate(?)
- Hermopolis parva
  - Unexplored building
- Athribis (Benha)
  - Unexplored building
- Fuah, Ganâg, and El-Mahalla el-Kubra
  - Unexplored buildings
- Memphis
  - Royal palace
  - Unexplored building
- Deir el-Abjad
  - Unexplored building at Neshau or Wannina
- Abydos
  - Tomb of king Djer: repair

AMASIS Khnumibre (570–526)
- Buto
  - Wadjet temple
- Mendes
  - Banebdjedet temple continued
- Behbeit el-Hagar
  - First Isis and Osiris temple(?)
- Sais
  - Neith temple: naos, pronaos, Sed-festival building(?)
- Nabesha
  - New temple and birth house of Wadjet
- Abu Yassin
  - Cemetery of sacred bulls
- Athribis
  - Khentikhety temple (date?)
- Memphis
  - Works in Ptah temple
  - Isis temple
- Saqqara
  - Anubieion
- Istabl 'Antar
  - Unexplored temple
- Abydos
  - Osiris-Khentimentiu temple

Coptos
 Osiris chapel
Karnak
 * Small chapel
Elephantine
 Satet temple
Philae
 Isis temple
'Ain el-Muftella
 *Main building
Qasr el-Ghueda
 *Amun temple
Siwa
 *Amun temple

Temple Buildings of the 27th (Persian) Dynasty

DARIUS I
 Busiris
 Osiris temple: decoration(?)
 El-Kâb
 Nekhbet temple: decoration
 El-Kharga/Hibis
 *Amun temple: decoration
 Qasr el-Ghueda
 Amun temple: decoration

Temple Buildings of the 29th Dynasty

NEPHERITES I Nayf-aau-rud (398/397–392/391)
 Tell Tmai
 Unexplored building
 Mendes
 Unexplored building
 Karnak
 *Turning station for barks
 *Birth house of Harpare
 Shena-wab (brick)

PSAMUTHIS (Psamut) Weser-Re setepen-Ptah (393)
 Karnak
 *Turning station for barks: continuation
 Shena-wab (brick): continuation

HAKORIS Maat-Khnum-Re (392/391–379/378)
 Letopolis
 Temple of Khenti-irti

Saqqara
 Beginning of new Serapeum
Medamoud
 Unexplored building
Karnak
 *Birth house of Harpare: Hypostyle
Medinet Habu
 *Side wing, roof supports
El-Tôd
 *Temple of Monthu: beginning of
 reconstruction(?)
El-Kâb
 Temple of Nekhbet: hypostyle
Elephantine
 New temple (found 1997)
 Khnum temple: additions
El-Kharga/Hibis
 *Amun temple: hypostyle hall

Temple Buildings of the 30th Dynasty

NECTANEBO I Kheperkare (379/378–361/360)
 Tell el-Balamun
 New Amun temple
 Birth house with Pronaos
 Tanis
 Khonsu-Neferhotep temple
 Huge entrance kiosk for Amun
 Entrance kiosk for Anta
 Qantir
 Unexplored building
 Saft el-Henne
 New Sopdu temple
 Munagat el-Kubra
 Unexplored building
 Mendes
 Relief blocks and naos
 Hermopolis parva
 Extension of Thoth temple
 Sais
 Unexplored buildings (screen walls in Atum
 temple)
 Athribis (Benha)
 "Chapel of the Seventy"
 Naucratis
 "Great Temenos"
 Memphis
 Addition to Ptah temple

Saqqara
  Serapeum: continuation, sphinx allée,
    dromos
  Hathor/Isis temple
  Anubieion: extension
  Bubasteion (date?)
Hermopolis magna
  +New Thoth temple
  New Nehemet-'awy temple
Abydos
  New Osiris temple
  Enclosure wall of Kom el-Sultan (date?)
Dendera
  *Birth house of Hathor
  Birth house of Isis
Coptos
  Enclosure wall and naos
Karnak
  First pylon
  *Great brick enclosure walls of major
    temples
  *West gate of Opet temple
  *Gate of the Maat temple
  *North gate of main enclosure
  New Opet temple planned (or begun?)
  *Sphinx allée to Luxor
  *Sphinx allée to Mut precinct
Medinet Habu
  *Gate in new enclosure wall
Armant
  Enclosure wall (date?)
El-Tôd
  Renewal of Monthu temple(?)
Mo'alla
  Unexplored Hemen temple
El-Kâb
  Entrance Kiosk
  Birth house(?)
Elephantine
  Smaller works
Philae
  *Isis temple begun(?)
  *Enclosure walls with monumental gate
  *Kiosk
  *Birth house begun(?)
El-Kharga/Hibis
  *Entrance kiosk of Amun temple

TEOS (Tachos) (361/360–359/358)
  Matariya (Lake Menzaleh)
    Unexplored building (Tanis?)
  Qantir(?)
    Relief fragments
  Athribis
    Unexplored building
  Karnak
    *Khonsu temple decoration

NECTANEBO II (Nakhtherheb)
    (359/358–342/341)
  Tanis
    Horus temple
  Horbeit
    Pronaos of temple of Hor-merty and obelisks
  Tell el-Ahmar
    Unexplored temple(?)
  Bubastis
    New temple of Bastet
  Saft el-Henne
    Temple of Sopdu: continuation
  Pithom
    Extension of temple of Atum
  Bilbeis
    Unexplored temple of Bastet(?)
  Hermopolis parva
    Extension of temple of Thoth
  Behbeit el-Hagar
    New(?) Isis temple, enclosure wall
  Sebennytos
    New temple of Onuris
  Sais
    Obelisks(?)
  Memphis
    *Granite doorjamb
  Saqqara
    East temple of Serapeum
    Precinct of animals catacombs
  Abusir el-Melek
    Temple of Ptah-Sokar-Osiris
  El-Hibe
    *Pronaos (date?)
  Hermopolis magna
    +Continuation of Thoth temple
  Abydos
    Unexplored building

Coptos
    Geb chapel with gate
Qûs
    New Haroeris and Heqat temple(?)
Karnak
    *Amun temple: central bark shrine(?)
    *East Gate (Bab el-Malakha)
    *Extension of Khonspakhered temple
    Shena wab of Mut temple
    Shena wab of Amunra-Monthu temple
Medinet Habu
    Sacred well
Armant
    Bucheum
Edfu
    Adaption of Horus temple(?)
El-Kâb
    Pylons and birth house
Elephantine
    New Khnum temple
El-Kharga/Hibis
    *Additions to Amun temple
Oasis Siwa
    +Temple of Umm Ubayda

Temple Buildings of the Macedonians

ALEXANDER the Great (332–323)
    Athribis
        Unexplored building
    Hermopolis magna
        +Continuation of Thoth temple
    Karnak
        *Royal cult chapel in Akhmenu
    Luxor
        *Bark Shrine
    Qasr el-Megysbeh
        *Amun and Horus temple

PHILIPPUS III Arrhidaeus (323–316)
    Tûkh el-Qarâmûs
        Unexplored building
    Sebennytos
        Decoration of Onuris temple
    Nûb Taha
        *Door lintel
    Hermopolis magna
        +Decoration of Thoth temple

Karnak
    *Decoration of bark shrine of Amun

ALEXANDER IV (316–304)
    Sebennytos
        Decoration of Onuris temple
    Elephantine
        *Decoration of gate of Khnum temple

Temple Buildings of the Ptolemaic Period

PTOLEMY I Soter (323–284 or 304–284)
    Tanis
        New east gate of Amun temple
    Tarraneh (Therenutis)
        Hathor-Thermutis temple
    Naucratis
        Unexplored building
    Tebtynis
        Soknebtunis temple
    Per-khefet
        Unexplored temple
    Sharuna
        Unexplored temple
    Cusae
        Unexplored temple
    Tuna el-Gebel
        *Chapels in Ibis-Galleries
        *Petosiris funerary temple

PTOLEMY II Philadelphus (284–246)
    Tanis
        Small chapel
    Pithom
        Temple fortress
    Behbeit el-Hagar
        Extension and decoration
    Sebennytos
        Decoration of Onuris temple
    Naucratis
        Unexplored building
    Arsinoe/Krokodilopolis
        New Sobek temple of Shedet
    Theadelphia
        Pnephoros temple
    Bacchias(?)
        Sokanobkonneus temple
    Medinet Madi
        *Extension of Renenutet temple

Dendera
    *Extension of the old birth house
Coptos
    New Min temple
Qûs
    Naos and decoration of Haroeris and Heqat
        temple(?)
Medamoud
    Sed-festival gate and other buildings
Karnak
    *Gate of Mut complex
Philae
    *Continuation or beginning of Isis temple
        and birth house

PTOLEMY III Euergetes I (246–221)
    Akhmim (Panopolis)
        +New Min temple house(?)
    Medamoud
        Birth house(?) begun and a gate
    Karnak
        *Gate of Khonsu temple (Bab el-Amara)
        *Ptah temple: entrance kiosk
        *Opet temple continued or begun
    Karnak-North
        *Processional approach
        *North gate (Bab el-ʿAbd)
    Kôm el-Deir (Esna-North)
        +Khnum temple with pronaos
    Edfu
        *New Horus temple
    Aswan
        *Isis temple
    Philae
        *Extension of birth house
    Qasr el-Ghueda (El-Kharga Oasis)
        *Addition of pronaos
    Hibis (El-Kharga Oasis)
        Shena wab of the Amun temple

PTOLEMY IV Philopator (221–205)
    Tanis
        New Mut/Anta temple with entrance kiosk
    Memphis
        Gate in enclosure of Ptah temple
    Akhmim (Panopolis)
        +Addition of pronaos to Min temple(?)
    Antaeopolis
        New temple house(?)

Medamoud
    Continuation of birth house, gate
Karnak
    *Osiris tomb
Deir el-Medine
    *New Hathor temple
El-Tôd
    *Adaption of Monthu temple with hypostyle,
        pronaos, and enclosure walls
Edfu
    *Completion of Horus temple
Elephantine
    Unexplored Osiris tomb
Philae
    *Arsnouphis temple

PSAMETIK-SA NEITH MENKHEPERRE
    (period of 207–186)
    Asfûn el-Matâʿna
        Extension of unexplored temple

ERGAMENES II (Arqamani, 218–200)

ADIKHALAMANI (Azechramun) (ca. 200–190)
    Philae
        Continuation of decoration
    Dabod
        Chapel of Amun/Isis
    Dakka
        *Chapel of Thoth/Isis

PTOLEMY V Epiphanes (205–180)
    Leontopolis
        Unexplored Mihos temple
    Memphis
        Restoration works and new Anubieion
    Esna
        New Khnum temple
    Kôm el-Deir
        Decoration of Pi-Khnum
    El-Kâb
        Restoration of unknown building
    Philae
        *First Pylon of Isis temple
        *Chapel of Imhotep
        *Extension of Arsnouphis temple

PTOLEMY VI Philometor (180–145)
    Tanis
        New temple complex of Horus(?)

Tell el-Yahudiya
  Jewish temple of Onias
Antaeopolis
  +Pronaos of Anty temple
Diospolis parva (Hiw)
  Hathor temple with +Osiris chapel
Dendera
  Extension of birth house of Isis
Karnak
  Smaller buildings
Armant
  Unexplored building
Kom Ombo
  *New Horus and Sobek temple
Elephantine
  Pronaos of Khnum temple
  New Satet temple with a kiosk
Philae
  *Second pylon of Isis temple
  *Court/pronaos of Isis temple
  *Entrance kiosk of Arsnouphis temple
  *Small Hathor temple
Dabod
  *Extension of Isis temple

PTOLEMY VIII Euergetes II (164–163 and 145–116)
Taposiris magna
  Osiris temple (date?)
Dendera
  Bark chapel
Coptos
  *Small gate
Qûs
  Inner monumental gate and temple of
    Haroeris/Heqat temple
Medamoud
  *Adaption of Monthu temple with pylon,
    forecourt, and pronaos
Karnak
  *Opet temple
Deir el-Medine
  *Small birth house and enclosure wall
Medinet Habu
  *Pylon and entrance kiosk of Amun temple
Qasr el-'Aguz
  *Thoth temple
Deir el-Bahari
  *Sanctuary of Imhotep and kiosk

Edfu
  *Addition of pronaos to Horus temple
  Birth house
Kom Ombo
  +Birth house
Elephantine
  Osiris/Khnum temple
  Khnum temple: completion
  Satet temple: addition of pronaos
Philae
  *Extension of birth house
  *Pair of obelisks at first pylon
  *Extension of Hathor temple
  *Extension of Arsnouphis temple
Dakka
  *Addition of pronaos to Thoth temple

PTOLEMY IX Soter II, called Lathyros or Physkon
    (116–107 and 88–80)
Athribis (Wannina)
  New Triphis temple
Karnak-North
  Entrance porch of Amunra-Monthu temple
El-Hilla (Contralatopolis)
  +Isis temple
El-Kâb
  +Kiosk of desert temple of Nekhbet
  Pronaos of Amenhotep III temple
Edfu
  *Continuation of enclosure wall
  *Entrance kiosk of birth house
Kalabsha
  *New Mandulis temple

PTOLEMY X Alexander I (107–88)
Banawît
  Unexplored temple
Dendera
  Ambulatory of birth house of Isis
Qûs
  +Outer monumental gate of Haroeris/Heqat
    temple
Medinet Habu
  Smaller works in Amun temple

PTOLEMY XII Neos Dionysos, called Auletes
    (80–58, 55–51)
Athribis (Wannina)
  "Birth house"

Akhmim
    Unexplored building
Dendera
    *New Hathor temple
Coptos
    *South gate at Geb temple
Karnak
    Smaller buildings
Deir el-Medine
    *Enclosure wall with gate
Edfu
    *Forecourt and pylon of Horus temple
Kom Ombo
    *Monumental gate and pronaos
Philae
    *Transfer of kiosk of Nectanebo I
Biggeh
    *Pronaos of the Osiris temple

CLEOPATRA VII Philopator (51–30)
    Dendera
        *Continuation of Hathor temple
    Coptos
        Geb temple: bark chapel
    Armant
        +Birth house of Monthu temple

Temple Buildings of the Roman Period

AUGUSTUS (30 B.C.–A.D. 14)
    Dendera
        *Completion of Hathor temple
        *New sanctuary of birth house of Isis
    El-Qal'a
        *New Isis temple
    Shanhour
        *Mut/Isis temple
    Deir el-Shelouit
        *Isis temple (date?)
    Kom Ombo
        *Forecourt and gate
    Elephantine
        Pylon and cult terrace of temple of Khnum
            (date?)
    Philae
        *Kiosk of "Trajan" (date?)
        *Colonnades of forecourt
        *Augustus temple

Biggeh
    *Pylon of Osiris temple
Dabod
    *Extension of temple
Qertassi
    *Kiosk (date?)
Taffeh
    *South Isis temple
    *North Isis temple
Kalabsha
    *New Mandulis temple
Dendur
    *Isis Temple and cult terrace
Dakka
    *Extension of Thoth temple
Maharraqa
    *Isis/Serapis temple (date?)
'Ain Amur
    *Amun temple
'Ain Birbijeh
    *Amun-nakht temple with gate of Augustus

TIBERIUS (A.D. 14–37)
    Dendera
        *Pronaos of Hathor temple
    Medamoud
        Monumental gate
    Philae
        *Extension of Hathor temple

CALIGULA (A.D. 37–41)
    Coptos
        Geb temple: Two gates

CLAUDIUS (A.D. 41–54)
    Esna
        *Addition of pronaos
    Philae
        *Harendotes temple

NERO (A.D. 54–68)
    Karanis
        *South Temple (Pnepheros and Petesukhos)
    Dîmeh
        Two temples (date?)
    Dionysias (Qasr Qarûn)
        *Temple of Sobek (date?)
    Tehna el-Gebel
        Three small temples

Dendera
  *New birth house of Hathor
Deir el-Haggar
  *Amun temple

VESPASIAN (A.D. 69–79)
  Nag'el-Hagar
    Unexplored temple

DOMITIAN (A.D. 81–96)
  Hermopolis magna
    Temple in Nehemet- 'awy complex
  Dendera
    *Monumental north gate
  Kom el-Resrâs
    Unexplored temple
  Aswan
    *Khnum/Satet/Anuket temple
  Qasr el-Dush
    *Isis/Serapis/Horus temple

NERVA (A.D. 96–98)
  Diospolis parva (Hiw)
    Unexplored Hathor(?) temple

TRAJAN (A.D. 98–117)
  Akhmim
    Monumental gate of the Min temple
  Shanhour
    *Extension of Mut/Isis temple with pronaos
  Qasr el-Dush
    *Forecourt and gate of Isis temple

HADRIAN (A.D. 117–138)
  Armant
    Pronaos of Monthu temple
  Ismant el-Kharab
    Tutu temple

ANTONINUS PIUS (A.D. 138–161)
  Dendera
    *East gate leading to birth house of Isis
  Medinet Habu
    *Entrance kiosk and court of Amun temple
      begun
  Armant
    *Stone gate
  El-Hilla (Contralatopolis)
    +Addition of pronaos to Isis temple
  Kommir
    *Anuket temple
  Nadûra
    *Temple A
    *Temple B
  Qasr 'Ain el-Zaiyan
    *Amun temple
  Near Qasr el-Dush
    Temple
  Near El-Deir
    Temple
  Belâd El-Rûm
    "Doric" temple

MARCUS AURELIUS (A.D. 161–180) and
LUCIUS VERUS (A.D. 161–169)
  Karanis
    *"North temple"
  Asfûn el-Matâ'na
    Addition of pronaos

COMMODUS (A.D. 180–192)
  Tahta
    Unexplored building

NOTES

Abbreviations

AJA	*American Journal of Archaeology* (New York)
Alexandria	Greco-Roman Museum, Alexandria
ASAE	*Annales du Service des Antiquités de l'Égypte* (Cairo)
Baltimore	The Walters Art Gallery, Baltimore
BASOR	*Bulletin of the American School of Oriental Research* (New Haven)
Berlin	Staatliche Museen zu Berlin, Stiftung Preussischer Kulturbesitz, Ägyptisches Museum, Berlin
BemerkungenAR (I/II)	Herbert Ricke, *Bemerkungen zur Ägyptischen Baukunst des Alten Reiches: Beiträge zur Ägyptischen Bauforschung und Altertumskunde*, vols. 4–5 in 2 parts (I–II) (I: Zurich, 1944; II: Cairo, 1950).
BIFAO	*Bulletin de l'Institut français d'Archéologie orientale* (Cairo)
Bologna	Museo Civico, Bologna
Boston	Museum of Fine Arts, Boston
Brit. Mus.	British Museum, London
Brooklyn	The Brooklyn Museum
Budapest	Museum der Bildenden Künste, Budapest
CAH	The Cambridge Ancient History, 2nd ed., 13 vols. (Cambridge, 1970–). Especially vol. 3, pts. 2 (*The Assyrian and Babylonian Empires and Other States of the Near East*, edited by John Boardman [1991]) and 3 (*The Expansion of the Greek World*, edited by John Boardman [1982]).
Cairo	Egyptian Museum, Cairo
CG	Catalogue Général des Antiquitées Égyptiennes, Cairo
JdE	Journal d'Entrée, Cairo
CdE	*Chronique d'Égypte* (Brussels)
Description [I–X]	*Description de l'Égypte, contenant plusieurs remarques curieuses sur la Géographie ancienne et moderne de ce Païs, sur ses Monuments anciens*, etc., 10 plate vols. (I–X) (Paris, 1809–28).
Description, Text	*Description de l'Égypte ou receuil des observations et des recherches qui ont été faites en Égypte pendant l'expédition de l'armée française*, 24 text vols. (Paris, 1821–29).

Florence	Museo Egizio, Florence
Glasgow	The Hunterian Museum, Glasgow
GM	*Göttinger Miszellen* (Göttingen)
Hildesheim	Roemer- und Pelizaeus-Museum, Hildesheim
JARCE	*Journal of the American Research Center, Egypt* (Cairo)
JEA	*Journal of Egyptian Archaeology* (London)
JNES	*Journal of Near Eastern Studies* (Chicago)
JSSEA	*Journal of the Society for the Study of Egyptian Antiquities* (Toronto)
Karnak	*Cahiers de Karnak* (Cairo), 10 vols. (1968–95). Note: vol. 1 = *Kêmi* 18 (1968); vol 2 = *Kêmi* 19 (1969); vol 3 = *Kêmi* 20 (1970); vol. 4 = *Kêmi* 21 (1971).
LÄ	*Lexikon der Ägyptologie*, 7 vols. and 3 supplements, edited by Wolfgang Helck and Eberhard Otto (Wiesbaden, 1975–92).
LD [I–VI]	Carl Richard Lepsius, *Denkmaeler aus Aegypten und Aethiopien*, 6 parts (I–VI) in 12 plate vols. (Berlin, 1849–59).
LD Text	Carl Richard Lepsius, *Denkmaeler aus Aegypten und Aethiopien*, 5 text vols., edited by Edouard Naville (Berlin, 1897–1913).
London, University College	Petrie Museum of Egyptian Archaeology, University College, London
Louvre	Musée du Louvre, Paris
MDAIK	*Mitteilungen des Deutschen Archäologischen Instituts Abteilung Kairo* (Cairo)
MMA	The Metropolitan Museum of Art, New York
Munich	Staatliche Sammlung Ägyptischer Kunst, München
Oxford	Ashmolean Museum, Oxford
Philadelphia	University Museum, University of Pennsylvania, Philadelphia
Princeton	Art Museum, Princeton University
RdE	*Revue d'Égyptologie* (Paris)
Rome	Musei Capitolini, La Collezione Egizia, Rome
RT	*Recueil de Travaux Relatifs à la Philologie et à l'Archéologie égyptiennes et assyriennes pour servir de bulletin à la mission française du Caire* (Paris)
SAK	*Studien zur altägyptischen Kultur* (Hildesheim)
Turin	Museo Egizio die Torino, Turin
Vatican	Museo Gregoriano Egizio, Rome
Vienna	Ägyptisch-Orientalische Sammlung, Kunsthistorisches Museum, Wien
ZÄS	*Zeitschrift der Ägyptischen Sprache und Altertumskunde* (Berlin)

Introduction

1. Exceptions are Gustave Jéquier, *L'architecture et la decoration dans l'ancienne Égypte,* vol. 3 (Paris, 1924); Serge Sauneron and Henri Stierlin, *Die letzten Tempel Ägyptens* (Zurich, 1978); François Daumas, "Architektur der Spätzeit," in *Das Alte Ägypten: Propyläenkunstgeschichte,* edited by Claude Vandersleyen (Berlin, 1975), pp. 196–205, and in *Ägypten, Spätzeit und Hellenismus,* edited by Jean Leclant, (Munich, 1981), pp. 17–123; Dietrich Wildung, *Egypt: From Prehistory to the Romans* (Cologne, 1997), pp. 169–77, 193–221.

2. In general: F. Daumas, "L'interprétation des temples égyptiens anciens à la lumière des temples gréco-romains," in *Karnak,* vol. 6 (1980),

pp. 261–84; Jean Yoyotte and Pascal Charvet, *Strabon: Le Voyage en Égypte* (Paris, 1997). The Egyptian reports of other ethnographers like Hecataeus of Abdera (ca. 360–290 B.C.) are mainly lost.

3. For details: S. Handler, "Architecture on the Roman Coins of Alexandria," *AJA* 75 (1971): 57–74; Henner von Hesberg, "Zur Entwicklung der Griechischen Architektur im ptolemäischen Reich," in *Das ptolemäische Ägypten,* edited by H. Maehler and V. M. Strocka (Mainz, 1978), pp. 137–45; Patrizio Pensabene, "Elementi architecttonici di Alessandria e di altri siti egiziani," in *Repertorio d'arte dell'Egitto greco-romano,* serie C, vol. 3 (Rome, 1993). For the connection between Egyptian and Greek art, see F. Le Corsu,

"Quelques motifs égyptiennes survivant dans l'architecture religieuse alexandrine," *RdE* 18 (1966): 37–44; John Boardman, *The Diffusion of Classical Art in Antiquity* (Washington, D.C., 1994), pp. 154–81.

Chapter 1

1. Samuel Birch, *Facsimile of an Egyptian Hieratic Papyrus of the Reign of Ramesses III, now in the British Museum* (London, 1876). James Henry Breasted, trans., *Ancient Records of Egypt*, vol. 4 (New York, 1906), pp. 87–206; Pierre Grandet, *Papyrus Harris I*, 2 vols. (Cairo, 1994).

2. A reconstruction drawing in Georges Perrot and Charles Chipiez, *A History of Art in Ancient Egypt* (London, 1883), p. 349, fig. 208. The architecture of the temple will be published in Françoise Laroche-Traunecker, *The Temple of Khonsu* (forthcoming). See also Claude Traunecker, "La chapelle de Khonsou du mur d'enciente et les travoux d'Alexandre," in *Karnak*, vol. 8 (1987).

3. Uvo Hölscher, *The Excavations of Medinet Habu*, 5 vols. (Chicago, 1934–54)—namely, vol. 2, *The Temples of the Eighteenth Dynasty*; vols. 3 and 4, *The Mortuary Temple of Ramses III*; and vol. 5, *Post-Ramessid Remains*.

Chapter 2

1. Malte Römer, *Gottes- und Priesterherrschaft in Ägypten am Ende des Neuen Reiches: Ein religionsgeschichtliches Phänomen und seine sozialen Grundlagen*, Ägypten und Altes Testament, no. 21 (Wiesbaden, 1994).

2. For example, the bronze statue of the princess Karomama in the Louvre (N 500) or the royal treasures of Tanis in Cairo.

3. See Henri Frankfort, *The Art and Architecture of the Ancient Orient* (New Haven, 1996), pp. 312–31; Rivka Gonen, "The Late Bronze Age," in *The Archaeology of Ancient Israel*, edited by Amnon Ben-Tor (New Haven, 1992), pp. 254–57.

4. A monumental cavetto (and even a pyramid?) topped the Iron Age rock tomb of "Pharaoh's daughter" at Silwan (eighth century B.C.) and survived to the first century B.C. or A.D. in the Lebanese towerlike "altars." See G.R.H. Wright, *Ancient Building in South Syria and Palestine*, 2 vols. (vol. 1 = text; vol. 2 = plates), Handbuch der Orientalistik VII (Leiden, 1985), pp. 326–27, pl. 277; H. Kalyan, "Rapport préliminaire sur les travaux de reconnaissance du site de Maschnak," *Bulletin du Musée de Beyrouth* 17 (1964): 105–110.

5. Wright, *South Syria and Palestine*, pl. 43[1].

6. P. P. Betancourt, *The Aeolic Style in Architecture* (Princeton, 1977); Yigal Shiloh, *The Proto-Aeolic Capital and Israelite Ashlar Masonry*. (= *Qedem* 11) (Jerusalem, 1979); Werner Kirch, *Die Entwicklung des ionischen Volutenkapitells im 6. and 5. Jhd. and seine Entstehung* (Bonn, 1988).

7. Yigal Shiloh, *The Proto-Aeolic Capital and Israelite Ashlar Masonry*; Gabriel Barkay, "The Iron Age II–III," in *The Architecture of Ancient Israel*, edited by Aharon Kempinski and Ronny Reich (Jerusalem, 1992), pp. 315–17. According to the Bible, the house of David and the Temple of Solomon were built of stone with the help of craftsmen sent by Hiram of Tyre (1 Kings 5:18; 1 Chron. 22:2, 14–15).

8. Dieter Arnold, *Building in Egypt: Pharaonic Stone Masonry* (New York, 1991), pp. 148–57.

9. For the excavation and building history of the temples of Tanis, see William M. Flinders Petrie, *Tanis I (1883–4)* (London, 1885); idem, *Tanis II* (London, 1882); Pierre Montet, *Les nouvelles fouilles de Tanis (1929–1932)* (Paris, 1933); idem, "Les fouilles de Tanis en 1933 et 1934," *Kêmi* 5 (1935/37): 1–18; idem, "Les obélisques de Ramsès II," *Kêmi* 5 (1935/37): 104–114; J.-L. Fougerousse, "Études sur les constructions de Tanis," *Kêmi* 5 (1935/37): 19–63; A. Lézine, "Le temple nord à Tanis," *Kêmi* 12 (1952): 46–58; and Pierre Montet, *Le lac sacré de Tanis,* (Paris, 1966). For recent excavations, see Philippe Brissaud, *Cahiers des Tanis*, vol. 1 (Paris, 1987), and subsequent volumes in this series.

10. Rudolf Anthes, *Mit Rahineh* (Philadelphia, 1965), pp. 92–95, pl. 31.

11. Cairo, JdE 37478 + CG 639, and Louvre, A 23; Biri Fay, *The Louvre Sphinx and Royal Sculpture from the Reign of Amenemhat II* (Mainz, 1996).

12. C. C. Edgar, "Notes from My Inspectorate," *ASAE* 13 (1913): 277–78.

13. Reginald Engelbach, *Riqqeh and Memphis VI* (London, 1915), pl. 57[24].

14. Hermann Ranke, *Koptische Friedhöfe bei Karâra und der Amontempel Scheschonks I. bei El Hibe* (Berlin, 1926), pp. 58–68.

15. Eberhard Otto, *Werke der Kunst in Heidelberg: Aus der Sammlung des Ägyptologischen Institutes der Universität Heidelberg* (Berlin, 1964), pp. 18, 94, pl. 18; E. Feucht, "Zwei Reliefs Scheschonks I. aus El-Hibeh," *SAK* 6 (1978): 69–77.

16. According to J.-F. Carlotti, "Contribution à l'étude métrologique de quelques monuments du temple d'Amon-Rê à Karnak," in *Karnak*, vol. 10 (1995), pp. 65–125.

17. It is also considered as part of the enclosure wall of the Amun precinct built by Nectanebo I.

18. See Edouard Naville, *Bubastis (1887–1889)* (London, 1891); idem, *The Festival-Hall of Osorkon II in the Great Temple of Bubastis (1887–1889)* (London, 1892); Labib Habachi, *Tell Basta* (Cairo, 1957); Ch. Tietze and M. Omar, *Tell Basta: Geschichte einer Grabung*, Arcus, no. 4 (Berlin, 1996).

19. One of the decorated blocks in Philadelphia (E-224).

20. The use of such columns in the nave of a hypostyle hall is unusual. The best capital example is in Boston (89.555).

21. Tietze and Omar, *Tell Basta*, p. 7, reconstruct instead of two hypostyles a colonnade of about two-by-fifteen papyrus-bundle columns, similar to the colonnade of the Luxor Temple, crossing a deep, wide court enriched with numerous Ramesside statues. They seem to allocate the remaining column and pillar types to another building in the south.

22. Naville, *Bubastis*, pp. 60–62.

23. Glyptothek Munich, no. 78, see Hans Wolfgang Müller, *Staatliche Sammlung Ägyptischer Kunst*, no. 73 (Munich, 1972).

24. W. M. Flinders Petrie and Ernest Mackay, *Heliopolis, Kafr Ammar and Shuraf* (London, 1915), pl. 40.

25. For the possible origin of the granite columns, see D. Arnold, "Hypostyle Halls of the Old and Middle Kingdom?" in *Studies in Honor of William Kelly Simpson*, edited by Peter Der Manuelian, vol. 1. (Boston, 1996), pp. 39–54.

26. The Hathor capitals are cut from relief blocks of Osorkon I, still preserved at the underside. Five examples are in the Brit. Mus. (1107), in Boston (89.555), in the Louvre (E 10590), in Berlin (10834), and in the Nicholson Museum, Sydney. For their date see A. W. Shorter, "A Hathor-capital from Bubastis," *British Museum Quarterly* 10 (1936): 172–74. E. von Mercklin, "Das aegyptische Figuralkapitell," in *Studies Presented to David Moore Robinson*, vol. 3 (St. Louis, 1951), pp. 199–201; and J. L. Haynes, "Redating the Bat Capital in the Museum of Fine Arts, Boston," in *Studies in Honor of William K. Simpson*, edited by Peter Der Manuelian, vol. 1 (Boston, 1996), pp. 399–408. Because of the hairstyle of the Hathor heads, they were already thought to be of Middle Kingdom origin.

27. Naville, *The Festival-Hall of Osorkon II*; Ch. C. Van Siclen, "The Shadow of the Door and the Jubilee Reliefs of Osorkon II from Tell Basta," *Varia Aegyptiaca* 7 (1991): 81–87. Some blocks are in the Brit. Mus. (1105, 1077), in Philadelphia (E-225), in Boston (89.557, 90.235), and in Berlin (10838).

28. Sheshonq V at Tanis and Shabaka in front of the temple of Ptah of Thutmosis III at Karnak (gate no. 2). A list of early examples is provided in Dieter Arnold, "Royal Cult Complexes of the Old and Middle Kingdoms," in *Temples of Ancient Egypt*, edited by Byron E. Shafer (Ithaca, 1997), pp. 269–70 n. 151.

29. C. Sambin and J.-F. Carlotti, "Une porte de fête-sed de Ptolémée II remployée dans le temple de Montou à Médamoud," *BIFAO* 95 (1995): 383–457.

30. The motive goes back to Thinite times and was amplified for the chapel court of the Djoser complex and the decoration program of the square antechambers of the pyramid temples. See Arnold, "Royal Cult Complexes of the Old and Middle Kingdoms," in *Temples of Ancient Egypt*, edited by Byron E. Shafer (Ithaca, 1997), pp. 32–39.

31. Cairo, CG 70006.

32. Naville, *Bubastis*, pp. 12–13; Habachi, *Tell Basta*, pp. 46–55. One fragment is in the Louvre (B 55).

33. A stela of Osorkon II found not far south of Mît Yaîsh may also originate at Leontopolis.

34. Naville, *Bubastis*, p. 52.

35. Claude Robichon, P. Barguet, and J. Leclant, *Karnak-Nord IV (1949–1951)* (Cairo, 1954), pp. 66–67, pl. 60.

36. Jean Leclant and Gisèle Clerc, "Fouilles et travaux en Égypte et au Soudan," *Orientalia* (Rome) 66 (1997): 235.

37. A. J. Spencer, *Excavations at Tell el-Balamun* (London, 1996).

38. Edouard Naville, *The Mound of the Jew and the City of Onias* (London, 1890), pp. 28–30.

39. C. C. Edgar, "Report on an Excavation at Tell Om Harb," *ASAE* 11 (1911): 165–69; G. Daressy, "Mostai, Tell Omm Harb," *ASAE* 12 (1912): 209–213.

40. G. Daressy, "Le nom de Horus du roi Chéchanq III," *ASAE* 13 (1914): 86.

41. G. Daressy, "Rapport sur Kom el-Hisn," *ASAE* 4 (1903): 283–84.

42. G. Daressy, "Bendarieh," *ASAE* 12 (1912): 205–206.

43. R. A. Schwaller de Lubicz, G. de Miré, and V. de Miré, *Les temples de Karnak*, 2 vols. (vol. 1 = text; vol. 2 = plates) (Paris, 1982), pls. 234–35.

44. Pierre Montet, *Le Lac sacrée de Tanis* (Paris, 1966), pp. 57–61. Some of the blocks show priests' processions and rituals connected with the Sed festival.

Chapter 3

1. For an introduction into Kushite history and culture, see Derek A. Welsby, *The Kingdom of Kush* (London, 1996), and Dietrich Wildung,

Sudan: *Antike Königreiche am Nil*, exhibition catalogue, Munich (1997).

2. The events of the conquest are recorded on the famous stela of Piankhi from the Gebel Barkal in Cairo. (JdE 48862). See Nicolas Grimal, *La stèle triomphale de Pi('ankh)y au Musée de Caire* (Cairo, 1981).

3. Comprehensive: Jean Leclant, *Recherches sur les monuments thébains de la XXVe dynastie dite éthiopienne*, 2 vols., Bibliothèque d'Étude, no. 36 (Cairo, 1965).

4. It seems unlikely, for that reason, that the green schist parapet slabs of Psametik I and II from a temple in Sais (figs. 34, 37) are, despite iconographic similarities of Kushite origin; see note 65, chapter 4.

5. For the Theban area, see Leclant, *Monuments thébains*.

6. Michel Azim points at features of an autonomous building activity of the Kushites in Egypt in "A propos du pylône du temple d'Opet à Karnak," in *Karnak*, vol. 8 (1987), pp. 66–67.

7. Leclant, *Monuments thébains*, vol. 1, pp. 216–19.

8. Bernhard V. Bothmer, *Egyptian Sculpture of the Late Period 700 B.C. to A.D. 100* (Brooklyn, 1960), p. 1.

9. Manfred Bietak and Elfried Reiser-Haslauer, *Das Grab des 'Anch-Hor*, vol. 2 (Vienna, 1982), pp. 232–40.

10. The grid that was used for proportioning the human figure was now divided into twenty-one squares (not the earlier eighteen) from the baseline to the root of the nose, significantly elongating the figure; see Gay Robbins, *Proportion and Style in Ancient Egyptian Art* (Austin, 1994), pp. 160–64.

11. Leclant, *Monuments thébains*, vol. 1, pp. 204–205.

12. Comprehensive in documentation and analysis: Diethelm Eigner, *Die monumentalen Grabbauten der Spätzeit in der thebanischen Nekropole* (Vienna, 1984).

13. For example, the tombs of Harwa (715–685), Pedamenophis (675–665), and Montemhet (675–660).

14. The theory that Kushite domination might have advanced the use of iron in Egypt cannot be substantiated any longer. The output of iron in the Sudan increased only after the end of the Kushite rule in the fourth century B.C. See A. A. Hakem, "The Civilization of Napata and Meroe," in *Ancient Civilizations of Africa*, vol. 2 of *General History of Africa*, edited by Gamal Mokhtar (Paris, 1981), p. 312.

15. Eigner, *Monumentale Grabbauten*, p. 84, pl. A-B; O. Palaga and R. S. Bianchi, "Who Invented the Claw Chisel?" *Oxford Journal of Archaeology* 13 (1994): 185–97.

16. The first true stone vaults appear in Egypt already in the 4th Dynasty at Dahshur (ca. 2550) and in a few later Old Kingdom tombs; see Rainer Stadelmann, Nicole Alexanian, Herbert Ernst, Günter Heindl, and Dietrich Raue, "Pyramiden und Nekropole des Snofru in Dahschur," *MDAIK* 49 (1993): 290, pl. 59b. Thereafter, Egyptian builders showed little inclination for building stone vaults and preferred "false" vaults that consisted of horizontal or slanting ceiling beams, carved from below into the shape of a vault; see Arnold, *Building in Egypt*, pp. 200–201, fig. 4.141.

17. Hölscher, *Post-Ramessid Remains*, vol. 5 of *The Excavations of Medinet Habu*, pp. 17–30; J. Brinks, "Gewölbe," in *LÄ*, vol. 2 (1977), pp. 589–94; Eigner, *Monumentale Grabbauten*, pp. 78–79; M. Verner, "La tombe d'Oudjahorresnet," *BIFAO* 89 (1989): 283–90.

18. Welsby, *The Kingdom of Kush*, fig. 36.

19. Th. D. Boyd, "The Arch and the Vault in Greek Architecture," *AJA* 82 (1978): 83–100. Structures that have the aspect of a vault but are produced by different means are, of course, older.

20. See Fritz Hintze, *Der Löwentempel: Musawwarat es Sufra*, vol. 1, pt. 2. (Berlin, 1971); F. W. Hinkel, "Säule und Interkolumium in der meroitischen Architektur," *Meroitica* 10 (1989): 231–67; idem, "Grundsätze der Architekturanalyse und einige Aspekte in der Untersuchung von meroitischen Baudenkmälern," *Meroitica* 12 (1991): 143–64; Welsby, *The Kingdom of Kush*, pp. 99–136; F. W. Hinkel, "Meroitische Architektur, 300 v.Chr.-350 n.Chr.," in Wildung, *Sudan*, pp. 393–415.

21. Leclant, *Monuments thébains*, vol. 1, pp. 36–41; vol. 2, pl. 16.

22. Ibid., vol. 1, pp. 19–23.

23. Ibid., vol. 1, p. 19.

24. Ibid., vol. 1, pp. 41–47; vol. 2, pls. 17–20.

25. Ibid., vol. 1, pp. 93–105. The chapel contained the beautiful alabaster statue of Amenirdis I, now in Cairo (JdE 3420); see ibid., vol. 2, pl. 61, and A. Mariette, *Karnak* (Paris, 1875), pp. 68–69, pl. 45e.

26. See Herbert Ricke, *Das Kamutef-Heiligtum Hatschepsuts und Thutmosis' III. in Karnak* (Cairo, 1954), pp. 14–15, plans 1 and 4.

27. Leclant, *Monuments thébains*, vol. 1, pp. 137–39.

28. See ibid., vol. 1, pp. 145–52. For the latest investigations by the Oriental Institute of the University of Chicago, see P. Dorman, "Epigraphic Survey," in *The Oriental Institute: 1996–97 Annual Report* (Chicago, 1997), pp. 40–41.

29. The oldest cartouches began with *Re-///-///*, which unfortunately fits most of the royal names of the 25th and 26th Dynasties. Since the kiosk covers the grooves for the flagpoles of the pylon, the kiosk must be added later. Because of the meager building activity of the 26th Dynasty at Thebes, one would like to exclude that period. C. Traunecker suggests instead Hakoris of the 29th Dynasty ("Essai sur l'histoire de la XXIXe dynastie," *BIFAO* 79 [1979]: 434).

30. For example, the naos in Cairo (CG 70007).

31. Leclant, *Monuments thébains*, vol. 1, pp. 47–54; vol. 2, pls. 21–28.

32. Ibid., vol. 1, pp. 59–61.

33. Statue, Cairo, CG 655 (relief lost).

34. For Taharqa's building activity: J. Leclant, "Taharqa," in *LÄ*, vol. 6 (1986), pp. 156–84; K. A. Kitchen, *The Third Intermediate Period (1100–650 BC)* (Warminster, 1986), pp. 389–90.

35. Shown in the north palace of Nineveh on the relief slab (Brit. Mus., W 124 928); see Julian Reade, *Assyrian Sculpture: British Museum*, (Cambridge, Mass., 1983), fig. 99.

36. Hans-Ulrich Onasch, *Die assyrischen Eroberungen Ägyptens*, Ägypten und Altes Testament, no. 27 (Wiesbaden 1994).

37. Leclant, *Monuments thébains*, vol. 1, pp. 8–13.

38. With abacus but without base, corresponding to 35 cubits.

39. A forerunner of the Greek sphinx column? See Klaus Hoffelner and Michael Kerschner, *Die Sphinxsäule* (Mainz, 1996).

40. Leclant, *Monuments thébains*, vol. 1, pp. 63–76; vol. 2, pls. 38–49; Richard A. Parker, Jean Leclant, and Jean-Claude Goyon, *The Edifice of Taharqa* (Providence, 1979).

41. Leclant, *Monuments thébains*, vol. 1, pp. 61, 77–78.

42. Leclant, *Monuments thébains*, vol. 1, pp. 23–36, 110–13; vol. 2, pls. 68–70.

43. Robichon, Barguet, and Leclant, *Karnak-Nord*, pp. 109–135; Leclant, *Monuments thébains*, vol. 1, pp. 91–93, and vol. 2, pls. 56–60.

44. This type of depicting architecture in Egypt goes back to the Djoser complex of the 3rd Dynasty and is quite common in Late Egyptian building. For example, the facade of engaged half-columns with Hathor capitals at the temple of Mut at Karnak (see the buildings of Taharqa, this chapter) or the bark station of Cleopatra VII in the temple of Geb at Coptos (see chapter 7).

45. M. Abdul-Qader Muhammad, "Preliminary Report on the Excavations Carried Out in the Temple of Luxor Seasons 1958–1959 &

1959–1960," *ASAE* 60 (1968): 244–47, pls. 14–18; Leclant, *Monuments thébains*, vol. 2, pl. 76.

46. Robichon, Barguet, and Leclant, *Karnak-Nord*, pp. 5–6, 106–109. A similar building was dedicated by Nectanebo I on Philae; see fig. 74, this volume.

47. Two quite similar contemporary features are found in the enclosure of Monthu and in front of the Luxor Temple.

48. Figure 27 attempts to incorporate results from the excavation by The Brooklyn Museum of Art; see R. Fazzini, "The Precinct of Mut during Dynasty 25 and Early Dynasty 26," *JSSEA* 11 (1981): 115–16; idem, "Precinct of the Goddess Mut," *Archaeological News* 16 (1991): 71ff.; idem, "Excavating the Temple of Mut," *Archaeology* 36 (1983): 16–23; idem, "Report on the 1983 Season of Excavation at the Precinct of the Goddess Mut," *ASAE* 70 (1984/85): 287–307.

49. Leclant, *Monuments thébains*, vol. 1, pp. 114–15.

50. M. Pillet, "Le temple de Khonsou dans l'enceinte de Mout à Karnak," *ASAE* 38 (1938): 469–78.

51. As suggested by birth and circumcision scenes: see M. Pillet, "Les scènes de naissance et de circoncision dans le temple nord-est de Mout, à Karnak," *ASAE* 52 (1952): 77–104; François Daumas, *Les mammisis des temples égyptiens* (Paris, 1958), pp. 44–54.

52. Leclant, *Monuments thébains*, vol. 1, p. 84.

53. Some of the columns were reconstructed by Chevrier in 1952; see Leclant, *Monuments thébains*, vol. 1, pp. 56–58, and vol. 2, pls. 31–35; idem, "La colonnade éthiopienne à l'est de la grande enceinte d'Amon," *BIFAO* 53 (1953): 113–72.

54. Robichon, Barguet, and Leclant, *Karnak-Nord*; Leclant, *Monuments thébains*, vol. 1, pp. 85–86, and vol. 2, pls. 50–53.

55. W. Y. Adams, "The Napatan/Meroitic Temple Complex," *JEA* 65 (1979): 32–33.

56. D. Meeks, "Une fondation memphite de Taharqa," in *Hommages à Serge Sauneron* (Cairo, 1979), pp. 221–59.

57. See Francis Ll. Griffith, "Oxford Excavations in Nubia," *Annals of Archaeology and Anthropology* 9 (1921/22): 74–76; M. F. Laming Macadam, *The Temples of Kawa*, 2 vols. (London, 1955), esp. part 2, "History and Archaeology of the Site"; Helen Jacquet-Gordon, Charles Bonnet, and Jean Jacquet, "Pnubs and the Temple of Tabo on Argo Island," *JEA* 55 (1969): 103–111.

58. Macadam, *The Temples of Kawa*, vol. 2, p. 15, pls. 9–12.

59. The shrine from Kawa now in Oxford (no. 1936.661).

60. Most Egyptian temples also housed

images of minor deities, who were part of the main god's family or local cult community, similar to the cult of saints in medieval churches.

61. A column in Queen's College at Oxford.

62. LD I, pl. 127; LD V, pl. 6.

Chapter 4

1. For the history, see Friedrich Karl Kienitz, *Die politische Geschichte Ägyptens vom 7. bis zum 4. Jahrhundert vor der Zeitwende* (Berlin, 1953); T.G.H. James, "Egypt: The Twenty-fifth and Twenty-sixth Dynasties," CAH, vol. 3, pt. 2, pp. 708–738.

2. T.F.R.G. Braun, "The Greeks in Egypt," CAH, vol. 3, pt. 3, pp. 32–52.

3. Blocks from Sais, for example, were shipped 65 km down the Nile to Damietta.

4. Under Psametik I, in contrast to the deficiency of royal building projects at Thebes, monumental private tombs of Basa, Pabasa (625–610), and Ibi (635–625) were built, followed by the giant late 26th Dynasty tombs of Pedihor-resnet (610–595) and Ankhhor (595–585).

5. A stylistic rift separates reliefs of the early 26th Dynasty (Psametik I) from those of the later succeeding kings (Apries and Amasis).

6. Eigner, *Monumentale Grabbauten*, pp. 17–18.

7. It seems significant that, instead, the sanctuaries of gods' temples were occasionally furnished with colossal, monolithic hard stone naoi. Typically, the largest of the naoi was dedicated not to Amun of Karnak but to Neith of Sais.

8. As designated by George Foucart, *Histoire de l'ordre lotiforme* (Paris, 1897), and A. Köster, "Die ägyptische Pflanzensäule der Spätzeit," *Recueil de travaux* 25 (1903): 110–19.

9. Although Old Kingdom foundations were far from technically sound; see Arnold, *Building in Egypt*, pp. 109–111.

10. D. P. Hansen, "The Excavations at Tell el Rub'a," *JARCE* 6 (1967): 5–8.

11. The foundation pits for temples and pyramids of the 12th Dynasty were already cased with brick and the floor of the pit covered with bricks or sand.

12. Angela Schwab, "Die Sarkophage des Mittleren Reiches" (Ph.D. diss., University of Vienna, 1989), pp. 15–18.

13. Comprehensive: J.-F. Carlotti, "Quelques réflexions sur les unités de mesure utilisées en architecture à l'époque phraonique," in *Karnak*, vol. 10 (1995), pp. 127–39.

14. Diodorus (I.98) mentions Solon of Athens, Plato, Pythagoras of Samos, Eudoxus, Democritus of Abdera, and Oenopides of Chios,

and the sculptors Telecles and Theodorus of Samos. Herodotus (II.143) specifies Hecataeus of Miletus, and Thales is said to have measured the pyramids.

15. J. J. Coulton, *Ancient Greek Architects at Work* (Ithaca, 1977); G. Hölbl, "Ägyptischer Einfluß in der griechischen Architektur," *Jahreshefte des Österreichischen Archäologischen Institutes in Wien* 55 (1984): 1–18. Early Ionic temples were the older Artemision of Ephesos (ca. 560 B.C.), the older Didymaion (ca. 540 B.C.), the Heraion III of Rhoikos on Samos (ca. 540 B.C.), and the Heraion IV of Polykrates on Samos (ca. 525 B.C.).

16. Coulton, *Ancient Greek Architects*; Wolfgang Müller-Wiener, *Griechisches Bauwesen in der Antike* (Munich 1988); Manolis Korres, *From Pentelicon to the Parthenon* (Athens, 1995).

17. Dieter Mertens, *Der alte Heratempel in Paestum und die archaische Baukunst in Unteritalien* (Mainz, 1993), p. 6; Arnold, *Building in Egypt*, pp. 110–11.

18. Arnold, *Building in Egypt*: anathyrosis, p. 123; cramps, pp. 124–28; square levels, pp. 253–55.

19. See G.R.H. Wright, *Ancient Building in Cyprus*, 2 vols. (vol. 1 = text; vol. 2 = plates), Handbuch der Orientalistik VII (Leiden, 1992), pls. 202–204.

20. For the temple of Hera I at Paestum of ca. 545, see Mertens, *Der alte Heratempel*. For Attic gravestones of 610–525 with cavetto and sphinxes, see Gisela Richter, *The Archaic Gravestones of Attica* (London, 1961), pp. 2–3, figs. 1–3, 66–76. For Etruscan tombs from ca. 590 to the third century A.D., see Axel Boethius, *Etruscan and Roman Architecture* (New Haven, 1995), figs. 60, 84.

21. Mertens, *Der alte Heratempel*, p. 65, figs. 52, 70–73, 114, pls. 90–91.

22. Helmut Berve and Gottfried Gruben, *Griechische Tempel und Heiligtümer* (Munich, 1961), pp. 216–18. In the Olympieion of Agrigent (temple "B," ca. 480), in which one had already noticed Phoenician-Cartagan elements, the intercolumniations were completely closed (Berve and Gruben, pp. 226–29).

23. See William M. Flinders Petrie, *Naukratis*, vol. 1 (London, 1886), pl. 53. At the same time (ca. 560), Ionic capitals appear in the Artemision of Ephesos. The capitals of the slightly older (570) Heraion of Samos are lost.

24. See Wright, *Cyprus*, p. 535.

25. Aharon Kempinksi and Ronny Reich, eds., *The Architecture of Ancient Israel* (Jerusalem, 1992), pp. 305–306.

26. Helmut Berve and Gottfried Gruben, *Griechische Tempel und Heiligtümer* (Munich, 1961), pp. 134–37.

27. The assumption of Köster, that the Ptolemaic capitals show a certain adaption to the Corinthian capital imported by the Greeks (Köster, "Pflanzensäule," p. 87), cannot be substantiated any longer, because the Egyptian composite capital appears already at 600 B.C. According to Vitruvius (IV.1.9–10), the first Corinthian capital was invented in the second half of the fifth century by the sculptor Kallimachos. The earliest known example (now lost) was found in the temple of Bassai Phigalia (ca. 429–427); see A. W. Lawrence, *Greek Architecture*, rev. 4th ed. (New Haven, 1996), p. 223 n. 7.

28. Anton Bammer and Ulrike Muss, *Das Artemision von Ephesos* (Mainz, 1996), pp. 49–57.

29. Serena Ensoli Vittozzi, *Musei Capitolini: La Collezione Egizia* (Rome, 1990), pp. 59–70.

30. The temple of Apollo of Bassai Phigalia (ca. 420) and the temple of Lousoi in Arcadia of the fourth—or rather, more likely, the third—century B.C.

31. *BemerkungenAR I*, pp. 138–39.

32. Coulton, *Ancient Greek Architects*, pp. 32–33.

33. O. Palaga and R. S. Bianchi, "Who Invented the Claw Chisel?" *Oxford Journal of Archaeology* 13 (1994): 188.

34. Jean-Pierre Protzen, *Inca Architecture and Construction* (New York, 1993), pp. 165–90.

35. Erich Friedrich Schmidt, *Persepolis*, 3 vols. (Chicago, 1953–70), vol. 1, pp. 26–28.

36. Bastan Museum, Teheran; see J. Yoyotte, "Les inscriptions hiéroglyphiques: Darius et l'Égypte," *Journal Asiatique* 260 (1972): 235–66. In case that the material is gray-green graywacke, its origin from the quarries of the Wadi Hammâmât should be substantiated. It is also called "gray limestone" from Zakros. The transport of a 3 m long limestone block to Egypt only for sculpting seems to be excessive considering the beautiful stone material available in Egypt itself. There is no evidence in the text for a temporary installation in Egypt; see also O. W. Muscarella, *The Royal City of Susa*, exhibition catalogue, MMA (New York, 1992), pp. 219–21.

37. Schmidt, *Persepolis*, vol. 1, pls. 178–79. The doors are framed, however, by a non-Egyptian double recess.

38. Ibid., vol. 3, pls. 20, 53, 58, 64[A]. From Persepolis, the Egyptian cavetto was even transplanted to the Sassanian palace of Firuzabad of the early third century A.D.; see Arthur Pope and Upham Pope, *Persian Architecture* (New York, 1965), pp. 54–55, fig. 42.

39. The assumption (often repeated after Schmidt, *Persepolis*, vol. 1, pp. 26–27) that the plan of the Amun temple of Hibis in El-Kharga could have determined the plan of the palace of Darius is unconvincing. The temple of Hibis was a rather insignificant temple of the oases and was not situated in the main architectural stream of its time. Egyptian architects in Persian service could have offered better architectural examples than the temple of Hibis.

40. Klaus P. Kuhlmann, *Das Ammoneion: Archäologie, Geschichte und Kultpraxis des Orakels von Siwa* (Mainz, 1988), pp. 31–33.

41. See n. 15, this chapter. The hypaetral temple of Apollo at Didyma and the Olympieion at Agrigent are somewhat later (540–520 and ca. 500 B.C.).

42. The fortress could not, however, resist the Persian assault of 525 and, along with the Amun temple, was destroyed.

43. T.F.R.G. Braun, "Naucratis," in CAH, vol. 3, pt. 3, pp. 37–43.

44. Labib Habachi, "Sais and Its Monuments," *ASAE* 42 (1943): 369–407, and Ramadan el-Sayed, *Documents relatives à Sais et ses divinitées* (Cairo, 1975), pp. 177–213.

45. Neith, mistress of Sais, was an archaic goddess of the primordial ocean, the creation, and the mother of the sun.

46. The sphinx is in the Museum of Alexandria; see G. Daressy, "Inscriptions hiéroglyphiques du Musée d'Alexandrie," *ASAE* 5 (1904): 126. The column is in the Brit. Mus. (946). A relief block of Psametik I was also found under "Pompey's" Pillar.

47. Brit. Mus., EA 20 [800] (from Rosetta); see T.G.H. James, *Ancient Egypt* (Austin, 1988), fig. 3.

48. The continuous sequence of relief decoration proves that the slabs were not separated by columns and therefore cannot have belonged to a kiosk or roof chapel.

49. Spencer, *Tell el-Balamun*.

50. L. Habachi, "Notes on the Delta Hermopolis," *ASAE* 53 (1955): 441–80; Alain Pierre Zivie, *Hermopolis et le nome de l'Ibis* (Cairo, 1975).

51. For the naos (JdE 25796, CG 70008) and the other monuments, see Zivie, *Hermopolis*, pp. 104–113.

52. Cairo, JdE 47580; see H. Gauthier,"A travers la Basse-Egypte," *ASAE* 23 (1923): 170–71.

53. M. Jones and A. Jones, "The Apis House Project at Mit Rahina," *JARCE* 19 (1982): 51–58; 20 (1983): 33–45; 22 (1985): 17–28; and 24 (1987): 35–46.

54. For the pre-Ptolemaic Sarapis, see Werner Huß, *Der makedonische König und die ägyptischen Priester* (Stuttgart, 1994), pp. 58–61.

55. In the chapel of Ameniridis stood the beautiful, life-size alabaster statue of Amenirdis (daughter of Kaschta, divine consort under

Piankhi), in Cairo (CG 565); see Regine Schulz and Matthias Seidel, *Ägypten: Die Welt der Pharaonen* (Cologne, 1997), p. 274.

56. Somers Clark, "El-Kâb and Its Temples," *JEA* 8 (1922): 16–40.

57. For the history see Donald B. Redford, *Egypt, Canaan, and Israel in Ancient Times* (Princeton, 1992), pp. 430–69.

58. Persian ships later actually used the sea route around the Arabian Peninsula to the Red Sea harbors of Egypt. For the canal see T.G.H. James, "Egypt: The Twenty-fifth and Twenty-sixth Dynasties," in CAH, vol. 3, pt. 2, p. 722.

59. Habachi, "Sais," pp. 378–82.

60. W. M. Flinders Petrie, *A History of Egypt from the XIXth to the XXXth Dynasties* (London, 1985), p. 337.

61. Naville, *The Mound of the Jew*, pp. 60–61, pl. 20[4].

62. Marie-Louise Buhl, *The Late Egyptian Outer Stone Sarcophagi* (Copenhagen, 1959).

63. J.-Y. Empereur, "Alexandria: Underwater Site near Qait Bey Fort," *Egyptian Archaeology* 8 (1996): 7–10; idem, *Alexandria Rediscovered* (New York, 1998), pp. 68–79.

64. The Brit. Mus. label dates the head to the "Eighteenth Dynasty, about 1520(?)."

65. One slab (Vienna, ÄS 213) was found in Alexandria inscribed with the name of Psametik II, which replaced the cartouches of a predecessor, perhaps of Psametik I, who probably started the building. Since the king wears a skullcap with streamers of Kushite style and figures have been scratched out, a 25th Dynasty origin cannot be ruled out. See Bothmer, *Egyptian Sculpture*, p. 91; M. Eaton-Krauss, "A Falsely Attributed Monument," *ASAE* 78 (1992): 285–877; and Jack A. Josephson, *Egyptian Royal Sculpture of the Late Period, 400–246 B.C.* (Mainz, 1997), p. 14.

66. Habachi, "Sais," pp. 398–99. LD Text, vol. I, p. 4. The formidable ancient remains at the site may contradict the possibility that the blocks were moved from Sais.

67. *Description*, Text, vol. 5, pp. 166–69; *Description* V, pl. 30.

68. J. Vandier d'Abbadie, *Nestor l'Hôte (1804–1842)* (Leiden, 1963), p. 16.

69. Does it refer to Horus Khentikhety, Lord of the Black-Bull-Nome? That was located, however, far to the south (Athribis).

70. It was reerected as gnomon of his gigantic sundial on the Campus Martius, the *horologium solarium Augusti*. The obelisk fell during either an earthquake in 849 or the fire set by Robert Guiscard in 1084. Only in 1792 could it be reconstructed in front of the Palazzo di Montecitorio. See Erik Iversen, *Obelisks in Exile*, 2 vols. (Copenhagen, 1968 and 1972), vol. I, pp. 142–60; Edmund Buchner, *Die Sonnenuhr des Augustus* (Mainz, 1982).

71. Strabo's description of the situation is not clear. Allegedly the walls at first ran parallel and narrowed thereafter.

72. The Persians used the simple trick of destroying obelisks by blowing off the lower edges with fire, thus reducing the footing so that the obelisk fell. Traces of this firing can be observed on the New York obelisk of Thutmosis III from Heliopolis; see Henry H. Gorringe, *Egyptian Obelisks* (New York, 1882), chromolithograph between pp. 58 and 59.

73. Cairo, CG 17028.

74. Sales catalogue of Sotheby's New York, no. 41 (June 1, 1995). For the monuments of Elephantine, see Werner Kaiser, *Elephantine: Die Antike Stadt* (Cairo, 1998).

75. Gerhard Haeny, "A Short Architectural History of Philae," *BIFAO* 85 (1985): p. 203, fig. 1.

76. Haeny, "Philae," p. 202.

77. Through careful studies of the progression of the decoration process, E. Cruz-Uribe could demonstrate that the temple was a Saite, not a Persian, project; see E. Cruz-Uribe, "The Hibis Temple Project," *JARCE* 23 (1986): 157–66; idem, "Hibis Temple Project," *Varia Aegyptiaca* 3 (1987): 215–30. For the decoration program, see Jürgen Osing, "Zur Anlage und Dekoration des Temples von Hibis," *Studies in Egyptology Presented to Miriam Lichtheim*, vol. 2 (Jerusalem, 1990), pp. 751–67.

78. Herbert E. Winlock, *The Temple of Hibis in El Khargeh Oasis*, part I: "The Excavations" (New York, 1941), pl. 19B.

79. In contrast to the Osiris tomb of Sethos I at Abydos, the Sais tomb was probably an above-ground temple.

80. Cairo, 22/12/20/2; see H. Gauthier, "Un édifice hathorique à Sais," *ASAE* 22 (1922): 199–202, 239; *Nofret die Schöne*, exhibition catalogue, Munich (1985), no. 90.

81. In 1737 an obelisk was restored from fragments in the Piazza del Duomo at Urbino. The better preserved 5.47 m long pendant was erected in 1667 after designs by Gianlorenzo Bernini on the Piazza della Minerva in Rome, on top of an elephant (Iversen, *Obelisks in Exile*, vol. I, pp. 93–100). A beautifully carved and polished sphinx from Hadrian's villa (Munich, Gl. WAF 16) also may originate from this building.

82. An ushabti of Apries was found at Sais: G. Daressy, "Rapport sur des fouilles à Sa El-Hagar," *ASAE* 2 (1901): 237.

83. Habachi, "Sais," p. 405.

84. Montet, *Les nouvelles fouilles*, pp. 89–103. Examples in Cairo and the Louvre.

85. Herman De Meulenaere and Pierre Mackay, *Mendes II* (Warminster, 1976), p. 6.

86. Christine L. Soghor, "Inscriptions from Tell el Rub'a," in *JARCE* 6, special edition (1967): 5–51; B. V. Bothmer, "The Great Naos of Mendes," in *The Archaeology of the Nile Delta*, edited by E.C.M. Brink (Amsterdam, 1988), pp. 205–209.

87. Cairo, JdE 50039; see De Meulenaere and Mackay, *Mendes II*, p. 194[25], pl. 13.

88. Cairo, CG 70008.

89. Edgar, "Notes from My Inspectorate," p. 281.

90. G. Daressy, "Inscriptions hiéroglyphiques du Musée d'Alexandrie," *ASAE* 5 (1904): 127[XL].

91. W. Kaiser, "Die ältere Torfassade des spätzeitlichen Palastbezirkes von Memphis," *MDAIK* 43 (1986): 123–44.

92. W. M. Flinders Petrie, *Athribis* (London, 1908), pp. 10–11, 14.

93. Eigner, *Monumentale Grabbauten*.

94. M. V. Seton-Williams, "The Tell el-Farâ'in Expedition, 1968," *JEA* 55 (1969): 5–22.

95. Habachi, "Sais," pp. 385–86.

96. Rome, no. 35.

97. Their sarcophagi are in the Hermitage in St. Petersburg (766–7); see Henri Gauthier, *De la XXVe dynastie à la fin des Ptolemées*, vol. 4 of *Le livre des rois d'Égypte*, 5 vols. (Cairo, 1907–17), pp. 129–30.

98. Not to be confused with the more important temple of Wadjet at Buto in the Western Delta (Tell el-Farâ'in), visited by Herodotus (II.155–56). For finds, see Bertha Porter and Rosalind Moss, *Topographical Bibliography of Ancient Egyptian Hieroglyphic Texts, Reliefs, and Paintings*, 12 vols. (Oxford, 1960–81), vol. 4, p. 8.

99. W. M. Flinders Petrie, *Nabesha and Defenneh* (London, 1888), pp. 8–15.

100. A. Abdel Salam, "Rapport sur les fouilles du Service des Antiquités à Abou Yassin," *ASAE* 38 (1938): 609–614.

101. For finds see Bertha Porter and Rosalind Moss, *Topographical Bibliography of Ancient Egyptian Hieroglyphic Texts, Reliefs, and Paintings*, 12 vols. (Oxford, 1960–81), vol. 4, pp. 65–67.

102. Edgar, "Notes from My Inspectorate," pp. 280–81.

103. B. Ruszczyc, "Le temple d'Amasis à Tell-Atrib," *Études et Travaux* 9 (1976): 117–27.

104. Cairo, JdE 70011; Louvre, D 29. Pascal Vernus, *Athribis*, Bibliothèque d'Étude, no. 74 (Cairo, 1978), pp. 84–88.

105. Ibid., pp. 200–201.

106. Cairo, JdE 37494.

107. Apries ("Wahibre") carries out the dedication of the temple, followed by the Ka with the Horus name of Amasis ("Smen-Maat").

108. W. M. Flinders Petrie, *Meydum and Memphis III* (London, 1910), p. 39, pls. 29[4–5], 32[4–7].

109. Now in Memphis, Tennessee, at the Institute of Egyptian Art and Archaeology of Memphis State University. Published: Karol Mysliwiec, *Royal Portraiture of the Dynasties XXI–XXX* (Mainz, 1988), pl. 72.

110. Cairo, JdE 70010.

111. W. Golénischeff, "Lettre à M. G. Maspero surtrois petites trouvailles égyptologiques," *RT* 11 (1889): 98–99.

112. Charles Kuentz, *Obélisques* (Cairo, 1932), pp. 59–60, pl. 15 (CG 17029).

113. The text on the dorsal pillar quotes "Khnum, lord of Elephantine"; see O. Lollio Barberi, G. Parola, and M. P. Toti, *Le Antichità Egiziane di Roma Imperiale* (Rome, 1995), pp. 143–44.

114. W. Kaiser, "Stadt und Tempel von Elephantine," *MDAIK* 53 (1997): 173–82. In 1996, column bases of a structure of Amasis were found between the pronaos and kiosk of the Satet temple; see Leclant and Clerc, "Fouilles et travaux," p. 314.

115. S. Farag, G. Wahba, and A. Farid, "Reused Blocks from a Temple of Amasis at Philae," *Oriens Antiquus* 16 (1977): 315–24.

116. Ahmed Fakhry, *Bahria Oasis*, vol. 1 (Cairo, 1942), pp. 150–71. See also the reconstruction drawing in Sydney Aufrère, Jean-Claude Golvin, and Jean-Claude Goyen, *Sites et temples des déserts*, vol. 2 of *L'Égypte reconstituée*, 3 vols. (Paris, 1991–97), p. 131.

117. Rudolf Naumann, "Bauwerke der Oase Khargheh," *MDAIK* 8 (1939): 4–7.

118. Kuhlmann, *Das Ammoneion*. See the reconstruction drawing in Sydney Aufrère, Jean-Claude Golvin, and Jean-Claude Goyon, *Sites et temples des déserts*, vol. 2 of *L'Égypte reconstituée*, 3 vols. (Paris, 1991–97), p. 155.

119. Strabo, *Geography*, XVII.1.27. The sacking of Egypt is also recorded by Diodorus (I.46).

120. Kaiser, "Stadt und Tempel," pp. 178–83.

121. Herodotus, III.25–26.

122. G. Posener, *La première domination Perse en Égypte*, Bibliothèque d'Étude, no. 11 (Cairo, 1936), pp. 164–91.

123. For the history of the period, see A. T. Olmstead, *History of the Persian Empire* (Chicago, 1959), pp. 227, 234–36, 303–334; J. D. Ray, "Egypt 525–404 B.C.," in CAH, vol. 4, pp. 254–86.

124. For the building activities of the Persians in Egypt, see M. Cool Root, *The King and Kingship in Achaemenid Art* (Leiden, 1979), pp.

123–28, where she also upgrades the temple of Hibis to outstanding significance.

125. C. Traunecker, "Un document nouveau sur Darius Ier à Karnak," in *Karnak*, vol. 6 (1980), pp. 209–213.

126. W. H. Shea, "A Date for the Recently Discovered Eastern Canal of Egypt," *BASOR* 226 (1977): 31–38.

127. Fragments of the stelae are in the museums of Cairo and Ismailiya. See Posener, *Le première domination Perse*, pp. 48–87; idem, "Le canal du Nil à la Mer Rouge," *CdE* 13 (1938): 259.

128. Bothmer, *Egyptian Sculpture*, p. 82.

Chapter 5

1. For the history see Kienitz, *Die politische Geschichte Ägyptens*; Traunecker, "Essai"; A. B. Lloyd, "Egypt, 404–332 B.C." in CAH, vol. 6, pp. 337–60.

2. For the sequence of kings, see Huß, *Der makedonische König*, pp. 143–53.

3. The heavily fortified temples of Jerusalem, the Acropolis of Athens, and the Capitoline Temple in Rome come to mind.

4. In the case of unstamped bricks, the exact date of brick walls is often difficult to determine. Brick format is not always a reliable indicator; see A. J. Spencer, *Brick Architecture in Ancient Egypt* (Warminster, 1979), pp. 106–110. Enclosure walls at Pelusium, Tanis, Tûkh el-Qarâmus, Behbeit el-Hagar, and Saft el-Henne, of the Anubieion and Serapeum of Memphis, and at Hermopolis magna, Abydos, Dendera, Thebes, Armant, and El-Kâb might cautiously be attributed to the 30th Dynasty.

5. Sebennytos was the home of the priest and historian Manetho (ca. 290 B.C.).

6. Spiegelberg, *Der demotische Text der Priesterdekrete von Kanopus und Memphis (Rosettana)* (Heidelberg, 1922).

7. Günther Hölbl, *Geschichte des Ptolemäerreiches* (Darmstadt, 1994), p. 239.

8. Edouard Naville, *The Shrine of Saft El Henneh and the Land of Goshen* (London, 1887), p. 3.

9. G. Steindorff, "Reliefs from the Temples of Sebennytos and Iseion in American Collections," *The Journal of the Walters Art Gallery* 7/8 (1944–46): 59.

10. "Archaic" means in the style of ancient periods; "archaistic" means an artificial imitation of the art of a valued, older period.

11. Bothmer, *Egyptian Sculpture*, p. 89.

12. R. S. Bianchi, "The Pharaonique Art in Ptolemaic Egypt," in *Cleopatra's Egypt: Age of the Ptolemies*, exhibition catalogue, Brooklyn (1989), pp. 67–69.

13. For pharaonic building methods, see Somers Clark and Reginald Engelbach, *Ancient Egyptian Masonry* (Oxford, 1930), and Arnold, *Building in Egypt*. For Ptolemaic building methods, see J.C. Golvin and J. Larronde, "Étude des procédés de construction dans l'Égypte ancienne," *ASAE* 68 (1982): 165–90, and 70 (1984/85): 371–81; J.-Cl. Golvin and R. Vergnieux, *Hommages à François Daumas* (Montpelier, 1988), pp. 299–320; Jean-Claude Golvin and Jean-Claude Goyon, *Les bâtisseurs de Karnak* (Paris, 1987), pp. 88–137. For Roman building methods, see Roberto Marta, *Architettura Romana: Tecniche costrutive e forme architettonichi del mondo romano* (Rome, 1990), and Jean-Pierre Adam, *Roman Building: Materials and Techniques* (Bloomington, 1994).

14. Arnold, *Building in Egypt*, p. 122.

15. U. Hölscher, "Der Erste Pylon von Karnak," *MDAIK* 12 (1943): 139–49.

16. The use of dovetail-shaped cramps (generally of wood, rarely of metal or stone) was not a Late Period innovation; dovetail cramps are found as early as the Old Kingdom.

17. The masonry of the 30th Dynasty has not yet been studied in detail, but see M. Azim, "A propos du pylône du temple d'Opet à Karnak," in *Karnak*, vol. 8 (1987), p. 66.

18. Description following U. Hölscher, "Der Erste Pylon von Karnak," *MDAIK* 12 (1943): 147.

19. MMA, Rogers Fund, 1910 (10.177.2), first observed by Anne Heywood of the Objects Conservation Department, MMA.

20. In contrast to Greek temple building, where wood was used together with stone from the beginning; see A. T. Hodge, *The Woodwork of Greek Roofs* (Cambridge, 1960).

21. Alexandrian examples: Pensabene, *Repertorio d'Arte*, pp. 133–35, fig. 107, pl. 117; P. Gilbert, "Le fronton arrondi en Égypte," *CdE* 33 (1942): 83–90. In the pronaos of Dendera a kiosk with a flat pediment is depicted in the second scene of the second register on the west wall: Ludwig Borchardt, *Ägyptische Temple mit Umgang* (Cairo, 1938), figs. 5 and 6.

22. W. Weber, "Ein Hermes-Tempel des Kaisers Marcus," *Sitzungsberichte der Heidelberger Akademie der Wissenschaften* (1910): 10–54; *Iside: Il mito, il mistero, la magia*, exhibition catalogue, Milan (1997), p. 122.

23. From the temple of Fortuna Primigenia, ca. 80 B.C. The date of the mosaics is controversial, probably they are from the imperial age. See Pietro Romanelli, *Palestrina* (Naples, 1967), pls. 29–30, figs. 86–88.

24. Valdemar Schmidt, *Levende og Dode i det Gamle AEgypten/Album* (Copenhagen, 1919), pp. 228–33.

25. Probably from the Serapeum at Memphis, where it may have been a pendant to a sphinx of Hakoris. It was later moved to the Iseum in

Rome. Both sphinxes are now in the Louvre (A 26 and A 27); see Lollio Barberi et al., *Le Antichità Egiziane*, pp. 200–202.

26. A clear parallel to the two famous heraldic pillars of Thutmosis III in front of the main bark shrine of Karnak; see R. A. Schwaller de Lubicz, G. de Miré, and V. de Miré, *Les temples de Karnak*, vol. 2, (Paris, 1982), pls. 131–37. Similar heraldic pilasters are found in the room between the "Darius" sanctuary and the hypostyle hall of Akoris in the temple of Nekhbet at El-Kâb.

27. Traunecker, "Les >temples hautes< de Basse Époque," *RdE* 38 (1987): pp. 147–62.

28. D. B. Redford, "Mendès, une capitale éphémère, *Dossiers d'Archéologie* 213, special edition (1996): 78–81.

29. MMA, Rogers Fund, 1927 (27.2.1). See Traunecker, "Essai," p. 411.

30. Cairo, JdE 45936.

31. Louvre, A 27; see Lollio Barberi et al., *Le Antichità Egiziane*, pp. 200–202.

32. Now in Cairo (JdE 41534); see J. E. Quibell, *The Monastery of Apa Jeremias* (Cairo, 1912), p. 146, pl. 85. Quibell suspected a Late Period temple in the area later occupied by the monastery.

33. Cairo, JdE 67346; see F. Bisson de la Roque, *Tôd (1934 à 1936)* (Cairo, 1937), pp. 142–43.

34. These alternations have parallels in the addition by Hakoris of a hypostyle hall to the temple of Hibis at El-Kharga.

35. For example, the great hypostyle hall of Karnak and the Ramesseum. The hypostyle halls of the temple of Ptah at Memphis and of the temple of Ramesses III of Medinet Habu are destroyed.

36. *Description* I, p. 66.

37. Kaiser, "Stadt und Tempel," pp. 177–78.

38. Nectanebo I added a kiosk to the front of the already existing hall. The hall therefore would date into the period between the 26th and 30th Dynasties.

39. H. Gauthier, "Un ouchebti du roi Achôris," *ASAE* 22 (1922): 208.

40. J. Yoyotte, "Nectanébo II comme faucon divin?" *Kêmi* 15 (1959): 70–74.

41. J.-C. Golvin, "Essai d'explication des murs à assises courbés," *Comptes rendues de l'Academie des Inscriptions et Belles-Lettres* (Paris) (1990): 905–943. The appearance of the walls has been intrepreted as a representation of the primordial ocean encircling the sacred mound; see Paul Barguet, *Le temple d'Amon-Rê à Karnak* (Cairo, 1962), p. 32.

42. For a list of the monuments of Nectanebo I, see Kienitz, *Die politische Geschichte*

Ägyptens, pp. 199–212, augmented by H. De Meulenaere, "Nektanebos I," in *LÄ*, vol. 4 (1982), pp. 450–51.

43. Spencer, *Tell el-Balamun*.

44. A. Lézine, "Le temple du nord à Tanis," *Kêmi* 12 (1952): 46–48.

45. Montet, *Les nouvelles fouilles*, pp. 63–73 and 118–23.

46. Wilhem Spiegelberg, "Reliefbruchstücke aus der Zeit der 30. Dynastie," *ZÄS* 65 (1930): 102–104.

47. For the obelisk, see Charles Kuentz, *Obélisques* (Cairo, 1932), pp. 62–63 (CG 17031). For the tomb, see A. Abdel Salam, "Rapport sur les fouilles du Service des Antiquités à Abou-Yassin," *ASAE* 38 (1938): 607–622.

48. Naville, *The Shrine of Saft El Henneh*, p. 2.

49. Five fragments of the naos were rescued and put together in Cairo (CG 70021); several others were built into the bridges of Saft and Tahra. The naos was 1.87 m broad, 2.13 m deep, and 4 to 6 m high.

50. De Meulenaere and Mackay, *Mendes II*, pp. 191, 195. The naos was found in 1911 far from the temple and is now in Cairo (CG 70022).

51. Günther Roeder, *Naos* (Cairo, 1914), pp. 57–58 (CG 70020).

52. Brit. Mus., 926 (from Rosetta) and 927 (from Alexandria), see Silvio Curto, *L'Egitto antico nelle Collezioni dell'Italia settentrionale*, exhibition catalogue, Bologna (1961), pp. 88–90, pl. 9, and W. Stevenson Smith, *The Art and Architecture of Ancient Egypt*, rev. ed., edited by W. K. Simpson (New Haven, 1998), pp. 244–45, fig. 409. Bologna, B. 1870 (from the Aventin in Rome), see Curto, *L'Egitto antico nelle Colleziono dell'Italia senttentrionale*, pp. 88–90, pl. 39, and Sergio Pernigotti, *La collezione egiziana: Museo Civico archeologico di Bologna* (Bologna, 1994), p. 103.

53. Alain Pierre Zivie, "Hermopolis: El Baqlieh et le nome de l'Ibis," *Annuaire de l'Ecole Pratique des Hautes Etudes* 79 (1971–72): 491–94; L. Habachi, "Delta Hermopolis," pp. 441–80.

54. Vatican, 22676–77. For these monuments see Zivie, *Hermopolis*, pp. 122–34

55. Pascal Vernus, *Athribis*, Bibliothèque d'Étude, no. 74 (Cairo, 1978), pp. 135–71.

56. MMA, Edward S. Harkness Fund, 1928 (28.9.7).

57. Petrie, *Naukratis*, vol. 1, pp. 23–30.

58. W. M. Flinders Petrie, *Meydum and Memphis III* (London, 1910), pl. 32[1]; Engelbach, *Riqqeh and Memphis*, pl. 57[25].

59. August Mariette, *Choix de monuments et de dessins découverts ou exécutés pendant le déblaiement du Sérapéum de Memphis* (Paris, 1856), pl. 4. Mariette only produced sketches,

incorporated by De Morgan into his *Carte de la nécropole memphite* (Cairo, 1897), pls. 9–10, so that our reconstruction attempt (see here plan III) remains conjectural. See also M. Guilmot, "Le Sarapieion de Memphis," *CdE* 37 (1962): 359–81; S. Davies and H. S. Smith, "Sacred Animal Temples at Saqqara," in *The Temple in Ancient Egypt*, edited by Stephen Quirke (London, 1997), p. 120.

60. A few are left in the inspectorate of Saqqara, five are in Cairo (CG 685, 1193–6), two in Berlin (7777–8), six in the Louvre (N 391), and twelve in Vienna (Inv. 5756–67).

61. Louvre, N 390; see Guillemette Andreu, Marie-Hélèn Rutschowscaya, and Christine Ziegler, *L'Égypte ancienne au Louvre* (Paris, 1997), pp. 101–102.

62. J.-Ph. Lauer and Ch. Picard, *Les statues ptolémaiques du Sarapieion de Memphis* (Paris, 1955).

63. See M. Malinine, G. Posener, and J. Vercoutter, *Catalogue des stèles du Sérapéum de Memphis* (Paris, 1968).

64. Mariette's excavation of 1850–1854 was one of the earliest in Egypt and completely neglected architectural concerns. Since the building probably was the prototype for the Alexandrian Serapeum, our inadequate knowledge is especially deplorable, and the reexcavation of the area at Saqqara of great importance.

65. An ushabti of Nectanebo I was found at Memphis, and parts of his graywacke sarcophagus were found in Cairo (JdE 34673); see G. Daressy, "Inscriptions hiéroglyphiques trouvés dans le Caire," *ASAE* 4 (1903): 105–109.

66. Davies and Smith, "Sacred Animal Temples at Saqqara," pp. 112–31.

67. D. G. Jeffreys and H. S. Smith, *The Anubieion at Saqqara*, vol. 1 (London, 1988).

68. G. Roeder, "Zwei hieroglyphische Inschriften aus Hermopolis," *ASAE* 52 (1952–54): 353–409; Eberhard Otto, *Die biographischen Inschriften der ägyptischen Spätzeit* (Leiden, 1954), p. 179; A. J. Spencer, *Excavations at El-Ashmunein* (London, 1989), pp. 71–73.

69. Steven Snape and Donald Bailey, *The Great Portico at Hermopolis Magna: Present State and Past Prospects* (London, 1988); D. Arnold, "Zur Rekonstruktion des Pronaos von Hermopolis," *MDAIK* 50 (1994): 13–22; Klaus Parlasca, ">Verschränkte Kreise< bei Decken und Mosaiken: Zur Dekoration des großen Portikus des Thot-Tempels von Hermopolis Magna," in *Themelia*, edited by Martin Krause and Sofia Schaten (Wiesbaden, 1998), pp. 267–71.

70. E. F. Jomard's and L. Reybaud's suggestion (see Steven Snape and Donald Bailey, *The Great Portico at Hermopolis Magna: Present State and Past Prospects* [London, 1988], pp. 19, 21) that the pronaos of Hermopolis consisted originally of eighteen or twenty-four columns, that is, of three or four rows, was clearly contradicted by the location of the rear wall of the pronaos behind the second row.

71. A. Köster even went so far as to date the pronaos to the 18th Dynasty; see "Zum Tempel von Aschmunein," *ZÄS* 39 (1901): 141–43.

72. Now in Cairo (CG 70018).

73. Even more amazing is the fact that the Thutmoside Horus temple of Hierakonpolis was apparently never replaced by a later king.

74. A composite corner capital in MMA, Rogers Fund, 1910 (10.177.2).

75. Inscriptions of the Ptolemaic temple mention temple building by Kheops, Pepi I, Senwosret I, and Thutmosis III at Dendera.

76. Cairo, CG 70019. Its original location in the temple is unknown.

77. M. Abd el-Raziq, "Study on Nectanebo Ist in Luxor temple and Karnak," *MDAIK* 22 (1968): 159.

78. Claude Traunecker, "Un exemple de rite de substitution: Une stèle de Nectanébo Ier," in *Karnak*, vol. 7 (1982), pp. 339–54.

79. Photos in Mysliwiec, *Portraiture*, pls. 81–84. Mahmud Abd el- Razik, "Study on Nectanebo Ist in Luxor Temple and Karnak," *MDAIK* 23 (1968): 156–59.

80. Fine photos in Mysliwiec, *Portraiture*, pl. 76.

81. G. Pierrat et al., "Fouilles du Musée du Louvre à Tôd 1988–1991," in *Karnak*, vol. 10 (1995), pp. 442 n. 80, 498 n. 141.

82. *Description*, Text, vol. 1, p. 410.

83. G. Gabra, "Hemen and Nectanebo I in Mo'alla," *CdE* 49 (1974): 234–37.

84. W. Kaiser, "Stadt und Tempel," p. 177.

85. H. G. Lyons, *A Report on the Temples of Philae* (Cairo, 1908), pl. 6 (hereafter, *Temples*); idem, *A Report on the Island and Temples of Philae* (Cairo, n.d.), p. 22, pls. 3–4 (hereafter, *Island and Temples*).

86. A complete architectural survey is missing; see, at least, *Description* 1, pls. 5–9; Lyons, *Island and Temples*, plan 5.

87. Lyons, *Temples*, pl. 11; Haeny, "Philae," pp. 210–22, assumes that the core building and the front part of the ambulatory formed a unit.

88. A list of the monuments of Teos can be found in Kienitz, *Die politische Geschichte Ägyptens*, pp. 212–14.

89. The block may be taken from Tanis; see Edgar, "Notes from My Inspectorate," p. 277.

90. Wilhelm Spiegelberg, "Reliefbruchstücke aus der Zeit der 30. Dynastie," *ZÄS* 65 (1930): 102–104.

91. See G. Daressy, "Le roi Téôs à Athribis," *ASAE* 17 (1917): 42.

92. In general: P. Barguet, "Quelques fragments nouveaux au nom de Nekhthorheb," *Kêmi* 13 (1954): 87–91.

93. J. Yoyotte, "Nectanébo II comme faucon divin?" *Kêmi* 15 (1959): 70–74; H. De Meulenaere, "Les monuments du culte des rois Nectanébo," *CdE* 35 (1960): 92–107; T. Holm-Rasmussen, "On the Statue Cult of Nektanebos II," *Acta Orientalia* 40 (1979): 21–25. Cults are established for the Iseum, Heliopolis, Bubastis, Memphis, Abydos, Thebes, and Coptos. A remarkably fine falcon statue is in MMA, Rogers Fund, 1934 (34.2.1). Graywacke, height with crown and base 72 cm (fig. 82).

94. A list of the monuments of Nectanebo II can be found in Kienitz, *Die politische Geschichte Ägyptens*, pp. 214–30, augmented by H. De Meulenaere, "Nektanebos II," in *LÄ*, vol. 4 (1982), pp. 451–53.

95. It could have been the uninscribed obelisk (though only 25.37 m high) on St. Peter's Square, which was erected by Augustus on the Forum Julium in Alexandria and removed in A.D. 37 under Caligula on a special boat to Rome. There it was erected on the spina of the Circus Vaticanus, where it survived as the only upright standing obelisk until 1586. At that time it was transferred, under Pope Sixtus V, by the architect Domenico Fontana to St. Peter's Square.

96. Edouard Naville, *Détails relevés dans les ruines de quelques temples égyptiens* (Paris, 1930), pp. 40–55; A. Lézine, "État présent du temple de Behbeit el Hagar," *Kêmi* 10 (1949): 49–57; Ch. Favard-Meeks, "Un temple d'Isis à reconstruire," *Archaeologia* 263 (1993): 26–33.

97. Museo Nazionale, Rome, 52045; see Lollio Barberi et al., *Le Antichità Egiziane*, pp. 131–32.

98. *Description*, Text, vol. 5, pp. 160–66; *Description* V, pl. 30. The temple's estimated long proportions of 25 x 58 m suggest the existence of a pronaos, but this assumption disagrees with other observations. The halls that normally follow behind the pronaos would also require columns, although of somewhat smaller size. No such columns have been observed, and no traces of screen walls, which should have connected the front columns, were found.

99. The wall decoration of this part has been reconstructed by Christine Favard-Meeks in *Le temple de Behbeit el-Hagara* (Hamburg, 1991)—however, without much advancement of the temple's plan.

100. Ahmed Bey Kamal, "Sébennytos et son temple," *ASAE* 7 (1906): 87–94; C. C. Edgar, "The Temple of Samanoud," *ASAE* 11 (1911): 90–96. A granite block with the name of Alexander, son of Alexander the Great, is in the Louvre (E 10970), and blocks of Nectanebo II are in Baltimore (22.119) and in MMA, Edward S. Harkness Fund, 1912 (12.184.4B). See G. Steindorff, *Catalogue of the Egyptian sculpture in the Walters Art Gallery* (Baltimore, 1946), no. 253, pl. 47; Maria Mogensen, *La Glyptothèque Ny Carlsberg: La collection égyptienne* (Copenhagen, 1930), p. 108, pl. 118 (A 772); P. Barguet, "Quelques fragments nouveaux au nom de Nekhthorheb," *Kêmi* 13 (1954): 87–91; and N. Spencer, "The Temple of Onuris-Shu at Samanud," *Egyptian Archeology* 14 (1999): 7–9.

101. Cairo, CG 70015, CG 70012.

102. Huß, *Der makedonische König*, pp. 133–37.

103. Kamal, "Sébennytos," p. 93.

104. Vandier d'Abbadie, *Nestor l'Hôte*, pp. 17–18.

105. Brit. Mus., 523–24, 919–20, and Cairo, JdE 55312, CG 17030. See Iversen, *Obelisks in Exile*, vol. 1, pp. 51–61, pl. 43–44.

106. Rome, nos. 26, 32.

107. Naville, *The Shrine of Saft El Henneh*, p. 4.

108. The reconstruction of the temple by Ch. Van Siclen—in "Nectanebo II's Great Naos of Bastet," in *Essays in Egyptology in Honor of Hans Goedicke*, edited by Betsy M. Bryon and David Lorton (San Antonio, 1994), pp. 321–32, fig. 8—underestimates the huge dimensions of both temples.

109. A relief block now in Boston (90.233).

110. Tietze and Omar, *Tell Basta*, pp. 8–9.

111. One fragment of the naos is in Cairo (CG 70016) and two are in the Brit. Mus. (1106). For the site, see Naville, *Bubastis* and *The Festival-Hall of Osorkon II*; Habachi, *Tell Basta*; Tietze and Omar, *Tell Basta*.

112. Naville, *The Shrine of Saft El Henneh*, p. 4.

113. The famous naos in Cairo (CG 70021) with the catalogue of deities; see Naville, *The Shrine of Saft El Henneh*.

114. Flinders Petrie, *Tanis I, (1883–4)* (London, 1885), p. 28; Jean Clédat, "Notes sur l'isthme de Suez," *RT* 36 (1914): 103–112.

115. See Naville, *The Mound of the Jew*, pp. 22–23; Habachi, *Tell Basta*, pp. 123–40.

116. Ahmed Moussa, "A Red Granite Door-Jamb Bearing the Name of Nectanebo II," *ASAE* 70 (1984/85): 37–38.

117. Limestone reliefs in the Louvre (N 402, 423). See also "De l'Égypte au Louvre: Les plus belles oeuvres du Musée," *Ulisse*, special edition (1997): 72.

118. In the Brit. Mus. (EA 10). See *Description* V, pls. 39–41

119. See Henri Gauthier, *De la XXVe dynastie à la fin des Ptolemées* , vol. 4 of *Le livre des rois d'Égypte*, 5 vols. (Cairo, 1907–17), p. 179. The ushabti might indicate that the king's body was transferred from Upper Egypt, where he died, to Memphis and buried in his tomb.

120. Suggested by superbly decorated limestone slabs and parts of a 97 cm high cavetto with a frieze of cartouches; see Geoffrey T. Martin, *The Tomb of Hetepka* (London, 1979), pp. 89–99, pls. 65–74. For the excavation, see W. B. Emery, "Preliminary Report on the Excavations at North Saqqâra, 1968," *JEA* 55 (1969): 31–35; idem, "Preliminary Report on the Excavations at North Saqqâra, 1969–70," *JEA* 57 (1971): 3–13.

121. See W. B. Emery, "Preliminary Report on the Excavations at North Saqqâra, 1968," pp. 34–35, pl. 10. Similar to the facade decoration of cult niches in Theban Late Period tombs; for example, Jan Assmann, *Das Grab des Basa (Nr. 389) in der thebanischen Nekropole* (Mainz, 1973), pp. 32–33.

122. G. Daressy, "Rapport sur la découvert d'une grande cuve à Mit Rahineh," *ASAE* 2 (1901): 240–43.

123. Georg Möller and Alexander Scharff, *Die archäologischen Ergebnisse des vorgeschichtlichen Gräberfeldes von Abusir el-Meleq* (Leipzig, 1915) p. 102, pl. 77.

124. See W. M. Flinders Petrie, *Ehnasya, 1904* (London, 1905), p. 17. The naos measured about 1.50 x 1.50m.

125. Nectanebo II's naos to Thoth: CG70014. Major parts of two obelisks possibly from the temple of Thoth are in London (see *British Museum: A Guide to the Egyptian Galleries* [Sculpture] [London, 1909], p. 247, nos. 919–920/ 523–524). A fragment of one of them or of another obelisk is in Cairo (see Kuentz, *Obelisques*, pp. 61–62 [CG 17130]). The provenance is uncertain because the inscriptions refer to the temple of Thoth either of Hermopolis magna or of Hermopolis parva.

126. Cairo, CG 70017. Perhaps the so-called Osiris bed from Abydos also dates to Nectanebo II.

127. Its well-decorated gate was preserved in 1910 (see A. J. Reinach, *Rapports sur les fouilles de Koptos* [Paris, 1910], pl. 1) but has now disappeared; see Claude Traunecker, *Coptos: Hommes et dieux sur le parvis de Geb*, Orientalia Lovaniensia Analecta, no. 43 (Leuven, 1992).

128. The following hypothesis is not based on written evidence but tries to explain the unusual condition of the central part of the Amun temple. In contrast to the well-preserved other parts of Karnak, the area of the temple of the Middle Kingdom is completely flattened.

129. The old bark shrine of Thutmosis III was an early example of a free-standing bark shrine. See Paul Barguet, *Le temple d'Amon-Rê à Karnak* (Cairo, 1962), pp. 136–37.

130. One block is in Boston (75.11 a-d): B. Von Bothmer, "Ptolemaic Reliefs I," *Bulletin of the Museum of Fine Arts Boston* 50 (1952): 19–27.

131. D. Redford, "Three Seasons in Egypt: The Excavation of Temple C," *JSSEA* 18 (1988): 1–13, dates both phases to the third century B.C. The use of papyrus-bundle columns and the lack of mortar grooves might suggest an earlier date. The reconstruction of the columned front (see Redford, fig. 4) with engaged three-quarter columns is not supported by the published plan (see Redford, fig. 2).

132. See M. Dewachter, "Un bloc du 'temple haut' de Karnak Nord au Musée de Grenoble," *CdE* 49 (1974): 52–58.

133. Buchis was the sacred bull of the god Monthu.

134. Sir Robert Mond and Oliver H. Myers, *The Bucheum*, 3 vols. (London, 1934).

135. The naos originally stood in the corner of the room. In 1903, A. Barsanti had it pushed into the center of the sanctuary and on that occasion also restored the missing roof slabs. See "Rapport sur les trauvaux exécutés à Edfou en 1902–1905," *ASAE* 7 (1906): 105–107.

136. Unpublished; see Jean Leclant, "Fouilles et travaux en Égypte et au Soudan, 1984–85," *Orientalia* (Rome) 55 (1986): 287.

137. A publication by W. Niederberger and H. Jenni will appear soon; see Ewa Laskowska-Kusztal, *Die Dekorfragmente der ptolemäisch-römischen Tempel von Elephantine* (Mainz, 1996), pp. 6–14; Werner Kaiser, *Elephantine: Die Antike Stadt* (Cairo, 1998), p. 35, fig. 8.

138. Winlock, *The Temple of Hibis*, pp. 34–38.

139. Kuhlmann, *Das Ammoneion*, pp. 37–41.

140. Since lotus columns were extremely rare in that period, Cailliaud may actually have seen the rather similar papyrus-bundle columns.

Chapter 6

1. The military details of the conquest of Egypt is recorded in Diodorus (XVI.46–51).

2. D. B. Redford, "Mendès, une capitale éphémère," *Dossiers d'Archéologie* 213, special edition (1996): 78–81.

3. See Handler, "Roman Coins," pp. 57–74.

4. Diodorus, XVI.46–51. G. Daressy, "Remarques et notes," *RT* 10 (1888): 143. For a limestone block with cartouches of Alexander and the name of Thoth of Hermopolis, see the sales catalogue of Bonhams, Knightsbridge, vol. 40, no. 193 (December 1996).

5. C. Traunecker, "La chapelle de Khonsou du mur d'enceinte et les travaux d'Alexandre," in *Karnak*, vol. 8 (1987), pp. 347–54.

6. For traces on the floor, see R. A. Schwaller de Lubicz, *The Temple of Man*, 2 vols. (Rochester, 1998), vol. 2, pls. 83, 90.

7. A. Fakhry, "A Temple of Alexander the Great at Bahria Oasis," *ASAE* 40 (1941): 823–28.

8. Alexander the Great was Alexander III of Macedonia, and thus his son could be counted as Alexander IV. If Alexander the Great is considered as Alexander I, his son is Alexander II.

9. C. C. Edgar, "The Temple of Samanoud," *ASAE* 11 (1910): 91–92. One block is in the Louvre (10970).

Chapter 7

The counting of Ptolemaic royal names after Ptolemy VI is confused by the fact that Ptolemy Neos Philopator, the former Ptolemy VII, has been eliminated as a ruling king. In order not to alter the numbering of the following kings, I retain the familiar counting (Ptolemy Euergetes II = Ptolemy VIII, etc.). To be on the safe side, their epithets are added.

1. For a long list of private contributors to temple building, see Huß, *Der makedonische König*, pp. 20–25.

2. Hölbl, *Ptolemäer*, p. 62.

3. J. Kügler, "Propaganda oder performativer Sprechakt?" *GM* 142 (1994): 83–92.

4. For example, in the sanctuary of the Great Gods on the Island of Samothrace; see James R. McCredie, Georges Roux, Stuart M. Shaw, and John Kurtich, *The Rotunda of Arsinoe*, vol. 7 of *Samothrace*, Bollingen Series, no. 60 (Princeton, 1990). For more examples, see Hölbl, *Ptolemäer*, p. 89. For a Ptolemeion in Hermopolis magna, see A.J.B. Wace et al., *Hermopolis Magna, Ashmunein: The Ptolemaic Sanctuary and the Basilica* (Alexandria, 1959), pp. 4–11.

5. See chapter 7, this volume, note 95.

6. See Hölbl, *Ptolemäer*, pp. 77–82.

7. See P. Gilbert, "Éléments hellénistiques de l'architecture de Philae," *CdE* 36 (1961): 196–208.

8. Such transformations occurred, for example, in the period between Djoser and Snofru or with the Amarna reformation.

9. For the equal dimensions of blocks of the temple of Sharuna, see L. Gestermann, "Zum Dekorationsprogramm des ptolemäischen Tempels," *MDAIK* 48 (1992): 21.

10. E. Winter, "Untersuchungen zu den ägyptischen Tempelreliefs der Griechisch-Römschen Zeit," *Denkschriften der Österreichischen Akademie der Wissenschaften Wien* 98 (1968); D. Kurth, "Die Friese innerhalb der Tempeldekoration griechisch-römischer Zeit," in *Aspekte spätägyptischer Kultur: Festschrift Erich Winter*, edited by Martina Minas and Jürgen Zeidler (Mainz, 1994), pp. 191–201; D. Kurth, "Die Säulendekoration im Tempel von Edfu," *Studien zur Altägyptischen Kultur* 23 (1996): 255–80.

11. The frontally half-open pronaoi are still connected with the interior of the temple by only a small door.

12. For example, Edfu, Kom Ombo, and later Kalabsha.

13. *Description* I, pls. 16, 18; II, pl. 37; III, pl. 34, IV, pl. 12. See also LD I and David Roberts, *Egypt and Nubia*, 3 vols. (London, 1846–49).

14. Kiosk of Nectanebo I at the temple of Hibis; see, here, figs. 68–70.

15. Also in Hellenistic architecture, the Doric, Ionic, and Corinthian orders can only be superimposed in double-tiered colonnades. Occasionally in Hellenistic temples, different orders were used inside and out, or the rear portico of a court was emphasized by a different order. In Roman architecture, different column capitals were only used in the same row as late as the basilicas of the time of Constantine the Great—for example, San Giovanni in Laterano (313), San Pietro in Vaticano (324–344), and San Paolo fuori le mura (ca. 390). See, in general, Beat Brenk, "Spolien und ihre Wirkung auf die Ästhetik der varietas," in *Antike Spolien in der Architektur des Mittelalters und der Renaissance*, edited by Joachim Poeschke (Munich, 1996), pp. 49–92.

16. See Margaret Lyttelton, *Baroque Architecture in Classical Antiquity* (Ithaca, 1974), pp. 40–60.

17. *BemerkungenAR* I. The depiction of wooden structures in stone—for example, of false doors or tree trunks as rounded ceiling beams in tombs—also comes to mind.

18. For example, the front of the Hathor chapel at Deir el-Bahari (Edouard Naville, *The Temple of Deir el Bahari*, vol. 4 [London, 1901], pl. 103) or of a chapel in the Akhmenu of Karnak (Golvin and Goyon, *Les bâtisseurs de Karnak*, fig. p. 46).

19. For a forerunner of Nectanebo I at Hermopolis, see Günther Roeder, *Hermopolis 1929–1939* (Hildesheim, 1959), p. 286, pl. 57 b-c.

20. Cairo, CG 701, CG 1230.

21. M.-C. Bruwier, "La collection égyptienne de Raoul Warocqué," *Cahiers Mariemont* 20–21 (1989–90): 32–35.

22. *La gloire d'Alexandrie*, exhibition catalogue, Paris (1998), pp. 103–104, 307; Empereur, *Alexandria Rediscovered*, pp. 64–81.

23. G. Steindorff, "Reliefs from the Temples of

Sebennytos and Iseion in American Collections," *Journal of the Walters Art Gallery* 7/8 (1944–46): 38–59; and B. Von Bothmer, "Ptolemaic Reliefs III," *Bulletin of the Museum of Fine Arts* 51 (1953): 1–7.

24. Eleni Vasilika, *Ptolemaic Philae* (Leuven, 1989), pp. 151–54, 207–209.

25. Achille Adriani, *Repertorio d'arte dell'Egitto greco-romano*, serie C, 2 vols. (Palermo, 1963), pp. 127, 47[178–79]. See this work also (pl. 19 [66]) for two similar granite blocks in the Museum of Alexandria.

26. Ibrahim Noshy, *The Arts in Ptolemaic Egypt* (London, 1937), pp. 64–65; F. Le Corsu, "Quelques motifs égyptiennes survivant dans l'architecture religieuse alexandrine," *RdE* 18 (1966): 37–44. For Cyprus see Wright, *Cyprus*, pp. 534–37.

27. Wright, *Cyprus*, pl. 201.

28. Theodore Fyfe, *Hellenistic Architecture: An Introductory Study* (Cambridge, 1936), pp. 75–76.

29. G.R.H. Wright, "A Nabataean Capital . . . and Its Possible Background," in *Proceedings of the First National Congress of Cypriote Studies* 1 (n.p., 1972), pp. 175–78.

30. McCredie et al., *The Rotunda of Arsinoe*, pls. 77–78.

31. Gates with a lintel on two pillars are known worldwide, from the "Trilith" in Stonehenge of Salisbury to the Gate of the Sun at Tiahuanaco. Closer parallels are found in Hellenistic architecture, such as the Aristaeneta monument at Delphi and at the side entrances (*parodoi*) between audience and stage house of the theater of Epidauros (beginning of third century B.C.).

32. See Jacke Phillips, "Some Non-Egyptian Obelisks," *JSSEA* 24 (1997): 103–115.

33. A. W. Lawrence, *Greek Architecture*, rev. 4th ed. (New Haven, 1996), p. 151.

34. Studies of Greek building techniques are numerous—for example, Coulton, *Ancient Greek Architects*; Manolis Korres, *From Pentelicon to the Parthenon* (Athens, 1995); Roland Martin, *Dictionnaire méthodique de l'architecture grecque et romaine*, vol. 1 (Athens, 1985); René Ginouvès, *Dictionnaire méthodique de l'architecture grecque et romaine*, vol. 2 (Athens, 1992).

35. S. Cauville and D. Devauchelle, "Les mesures réelles du temple d'Edfou," *BIFAO* 84 (1984): 23–34. For the ancient Egyptian cubit, see W. F. Reineke, "Untersuchungen zur altägyptischen Elle," *Meroitica* 12 (1990): 257–63.

36. The coordination of architecture and inscription is difficult. Scribes frequently overestimated the available wall space and had to condense their text at the end. One may suspect that the great length of royal tombs of the New Kingdom was prompted partially by the demand for wall surface to accommodate the required texts.

37. Isodomic masonry is already found in the Djoser complex at Saqqara, in the "chapelle rouge" of Hatshepsut at Karnak, and in the form of *talatat* in the Amarna Period.

38. J.-C. Golvin and R. Vergineux, "Étude des techniques de construction dans l'Égypte ancienne," in *Mélanges Gamal Eddin Mokhtar*, vol. 1, edited by Paule Posener-Krieger (Cairo, 1985), pp. 325–38; Golvin and Goyon, *Les bâtisseurs de Karnak*.

39. Pierre Zignani, "Monolithisme et élasticité dans la construction égyptienne," *BIFAO* 96 (1996): pp. 453–85.

40. Arnold, *Building in Egypt*, pp. 123, 266–67.

41. During the laying of the ceiling blocks, mortar ran over already finished reliefs: E. Winter, "A Reconsideration of the Newly Discovered Building Inscription on the Temple of Denderah," *Göttinger Miszellen* 108 (1989): 79; Zignani, *Monolithisme*, p. 68.

42. Zignani, *Monolithisme*, pp. 470–85.

43. Ludwig Borchardt, "Altägyptische Werkzeichnungen," *ZÄS* 34 (1896): 70–74; H. Riemann, "Ägyptische Säulenmaße," *ZÄS* 72 (1936): 68–71.

44. See Dietrich Conrad, *Kirchenbau im Mittelalter* (Leipzig, 1990), pp. 83–84; François Icher, *Building the Great Cathedrals* (New York, 1998), pp. 96–99.

45. The whereabouts of the giant obelisk is unknown. It should show a dedication by Ptolemy II. Is it the (uninscribed) obelisk on St. Peter's Square in Rome?

46. See Coulton, *Ancient Greek Architects*.

47. Huß, *Der makedonische König*, pp. 51–52.

48. Erich Winter, *Der Herrscherkult in den ägyptischen Ptolemäertempeln* (Berlin, 1976).

49. Huß, *Der makedonische König*, pp. 58–68.

50. The famous statue by the Greek sculptor Bryaxis (second half of the 4th century B.C.) showed a seated, bearded god with the basket-shaped Kalathos crown.

51. W. Swinnen, "Sur la politique religieuse de Ptolémé Ier," in *Les syncrétismes dans les religions grecque et romaine* (Paris, 1973), pp. 115–33.

52. Manetho, *Aegyptiaca*, edited and translated by W. G. Wadell (London, 1940). Manetho also devised the dynastic counting system.

53. Today El-Manschâh or El-Minschiîya on the east bank south of Akhmim, archaeologically unexplored.

54. Naville, *The Mound of the Jew*, pp. 60–64.

55. In the museums of Boston (89.559-60), Philadelphia (E 221-223), Princeton (50-129),

Oxford (1889.182), Glasgow (94.118), and in the Brit. Mus. (EA 651-3); see B. Von Bothmer, "Ptolemaic Reliefs II," *Bulletin of the Museum of Fine Arts* 281 (1952): 49–56.

56. A. Badawy, "A Sepulchral Chapel of Greco-Roman Times at Kom Abu Billo," *JNES* 16 (1957): 52–54.

57. The basalt blocks were moved to Tanta; see C. C. Edgar, "Some Hieroglyphic Inscriptions from Naukratis," *ASAE* 22 (1922): 1–6.

58. See Carlo Anti,"Scavi di Tebtynis, 1930–1935," *Aegyptus* 5 (1936): 473–78; Gilberto Bagnani, "Gli scavi di Tebtunis," *Bolletino d'arte* 27 (1933): 119–34.

59. Unfortunately, they were never revealed by the excavators in a proper publication.

60. Serge Sauneron, *Villes et Légendes d'Égypte*, 2nd ed., Bibliothèque d'Étude, no. 90 (Cairo 1983), pp. 114–17. For blocks in Leiden (F 1961/12.3, F 1994/3.1–2), see M. J. Raven and H. D. Schneider, "Recent Acquisitions. I Egypt," *Oudheidkundige Mededelingen* 75 (1995): 137.

61. Six in Budapest (51.2156–60) and three in Vienna (6694); see W. Wessetzky, "Reliefs aus dem Tempel Ptolemaios'I. in Kom el Ahmar-Sharuna," *MDAIK* 33 (1977): 133–41.

62. F. G. Newton, "Excavations at El-'Amarnah," *JEA* 10 (1924): 305, pl. 37[3]. The relief probably is in the University Museum of Sidney.

63. Now in Cairo and Hildesheim; see Philippe Derchain, *Zwei Kapellen des Ptolemäus I Soter in Hildesheim* (Hildesheim, 1961).

64. Similar Ptolemaic chapels stood in the cemetery of Kom Abu Billo in the southwestern Delta (see above and Badawy, "A Sepulchral Chapel of Greco-Roman Times at Kom Abu Billo," *JNES* 16 (1957): 52–55.

65. Gustave Lefebvre, *Le tombeau de Petosiris* (Cairo, 1924); Sami Gabra, *Rapport sur les fouilles d'Hermoupolis ouest (Touna el-Gebel)* (Cairo, 1941); S. Nakaten, "Petosiris," in *LÄ*, vol. 4 (1982), pp. 995–98; Michael Sabottka, "Tuna el-Gebel: Grab des Djed-Thot-iw-ef-ankh. Vorbericht," *ASAE* 69 (1983): 147–51; D. Keßler, "Tuna el-Gebel," in *LÄ*, vol. 6 (1986), pp. 797–804.

66. The beginning of the construction is dated to the reign of Ptolemy II. The lighthouse was destroyed by an earthquake on August 8, 1303. See Strabo, *Geography*, XVII.8.23; Josephus, *The Judean War*, IV.10.5; Pliny, *Natural History*, XXXVI.12.83; H. Thiersch, *Der Pharos* (Lipsia, 1909). Numerous architectural and sculptural fragments were found in 1994–1995 in front of the island by Jean-Yves Empereur. A smaller replica is the better preserved lighthouse of Taposiris: A. Adriani, "Travaux de fouilles et de restaurations dans la région d'Abousir (Maréo-

tis)," *Annuaire du Musée Gréco-Romain* 3 (1940–50): 132–35.

67. McCredie et al., *The Rotunda of Arsinoe*, and Frazer, *The Propylon of Ptolemy II*.

68. Athenaios, *The Deipnosophistes*, II.387–419, V.196–203.

69. Descriptions by Kallixeinos in Athenaios, *The Deipnosophistes*, II.387–393, V.196–197; Gerhard Haeny, *Basilikale Anlagen in der ägyptischen Baukunst des Neuen Reiches* (Wiesbaden, 1970), p. 76, fig. 29a.

70. Petrie, *Naucratis*, vol. 1, p. 28.

71. Now in the Vatican (22681, 22682): Giuseppe Botti and Pietro Romanelli, *Le sculture del Museo Gregorino Egizio* (Rome, 1951), pp. 22–24, nos. 31–32.

72. The statues found in Rome are thought to have originated in Heliopolis because the text on the dorsal pillar of the statues ends with ". . . Reharahkte" and "beloved by Atum, Lord of the Two Countries of . . ." This attribution is not compelling, however, because Late Period temples of Atum and Reharakhte were built in Sais, Bubastis, and Pithom.

73. Even Strabo found only a few priests and tour guides left (*Geography*, XVII.1.27).

74. In the Villa Albani Torlonia. The text on the dorsal pillar mentions the goddess Bastet; see Lollio Barberi et al., *Le Antichità Egiziane*, pp. 141–42.

75. Empereur, *Alexandria Rediscovered*, pp. 64–81.

76. W. M. Flinders Petrie, *Hawara, Biahmu, and Arsinoe* (London, 1889), pp. 56–57, pl. 29. The huge dimensions suggest a second enclosure wall that contained the actual temple house.

77. Evaristo Breccia, *Monuments de l'Égypte gréco-romain*, vol. 1 (Bergamo, 1926), pp. 97–121. The three gates, the chapel, and the crocodile stretcher were transferred to the Graeco-Roman Museum in Alexandria; see Jean-Yves Empereur, *A Short Guide to the Graeco-Roman Museum, Alexandria* (Alexandria, 1995), pp. 9–10.

78. Only an incomplete sketch published by David G. Hogarth in B. P. Grenfell, Arthur S. Hunt, and David G. Hogarth, *Fayûm Towns and Their Papyri* (London, 1900), pp. 36–38.

79. Achille Vogliano, *Primo rapporto degli Scavi condotti dalla missione archaeologica d'Egitto della R. Universita di Milano . . . di Madînet Mâdi* (Milan, 1936); idem, *Secondo rapporto . . .* (Milan, 1937).

80. A. Vogliano, "Rapporto preliminare della IVa campagna di scavo a Madînet Mâdi," *ASAE* 38 (1938): 538–43.

81. A screen wall of blocks with the representation of the deified Ptolemy I in the Ashmolean Museum Oxford (1984.106). See M. A.

Murray, "Sculpture of Ptolemy I," *Ancient Egypt* (1917): 168–69.

82. *Description* IV, pl.1. The ground-plan dimensions are only 0.84 x 0.95 m!

83. Shabaka may have built an entrance porch at Medamoud; see Leclant, *Monuments thébains*, vol. 1, p. 131.

84. See excavation reports by F. Bisson de la Roque, *Rapport sur les fouilles de Médamoud 1925–26, 1927–28, 1929, 1929–32* (Cairo, 1926–33). For the intricate history of the excavation, see idem, "Les fouilles de l'Institut Français à Médamoud," *RdE* 5 (1946): 25–44. For later constructions, see the discussion of the buildings of Ptolemy VIII, this chapter.

85. See Serge Sauneron, *La porte Ptolémaïque de l'enceinte de Mout à Karnak* (Cairo, 1983).

86. The visible, formerly touching faces in the upper part of the building show *anathyrosis* and mortar grooves that are typical for Ptolemaic buildings.

87. Haeny assumes that the first two rooms of the core building and the colonnaded ambulatory were planned under Ptolemy II and begun under Ptolemy III (Haeny, "Philae," p. 211).

88. Lyons, *Temples*, pp. 13–14, pl. 11.

89. Pensabene, "Elementi architettonici," in *Repertorio d'arte*, pp. 195–99; Handler, "Roman Coins," pp. 64–68.

90. Excavation report by Alan Rowe, *The Discovery of the Famous Temple and Enclosure of Serapis at Alexandria*, ASAE supplement vol. 2 (1946).

91. Following a description in Rufinus, *Historia Ecclesiae*, XI.23.

92. E. Breccia, *Le rovine e i monumenti di Canopo* (Bergamo, 1926).

93. Pensabene, "Elementi architettonici," in *Repertorio d'arte*, pp. 217–18.

94. Daninos-Pacha, "Note sur les fouilles d'Abouqir," *RT* 12 (1892): 209–214; Evaristo Breccia, *Monuments de l'Égypte gréco-romain*, vol. 1 (Bergamo, 1926), pp. 51–82.

95. According to Diodorus (XX.100.4), a Ptolemeion was already dedicated to Ptolemy I on the island of Rhodes. See J. B. Ward-Perkins, *Roman Imperial Architecture* (1st ed., 1981; New Haven, 1990), p. 366; Duane W. Roller, *The Building Program of Herod the Great* (Berkeley, 1998), p. 92.

96. Klaus P. Kuhlmann, *Materialien zur Archäologie und Geschichte des Raumes von Achmim* (Mainz, 1983), pp. 14–49.

97. The gate was 3.75 m wide and 4.45 m high, excluding the cavetto; see Ch. Sambin, "Les portes de Médamoud du Musée de Lyon," *BIFAO* 92 (1992): 148–61; Genevieve Galliano, *Musée des Beaux-Arts de Lyon, Guide des Collections: Les Antiquitées* (Paris, 1997), pp. 28–29.

98. In Sydney Aufrère, Jean-Claude Golvin, and Jean-Claude Goyon, *Sites et temples des déserts*, vol 2 of *L'Égypte restituée* (Paris, 1991–97), p. 97—probably unnecessarily—three rows of columns are reconstructed.

99. Zignani, *Monolithisme*, pp. 457–58.

100. Heike Sternberg-El Hotabi, *Der Propylon des Monthu-Temples in Karnak-Nord: Zum Dekorationsprinzip des Tores*, Göttinger Orientforschungen, 4th series (Wiesbaden, 1993), p. 25.

101. Maurice Alliot, *Le culte d'Horus à Edfou au temps des Ptolémées*, Bibliothèque d'Étude, no. 20 (Cairo, 1954); S. Cauville and D. Devauchelle, "Le Temple d'Edfou: Étapes de la construction nouvelles données historiques," *RdE* 35 (1984): 31–55; Sylvie Cauville, *Essai sur la théologie du temple à Edfou*, Bibliothèque d'Étude, no. 102 (Cairo, 1987); Dieter Kurth, *Treffpunkt der Götter: Inschriften aus dem Tempel des Horus von Edfu* (Zurich, 1994).

102. The oldest examples known to me are in the pronaos of the temple of Hibis (from the time of Psametik II?).

103. Edda Bresciani, *Il tempio tolemaico di Isi* (Pisa, 1978).

104. Lyons, *Temples*, pp. 13–14, pl. 11.

105. Atheneios, *The Deipnosophistes*, II.421–33, V.203–206.

106. Three names are recorded: Psametik-sa-Neith Menkheperre, Hor-nefer, and Anch-wen-nefer.

107. E. Lanciers, "Die ägyptischen Tempelbauten zur Zeit des Ptolemaios V. Epiphanes (204–180 BC)," *MDAIK* 42 (1986): 81–98, and 43 (1986): 173–82.

108. A kiosk of the 26th to 30th Dynasties stood in the court north of the temple house.

109. Kuhlmann, *Achmim*, pp. 14–49; Sauneron, *Villes*, pp. 51–61.

110. The original reading by Champollion was later changed into Ptolemy Philometor (Ptolemy X Alexander I); see Kuhlmann, *Achmim*, p. 46 n. 223. Since no significant buildings of Ptolemy X exist, it seems improbable that he would have built such a monumental pronaos.

111. Unpublished manuscript of Sir J. Gardner Wilkinson (I.88, top) in the Bodleian Library, Oxford.

112. Ch. Sambin, "Les portes de Médamoud du Musée de Lyon," *BIFAO* 92 (1992): 162–70; Genevieve Galliano, *Musée des Beaux-Arts de Lyon, Guide des Collections: Les Antiquitées* (Paris, 1997), pp. 28–29.

113. F. Leclère, "A Cemetery of Osiride Figurines at Karnak," *Egyptian Archaeology* 9 (1996): 9–12.

114. Similar to the front part of the Isis temple on Philae.

115. Similar to the example from Dendera in the Brit. Mus. (1153).

116. Ch. Desroches Noblecourt, "Considerations sur l'existence des divers temples de Monthou à travers les âges, dans le site de Tôd," *BIFAO* 84 (1984): 81–109; G. Pierrat et al., "Fouilles du Musée du Louvre à Tôd, 1988–1991," in *Karnak*, vol. 10 (1995), pp. 405–503.

117. Laskowska-Kusztal, *Elephantine*, pp. 15–21.

118. Lyons, *Island and Temples*, pp. 22–25, pls. 5–8, plan 2.

119. Despite the royal name, which points to a 26th Dynasty date, the building was attributed, for stylistic reasons, to the Ptolemaic or the Roman Period; see G. Maspero, "La Chapelle d'Asfoun," *ASAE* 7 (1906): 58–60, and E. P. Weigall, "Report on the Discovery of Part of a Temple at Asfoun," *ASAE* 8 (1907): 106–107.

120. E. Winter, "Ergamenes II., seine Datierung und seine Bautätigkeit in Nubien," *MDAIK* 37 (1981): 509–513.

121. Since Ptolemy IV died in 205, before Upper Egypt and Nubia could be reconquered (187/186), the name of Ptolemy IV could only have been added posthumously.

122. Brit. Mus., EA 24. The decree of March 27, 196, was written in hieroglyphic and demotic Egyptian and Greek versions.

123. M. Alliot, "La Thebaide en lutte contre les rois d'Alexandrie sous Philopator et Epiphanes (216–184)," *Revue Belge de Philologie et d'Histoire* (Brussels) 29 (1951): 424–43; W. Peremans, "Les revolutions égyptiennes sous les Lagides," in *Das ptolemäische Ägypten: Akten des internationalen Symposions Berlin 27.-29. September 1976* (Mainz, 1978), pp. 39–49; Lanciers, "Die ägyptischen Tempelbauten," 42:81–98 and 43:173–82.

124. D. G. Jeffreys and H. S. Smith, *The Anubieion at Saqqara*, vol. 1 (London, 1988), pl. 62.

125. Lyons, *Island and Temples*, p. 26, pls. 10–11.

126. Sydney Aufrère, Jean-Claude Golvin, and J.-Cl. Goyon, *Sites, temples, et pyramides de Moyenne et Basse Egypte*, vol. 3 of *L' Égypte reconsituée*, 3 vols. (Paris, 1991–97), pp. 309–319.

127. Josephus, *Jewish Antiquities*, XIII.73.387–88, and *The Judean War*, VII.426–30.

128. W. Flinders Petrie, *Hyksos and Israelite Cities* (London, 1906), pp. 19–27, pls. 22–27. For historical events see Joseph M. Modrzejewski, *The Jews of Egypt* (Edinburgh, 1995), pp. 124–33.

129. *Description*, Text, vol. 4, pp. 103–111; Henri Gauthier, *De la XXVe dynastie à la fin des Ptolemées*, vol. 4 of *Le livre des rois d'Égypte*, 5 vols. (Cairo, 1907–17), p. 302. A Greek restoration text of the Roman emperors Marcus Aurelius and Lucius Verus were added June 3, A.D. 164.

130. *Description* IV, pls. 38–43; *Description*, Text, vol. 4, pp. 75–124.

131. The intercolumnations measured 10 cubits (5.25 m). Only the central nave was 14½ cubits (7.61 m). The addition of the detail measurements produces the interior width (in cubits):

$$10 + 10 + 10 + 14\tfrac{1}{2} + 10 + 10 + 10 = 74\tfrac{1}{2}$$

Adding the presumed thickness of the lateral walls of 5¼ cubits one can estimate the total width of the pronaos as 85 cubits (44.625 m). The survey of the Napoleonic expedition records an intercolumniation in the depth of 5.13 m, which suggests the following distance between the front column and the rear wall:

$$5 \text{ c. } 2 \text{ p.} + 4 \text{ c. } 3 \text{ p.} + 5 \text{ c. } 2 \text{ p.} + 4 \text{ c. } 3 \text{ p.}$$
$$+ 5 \text{ c. } 2 \text{ p.} = 24 \text{ c. } 5 \text{ p. } (12.975 \text{ m})$$

The total depth of the pronaos (outside) would have been 29 c. 5¼ p. (15.619 m).

132. Temple houses with several parallel approach paths also occured at Kom Ombo and Medamoud.

133. Vandier d'Abbadie, *Nestor l'Hôte*, pp. 33–34.

134. W. M. Flinders Petrie, *Diospolis Parva: The Cemeteries of Abadiyeh and Hu* (London, 1901), pp. 54–55, pl. 43.

135. Lanciers, "Die ägyptischen Tempelbauten," 43:174.

136. In Cairo (758); see J. De Morgan et al., *Kom Ombos: Catalogue des monuments et inscriptions de l'Égypte antique*, 2 vols. (Vienna, 1895 and 1909), vol. 2, pp. 348–49 (no. 1077).

137. Recorded by Adolphe Gutbub and Danielle Inconnu-Bocquillon, *Kôm Ombo* (Cairo, 1995).

138. Laskowska-Kusztal, *Elephantine*, p. 8.

139. The foundation ceremony was carried out on February 4, 164 B.C., during the joint reign of Ptolemy VI, Ptolemy VIII, and Cleopatra II; see G. Vittmann, "Das demotische Graffito vom Satettempel auf Elephantine" *MDAIK* 53 (1997): 263–81. For the temple, see Herbert Ricke, *Die Tempel Nektanebos' II. in Elephantine*, (Cairo, 1960).

140. Recently the possibility was raised that the kiosk was not freestanding but instead was connected to another building in the north; see Laskowska-Kusztal, *Elephantine*, p. 14.

141. LD IV, pl. 27b.

142. *Description*, Text, vol. 1, pp. 59–60. In the drawing of *Description* I, pl. 18, the capitals of the two innermost corner columns are switched; cf. Sauneron and Stierlin, *Letzte Tempel*, p. 166.

143. Lyons, *Island and Temples*, plan 2. Compare Haeny's reconstruction: "Philae," p. 225, fig. 4.

144. Lyons, *Island and Temples*, pp. 27–28, pls. 12–15, plan 6.

145. Carmen Priego and Alfonso Martin Flores, *Templo de Debod* (Madrid, 1992).

146. For the complicated history of kings of the time, see M. Chauveau, "Un été 145," *BIFAO* 90 (1990): 135–68.

147. E. Breccia, *Alexandria ad Aegyptum* (Bergamo, 1914), pp. 123–30; J. Y. Brinton, "Restoration of the Temple of Abusir," *Archaeology* 1 (1948): 186–87; Achille Adriani, *Annuaire du Musée Gréco-Romain*, vol. 3 (1940–1950) (Alexandria, 1952), pp. 130–32.

148. For early examples of this practice, see *Bemerkungen AR I*, p. 64

149. A. Piankoff, "Le naos D 29 du Musée du Louvre," *RdE* 1 (1933): 161–79.

150. S. Cauville, "La chapelle de la barque à Dendera," *BIFAO* 93 (1993): 79–172.

151. The blocks are now reconstructed in Boston (24.1632–33); see Thomas Nancys, *The American Discovery of Ancient Egypt* (New York, 1995), pp. 218–21.

152. Ahmed Bey Kamal, "Le pylône de Qous," *ASAE* 3 (1902): 232–35.

153. The reconstruction plan presented by C. Robichon and A. Varille in *Description sommaire du temple primitif de Médamoud* (Cairo, 1940), fig. 1, suggests several alterations of the original site plan published by F. Bisson de la Roque, "Les fouilles de l'Institut Français à Médamoud," *RdE* 5 (1946): 41–43. A new survey is urgently required.

154. They resemble the papyrus-bundle columns of Hermopolis magna; see fig. 253.

155. C. De Witt, *Les inscriptions du temple d'Opet à Karnak*, 2 vols. (Brussels 1958, 1960).

156. A fine sequence of reliefs is in Berlin (2115).

157. A relief block of the temple is in Berlin (2116).

158. That such Ptolemaic-Roman festivities could occasionally imply menacing aspects is suggested by a sandstone altar found in 1907 near the temple. It depicts rows of nude, shackled juveniles who are being assaulted by priests with knives. See A. Weigall, "A Report on Some Objects Recently Found," *ASAE* (1907): 44–46.

159. Bes was the protector demon of birth.

160. The corresponding wall sections were probably already missing at the time of the Napoleonic expedition. Therefore, a building with a colonnaded ambulatory cannot be completely ruled out.

161. Laskowska-Kusztal, *Elephantine*, pp. 21–25.

162. The eastern one was removed in 1819 by Giovanni Belzoni on behalf of William J. Banks and reerected in 1839 in the park of Kingston Lacy, Wimborne in Dorset. The lower part of the western obelisk followed later; see Iversen, *Obelisks in Exile*, vol. 1, pp. 62–85. In 1816, W. J. Banks already recognized the name of Cleopatra in the hieroglyphic text of the obelisk, with the help of Greek inscriptions on the base.

163. Florence, 2612, and Louvre, D 30, height 2.25 and 2.36 m.

164. Brit. Mus., EA 962/1134, height 2.51 m.

165. *Description* I, pls. 84–88, *Description, Text*, vol. 1, pp. 384–92.

166. Philippe Derchain, *El Kab I: Les monuments religieux à l'entrée de l'Ouady Hellal* (Brussels, 1971); LD IV, pl. 68; LD Text, vol. 1, pp. 38–41.

167. At the now-lost chapel of Amenhotep III on Elephantine, two columns stood at the front and rear sides between corner pillars. They were not really alternating. Borchardt's addition of front columns to other chapels with pillar ambulatories is hypothetical: Borchardt, *Tempel mit Umgang*, pls. 20–23.

168. For example, Hagios Demetrios in Salonica, late fifth century; see Richard Krautheimer, *Early Christian and Byzantine Architecture*, 4th ed. (New Haven, 1985), figs. 81–82.

169. George H. Wright, *Kalabsha III: The Ptolemaic Sanctuary of Kalabsha* (Mainz, 1987).

170. See E. Winter, "Das Kalabsha-Tor in Berlin," *Jahrbuch Preußischer Kulturbesitz* 14 (1979): 59–71; H. De Meulenaere, "Ptolémé IX Sôter à Kalabcha," *CdE* 36 (1991): 98–105.

171. When the Augustan temple was dismantled in 1961–1963 for its transfer to Aswan, about 250 blocks from previous buildings were found in its foundations and walls. From these blocks the Ptolemaic chapel could be reassembled in 1974–1975 on the southern tip of Elephantine and the gate reerected in 1976 in Berlin. See Dieter Arnold, *Die Tempel von Kalabscha* (Mainz, 1975), and Hanns Stock, *Kalabsha: Der größte Temple Nubiens und das Abenteuer seiner Rettung* (Wiesbaden, 1965). A comprehensive publication is being prepared by Ewa Laskowska-Kusztal and Dieter Arnold.

172. Sir Gardner Wilkinson, *A Handbook for Travellers in Egypt* (London, 1885), p. 273.

173. Ibid., p. 304. Maghara is located 18 km north of Sohag.

174. One has to consider, however, that the kiosk of Qertassi, with similar dimensions, was indeed roofed with stone; see figs. 197–98.

175. *Description* IV, pl. 1; A. Bey Kamal, "Le pylône de Qous," *ASAE* 3 (1902): 215–35; Egon v.

Komorzynski, "Der Ptolemäertempel von Kus," *Archiv für aegyptische Archaeologie* 1 (1938): 235–39.

176. Unpublished data, communicated by Jean Jacquet.

177. For Ptolemy XI, Alexander II, see the buildings of Ptolemy X, Alexander I.

178. The country was ruled now by Berenike IV, Cleopatra VI Tryphanaia, and Archelaos.

179. The reconstruction offered here remains—in consequence of Petrie's rather confused excavation—completely hypothetical. See Petrie, *Athribis*.

180. The intercolumniations estimated by Petrie to have been up to 8.6 m should be reduced and screen walls added between the first row of columns. Petrie, *Athribis*, pl. 15.

181. Borchardt, *Tempel mit Umgang*, p. 11.

182. See Rifaat el-Farag, U. Kaplony-Heckel, and K. P. Kulman, "Recent Archaeological Explorations at Athribis," *MDAIK* 41 (1985): 1–4, pls. 7–8. The clear pharaonic forms of the facade decoration suggest that a rock tomb of the Late Period(?) was usurped by the Asclepius cult.

183. For the date see H. I. Amer and B. Moradet, "Les dates de la construction du temple majeur d'Hathor à Dendera," *ASAE* 69 (1983): 255–58.

184. The architecture of the building will be published by Pierre Zignani for the French Archaeological Institute in Cairo.

185. See G. Legrain, "Le logement et transport des barques sacrées et des statues des dieux dans quelques temples égyptiens," *BIFAO* 13 (1917): 1–76.

186. Borchardt and Ricke believed there were Hellenistic tendencies in the ceiling construction; see Borchardt, *Tempel mit Umgang*, p. 16.

187. Since 1823 in the Louvre (D 38); see Guillemette Andreu et al., *L'Égypte ancienne au Louvre* (Paris 1997), pp. 201–211.

188. See H. Chevrier, "Temple de Ptah," *ASAE* 53 (1955): 18–19, pl. 9.

189. One wonders whether these winding staircases of Ptolemaic towers led to the invention of the round spiral staircase, see fig. 207.

190. That such ornaments of gates may have existed elsewhere is suggested by two consoles that protrude from the High Gate of the temple of Ramesses III at Medinet Habu: Epigraphic Survey (Chicago), *The Eastern High Gate*, vol. 8 of *Medinet Habu*, 8 vols. (Chicago, 1930–70), pls. 611, 613

191. J. F. Pécoil, "Le soleil et la cour d'Edfou," *BIFAO* 86 (1986): 277–301.

192. The two northern front architraves were seen in 1996 on the ground north of the temple. The southern architrave was recorded in De Morgan et al., *Kom Ombos*, vol. 1, fig. 200. The fallen column parts have disappeared. For conservation work, see A. Barsanti, "Rapport sur les travaux de consolidation exécutés à Kom Ombo," *ASAE* 15 (1915): 168–76.

193. Hermann Junker, *Das Götterdekret über das Abaton* (Vienna, 1913).

194. For a splendid view, see David Roberts, *Egypt and Nubia*, vol. 1 (London, 1846); Aylward M. Blackman, *The Temple of Bigeh* (Cairo, 1915). The relatively high location of the temple prevented its permanent flooding and removal after the construction of the dam.

195. Claude Traunecker, *Coptos* (Leuven, 1992), pp. 49–50, figs. 10–11.

196. E. F. Jomard in *Description*, Text, vol. 1, pp. 412–34; vol. 10, pp. 95–99; *Description* I, pls. 91–97. Photographs by Maxime Ducampe (1849), Felix Teynard (1850–1851), and Frith (1857). Analysis by Borchardt, *Tempel mit Umgang*, pp. 9–11, pl. 4.

197. Excavation efforts by Sir Robert Mond's 1935 expedition were unsuccessful, because the area had been flattened beneath the level of the temple foundations; see Sir Robert Mond and Oliver H. Myers, *The Temples of Armant* (London, 1940), pp. 5, 8–9. For reconstruction see Dieter Arnold, "Zum Geburtshaus von Armant," in *Stationen: Beiträge zur Kulturgeschichte Ägyptens*, edited by Heike Guksch and David Polz (Mainz, 1998), pp. 427–30.

198. The relationship of the birth house to the main temple corresponded to that of the birth house of Isis to the Hathor temple of Dendera.

Chapter 8

1. For classical architecture see D. M. Bailey, "Classical Architecture in Roman Egypt," in *Architecture and Architectural Sculpture in the Roman Empire*, edited by M. Henig (Oxford, 1990), pp. 125–27; idem, *Hermopolis Magna: Buildings of the Roman Period, Excavations at El-Ashmunein*, vol. 4 (London, 1991); J. B. Ward-Perkins, *Roman Imperial Architecture* (1st ed., 1981; New Haven, 1990), pp. 363–68. For the history see J. G. Milne, *A History of Egypt under Roman Rule*, 2nd ed. (London, 1913); Judith McKenzie, "The Architectural Style of Roman and Byzantine Alexandria and Egypt," in *Archaeological Research in Roman Egypt*, edited by Donald M. Bailey (Ann Arbor, 1996), pp. 128–42.

2. Donald, M. Bailey. "Honorific Columns, Cranes, and the Turah Epitaph," in Bailey, *Roman Egypt*, pp. 155–68.

3. The largest new buildings, such as Shanhour, Kalabsha, and Maharraqa, were still

inferior in size to the main temples of the Ptolemaic Period.

4. O. E. Kaper, "A Painting of the Gods of Dakhla in the Temple of Ismant el-Kharab," in Quirke, *The Temple*, pp. 204–215.

5. According to the statistical study of M. Haneborg-Lühr, "Les chapiteaux composites: Étude typologique, stylistique et statistique," in *Amosiadès: Mélanges offerts au professeur Claude Vandersleyen par ses anciens étudiants*, edited by Claude Obsomer and Ann-Laure Oosthoek (Louvain-la-Neuv, 1992), pp. 125–52.

6. J. Clédat, "Fouilles à Qasr-Gheit," *ASAE* 12 (1912): 145–68.

7. Horst Jaritz, "Untersuchungen zum Tempel des Domitian in Assuan," *MDAIK* 31 (1975): 246–49. Comprehensive: J. C. Golvin and J. Larronde, "Étude des procédés de construction dans l'Égypte ancienne, I. L'édification des murs de grès en grand appareil à l'époque romaine," *ASAE* 68 (1982): 165–90; G.R.H. Wright, "The Works Organization of a Major Building Project in Roman Egypt," in Bailey, *Roman Egypt*, pp. 143–54.

8. Occasionally the top surface shows elongated sockets in the center, located beneath the joint of the next course, with corresponding, juxtaposed sockets in the upper block. Metal shims sat upright in the sockets and attached the upper block to the block beneath in order to prevent lateral shifting. The use of vertical shims is common in Greek architecture: Roland Martin, *Manuel d'architecture grecque*, vol. 1 (Paris, 1965), p. 282, fig. 125. They seem not to have been used in pre-Roman Egyptian buildings.

9. Jean-Pierre Adam, *Roman Building: Materials and Techniques* (Bloomington, 1994), pp. 43–50; Donald M. Bailey, "Honorific Columns, Cranes, and the Tuna Epitaph," in Bailey, *Roman Egypt*, pp. 157–68.

10. A model of such a contraption was successfully tested after excavation results at the seventh pylon of Karnak: M. Azim, J.-C. Golvin, et al., "Étude technique de l'abattage de l'obélisque ouest du VIIe pylône de Karnak," in *Karnak*, vol. 7 (1982), pp. 167–211.

11. Jean Lauffray could show that a cubit of 54 cm was used at the bark station of Hakoris at Karnak: *La chapelle d'Achôris à Karnak* (Paris, 1995), pp. 23ff.

12. Karl Georg Siegler, *Kalabsha: Architektur und Baugeschichte des Temples* (Berlin, 1970); idem, "Die Tore von Kalabsha," *MDAIK* 25 (1969): 145.

13. F. W. Hinkel, "Grundsätze der Architekturanalyse und einige Aspekte in der Untersuchung von meroitischen Baudenkmälern," *Meroitica* 12 (1990): 148. Hinkel also stressed the fundamental importance of the diameter of columns for the proportional system of a building: idem, "Säule und Interkolumnium in der meroitischen Architektur," *Studia Meroitica* 10 (1988): 231–67.

14. Jaritz, "Tempel des Domitian," pp. 252–57.

15. The Roman vassal Herod of Judea (37–34 B.C.); see Duane W. Roller, *The Building Program of Herod the Great* (Berkeley, 1998).

16. The western obelisk, overturned by an earthquake in A.D. 1303, was reerected in London in 1877–1878. The eastern obelisk was moved to New York in 1879–1880. See Gorringe, *Egyptian Obelisks*, pp. 59–76, 96–109.

17. Laure Pantalacci and Claude Traunecker, *Le temple d'El-Qal'a* (Cairo, 1990); L. Pantalacci, and C. Traunecker, "Le temple d'El-Qal'a à Coptos," *BIFAO* 93 (1993): 379–90; C. Traunecker, "Lessons from the Upper Egyptian Temple of El-Qal'a," in Quirke, *The Temple*, pp. 168–78.

18. Jan Quaegebeur, "Excavating the Forgotten Temple of Shenhur," in Quirke, *The Temple*, pp. 159–67; and idem, "Le temple romain de Chenhour," in 3. *Ägyptologische Tempeltagung*, edited by Dieter Kurth, Ägyten und Altes Testament, no. 33 (Wiesbaden, 1995), pp. 199–226.

19. Christiane M. Zivie, Michel Azim, Patrick Deleuze, and Jean-Claude Golvin, *Le temple de Deir Chelouit*, Étude architecturale, no. 4 (Cairo, 1992).

20. One could ask whether the obstruction of the Ptolemaic pronaos was politically motivated.

21. One can conclude from the lowermost preserved blocks that the double gate had no corner torus. Even without one, the gate could have had a cavetto. The vertical torus preserved at the side of the gate must have belonged to the cavetto that topped the enclosure wall.

22. Altars for festive open-air offerings also appear in the courts of Medamoud and Edfu and follow the old tradition of the Amarna Period and the Ramesseum.

23. Lyons, *Temples*, pls. 13–14; idem, *Island and Temples*, pls. 17–19.

24. "Though the architectural form of the Kiosk is perfectly in keeping with Late Ptolemaic rules, the mere size of the edifice gives the impression of a demonstration of power, and also of goodwill, at the beginning of Roman rule in Egypt" (Haeny, "Philae," p. 229).

25. Lyons, *Island and Temples*, pp. 2–5, pls. 29–45; idem, *Temples*, pls. 7–9.

26. This arrangement is certainly generated by the shape of the island. What is new, however, is that this shape was accepted and the platform not artificially extended to the southwest.

27. Pierre Gilbert, "Éléments hellénistiques de l'architecture de Philae," *CdE* 36 (1961): 196–208.

28. H. Jaritz, "Die Ostkolonnade von Philae," *MDAIK* 47 (1991): 179–86.

29. A few years earlier, temples were built for Augustus "Sebastos" by Herod the Great at Sebaste (Samaria), at the Paneion (Syria), and in Caesarea.

30. Lyons, *Island and Temples*, pp. 29–30, pls. 20–21. The front of the temple was once reconstructed in the Egyptian Museum, Cairo, but has since been removed.

31. Today in Madrid; see Carmen Priego and Alfonso Martin Flores, *Templo de Debod* (Madrid, 1992).

32. Günther Roeder, *Debod bis Bab Kalabsche* (Cairo, 1911–12), pp. 146–79. The kiosk was moved to the site of New Kalabsha, south of Aswan.

33. Franz Christian Gau, *Antiquité de la Nubie* (Stuttgart, 1822), pls. 10–11; M. J. Raven, "The Temple of Taffeh: A Study of Details," *Oudheidkundige Mededelingen uit het Rijksmuseum van Oudheden te Leiden* 76 (1996): 41–52.

34. Herbert Ricke, *Ausgrabungen von Khor-Dehmit bis Bet el-Wali* (Chicago, 1967), pp. 25–33.

35. In the Ägyptische Museum in Berlin-Charlottenburg since 1976. Since the gate is inscribed with the names of Ptolemy V Epiphanes, Ptolemy VIII Euergetes II, and Ptolemy IX Soter II, one would expect a corresponding date. Winter suggests that the construction of the gate was Ptolemaic but that the Ptolemaic cartouches were added under Augustus; see E. Winter, "Das Kalabsha-Tor in Berlin," *Jahrbuch Preußischer Kulturbesitz* 14 (1977): 59–71.

36. Kurt Siegler, *Kalabsha: Architektur und Baugeschichte des Temples* (Mainz, 1970).

37. A. M. Blackman, *The Temple of Dendur* (Cairo, 1911); Hassan el-Achiri, M. Aly, F.-A. Hamid, and Ch. Leblanc, *Le temple de Dandour*, 2 vols. (Cairo, 1972 and 1979); Cyril Aldred, "The Temple of Dendur," special edition of *The Metropolitan Museum of Art Bulletin* (New York, 1978).

38. Spiral staircases may have developed in Egypt from the square winding staircases found in Ptolemaic towers. Other examples appear in the triumphal gate of Antinoupolis, the theater of Oxyrhynchos, and the Roman gate of Bahariya. An early spiral staircase outside Egypt is known from the temple of Baal at Palmyra (A.D. 32).

39. Herbert E. Winlock, *Ed-Dakhleh Oasis* (New York, 1936), pp. 48–50.

40. A. J. Mills, "The Dakhle Oasis Project: Report on the 1990–1991 Field Season," *JSSEA* 20 (1990): 14–16.

41. On the cavetto of the facade, in Greek and Latin: "Under the Emperor Tiberius Caesar, new Augustus, sun of the divine Augustus, under/// the commander Serapion Truxambo, the citizens of the capital of the nome [consecrated] the pronaos to Aphrodite, the highest goddess and to the gods who are honored with her///." See *Description*, Text, vol. 3, pp. 396–97.

42. One single column type was used in the pronaoi of Dendera (Hathor columns), Antaeopolis (palm columns), and Hermopolis magna (papyrus-bundle columns). The Roman pronaos of the temple of Monthu at Medamoud contained papyrus-bundle columns except for the two columns at the center of the front row, which had quatrefoil composite capitals.

43. They differ from those of the hypostyle hall of the temple house because they lack composite capitals below the heads.

44. D. Valbelle, "La porte de Tibère," in *Hommages à Serge Sauneron*, vol. 1 (Cairo, 1979), pp. 73–85.

45. Lyons, *Island and Temples*, pp. 27–28, pls. 12–15, plan 6; F. Daumas, "Les propylées du temple d'Hathor à Philae et le culte de la déesse," *ZÄS* 95 (1968): 1–10.

46. Iversen, *Obelisks in Exile*, vol. 2, pp. 19–46. The first Iseum Campese was constructed on the Campus Martius in Rome, somewhat east of the church Santa Maria sopra Minerva and not far from the Pantheon.

47. A. J. Reinach, *Rapports sur les fouilles de Koptos* (Paris, 1910), pl. 2.

48. The latest inscription of Decius (249–51), the last emperor whose name was recorded in hieroglyphs anywhere, is on the interior west wall of the pronaos.

49. Lyons, *Island and Temples*, pp. 31–32, pls. 22–24, plan 9.

50. Two of its composite capitals are in MMA, Rogers Fund, 1911 (11.154.4–5). The block 11.154.3, with a cavetto outside and remains of a purification scene inside, is probably from one of the screen walls.

51. Josephus, *The Judean War*, II.18. The Romans were commanded by the renowned prefect Tiberius Julius Alexander, originally an Alexandrian Jew, who later became a fundamental figure in the conquest of the temple of Jerusalem in the year A.D. 70.

52. Arthur E. R. Boak and Enoch Peterson, *Karanis: Topographical and Architectural Report of Excavations during the Seasons 1924–28* (Ann Arbor, 1931), pp. 50–55.

53. Repeated in Sydney Aufrère, Jean-Claude Golvin, and Jean-Claude Goyon, *Sites, temples, et pyramides de Moyenne et Basse Égypte*, vol. 3 of *L'Égypte reconstituée*, 3 vols. (Paris, 1991–97), p. 193.

54. R. P. Bovier-Lapierre, "Les fouilles," *CdE* 7

(1932): 85–88; Édouard Dhorme, "Les fouilles," *CdE* 9 (1934): 77–78. For recent work, see C. Gallazzi, "Tebtunis: Piecing together 3000 Years of History," *Egyptian Archeology* 5 (1994): 27–29.

55. A. Vogliano, "Rapporto preliminare de la IVa campagna di scavo a Medînet Mâdi," *ASAE* 38 (1938): 538–43.

56. Hiroyuki Kawanishi, *Akoris: Report of the Excavations at Akoris in Middle Egypt, 1981–1992* (Kyoto, 1995), pp. 17–24, 43–143.

57. The first row of columns stood so close to the front wall of the temple that one might think of a pronaos, but the narrow space between columns and wall argues against such a reconstruction.

58. François Daumas, *Les mammisis de Dendara* (Cairo, 1959), nos. 19–22.

59. E. Prisse d'Avennes, *Architecture*, vol. 1 of *Atlas de l'art égyptien* (Paris, 1868–78), pl. 53.

60. M. Mustafa and H. Jaritz, "A Roman Fortress at Nag' el-Hagar," *ASAE* 70 (1984/85): 21–31

61. Parts of the ground plan are shown on marble fragments of the ancient plan of Rome (the Severan *Forma Urbis Romae*). A picture on a coin of Vespasian records the temple's front, and sporadic excavations contribute some building elements; see Michel Malaise, *Inventaire préliminaire des documents égyptiens découverts en Italie* (Leiden, 1972), pp. 187–214; Anne Roullet, *The Egyptian and Egyptianizing Monuments of Imperial Rome* (Leiden, 1972), pp. 23–35; Katja Lembke, *Das Iseum Campense in Rome* (Heidelberg, 1994); Lollio Barberi et al., *Le Antichità Egiziane*, pp. 57–69; *Iside*, pp. 297–305.

62. The plans of the exedra and apse are not Egyptian and must be derived from Roman secular buildings such as baths and forums.

63. Four obelisks of Ramesses II from Heliopolis are in the Piazza della Rotunda, the gardens of the Villa Celimontana, the Viale delle Terme di Diocleziano, and the Boboli Gardens of Florence. Two obelisks of Apries from Sais are in the Piazza della Minerva and the Piazza del Duomo at Urbino. One obelisk made for Domitian is in the Piazza Navona in Rome.

64. Parts of three columns are in Rome, and of another in the Museo Archeologico, Florence; see Ensoli Vittozzi, *Musei Capitolini*, pp. 59–70.

65. For the finds see Malaise, *Inventaire*, pp. 187–214; Roullet, *Egyptianizing Monuments*, pp. 23–35; Ensoli Vittozzi, *Musei Capitolini*.

66. Erected by Lucilius Rufus in the eighth year of Domitian (*Iside*, p. 503). Two others are found at Praeneste in the Museo Nazionale, Naples (Collection Borgia) and in Munich (the so-called Albani-Obelisk); see Gorringe, *Egyptian Obelisks*, p. 137. For the Iseum of Benevent: Hans Wolfgang Müller, *Der Isiskult im antiken Benevent* (Berlin, 1969).

67. S. R. Snape, *A Temple of Domitian at El-Ashmunein* (London, 1989).

68. *Description* IV, pls. 4–5, still shows the cavetto on the front.

69. H. A. Sayce, "Excavations at Gebel Silsila," *ASAE* 8 (1907): 102–105.

70. *Description* I, p. 38; Jaritz, "Tempel des Domitian," pp. 237–57.

71. R. Nauman, "Bauwerke der Oase Khargeh," *MDAIK* 8 (1939): 6–8; S. Sauneron, "Douch-Rapport prélimiaire de la campagne de fouilles 1976," *BIFAO* 78 (1978): 5–10.

72. Petrie, *Diospolis Parva*, p. 55.

73. Remains of figural decoration at the corners of the block contradict Kuhlmann's assumption that it was the architrave of a colonnade (Kuhlmann, *Achmim*, pp. 41–44).

74. Excavation and documentation of the temple are in progress and may soon produce new results. See Jan Quaegebeur, "Excavating the Forgotten Temple of Shenhur," in Quirke, *The Temple*, pp. 159–67; Leclant and Clerc, "Fouilles et travaux," 284–86.

75. Huge numbers of columns, bases, capitals, colossal statues, and sphinxes were discovered in 1994–1995 in the sea northeast of the modern Qait Bey fort. Some pieces have been hauled out and stored in Alexandria; see Empereur, *Alexandria Rediscovered*, pp. 62–81.

76. The ruin site with impressive public buildings, documented by the Napoleonic expediton (*Description* IV, pls. 53–61), has disappeared without proper excavations. Some composite capitals from the area suggest a small temple in the Egyptian style; see Vincent Rondot, "Note sur six chapiteaux composites réutilisés dans la mosqué Al-Yusufi à Mellawi," *ASAE* 70 (1984/85): 143–49.

77. T. Kraus and J. Roeder, "Mons Claudianus," *MDAIK* 18 (1962): 91–97; T. Kraus, J. Roeder, and W. Müller-Wiener, "Mons Claudianus—Mons Porphyrites," *MDAIK* 22 (1967): 172–81.

78. See Jean-Claude Golvin, Francois Dunand, Guy Wagner, and Sayed Abd el-Hamid, "Le petit Serapeum de l'époque d'Hadrien," *Dossiers Histoire et Archéologie* 101 (1986): 66–68.

79. LD Text, vol. 4, p. 1. Some relief fragments are in the Musée des Beaux-Arts, Grenoble (1974, 1980).

80. Hermann Junker, *Das Götterdekret über das Abaton* (Vienna, 1913).

81. Haeny, "Philae," p. 215, pl. 36.

82. C. A. Hope, "Dakhle Oasis Project: Report on the 1987 Excavations at Ismant el-Gharab," *JSSEA* 16 (1986): 74–91; idem, "Dakhle Oasis

Project: Ismant el-Kharab 1991–92," *JSSEA* 19 (1989): 6–10.

83. O. E. Kaper, "A Painting of the Gods of Dakhla in the Temple of Ismant el-Kharab," in Quirke, *The Temple*, pp. 204–215.

84. For the diffusion of the cult of Isis in the Near East, see Francesco Tiradritti, "La diffusione del culto di Iside in Oriente e in Nord Africa," in *Iside*, pp. 541–50.

85. See, for example, Euphrosyne Doxiades, *The Mysterious Fayum Portraits* (London, 1995).

86. Hölscher, *The Temples of the Eighteenth Dynasty*, vol. 2 of *The Excavations of Medinet Habu*, pp. 59–62.

87. Good photos of the incomplete condition: J. C. Golvin and J. Larronde, "Étude des procédés de construction dans l'Égypte ancienne, I. L'édification des murs de grès en grand appareil à l'époque romaine," *ASAE* 68 (1982): 188, pls. 6–8.

88. *Description* I, pls. 84[1], 89, 90.

89. M. Es-Saghir and D. Valbelle, "Komir," *BIFAO* 83 (1983): 149–70.

90. In the reconstruction published in Sydney Aufrère, Jean-Claude Golvin, and Jean-Claude Goyon, *Sites et temples des déserts*, vol. 2 of *L'Égypte restituée* (Paris, 1991–97), p. 97, two more rows of interior columns are suggested in the interior.

91. Similar benches for priests' assemblies were preserved in the Ramesside Hathor temple of Deir el-Medine: Bernard Bruyère, *Rapport sur les fouilles de Deir el Médineh (1935–1940)* (Cairo, 1948), p. 101, pl. 10. Two similar assembly rooms with benches were found in the second-century mountain sanctuary of Bab Kalabsha; see Herbert Ricke, *Ausgrabungen von Khor-Dehmit bis Bet el-Wali* (Chicago, 1967), pp. 7–9, figs. 12–16.

92. Ahmed Fakhry, *Siwa Oasis* (Cairo, 1944), p. 70.

93. The use of the Doric order is unusual for this period and would actually point to a much earlier date.

94. Ezbet Bashandi in the El-Dakhla Oasis, the temple Hatiyet Abu-Shuruf, and the four chapels of the necropolis of Abu'l-Awaf in the Siwa Oasis. The temple of El-Zeitun was built in the Egyptian style. All were studied and published by Fakhry, *Siwa Oasis*.

95. Boak and Peterson, *Karanis*, pp. 14–16.

96. A. Farid, "New Roman Blocks from a Hypostyle-Hall Found at Asfoun el-Mata'na," *SAK* 13 (1986): 35–53.

97. J. Capart, "L'énigma de Tahta," *CdE* 29/15 (1940): 45–50; H. Grégoire, "L'énigma de Tahta," *CdE* 29/15 (1940): 119–23.

98. Roger S. Bagnall, *Egypt in Late Antiquity* (Princeton, 1993).

99. See ibid., pp. 261–68.

100. Mohammed el-Saghir, *Le camp romain de Louqsor* (Cairo, 1986); J.-C. Golvin et al., "Le camp romain," *Dossiers Histoire et Archéologie* 101 (1986): 69–78.

101. U. Monneret de Villard, *The Temple of the Imperial Cult at Luxor* (Oxford, 1953).

102. *Description* I, pl. 29; Lyons, *Island and Temples*, pl. 25.

103. Iversen, *Obelisks in Exile*, vol. 1, pp. 9–33. The erection of the obelisk in the hippodrome is depicted on the lower base block (Iversen, *Obelisks in Exile*, vol. 1, figs. 10–11).

104. De Lacy O'Leary, "The Destruction of Temples in Egypt," *Bulletin de la Société d'archéologie Copte* 4 (1938): 51–57.

105. The best example is the White Monastery at Sohag with a pharaonic cavetto on top of the high, battered walls. See Peter Grossmann, "Frühchristliche Baukunst in Ägypten," in *Spätantike und Frühes Christentum: Propyläenkunstgeschichte*, edited by Claude Vandersleyen (Frankfurt, 1977), pp. 234–38, and idem, "Altägyptische Elemente in der frühchristlichen Baukunst Ägyptens," in *Stationen: Festschrift Rainer Stadelmann* (Wiesbaden, 1998), pp. 443–58. See also F. W. Deichmann, "Zum Altägyptischen in der koptischen Baukunst," *MDAIK* 8 (1939): 34–37.

Chapter 9

1. See Sylvie Cauville, *Edfou* (Cairo, 1984), pp. 46–48, and idem, *Le temple de Dendera* (Cairo, 1990), pp. 60–62.

2. Hölscher, *The Mortuary Temple of Ramses III*, vol. 3 of *The Excavations of Medinet Habu*, p. 15, fig. 8, with several examples.

3. See Haeny, *Basilikale Anlagen*.

4. The pronaos of the temple of Sheshonq I at El-Hibe (fig. 239) has been dated tentatively here to the 30th Dynasty.

5. D. Kurth, *Die Dekoration der Säulen des Pronaos des Temples von Edfu* (Wiesbaden, 1983); Cauville, *Edfou*, pp. 18–23.

6. For the Kushite examples at Thebes, see Leclant, *Monuments thébains*, vol. 1, pp. 200–216.

7. For example, the two-by-four column porch of the sanctuary of the great temple of Aton and the four-by-four porch of the palace. J.D.S. Pendlebury, *The City of Akhenaten*, pt. 3 (London, 1951), pls. 2, 8–9, 13B, 15[2].

8. S. Wenig, "Gedanken zu einigen Aspekten der kuschitischen Tempelarchitektur," *Meroitica* 7 (1984): 404–408.

9. Several good examples are in Marsha Hill and Charles K. Wilkinson, *Egyptian Wall Paint-*

ings: *The Metropolitan Museum of Art's Collection of Facsimiles* (New York, 1983).

10. For example, the White Chapel of Senwosret I at Karnak; see Pierre Lacau and Henri Chevrier, *Une chapelle de Sésostris Ier*, 2 vols. (Cairo, 1956).

11. For example, the two bark stations of Hatshepsut and Thutmosis III on the processional approach to Deir el-Bahari; see Dieter Arnold and Jürgen Settgast, "Dritter Vorbericht über die vom Deutschen Archäologischen Institut Kairo im Asasif unternommenen Arbeiten," *MDAIK* 22 (1967): 22–24.

12. Examples are the original sanctuary of the Luxor temple, which contained a canopy of four stone columns, and the sanctuary of the temple of Amenhotep IV at Sesebi in the Sudan, with a similar canopy (A. M. Blackman, "Preliminary Report on the Excavations at Sesebi," *JEA* 23 [1937]: pl. 14). On a temple facade of Amarna, a kiosk with papyrus-bundle columns and corner pillars with papyrus bundles was represented (fig. 252, this volume).

13. For example, at Soleb, where Amenhotep III added a closed kiosk with four columns to the pylon.

14. See Irmgard Hein, *Die ramessidische Bautätigkeit in Nubien* (Wiesbaden, 1991). Dummy temple facades are an essential part of Nabataean rock architecture (Judith McKenzie, *The Architecture of Petra* [Oxford, 1990]) and of the Indian rock temples of Ajanta and Elura (Herbert Plaeschke and Ingeborg Plaeschke, *Indische Felsentempel und Höhlenklöster* [Wien, 1983]). Palace facades appear at the Persian royal tombs of Naksh-i Rustam (Schmidt, *Persepolis*, vol. 3).

15. For example, the Mut temple and the sanctuary of the divine consorts in the Amunra-Monthu complex at Karnak and the Sed-festival chapel at the Luxor temple, all from the reign of Taharqa. Engaged palm columns were cut from the rock at the rock temple of Asclepius at Athribis (Wannina). Doric half-columns were used on the Ammonieion of Amasis at Siwa, and Ionic half-columns occurred on a temple of Ptolemy II at Theadelphia.

16. Ancient Egyptian *per-meset*. Champollion introduced the term *mammisi*. See A. Badawy, "The Architectural Symbolism of the Mammisi-Chapels in Egypt," *CdE* 38 (1933): 78–90; Daumas, *Mammisis des temples égyptiens*; idem, "Birth House," in *LÄ*, vol. 2 (1977), pp. 462–75; Borchardt, *Tempel mit Umgang*; Francois Daumas, *Les mammisis de Dendara* (Cairo, 1959), nos. 19–22.

17. Jean Marcel Humbert, *L'Égyptomanie dans l'art occidental* (Paris, 1989), fig. p. 73.

18. In the morning, the young god as Re sitting on a lotus flower rises from the primordial ocean (associated with the mother-goddess Nun) to brighten the world with his radiance. See Daumas, *Mammisis des temples égyptiens*.

19. The oldest formal prototypes of this building appear in the Amarna Period. For example, such a kiosk is represented in relief on a chapel wall. It had three papyrus-bundle columns on the long sides and L-shaped corner pillars. The intercolumniations were closed with screen walls of leather matting topped with uraei friezes. A chapel is suggested inside and crowned by an uraeus frieze; see Rainer Hanke, *Amarna-Reliefs aus Hermopolis*, Hildesheimer Ägyptologische Beiträge, no. 2 (Hildesheim, 1978), fig. 24. Two juxtaposed kiosks on the island of Maru-Aton were reconstructed in a similar but rather imaginary way in T. Eric Peet, *The City of Akhenaten*, pt. 1 (London, 1923), p. 121, pls. 29–30.

20. Somers Clark and Reginald Engelbach, *Ancient Egyptian Masonry* (London, 1930), pp. 159–60, figs. 247.

21. Only the Augustan birth house of Kalabsha was a true *peripteros* (fig. 247).

22. Daumas, *Mammisis des temples égyptiens*, pp. 242, 270ff.

23. Borchardt, *Tempel mit Umgang*, pp. 3–12.

24. See Hölscher, *The Mortuary Temple of Ramses III*, vol. 4 of *The Excavations of Medinet Habu*, pp. 11–13; J. Lauffray, "Abords occidentaux du premier pylône de Karnak: Le dromos, la tribune et les aménagements portuaires," *Karnak* 4 (1971): 77–131; Horst Jaritz, *Die Terrassen vor den Tempeln des Chnum und der Satet*, vol. 3 of *Elephantine* (Mainz, 1980).

25. Some terraces were built in the desert far from any canal (Deir el-Medine, Qasr el-Ghueda).

26. For example, in the Theban tombs of Panehesi (no. 16) and Amenmose (no. 19).

27. A similarity to the valley temples of the pyramids of the Old and Middle Kingdoms is certainly not coincidental. In the valley temple the cult symbols of the king greeted, for example, the visiting gods Sokaris and Hathor; see Paule Posener-Krieger, *Les archives du temple funéraire de Néferirkarê-Kakai* (Cairo, 1976), pp. 549–60.

28. Jaritz, *Elephantine*, 3:59–65.

29. Herodotus, II.169.

30. Athenaios, *The Deipnosophistes*, II.387–393, V.196–197. Compare with the Roman tomb of Mafrûsa (Mex): Achille Adriani, *Repertorio dell'Egitto greco-romano*, serie C, vols. 1–2 (Palermo, 1963), pl. 70[235].

31. In figure 252, bundle columns are shown with open papyrus umbels, which are surrounded at their neck with a wreath of smaller

umbels and buds. The foot of the stems grew out of a wild papyrus swamp: Rainer Hanke, *Amarna-Reliefs aus Hermopolis*, Hildesheimer Ägyptologische Beiträge, no. 2 (Hildesheim, 1978), fig. 24.

32. For example, N. de G. Davies, *The Rock Tombs of El Amarna*, vol. 2 (London, 1905), pls. 3–4, 26. For more examples, possibly from the pre-Amarna period, see W. M. Flinders Petrie, *Memphis I* (London, 1909), pl. 25.

33. Gustave Jéquier, *Les temples ramessides et saites* (Paris, 1922), pls. 32–33, 35–36, 38, 41.

34. The better specimen is in Cairo (CG 41435), another is in Manchester; see Petrie, *Memphis I*, pls. 2, 25.

35. Examples in Prisse d'Avennes, *Architecture*, pls. 15, 17–20.

36. Western hall, second column from north.

37. Examples in Prisse d'Avennes, *Architecture*, pls. 17, 19.

38. D. Arnold, "New Evidence for Lilyform Capitals in Egypt," in *Chief of Seers: Studies in Memory of Cyril Aldred*, edited by Elizabeth Goring, Nicholas Reeves, and John Ruffle (London, 1997), pp. 20–29.

39. Single and eight-stem at the kiosk of Nectanebo I. Small Saite(?) fayence-capitals in Bologna and Berlin: Köster, "Pflanzensäule," p. 96, and *Staatliche Museen zu Berlin: Ausführliches Verzeichnis der ägyptischen Altertümer und Gipsabgüsse* (Berlin, 1899), p. 289 (no. 6610).

40. A. Andrén, "Palmetta," *Enciclopedia de l'arte antica*, vol. 5 (Rome, 1963), pp. 898–900

41. See Prisse d'Avennes, *Architecture*, pls. 17–20.

42. A late example survived in the Saite rock tomb at Giza. The columns of the *tetrastyle in antis* carried a unique combination of two super-imposed, open and closed papyrus capitals: LD I, pl. 27; LD Text, vol. 1, pp. 96–97.

43. For example, the lion cosmetic jar (no. 211), the boat-shaped "center-piece" of calcite (no. 578), and the fan handle (no. 415), here figure 257; see Nicholas Reeves, *The Complete Tutankhamun* (London, 1990), pp. 179, 198–99.

44. W. M. Flinders Petrie, *Tell el Amarna* (London, 1894), pl. 9.

45. Similar to the much later tree-shaped columns of the triumphal arch of Theodosisus I at Constantinople, their shaft imitated the irregular, flattened curves of a tree trunk.

46. Whereas a composite column carries several different capitals, a composite capital contains elements of different plants.

47. The northwestern column of hall B of the Hibis temple carries a capital with a bell-shaped core, surrounded at its neck with a wreath of lilies(?): Winlock, *The Temple of Hibis*, pls. 20–21, 35–36, 43. When the final sculpting was unexpectedly abandoned, the capital was molded with a heavy coat of mortar into a plain bell-shaped capital. The column, usually quoted as an early example of composite capitals in room L (pl. 19B), was, however, added as a repair in the time of Nectanebo I.

48. The observation that the exact shape of composite capitals was used for ornamentation of the so-called New Year's flasks of the 26th Dynasty also confirms the full development of composite capitals at that period.

49. Numerous examples: *Description* I–IV; Prisse d'Avennes, *Architecture*, pls. 17–20, 25, 47, 58–61; Jéquier, *L'architecture et la decoration*; Ludwig Borchardt, *Die aegyptische Pflanzensäule: Ein Kapitel zur Geschichte des Pflanzenornaments* (Berlin, 1897).

50. Following a suggestion by A. Oppenheim.

51. Jéquier defined twenty-seven types: G. Jéquier, *Manuel d'archéologie égyptienne: Les éléments de l'architecture* (Paris, 1924), pp. 230–74. See also M. Haneborg-Lühr, "Les chapiteaux composites: Étude typologique, stylistique et statistique," in *Amosiadès: Mélanges offerts au professeur Claude Vandersleyen par ses anciens étudiants*, edited by Claude Obsomer and Anne-Laure Oosthoek (Louvain-la-Neuv, 1992), pp. 125–52.

52. The parallel of the "Tuscan column" in Roman architecture comes to mind, with the planed-off lower part of the shaft, represented by numerous examples in Pompeii.

53. Ionic column bases occasionally sit on square plinths; see René Ginouvès, *Dictionaire méthodique de l'architecture greque et romaine*, vol. 2 (Athens and Rome 1992), pls. 36–37.

54. For example, in the Hathor chapel of Hatshepsut at Deir el-Bahari; see G. Haeny, "Hathor-Kapitell," in *LÄ*, vol. 2 (1997), pp. 1039–41.

55. As is already found in the temple of Hatshepsut at Deir el-Bahari (double-faced on a round column shaft).

56. With the exception of the old-fashioned granite columns of Osorkon I and Osorkon II at Bubastis; see, here, fig. 11.

57. Real examples appear in the kiosk of Nectanebo I and the birth house of Philae and in the temple of Opet at Karnak. An older origin of the column type is suggested by depictions of Mut chapels on mirrors of the 25th/26th Dynasty; see *Nofret die Schöne*, exhibition catalogue, Munich (1985), no. 55.

58. For example, at the birth houses of Philae, Edfu, and Dendera II; see figs. 100, 121, 154, 155, 158, 179–80, 222.

59. Temple B.300; see LD I, pl. 139; Welsby,

The Kingdom of Kush, fig. 47. Remains of a double Bes capital are also in the Museo Egizio, Florence (448).

60. See Welsby, *The Kingdom of Kush*, fig. 47. In the temple of Mut at Karnak, Bes figures were also attached to the foot of columns (fig. 263).

61. E. von Mercklin, "Das aegyptische Figuralkapitell," in *Studies Presented to David Moore Robinson*, vol. 3 (St. Louis, 1951), pp. 198–214.

62. Elaine Vergnolle, *L'art roman en France* (Paris, 1994), pp. 182–87.

63. Continued occasionally in the New Kingdom, see the granite papyrus-bundle columns from Alexandria (in Vienna; see E. von Bergmann, *Inschriftliche Denkmäler der Sammlung ägyptischer Altertümer*," *RT* 7 [1886]: 177–78), in the Brit. Mus. (EA 64), and at the Thutmoside bark station behind the pylon of the Luxor temple.

64. D. Wildung, "Schranken," in *LÄ*, vol. 5 (1984), pp. 690–93.

65. For example, N. de G. Davies, *The Rock Tombs of El Amarna*: vol. 1 (London, 1903), pl. 31; vol. 3 (London, 1905), pl. 14; vol. 6 (London, 1908), pls. 11–12, 14.

66. Wolfe-Larkin asks whether the real sun replaced the solar disk normally depicted in relief on closed lintels; see Diana Wolfe-Larkin, "The Broken-Lintel Doorway in Ancient Egypt and its Decoration" (Ph.D. diss., Institute of Fine Arts, New York University, 1994).

67. Lyttelton, *Baroque Architecture*, p. 52.

Chapter 10

1. For the history, see Kienitz, *Die politische Geschichte Ägyptens*, pp. 11–54. For the functional aspects, see Byron E. Shafer, ed., *Temples of Ancient Egypt* (Ithaca, 1997).

2. For example, pointed arches and ribbing or the ambulatory of the apse already appear as separate elements in Romanesque churches. Only their combination, in 1140, established the new Gothic style.

3. See Cauville, *Edfou*, pp. 28–31; idem, *Le temple de Dendera* (Cairo, 1990), pp. 30–32.

4. For example, the Opet temple at Karnak and the temples of Deir el-Medine, Qasr el-'Aguz, and Kalabsha.

5. For example, the temple of Amunra-Monthu of Amenhotep III and the temple of Khonsu at Karnak. A circular configuration is also found in New Kingdom bark stations with pillared ambulatories.

6. E.A.E. Reymond, *The Mythical Origin of the Egyptian Temple* (New York, 1969), pp. 316–22.

7. Barry J. Kemp, *Ancient Egypt: Anatomy of a Civilization* (London, 1989), p. 103.

8. H. Brunner, "Zum Verständnis der archaisierenden Tendenzen in der ägyptischen Spätzeit," *Saeculum* 21 (1970): 151–61; Anton Bammer, *Architektur als Erinnerung* (Vienna, 1977). Compare also the search for the lost original Mingtang building in imperial China: Nancy Shatzman Steinhardt, *Chinese Traditional Architecture* (New York, 1984), pp. 72–74.

9. See Alexandre Varille, *Quelques caractéristiques du temple Pharaonique* (Cairo, 1946); R. A. Schwaller de Lubicz, *Le temple de l'homme: L'Apet sud à Louxor*, vol. 3 (Paris, 1957), pp. 355–63; W. Helck, "Wiederverwendung," in *LÄ*, vol. 6 (1986), pp. 1264–65.

10. See Hans Goedicke, *Re-used Blocks from the Pyramid of Amenemhet I at Lisht* (New York, 1971).

11. V. Meinecke-Berg, "Spolien in der mittelalterlichen Architektur von Kairo," in *Ägypten Dauer and Wandel* (Mainz, 1985), pp. 131–42.

12. From Constantine basilicas to San Marco in Venice (829–1094) and the cathedral of Pisa (1063); see Joachim Poeschke, ed., *Antike Spolien in der Architektur des Mittelalters und der Renaissance* (Munich, 1996).

13. Gilbert even recognized "female aspects" in the dimensions and proportions of late buildings, see P. Gilbert, "Éléments hellénistiques de l'architecture de Philae," *CdE* 36 (1961): 196–208.

14. See W. Helck, "Bauleiter," in *LÄ*, vol. 1 (1975), pp. 654–65; Rosemarie Drenkhahn, *Die Handwerker und ihre Tätigkeit im Alten Ägypten* (Wiesbaden, 1976), pp. 89–94. The artist Petisis who was—according to a folk legend—ordered by Nectanebo II to complete the temple of Sebennytos, was probably a sculptor. See Kamal, "Sébennytos," p. 90.

15. Inscriptions of the royal chief of works, Khnumibre, in the Wadi Hammamat dates from the year 44 of Amasis and the years 24–30 of Darius I. He lists twenty-five generations of royal master builders as ancestors, who were related as father/son; see Posener, *La première domination Perse*, pp. 98–105.

16. For example, the classical architect Iktinos, the late classical-Hellenistic Philon of Eleusis, the architect Vitruvius of Augustean times, and the Byzantine Isidoros the Elder of Milet.

17. Werner Müller, *Architekten in der Welt der Antike* (Zurich, 1989), pp. 47–49.

18. Lyttelton, *Baroque Architecture*; J. McKenzie, "Alexandria and the Origins of Baroque Architecture," in *Alexandria and Alexandrianism* (Malibu, 1996), pp. 109–122. An example of the survival of Alexandrian baroque tendencies in the Middle Ages is the Romanesque facade of

Saint-Gilles-du-Gard (ca.1150), obviously influenced by Roman buildings in southern France.

19. The rigid, axial alignment of Egyptian temple courts corresponds, for example, to the organization of imperial fora, which display more complicated spatial features.

20. *BemerkungenAR I*, pp. 7–10.

21. Köster, "Pflanzensäule," pp. 106–107; Lyttelton, *Baroque Architecture*, pp. 40–52; Jean-Yves Empereur, *A Short Guide to the Catacombs of Kom el-Shoqafa Alexandria* (Alexandria, 1995), figs. 12, 19.

22. Reginald E. Witt, *Isis in the Greco-Roman World* (London, 1971); and *Iside*.

23. For the influence of the architecture of Alexandria on Petra, see Judith McKenzie, *The Architecture of Petra*, (Oxford, 1990), pp. 85–101, with numerous examples of segmented pediments and the Egyptian cavetto.

24. For Italy see Malaise, *Inventaire*; Roullet, *Egyptianizing Monuments*; and *Iside*.

25. For example, in the arcades of the Severian forum of Leptis Magna.

26. For a comprehensive history of obelisks in later times, see Iversen, *Obelisks in Exile*. For the sun dial see Edmund Buchner, *Die Sonnenuhr des Augustus* (Mainz, 1982).

27. Stimulated by the picturesque location of the temples of Isis and Serapis of Canopus east of Alexandria at the end of a canal.

28. Roberta Belli Pasqua, *Sculture di età romana in "basalto,"* Monografie Xenia Antiqua (Rome, 1995).

29. Huge Egyptian column shafts were used in the temple of Trajan in Rome (14.75 m high), the Pantheon of Hadrian (11.80 m), the column of Antoninus Pius in Rome (14.75 m), and the columns of the portico of the temple of Jupiter of Baalbek; see Donald M. Bailey, "Honorific Columns, Cranes, and the Turah Epitaph," in Bailey, *Roman Egypt*, pp. 157–68.

30. Forthcoming: Günther Hölbl, *Altägypten im römischen Reich: Der römische Pharao und seine Tempel*.

31. Earl Baldwin Smith, *Architectural Symbolism of Imperial Rome and the Middle Ages* (Princeton, 1956), pp. 120–24 and 152–65; Günther Bandmann, *Mittelalterliche Architektur als Bedeutungsträger*, 6th ed. (Berlin, 1979), pp. 191–96.

32. A classical example is the Theokoleon at Olympia (fourth century B.C.) with its cult place covered by a column construction. Magnificent Christian examples are S. Agostino at Spoleto (seventh century), Sant'Ambrogio in Milan (ca.

900), San Miniato al Monte in Florence (with vaulted roof, twelfth century), and Old Saint Peter's in Rome.

33. See P. Gilbert, "La conception architecturale de la salle hypostyle de Karnak," *CdE* 17 (1942): 169–76; idem, "La salle hypostyle égyptienne et la basilique latine," *CdE* 20 (1945): 47–48; Haeny, *Basilikale Anlagen*, pp. 1–4.

34. For example, the cathedrals of Speyer (1106) or Canterbury (1175–1185).

35. Kenneth J. Conant, *Carolingian and Romanesque Architecture*, 3rd ed. (London 1973), figs. 28–29.

36. Beautiful examples are found in the churches of Santa Maria in Cosmedin (ca. 1100) and Santa Maria Assunta at Torcello/Veneto (ca. 1008).

37. Compare, for example, the late Roman palm leaf capital on a pharaonic base from Memphis (Engelbach, *Riqqeh and Memphis*, pl. 62) with the capitals in the cloisters in Fontenay Abbey (France) of 1139 (Éliane Vergnolle, *L'art roman en France* [Paris, 1994], fig. 410).

38. See Smith, *Architectural Symbolism*, pp. 166–72. An early example is the early Carolingian abbey of Centula in Normandy (799).

39. At Ferrara (1135), Parma (1281), Modena (1099), Verona (end of eleventh century), Fidenza (beginning of thirteenth century), and San Ciriaco in Ancona (thirteenth century, see fig. 270).

40. Smith, *Architectural Symbolism*, pp. 10–51.

41. S. Sauneron, "La justice à la porte des temples," *BIFAO* 54 (1954): 116–27; Thomas Grothoff, *Die Tornamen der ägyptischen Tempel* (Aachen, 1996), pp. 248–49.

42. Miriam Lichtheim, *Ancient Egyptian Literature*, vol. 1 (Berkley, 1975), p. 231. Magnificent examples are the gate lions of north Italian church portals.

43. For example, B. Schweitzer, *Die spätantiken Grundlagen der mittelalterlichen Kunst* (Leipzig, 1946); Samuel Guyer, *Grundlagen mittelalterlicher abendländischer Baukunst* (Einsiedeln-Zurich-Cologne, 1950). The book *L'Egitto in Italia dall'antichitá al medioevo: Atti del III Congresso Internazionale Italo-Egiziano Roma, 1995* (Rome, 1998) is appearing too late to be taken into consideration.

44. See Jean-Marcel Humbert, *L'Égyptomanie dans l'art occidental* (Paris, 1989), pp. 34–95; Dietrich Wildung, *Egypt: From Prehistory to the Romans* (Cologne, 1997), pp. 225–29.

GLOSSARY

Abacus (pl. *abaci*). The uppermost member of a capital.

Acanthus. A prickly plant, the spiny leaves of which were copied in Greek decoration.

Anathyrosis. The smooth marginal dressing or contact band of a joint surface of which the central portion is roughened and sunk to avoid contact.

Anta (pl. *antae*). Pilaster or corner post of slight projection terminating the end of the lateral walls of a building. *In antis*: between the antae.

Ashlar. Building technique with squared and finished, rectangular building blocks.

Avant-porte. A smaller, supplementary gate in front of the main gate.

Basilica, basilica-like. In New Kingdom hypostyle halls, the roof of the central nave towers above the roofs of the side aisles—similar in conception to Roman basilicas. In both cases, the windows of the clerestory light up the central nave.

Bed, bedding joint. The horizontal joint separating the upper surface (upper bed) of the lower block from the underside (lower bed) of the upper block.

Bossage, bosses. Surface of blocks left projecting in the rough during construction, to be cut away after construction work. In Greek and Roman masonry, bossage was often created intentionally as a rusticated, decorative form.

Caesareum. A ceremonial court with an installation for the imperial cult; originating from the Ptolemeion.

Cavetto, or *cornice*. A concave molding, generally a quarter round; regularly springing off a *torus*.

Ciborium. In Christian churches, a baldachin of four columns supporting a heavy roof above an altar or saint's tomb.

Columna caelata (pl. *columnae caelatae*). Column shafts with figured reliefs.

Contra-temple, contra-chapel. A secondary temple built back-to-back with a major sanctuary and subsequently often reduced to a small chapel or a falsedoor.

Divine consort, or *divine adoratrice*. Chief priestess and "god's wife" of Amun and worldly ruler over Thebes. Barred from marriage, they secured their succession by adoption of royal princesses.

Distyle, or *distylos*, *in antis*. Temple or porch front with two columns between antae piers.

Entasis. Outward curvature of the column shaft; in Egypt it occurs above the retracted column foot.

Exedra. Semicircular place or hall with an open front.

Fictive architecture (German *Scheinarchitektur*). Full-scale stone models of wood or stone chapels either built as unusable dummy buildings or depicted three-dimensionally on the front of a functional building.

Galilee. In Medieval architecture, a porch added to the narthex for the grouping of participants in the Good Friday procession.

Hemispeos. A temple partially cut from the rock.

Hypaetral. A temple with a naos wholly or partially open to the sky.

Hypostyle hall. Hall with large and numerous columns in several rows, carrying the roof.

Isodomic. Regular masonry of square stone (ashlar) in courses of equal height.

Komasterion. In Roman architecture, a hall for the lining up of processions.

Maat. Goddess personifying truth, justice, and the harmony of the universe as a central concept of the Egyptian worldview.

Monolithic. Made of a single stone

Naos (pl. *naoi*). Small shrine or holy of holies, usually made of hard stone and intended to hold the cult image of a deity.

Orthostates. Stone slabs or pillars set upright as a *revetment* of the lower part of a wall.

Osireion. Sanctuary or tomb of Osiris.

Peripteral. A building surrounded by colonnades on all four sides.

Peripteros. A temple surrounded by a peristyle or colonnade.

Plinth. Square, flat slab forming the bottom of a column base.

Pronaos (pl. *pronaoi*). Columned hall with open or half-open facade at the front of a temple.

Propylon. Frequently used by Herodotus for a real pylon or for other building types at a temple entrance, indicating more the location than the form of a building.

Prostyle. Temple in Greek style having a portico of usually four columns at its front, where the antae do not extend to the line of columns.

Pseudo-isodomic. Irregular masonry of square stone (ashlar), usually with high and low, alternating courses.

Rising joint. The vertical joint separating two touching blocks; commonly known as "joints."

Rustica. Masonry type with joints sunk in channels and the face of the stone projecting and usually roughened.

Sebakhin. Peasants quarrying away mud-brick walls and debris from ancient sites.

Sed festival. Royal jubilee, an extravagant ritual of renewal and regeneration to be celebrated after a reign of thirty years.

Serapeum. Sanctuary of Serapis (Osiris-Apis).

Shena wab. Brick building on a high, square brick platform associated with Late Period temples. Originally for the preparation of food offerings, they develop their own offering cult.

Sistrum. Musical rattling instrument, consisting of a papyrus-shaped handle topped by a naos.

Speos. Cave-like temple or chapel cut from the rock.

Telatat. Building stones, typical for ashlar masonry of the Amarna Period, in the standardized format of approx. 27 x 27 x 54 cm.

Temenos. An area reserved for sacred purposes; a temple enclosure.

Temple house. The building unit that forms the core of a larger temple complex and is sealed from the outer world by a roof and four walls, with a single doorway in the front wall. Courts, pylons, kiosks, pronaoi, etc., are added to the front. In terminology of Greek architecture, this is a *naos*.

Tetrastyle in antis. Temple or porch front with four columns between the antae.

Torus (pl. *tori*). A bold, convex, projecting molding of a semicircular cross-section, along the lower edge of the cavetto and at the corner of a building.

Tumulus. Burial mound.

Trikonch-building. Building with three apses at the end that are covered by half-cupolas.

Uraeus (pl. *uraei*). The rearing, poison-spitting cobra (upon the head of the king); depicted in architecture in rows as a frieze, probably apotropaic.

Ushabti, ushebti, shawabti. Funerary statuettes placed in a tomb and meant to represent the deceased in performing any labor required in the afterlife.

Volute. A spiral scroll, mostly on capitals like the Ionic, Corinthian, and Egyptian lily.

Voussoir. Stone of an arch or vault cut with two converging, opposite planes into a wedge shape.

Wabet (Egyptian *w'b.t*, "the pure place"). In late temples, a chapel for the celebration of the New Year's rituals.

SELECT BIBLIOGRAPHY

In order to keep the number of notes within reasonable limits, the following standard bibliographies have been consulted but not consistently quoted.

Aufrère, Sydney, Jean-Claude Golvin, and Jean-Claude Goyon. *L'Égypte restituée*. 3 vols. Paris, 1991–97. Vol. 1, *Sites et temples de Haute Égypte* (1991); vol. 2, *Sites et temples des déserts* (1994); and vol. 3, *Sites, temples, et pyramides de Moyenne et Basse Égypte* (1997).

Gauthier, Henri. *Le livre des rois d'Égypte*. 5 vols. Cairo, 1907–17. See especially vol. 3, *De la XIXe à la XXIVe dynastie* (1914); vol. 4, *De la XXVe dynastie à la fin des Ptolemées* (1916); and vol. 5, *Les empereurs romains* (1917).

Porter, Bertha, and Rosalind L. B. Moss. *Topographical Bibliography of Ancient Egyptian Hieroglyphic Texts, Reliefs, and Paintings*. 7 vols. Oxford, 1927–81.

Sauneron, Nadia. *Temples ptolémaiques et romains d'Égypte: Études et puplications parues entre 1939 et 1954*. Bibliothèque d'Étude, no. 15. Cairo, 1956.

Arnold, Dieter. *Building in Egypt: Pharaonic Stone Masonry*. New York, 1991.

Badawy, Alexander. *A History of Egyptian Architecture*. 3 vols. Berkeley, 1954, 1966, 1968.

Bailey, Donald, ed. *Archaeological Research in Roman Egypt*. Ann Arbor, 1996.

Boak, Arthur E. R., and Enoch Peterson. *Karanis: Topographical and Architectural Report of Excavations during the Seasons 1924–28*. Ann Arbor, 1931.

Borchardt, Ludwig. *Ägyptische Tempel mit Umgang*. Cairo, 1938.

Bothmer, Bernhard V. *Egyptian Sculpture of the Late Period 700 B.C. to A.D. 100*. Brooklyn, 1960.

Cauville, Sylvie. *Edfou*. Cairo, 1984.

Coulton, J. J. *Ancient Greek Architects at Work*. Ithaca, 1977.

Daumas, François. *Les mammisis des temples égyptiens*. Paris, 1958.

De Meulenaere, Herman, and Pierre Mackay. *Mendes II*. Warminster, 1976.

De Morgan, J., et al. *Kom Ombos: Catalogue des monuments et inscriptions de l'Égypte antique*. 2 vols. Vienna, 1895 and 1909.

Edgar, C. C. "Notes from My Inspectorate." *ASAE* 13 (1913): 277–284.

Eigner, Diethelm. *Die monumentalen Grabbauten der Spätzeit in der thebanischen Nekropole*. Vienna, 1984.

Empereur, Jean-Yves. *Alexandria Rediscovered.* New York, 1998.

Engelbach, Reginald. *Riqqeh and Memphis VI.* London, 1915.

Ensoli Vittozzi, Serena. *Musei Capitolini: La Collezione Egizia.* Rome, 1990.

Frazer, Alfred. *The Propylon of Ptolemy II.* Vol. 10 of *Samothrace,* Bollingen Series, no. 60. Princeton, 1990.

Golvin, Jean-Claude, and Jean-Claude Goyon. *Les bâtisseurs de Karnak.* Paris, 1987.

Gorringe, Henry H. *Egyptian Obelisks.* New York, 1882.

Habachi, Labib. "Notes on the Delta Hermopolis." *ASAE* 53 (1955): 441–80.

Habachi, Labib. "Sais and its Monuments." *ASAE* 42 (1943): 369–407.

Habachi, Labib. *Tell Basta.* Cairo, 1957.

Haeny, Gerhard. *Basilikale Anlagen in der ägyptischen Baukunst des Neuen Reiches.* Wiesbaden, 1970.

Haeny, Gerhard. "A Short Architectural History of Philae." *BIFAO* 85 (1985): 197–233.

Handler, S. "Architecture on the Roman Coins of Alexandria." *AJA* 75 (1971): 57–74.

Hinkel, F. W. "Säule und Interkolumium in der meroitischen Architektur." *Meroitica* 10 (1989): 231–67.

Hölbl, Günther. *Geschichte des Ptolemäerreiches.* Darmstadt, 1994.

Hölscher, Uvo. *The Excavations of Medinet Habu.* 5 vols. Chicago, 1934–54.

Huß, Werner. *Der makedonische König und die ägyptischen Priester.* Stuttgart, 1994.

Iside: Il mito, il mistero, la magia. Exhibition catalogue, Milan. Milan, 1997.

Iversen, Erik. *Obelisks in Exile.* 2 vols. Copenhagen, 1968 and 1972.

Jaritz, Horst. "Untersuchungen zum Tempel des Domitian in Assuan." *MDAIK* 31.2 (1975).

Jéquier, Gustave. *L'architecture et la decoration dans l'ancienne Égypte.* 3 vols. Paris, 1911, 1920, and 1924.

Kaiser, W. "Stadt und Tempel von Elephantine." *MDAIK* 53 (1997): 173–82.

Kamal, Ahmed Bey. "Sébennytos et son temple." *ASAE* 7 (1906): 87–94.

Kienitz, Friedrich Karl. *Die politische Geschichte Ägyptens vom 7. bis zum 4. Jahrhundert vor der Zeitwende.* Berlin, 1953.

Köster, A. "Die ägyptische Pflanzensäule der Spätzeit." *RT* 25 (1903): 86–119.

Kuhlmann, Klaus P. *Das Ammoneion: Archäologie, Geschichte und Kultpraxis des Orakels von Siwa.* Mainz, 1988.

Kuhlmann, Klaus P. *Materialien zur Archäologie und Geschichte des Raumes von Achmim.* Mainz, 1983.

Lanciers, E. "Die ägyptischen Tempelbauten zur Zeit des Ptolemaios V. Epiphanes (204–180 BC)." *MDAIK* 42 and 43 (1986).

Laskowska-Kusztal, Ewa. *Die Dekorfragmente der ptolemäisch-römischen Tempel von Elephantine.* Mainz, 1996.

Leclant, Jean. *Recherches sur les monuments thébains de la XXVe dynastie dite éthiopienne.* 2 vols. Bibliothèque d'Étude, no. 36. Cairo, 1965

Leclant, Jean, and Gisèle Clerc. "Fouilles et travaux en Égypte et au Soudan," *Orientalia* (Rome) 66 (1997): 235.

Lollio Barberi, O., G. Parola, and M. P. Toti. *Le Antichità Egiziane di Roma Imperiale.* Rome, 1995.

Lyons, H. G. *A Report on the Island and Temples of Philae.* Cairo, n.d.

Lyons, H. G. *A Report on the Temples of Philae.* Cairo, 1908.

Lyttelton, Margaret. *Baroque Architecture in Classical Antiquity.* Ithaca, 1974.

Macadam, M. F. Laming. *The Temples of Kawa.* 2 vols. London, 1955.

Malaise, Michel. *Inventaire préliminaire des documents égyptiens découverts en Italie.* Leiden, 1972.

McCredie, James R., Georges Roux, Stuart M. Shaw, and John Kurtich. *The Rotunda of Arsinoe.* Vol. 7 of *Samothrace,* Bollingen Series, no. 60. Princeton, 1990.

Mertens, Dieter. *Der alte Heratempel in Paestum und die archaische Baukunst in Unteritalien.* Mainz, 1993.

Montet, Pierre. *Les nouvelles fouilles de Tanis (1929–1932).* Paris, 1933.

Mysliwiec, Karol. *Royal Portraiture of the Dynasties XXI–XXX.* Mainz, 1988.

Naville, Edouard. *Bubastis (1887–1889).* London, 1891.

Naville, Edouard. *The Festival-Hall of Osorkon II in the Great Temple of Bubastis (1887–1889).* London, 1892.

Naville, Edouard. *The Mound of the Jew and the City of Onias*. London, 1890.

Naville, Edouard. *The Shrine of Saft El Henneh and the Land of Goshen*. London, 1887.

Pensabene, Patrizio. *Repertorio d'arte dell'Egitto greco-romano*. Serie C, vol. 3. Rome, 1993.

Petrie, W. M. Flinders. *Athribis*. London, 1908.

Petrie, W. M. Flinders. *Diospolis Parva: The Cemeteries of Abadiyeh and Hu*. London, 1901.

Petrie, W. M. Flinders. *Memphis I*. London, 1909.

Petrie, William M. Flinders. *Naukratis*. London, 1886.

Posener, G. *La première domination Perse en Egypte*. Bibliothèque d'Étude, no. 11. Cairo, 1936.

Prisse d'Avennes, E. *Architecture*. Vol. 1 of *Atlas de l'art égyptien*. Paris, 1868–78.

Quirke, Stephen, ed. *The Temple in Ancient Egypt*. London, 1997.

Robichon, Claude, P. Barguet, and J. Leclant. *Karnak-Nord IV (1949–1951)*. Cairo, 1954.

Roullet, Anne. *The Egyptian and Egyptianizing Monuments of Imperial Rome*. Leiden, 1972.

Sauneron, Serge. *Villes et Légendes d'Égypte*. 2nd ed. Bibliothèque d'Étude, no. 90. Cairo 1983.

Sauneron, Serge, and Henri Stierlin. *Die letzten Tempel Ägyptens*. Zürich, 1978.

Schmidt, Erich Friedrich. *Persepolis*. 3 vols. Chicago, 1953–70.

Smith, Earl Baldwin. *Architectural Symbolism of Imperial Rome and the Middle Ages*. Princeton, 1956.

Spencer, A. J. *The Ecavations of Tell el-Balamun*. London, 1996.

Tietze, Ch., and M. Omar. *Tell Basta: Geschichte einer Grabung*. Arcus, no. 4. Berlin, 1996.

Traunecker, C. "Essai sur l'histoire de la XXIXe dynastie." *BIFAO* 79 (1979): 395–436.

Vandier d'Abbadie, J. *Nestor l'Hôte (1804–1842)*. Leiden, 1963.

Welsby, Derek A. *The Kingdom of Kush*. London, 1996.

Wildung, Dietrich. *Sudan: Antike Königreiche am Nil*. Exhibition catalogue, Munich. Munich, 1997.

Winlock, Herbert E. *The Temple of Hibis in El Khargeh Oasis*. Part I, "The Excavations." New York, 1941.

Wright, G.R.H. *Ancient Building in Cyprus*. 2 vols. (vol. 1 = text; vol. 2 = plates) Handbuch der Orientalistik VII. Leiden, 1992.

Wright, G.R.H. *Ancient Building in South Syria and Palestine*. 2 vols. (vol. 1 = text; vol. 2 = plates) Handbuch der Orientalistik VII. Leiden, 1985.

Zignani, Pierre. "Monolithism et élasticité dans la construction égyptienne." *BIFAO* 96 (1996): 453–87.

Zivie, Alain Pierre. *Hermopolis et le nome de l'Ibis*. Vol. 1. Cairo, 1975.

INDEX

Ptolemy XII, 39, 119, 150, 155, 176, 181, 202, 211–21, 223, 232
Ptolemy XIII, 221
Ptolemy XIV, 221
Ptolemy XV, 223, 225
pylons, 35, 38, 40, 46, 47, 50, 54, 55, 57, 59, 74, 76, 88, 97, 103, 107, 111, 113, 115, 119, 129, 130, 133, 134, 144, 155, 158, 174, 181, 187, 190, 193, 196, 197, 202, 206, 208, 216, 221, 235, 236, 237, 242–43, 244, 248, 264, 265, 271, 272
    of Ramesses II at Luxor, 47, 54
    of Ramesses III at Medinet Habu, 40
pyramid mansion (Illinois), 314
pyramid of Shabitku at Kurru, 45
pyramid of Taharqa at Nuri, 51
pyramid-shaped tombs, 68–69
pyramid temple of Niuserre, 59
pyramid temple of Pepy II, 59
pyramid temple of Sahure, 59
pyramid tomb of Shabaka at El-Kurru, 50

Qantir, 107, 124, 284
Qasr 'Ain el-Zaijan, 267
Qasr el-'Aguz, 198, 200, 308
Qasr el-Dush, 262–63, 267
Qasr el-Ghueda, 92, 308
Qasr el-Megysbeh, 138
Qasr Gheit, 226–28
Qasr Ibrim, 59
Qertassi, 237, 239–40, 243
Quban, 244
Qûs, 131, 161

Ramesses II, 30, 36, 38, 40, 47, 54, 76, 87, 107, 110, 111, 248, 271, 278, 308
Ramesses III, 25, 30, 35, 40, 47, 145, 149
Ramesses IV, 25, 28
Ramesses IX, 25
Reharakhte, 309
representative palace at Memphis, 82
Ricke, H., 68, 97
Roberts, D., 148–49
Roeder, G., 240
Roman architecture, 271–73, 311–12
Roman Empire, 260–61, 271–73, 301, 309, 312
Romanesque church portals, 313
roof chapel, 277
Rosetta, 71, 80, 85, 108, 150, 179
royal necropolis at Sais, 91

"Sacred Book of the Primitive Times of the Gods," 310
Sa el-Hagar, 70

Saft el-Henne, 95, 107, 129–30
Sahure, 59
Sais, 64, 70, 71, 75–76, 80, 84–85, 91, 92, 95, 105, 108, 125, 157, 292, 309
Samaria, 265
Samothrace, 157
Sanam, 44, 59–61, 306
sanctuaries, 30, 312
    of Amun at Deir el-Bahari, 200
    of Arsinoe at Cape Zephyrion, 157
    of Asclepius at Athribis, 212
    of Atum at Pithom, 39
    of cow cult at Atfih, 36
    of the Great Gods of Samothrace at Samothrace, 157
    of Isis at Philae, 119, 122, 171
    of Khnum on Elephantine, 306
    of Khonspakhered at Karnak, 132
    of Monthu at Medamoud, 167–68
    of Mut/Anta at Tanis (first), 173–74
    of Mut/Anta at Tanis (second), 174
    of Nectanebo II at Karnak, 140
    of Pnephoros at Theadelphia, 159
    of Ptah at Memphis, 72
    of Reharakhte at Pithom, 39
    of Renenutet at Medinet Madi, 159–60
    of Satet on Elephantine, 306
    of Shu at Pithom, 39
    of Tefnut at Pithom, 39
    of the Theban Triade at Pithom, 39
    of Thoth at Hermopolis parva, 82
    of Thoth at Mesdet, 40
    of Triphis at Athribis, 211–12
Saqqara, 45, 68, 72, 105, 109–111, 130–31, 180, 297
Sarapis, cult of, 309
Saudi Arabia, 311–12
screen walls, 58, 95, 102, 108, 115, 152, 160, 176, 206, 235, 240, 244, 265, 278, 282, 284, 286, 304, 312
    discussion of, 302–330
Sebakhin, 232
Sebennytos, 76, 93, 95, 127–28, 140, 141, 158, 309
Sed-festival building of Amasis at Sais, 85
Sed-festival chapel of Taharqa at Luxor, 55
Sed-festival gates, 38, 47, 50, 59, 162
    at Medamoud, 38, 157
    at Sais, 80
    at Tanis, 41
Sema (royal palace) at Alexandria, 154–55
Semna-West, 59
Senwosret I, 105, 176
Senwosret III, 36, 195
Septimius Severus, 271

of Wadjet at Buto, 66, 84
of Wadjet at Nabesha, 85–86
at the western oases, 267
temples, distributional trends, 309
Teos, 93, 107, 122, 124
Theadelphia, 159, 253
Thebes, 30, 43, 44, 45, 47, 51, 77, 115, 116, 183, 271, 309
Theodosius I, 264, 272–73
Theodosius II, 272
Theodosius III, 272
Thinis, 25
Thutmosis III, 87, 103, 131, 138, 177, 211, 221, 230, 244, 272, 273
Tiberius, 190, 193, 197, 202, 231, 248–50, 251, 255
Titus, 260
Tivoli, 260, 265
tomb chapel of Amenirdis I at Medinet Habu, 49
tombs
    of Ahmose at Giza, 85
    of Alexander at Alexandria, 154
    of Apries at Sais, 80
    of Djer at Abydos, 83
    of the Kem-wer at Abu Yassin, 86, 107
    of Nakhtes-Bastetreru at Giza, 85
    of Neferibre-sa-Neith at Saqqara, 297
    of Nepherites I at Mendes, 102
    of Nespekashuti at Thebes, 45
    of Osiris at Abydos, 83
    of Osiris at Biggeh, 264
    of Osiris at Elephantine, 178
    of Osiris at Karnak, 174
    of Osiris at Neith, 71
    of Osiris at Sais, 80, 85

of Pedineith at Thebes, 45
    at Tanis, 31
    of Zechariah at Jerusalem, 311
tombs, pyramid-shaped, 68–69
tomb shaft at Giza, 45
tomb shaft at Saqqara, 45
tools, 45, 67, 69, 153, 228
Trajan, 138, 163, 174, 231, 232, 235, 255, 257, 260, 263
Transjordan, 311
Triphis, 309
Tûkh el-Qarâmûs, 140
Tuna el-Gebel, 49, 131, 156
Tutankhamun, 297

Udjahorresnet, 92

Vespasian, 189, 232, 260

wabets (New Year's festival courts), 60, 66, 102, 122, 134, 171, 188, 231, 232, 254, 305, 306
    discussion of, 277
Wadsworth, Illinois, 314
Western architecture, 310–14
western oases, 267
Wilkinson, Sir Gardner, 184, 209
Winlock, Herbert E., 134, 244

Xerxes I, 75, 92
Xerxes, 69

Zignani, P., 153

GENERAL=KARTE
von
AEGYPTEN
und der
SINAI HALBINSEL
mit Benutzung der handschriftlichen hydrographischen Aufnahmen des Nilthales
von
Linant de Bellefonds,
bearbeitet und gezeichnet
von
H. KIEPERT.
STICH von J. SULZER.
BERLIN
1872.